The Politics of Expertise

This book collects case studies and theoretical papers on expertise, focusing on four major themes: legitimation, the aggregation of knowledge, the distribution of knowledge and the distribution of power. It focuses on the institutional means by which the distribution of knowledge and the distribution of power are connected, and how the problems of aggregating knowledge and legitimating it are solved by these structures. The radical novelty of this approach is that it places the traditional discussion of expertise in democracy into a much larger framework of knowledge and power relations, and in addition begins to raise the questions of epistemology that a serious account of these problems requires.

Stephen P. Turner is Distinguished University Professor in the Philosophy Department at University of South Florida.

Routledge Studies in Social and Political Thought

For a full list of titles in this series, please visit www.routledge.com.

44 **Counter-Enlightenments**
From the Eighteenth Century to the Present
Graeme Garrard

45 **The Social and Political Thought of George Orwell**
A Reassessment
Stephen Ingle

46 **Habermas**
Rescuing the Public Sphere
Pauline Johnson

47 **The Politics and Philosophy of Michael Oakeshott**
Stuart Isaacs

48 **Pareto and Political Theory**
Joseph Femia

49 **German Political Philosophy**
The Metaphysics of Law
Chris Thornhill

50 **The Sociology of Elites**
Michael Hartmann

51 **Deconstructing Habermas**
Lasse Thomassen

52 **Young Citizens and New Media**
Learning for Democratic Participation
Edited by Peter Dahlgren

53 **Gambling, Freedom and Democracy**
Peter J. Adams

54 **The Quest for Jewish Assimilation in Modern Social Science**
Amos Morris-Reich

55 **Frankfurt School Perspectives on Globalization, Democracy, and the Law**
William E. Scheuerman

56 **Hegemony**
Studies in Consensus and Coercion
Edited by Richard Howson and Kylie Smith

57 **Governmentality, Biopower, and Everyday Life**
Majia Holmer Nadesan

58 **Sustainability and Security within Liberal Societies**
Learning to Live with the Future
Edited by Stephen Gough and Andrew Stables

59 **The Mythological State and its Empire**
David Grant

60 **Globalizing Dissent**
Essays on Arundhati Roy
Edited by Ranjan Ghosh & Antonia Navarro-Tejero

61 **The Political Philosophy of Michel Foucault**
Mark G.E. Kelly

62 **Democratic Legitimacy**
Fabienne Peter

63 **Edward Said and the Literary, Social, and Political World**
Edited by Ranjan Ghosh

64 **Perspectives on Gramsci**
Politics, Culture and Social Theory
Edited by Joseph Francese

65 Enlightenment Political Thought and Non-Western Societies
Sultans and Savages
Frederick G. Whelan

66 Liberalism, Neoliberalism, Social Democracy
Thin Communitarian Perspectives on Political Philosophy and Education
Mark Olssen

67 Oppositional Discourses and Democracies
Edited by Michael Huspek

68 The Contemporary Goffman
Edited by Michael Hviid Jacobsen

69 Hemingway on Politics and Rebellion
Edited by Lauretta Conklin Frederking

70 Social Theory in Contemporary Asia
Ann Brooks

71 Governmentality
Current Issues and Future Challenges
Edited by Ulrich Bröckling, Susanne Krasmann and Thomas Lemke

72 Gender, Emotions and Labour Markets
Asian and Western Perspectives
Ann Brooks and Theresa Devasahayam

73 Alienation and the Carnivalization of Society
Edited by Jerome Braun and Lauren Langman

74 The Post-Colonial State in the Era of Capitalist Globalization
Historical, Political and Theoretical Approaches to State Formation
Tariq Amin-Khan

75 The Psychology and Politics of the Collective
Groups, Crowds and Mass Identifications
Edited by Ruth Parkin-Gounelas

76 Environmental Solidarity
How Religions Can Sustain Sustainability
Pablo Martínez de Anguita

77 Comedy and the Public Sphere
The Rebirth of Theatre as Comedy and the Genealogy of the Modern Public Arena
Arpad Szakolczai

78 Culture, Class, and Critical Theory
Between Bourdieu and the Frankfurt School
David Gartman

79 Environmental Apocalypse in Science and Art
Designing Nightmares
Sergio Fava

80 Conspicuous and Inconspicuous Discriminations in Everyday Life
Victor N. Shaw

81 Understanding the Tacit
Stephen P. Turner

82 The Politics of Expertise
Stephen P. Turner

The Politics of Expertise

Stephen P. Turner

NEW YORK   LONDON

First published 2014
by Routledge
711 Third Avenue, New York, NY 10017

Simultaneously published in the UK
by Routledge
2 Park Square, Milton Park, Abingdon, Oxfordshire OX14 4RN

First issued in paperback 2015

*Routledge is an imprint of the Taylor & Francis Group,
an informa business*

© 2014 Taylor & Francis

The right of Stephen P. Turner to be identified as author of this work has been asserted in accordance with sections 77 and 78 of the Copyright, Designs and Patents Act 1988.

All rights reserved. No part of this book may be reprinted or reproduced or utilised in any form or by any electronic, mechanical, or other means, now known or hereafter invented, including photocopying and recording, or in any information storage or retrieval system, without permission in writing from the publishers.

Trademark Notice: Product or corporate names may be trademarks or registered trademarks, and are used only for identification and explanation without intent to infringe.

Library of Congress Cataloging-in-Publication Data
Turner, Stephen P., 1951–
 The politics of expertise / by Stephen P. Turner.
  pages cm. — (Routledge studies in social and political thought ; 82)
 Includes bibliographical references and index.
 1. Policy sciences. 2. Expertise—Political aspects. 3. Research—Political aspects. 4. Political planning. 5. Decision making—Political aspects. I. Title.
 H97.T873 2014
 320.6—dc23
 2013022114

ISBN13: 978-1-138-92963-0 (pbk)
ISBN13: 978-0-415-70943-9 (hbk)

Typeset in Sabon
by IBT Global.

To Kim, who pulled me through

Contents

Acknowledgments	xi
Introduction	1

PART I
Some Basic Theory

1	What is the Problem with Experts?	17
2	Political Epistemology, Expertise, and the Aggregation of Knowledge	41

PART II
Aggregation

3	Truth and Decision	53
4	Expertise and Political Responsibility: The *Columbia* Shuttle Catastrophe	71
5	Balancing Expert Power: Two Models for the Future of Politics	93
6	Quasi-Science and the State: "Governing Science" in Comparative Perspective	114
7	The Pittsburgh Survey and the Survey Movement: An Episode in the History of Expertise	138

PART III
Expert Institutions

8 From Edification to Expertise: Sociology as a "Profession"   155

9 Scientists as Agents   179

10 Expertise and the Process of Policy Making: The EU's New Model of Legitimacy   197

11 Was Real Existing Socialism a Premature Form of Rule by Experts?   209

12 Blind Spot? Weber's Concept of Expertise and the Perplexing Case of China   223

PART IV
Collective Heuristics: Expertise as System

13 Double Heuristics and Collective Knowledge: The Case of Expertise   239

14 Normal Accidents of Expertise   257

15 Expertise in Post-Normal Science   277

Notes   297
Bibliography   311
Index   327

Acknowledgments

Chapter 1, "What Is the Problem with Experts?" was published in 2001 in *Social Studies of Science* 31(1): 123–49. Reprinted by permission of the publisher, SAGE Publications.

Chapter 2, "Political Epistemology, Expertise, and the Aggregation of Knowledge," was published in 2007 in *Spontaneous Generations: A Journal for the History and Philosophy of Science* 1(1): 36–47. Reprinted by permission of the publisher.

Chapter 3, "Truth and Decision," was published in 1989 in *Science off the Pedestal: Social Perspectives on Science and Technology*, edited by Daryl Chubin and Ellen W. Chu. Belmont, CA: Wadsworth, 175–88. Reprinted by permission of the publisher.

Chapter 4, "Expertise and Political Responsibility: the Columbia Shuttle Catastrophe," was published in 2005 in *Democratization of Expertise? Exploring Novel Forms of Scientific Advice in Political Decision-Making*, edited by Sabine Maasen and Peter Weingart. Dordrecht: Springer, 101–21. Reprinted by permission of the publisher.

Chapter 5, "Balancing Expert Power: Two Models for the Future of Politics," was published in 2008 in *Knowledge and Democracy: Is Liberty a Daughter of Knowledge*, edited by Nico Stehr. New Brunswick, NJ: Transaction, 119–41. Copyright © 2008 by Transaction Publishers. Reprinted by permission of the publisher.

Chapter 6, "Quasi-science and the State," was published in 2004 in *The Governance of Knowledge*, edited by Nico Stehr. New Brunswick, NJ: Transaction, 241–68. Copyright © 2004 by Transaction Publishers. Reprinted by permission of the publisher.

Chapter 7:, "The Pittsburgh Survey and the Survey Movement: An Episode in the History of Expertise," was published in 1996 in *Pittsburgh Surveyed:*

Social Science and Social Reform in the Early Twentieth Century, edited by Maurine W. Greenwald and Margo Anderson. Pittsburgh, PA: University of Pittsburgh Press, 35–49. Reprinted by permission of the publisher.

Chapter 8, "From Edification to Expertise: Sociology as a 'Profession,'" was published in 1992 with William Buxton as "From Education to Expertise: Sociology as a Profession" in *Sociology and Its Publics: The Forms and Fates of Disciplinary Organization*, edited by Terence C. Halliday and Morris Janowitz. Chicago, IL: University of Chicago Press, 373–407. Copyright © 1992 by The University of Chicago Press, Chicago.

Chapter 9, "Scientists as Agents," was published in 2002 in *Science Bought and Sold*, edited by Philip Mirowski and Esther-Mirjam Sent. Chicago, IL: University of Chicago Press, 362–84. Copyright © 2002 by The University of Chicago Press, Chicago.

Chapter 10, "Expertise and the Process of Policy Making: the EU's New Model of Legitimacy," was published in 2008 in *Building Civil Society and Democracy in New Europe*, edited by Sven Eliason. Cambridge: Cambridge Scholars Publishing, 160–75. Published with the permission of the publisher.

Chapter 11, "Was Real Existing Socialism a Premature Form of Rule by Experts?," was published in 2006 in *Democracy and Civil Society East of the Elbe*, edited by Sven Eliaeson. London: Routledge, 248–61. Reprinted by permission of the publisher.

Chapter 12, "Blind Spot? Weber's Concept of Expertise and the Perplexing Case of China," was published in 2008 in *Max Weber Matters: Interweaving Past and Present*, edited by Fanon Howell, Marisol Lopez Menendez, and David Chalcraft. Aldershot, UK: Ashgate Publishing, 121–34. Copyright © 2008. Reprinted in accordance with Ashgate/Gower re-use Policy.

Chapter 13, "Double Heuristics and Collective Knowledge: the Case of Expertise," was published in 2012 in *Studies in Emergent Order* 5: 82–103. Reprinted by permission of the publisher.

Chapter 14, "Normal Accidents of Expertise," was published in 2010 in *Minerva* 48: 239–58. Reprinted by permission of the publisher.

Chapter 15, "Expertise in Post-Normal Science." Copyright © Stephen Turner 2013.

Introduction

The standard issues with experts are about the nature of scientific expertise; problems of legitimacy and problems having to do with the limits of expertise; problems having to do with the place of experts in democratic politics and bureaucracies; as well as more general problems about the knowledge that experts possess: what the role of tacit knowledge and knowledge embodied in things and routines is, and to what extent expertise can be replaced or augmented by expert systems and technical means. The chapters collected in this volume will be concerned with all of these issues, with the exception of tacit knowledge and technological "expert systems," which will be the subject of a separate volume, *Understanding the Tacit*. The chapters in the present volume, however, go beyond the problem of scientific expertise, which will be treated as one type among many forms of expertise.

The chapters collected in this volume represent twenty-five years of thinking about these problems and their relations to one another. They did not lead to a "theory" of expertise, but rather to a set of questions, and especially to a consideration of the place of knowledge in society more generally, that is, to seeing the issues with expertise as part of a larger set of issues, and to seeing these highly complex issues one or two facets at a time. In what follows, I will identify some central themes that reappear in these chapters, and briefly describe them in terms of these themes. But the interest in most of these cases is in the details, and specifically in the huge variety of ways in which knowledge intertwines with social and organizational processes, and especially with those involving decision-making.

The reasoning that runs through these chapters evolved from posing a problem closely related to expertise: patronage. Why would patrons, especially democratic governments, pay for something, namely science, that they didn't understand and could not easily assess the value of? When I began to think about this question in the early 1980s, I looked at various examples of early democratic government funding of geology by state legislatures in the US, the federal funding that followed, as well as the state relationships that sustained funding for agricultural research (S. Turner 1987). I found that there were characteristic institutional forms of these relationships, and that these institutions typically originated in personal relationships of trust. Institutions of this kind continued to rely on trust, but in new forms: stable expectations and something like the output legitimacy earned by the production of useful products, such as geological surveys that aided settlement (S. Turner 1990).

The practice of patronage is a response to the fact that the distribution of wealth and the distribution of knowledge and knowledge-generating talent are misaligned. De Tocqueville considered science to require a leisure class, something that did not exist in the kind of democracy he found in nineteenth-century America. But, in fact, there were a few remnants of the pre-revolutionary order, and one of them, Stephen Van Rensselaer, did patronize science. Eventually, and to a quite astonishing extent, so did the states, most spectacularly with the New York geological survey. Patronage by the state, rather than grandees, meant that the state went into the business of assessing experts, choosing between them, and accepting the views of experts.

These institutions, which are created or developed to allow those with money to make use of or support science and for scientists to get access to money, constitute a kind of family with more or less common characteristics and variations. They do similar things, solve similar problems, face and resolve or fail to resolve similar dilemmas. One can always ask the money question about science: whether it is Tycho supporting himself, Newton at the Mint, or Galileo and the Medici (Biagioli 1993), or last year's Nobel Laureate and the bureaucratized funding system of national science organizations, there is an answer to this question. The institutions and patterns of personal relations can be described and classified.

The problem of patronage led to another, contiguous, question of trust: why do political leaders cede not only money but decision-making authority to experts? What is the nature of "expert power" in cases where the decision-making process is clear? What are the typical institutional forms through which experts influence decisions or policy carried out by others? This kind of question led to the larger question of what the relation of knowledge was to institutional forms generally, and especially to politics, democratic politics, markets, and authority broadly, and to the question of trust and legitimacy involved in the reliance on the knowledge of others.

This was largely terra incognita at the time I began writing about it, and for the most part still is, despite the large and confusing literature on democracy and science that has recently emerged. Systematic reasons for the neglect of these problems can be found in the disciplinary orientations of the various social sciences. The social world, the political world, and the world of organized effort on the whole, are normally thought of in terms that ignore knowledge. Even models of the market typically ignore information and knowledge in order to simplify. An organizational chart, or a civics account of how a bill becomes law, or an account of the structure of state authority, are all knowledge-free depictions. It is striking that in the indexes of the works of Max Weber, who used the terms *Experten* and *Spezialisten* frequently, the terms never appear. It is as though the topic did not exist for the sociologists who produced these indexes, but the omission is a huge distortion of social life.

A similar omission occurs in formal models, both in economics and social epistemology. Contemporary "formal" sociological theory, such as it is, also routinely assumes away differences in knowledge (S. Turner forthcoming 2014). But differences in knowledge between people is a pervasive fact that is entangled with all social relationships and relations of authority, and the problem of matching knowledge to power is a generic one. The people in the positions of power on organizational charts and in civics diagrams are people with knowledge, who act on knowledge, who acquire knowledge, who use and aggregate or synthesize the knowledge of others, and who are judged on their knowledge and their ability to employ it. Importantly, they systematically differ from one another with respect to the knowledge and abilities they have.

There are of course partial exceptions: Niklas Luhmann uses the notion of information, as Talcott Parsons himself did. But this notion differs systematically from "knowledge." There are economic theory uses of concepts such as information asymmetry. But the role of knowledge is characteristically muddled and addressed in conflicting (and implausible) ways in the economic literature (Mirowski 2009). In management theory there is work on practices and tacit knowledge, and something akin to the notion of tacit knowledge is central to the widespread use of "practice" notions in sociology and anthropology. There is even a field of "knowledge management." But there are large issues with most of these usages. None of them is especially helpful in discussing expert knowledge and its relation to politics or the generic problem of the relation between the distribution of knowledge and the distribution of power.

THE LARGE PROBLEM AND THE SMALL PROBLEM

Expertise is the biggest and most dramatic form of the inequality of knowledge. It is tempting to take it as paradigmatic. But the model of the individual scientist as the possessor of expertise misleads in many ways, including misleading about science and scientific knowledge itself. The picture is this: the scientific expert, possessing models and theories, and cognizant of the data and its significance, delivers truths that are policy relevant, speaking in a way that non-experts can understand the conclusions, if not the reasoning behind them. Truth is on one side, authority is on the other. The problem of the relationship is solved by truth speaking to power, and power listening. A variant form of the picture involves consensus. There is a scientific consensus that permits the scientist to do the same thing, and validates it, to the extent that it can be validated at the present time.

4 The Politics of Expertise

Science is apolitical, so there is no "politics" here except for resistance by the uncomprehending and vicious. The problem of truth speaking to power is solved, more prosaically, by the democratic and voluntary submission to the authority of science (cf. J. Brown 2001; S. Turner 2003a), which Kitcher calls "well-ordered relation of science to politics" (2001: 117).

Little about this model is *not* misleading, even if we limit it to science itself. Policy results do not directly appear from science: there are always many steps, including devising the policy as an executable plan, involving administration and implementation, goals and values, and interests that are benefitted or harmed. But these steps also involve knowledge and differences in knowledge. Scientist and experts have interests. Systems of expertise have biases, and there are risks, what I call in Chapter 14 of this volume "knowledge risk," in relying on them.

Expertise itself is dependent on other people's knowledge and on the systems that generate it. Experts aggregate knowledge from various sources; they are not solitary geniuses. The kinds of decisions that get made using expert knowledge reflect structures of decision-making, particularly national bureaucratic traditions which differ substantially in the ways that they use knowledge. And in these structures, there are always people who are employing specialized knowledge other than scientific knowledge, and people whose business it is to aggregate knowledge from others, often in order to make decisions. Many kinds of knowledge need to be made to work together in even the simplest cases of the use of expert knowledge.

But the issues go far beyond expertise in the narrow sense. There is no escape from the problems posed by differences in knowledge. Social organization is also essentially the organization of knowledge. The problem of expertise and politics is the tip of a very large iceberg. But characterizing this iceberg is not simple. I take the problem of the relation of politics to knowledge to have its intellectual origins in Plato's idea that philosophers should rule. But little of this formulation makes sense today. We no longer can think of either politics or knowledge as Plato did: there are neither kings nor forms. We need a much wider scope, with a wider conception.

The advantage of the science studies tradition, into which the chapters in this book fall, is that it grounds issues of this kind in cases with concrete implications and known historical outcomes. This book is largely a collection of case studies, with an eye to the general issues that these often tangled problems raise. But my concerns throughout will be theoretical: to understand the problem of expertise as a problem of knowledge and power, but also as a problem of the organization of knowledge and a wider conception of power and decision itself, especially the problem of the organized bringing together of bits of knowledge. A better model for this might be Durkheim's distinction between mechanical and organic solidarity. In the simplest societies, Durkheim thought, people had the same moral ideas and in complex societies with complex divisions of labor, they had different ones, corresponding to their occupation, which were needed to enable them to fit into an "organic" whole. The problem of knowledge is analogous: different people know different things, and the "problem" is to organize this knowledge for various purposes. Durkheim's solution was political, a kind of syndicalism. This is not enough. We need not only to widen the conceptions of knowledge and power, but to lengthen the list of solutions.

The case studies in the book primarily deal with the complexities of the relation of science and democracy. As I suggest, these are two distinct modes of aggregating knowledge. But the chapters also deal with a wider variety of claims to expert knowledge—wider both with respect to topics and with respect to the conception of knowledge. The book includes case-based material on a range of variant forms of the use of expertise: city planning, the decision to drop the A-bomb, national differences in responding to cholera epidemics, the Danish Planning tradition, the problem of water policy in the western US, the European Union, the "Social Survey" movement and its attempt to reform cities through the presentation of expert advice to the public, the Chinese bureaucracy, Communism, and the Rockefeller model of creating expertise. The same general themes reappear in one case after another, although with different emphases.

FOUR BASIC IDEAS

The four basic ideas that run through this volume are: the distribution of power, the distribution of knowledge, the aggregation of knowledge, and legitimacy (under which, or along with, I wish to include issues of trust and reliance on other people's knowledge). As I have suggested, the problem of the relation of knowledge to power is a generic one: the power to make authoritative decisions is distributed among people. Even if we consider only formal powers in an organized state governed by rules, there is a distribution. People are given different powers, countervailing powers, or very limited power. Kings have it, subjects don't. The rules more or less fix these powers, and rules govern changes in their distribution. Political authority, bureaucracies, and even markets may be understood in terms of the distribution of powers to decide. Knowledge is distributed as well, and differently.

The problem of aggregation links the first two ideas. If knowledge is distributed, it needs to be assembled in order to be employed for decision-making. To be assembled, there must be a process, or many processes. To be a process, there must be elements of organization. The organization of knowledge is the organization of other people's knowledge, and the structure of this organization involves trust, methods of certification and recognition filters that help to legitimate intellectual authority, and claims about the legitimacy of expertise that are intended to define boundaries with other kinds of legitimacy claims, notably those of politics. These terms—knowledge, power, distribution, aggregation, and legitimacy—all raise very large problems of their own. But elaborate definitions won't help much in clarifying the issues. It is more important to use cases to broaden our understanding of each of these elements.

Knowledge is distributed; different people know different things. This distribution is difficult to conceptualize and so is "knowledge." Some knowledge is relatively fungible and easy to distribute widely. But expertise is a particular kind of knowledge, and one that is either difficult to attain or inaccessible to others. So expert knowledge is a type of knowledge that is especially resistant to changes in the distribution of knowledge. Because scientific expertise is especially difficult to obtain, and relatively stable, it often serves as a proxy in our thinking about knowledge in society for all expertise as, similarly, expert knowledge serves as a proxy for all knowledge.

This substitution is potentially deceptive. The literature on expertise has responded by recognizing other kinds of "expertise" (cf. Collins and Evans 2007; Wynne 1996). But this is just a start. Herman Wouk, in *The Caine Mutiny*, has one of his characters say "the Navy is a master plan designed by geniuses for execution by idiots. If you're not an idiot, but find yourself in the navy, you can only operate well by pretending to be one" ([1951] 1979: 105). This raises questions about where expertise, and knowledge, actually is located. In this case the relevant knowledge is hidden in the routines that are carried out by the sailors and their commanders. Knowledge is also hidden in objects: drugs, weapons, and so forth are used by people who do not have the knowledge to make them. Finding a way to think about this kind of knowledge, and many other kinds, is a challenge.

Wouk's phrase suggests that there are originators and routine followers who are more or less mindless in their following of routines. This is similar to the kind of analysis promoted by Michel Foucault: to think of knowledge/power as one thing, enacted through or contained in the routines, which can only be understood through their originators. But this approach has its problems: one must infer the knowledge from the effects of the routines, by treating these effects as though they were intended. This kind of inference, even when it is bolstered by evidence from the words of the originators, is circular and suffers from the usual ills of functional explanation generally (Elster 2010). Moreover, Foucault's practice of inferring hidden meanings from the supposed oppressive consequences of a practice is dubious if it involves comparisons to a non-oppressive utopian state.[1] The problems addressed by "oppressive" practices, however badly, are usually real, and the practices appear oppressive rather than imperfect only if the problems are ignored. It is one thing to ridicule Victorian ideas about madness and the practices that they warranted, and it is another to abolish madness as a fact or to cure the mad.

In Wouk's case, we can see that this image of expertise is a caricature: the people involved know many things the originators do not. It may well be that the best way to succeed is to follow the routines. But doing so itself requires skills and knowledge: local knowledge of how to carry out the routines, tacit knowledge, embodied skills, and beliefs about what they are doing. These beliefs may be very limited, based as they are on institutionally constructed experiences which provide their basis. But they are part of the knowledge that needs to be aggregated in order to make the institution work, and it is normally not shared with the public, the originators, or the people on the top of the organizational hierarchy.

It is important, then, to see both what is true and false about this caricature. What is true is that the people who carry out routines often have a very limited perspective on the whole, and that what they "know" is shaped by experiences that are themselves limited. But it is also true that they know things that must be known for the institution to work, and know things about the failures and problems with the routines that the people in charge do not know. These types of knowledge aggregate, but they do not necessarily (or normally) get aggregated into a synthesis that is in the grasp of one person. Aggregation is organized, and in different ways. What comes out as a decision, or as accepted knowledge, is the product of organization, but it is the organization of people with knowledge. To understand this process we need to understand the varieties of knowledge that are involved in it. But we need to understand a few other things much more including: What motivates them to share knowledge? How it is codified to be shared? How do others assess knowledge claims? What are the many ways we rely on the knowledge of others?

The solution to these issues is not to caricature, but to enrich our notion of knowledge. A theory of knowledge is not, however, going to help much, and in the chapters on expertise and knowledge that follow in this volume, I make no attempt to provide a novel definition or theory of "knowledge." Knowledge is, in my view, a much too diffuse and confused concept to yield to "analysis" in the traditional philosophical sense. At best, we can work with a functional notion of knowledge: A routine can do things for us that a justified true belief can do; tacit knowledge can do what explicit knowledge can do; an instrument can do what a trained body can do; a person merely following a routine can do what a person who is knowledgeable about the process itself can do. Objects created by design can also serve as functional substitutes for knowledge. These enrichments of our notion of knowledge can be extended. This is perhaps the best we can do.

WHAT IS KNOWLEDGE AND WHAT IS "SOCIAL" ABOUT IT?

Our normal model of knowing is individual. Even "social epistemology," in its most common form, is concerned with the individual knower and how this knower can give and receive knowledge—with giving and receiving based on the model of testimony, an individual act articulated in speech, indeed in propositions, and capable of justification according to the traditional philosophical formula of knowledge as justified true belief. This is obviously very limiting. But we can say something about the "social" character of knowledge even with this impoverished vocabulary. Knowledge in the familiar propositional sense typically depends on other people's knowledge. Even the simplest justified true belief in science is not known directly, but instead by relying on machines, claims made and certified by others, rote learning of formulas, and so forth. Michael Polanyi was fond of saying that all knowledge was either tacit knowledge or depended on tacit knowledge. We can say similarly that (virtually) all knowledge is taken at least in part from other people or dependent on the knowledge of other people. This is the generic problem of which the problem of expert knowledge is a subspecies.

Expert knowledge exhibits this dependence in dramatic fashion: experts, particularly experts in science, are heavily dependent on other people's knowledge, whether it is taken from textbooks or journals, taught, learned by imitation and coaching, or built into instruments. What people understand and know depends on things they do not understand or know. Much of this knowledge is specialized knowledge that is more or less inaccessible, in a practical sense, to specialists of other kinds. This is true both of scientific knowledge in the narrow sense and of policy-related science and policy itself.

The standard philosophical formula "justified true belief" obscures all of this, and obscures the problem of distribution. Questions like "For whom is it 'justified'?" and "What does 'justified' mean for different persons?" are papered over by treating justification and truth as abstract and unlocated conditions. To be sure, there are numerous ways of revising our concepts of knowledge to overcome the problem of distribution. We can talk about distributed knowledge, with the thought that the knowledge contained in the whole of a group of cooperating individuals is greater than the knowledge possessed by any individual (Giere and Moffatt 2003). We can use the metaphor of the extended mind (Clark 1998) and deny that it is a metaphor (cf. Collins 2010). But metaphors are not enough, and these metaphors are less than helpful with the case of expertise.

The fact that knowledge is distributed, that we are dependent through and through on knowledge generated, warranted, secured, discovered, and constructed conceptually in communicable ways by others, means that our decisions—including our decisions (even our tacit "choices") to believe, accept, or act on knowledge—are decisions that depend on processes by which we aggregate knowledge from other sources and combine it with our own knowledge. The emphasis in several of the following chapters is on the inherent epistemic problems of the aggregation of knowledge, the judging of expert claims, and the translation of expertise into decisions. These chapters concern ways in which this goes wrong because of the inherent difficulties of making decisions involving expert knowledge, especially aggregated knowledge, and assessing expert claims.

For users of expert claims, including experts themselves, there are issues of trust. In large scale expert-audience relations, these are usually described as problems of legitimacy. Science as a whole rests on a vast amount of what is called output legitimacy as distinct from process legitimacy. Science is legitimated by the fact that it allows us to produce valuable results. Democracy rests on process legitimacy; the question of legitimacy is whether the rules of the process were followed. With experts we have a bit of both: Are the supposed experts really knowledgeable (an output problem), and is there a system of checks that assures us that they are speaking as experts rather than as interested parties (a process problem).

This is a problem that can be conceptualized in some respects in terms of agency theory and the idea of bonding as addressed in Chapter 9 of this volume. Is the lab that produced a result known for the quality of its work? Is the journal that published it known for its editorial strictness? Is the university from which it came jealous of its reputation? Do the professionals have a stake in their reputation that would prevent them from misleading? Within closer or more equal relations the issue of reliance is more readily described in terms of trust, but "legitimacy" is a flexible term. More to the point, much of what we "know" we have accepted because we think there is a system that assures that what we take to be fact is vetted or filtered through some sort of institutional process that minimizes error or corrects for it. But there are many systems of this sort. Markets are means of aggregating information about preferences, the quality of products, and the like. The politics of representative government is a means of testing the strength of the beliefs and desires and of revising them in the light of opposition and discussion under conditions of conflicting interests (see Chapter 5 of this volume).

Expertise has often been thought of as an alternative to politics and the market, and various forms for the use and assessment of expert opinion have been devised by states and polities. The German model involves bureaucracy-led negotiations between interested parties who have expert knowledge, with the aim of producing a consensus that politicians don't, and aren't in a position to, contest. The Imperial Chinese system relied on a class of bureaucrats who were literati and gained their positions through a system of literary testing, thus replacing politics with expertise (see Chapter 12 of this volume). Communism itself was largely understood by its promoters as a means of replacing the market with expert decision-making and party membership was a sign of ideological reliability (see Chapter 11 of this volume).

These systems all have had their critics, as well as their failures. But they are each attempts, typically attempts that are strongly marked by preexisting bureaucratic administrative traditions and forms, to solve the problem of taking knowledge that is widely distributed in society and organizing it in such a way that it can be used as a basis for state action. Even the ideological systems of Confucianism and Communism did this: they equipped their possessors with a common method of dealing with the specific knowledge-sensitive issues that arose in the course of governance.

These chapters are about "knowledge" in a much broader sense than scientific knowledge or expertise. The minimal sense of knowledge that is in common to all of these cases is functional: Knowledge is something cognitive in origin that enables someone to do something they could not otherwise do. Knowledge that is merely accepted or defined as knowledge politically fits this definition; the acceptance of a creed or ideology enables people in a group to do things they could not have done otherwise. This is not a notion of knowledge that matches up with "truth." But we can say something about the biases that are built into the construction of these forms of knowledge, and about the risks that they generate, because these are risks and biases on their own terms. Just as science operates with an idea of truth that can become discrepant from the products of its institutional processes, so can political or religious communities face conflicts between their "truths" and the truths produced by their institutional processes—Communists rejected the Communist regimes of which they were a part; Catholics can reject the Pope. One can be agnostic about metaphysical truth but acknowledge these kinds of conflicts, as well as such things as knowledge risk, failure, and the problems of aggregating knowledge. Indeed, these kinds of considerations are very much part of the self-reflection of members of knowledge communities themselves.

Science, as a system of indirect bonding that employs a large number of weak but redundant means of correction, is a very strong system over the long run. Its weaknesses are conservatism, the inability to give the answers that are demanded of it, and so forth. Solutions to these problems, such as the methods of the organization of knowledge production of post-normal science, create knowledge risks. We can say something about biases, and something about these risks. We can compare different forms of knowledge aggregation, such as liberal democracy and markets. We can also attempt to understand how knowledge works in complex organizations. We can even begin to think about the role of knowledge differences in ordinary social interaction. But thinking about these things is difficult. What this volume represents, for me, is a start on bringing considerations about knowledge into all of these domains, but doing so by generalizing the institutional problems of matching knowledge and power to the many domains in which it appears rather than by treating one of these domains, science, as paradigmatic.

PART I: SOME THEORY

Finding one's way around these problems even in a preliminary way requires "theory." The most minimal form of theory is taxonomy, and the most minimal form of taxonomy is a laundry list without even the pretense of completeness. Although the concerns of these chapters are "theoretical," the theoretical content appears primarily in the themes discussed above, rather than in any explicit theory. Nevertheless some explicit "theory" in the form of taxonomy can provide an orientation and motivation for the case studies.

Chapter 1, "What is the Problem with Experts?," is a taxonomy of expert-audience relations, with an eye to specifying the relations that are politically relevant and explaining why and how they are relevant. Several of the examples given in this chapter are elaborated in the case studies that follow.

Chapter 2, "Political Epistemology, Experts, and the Aggregation of Knowledge," provides a laundry list of forms of aggregation, which has no pretense of being complete. The case studies that follow discuss several of these.

PART II: AGGREGATION

Chapter 3, "Truth and Decision," is a discussion of a case in which multiple forms of expertise need to be integrated to solve a policy problem, in this case the nineteenth century settlement policy for the arid lands of the American West. This problem had multiple elements—legal, political, scientific, and a problem of experts against citizens. The policy at stake was homesteading—the welfare program of the American nineteenth century. The expert issues involved climate; the conflict was between the actual, but short term, experience of settlers and the experts' insistence that the land in question was undergoing a wet cycle that would not last. There was also expert disagreement; some scientists believed that "rain follows the plow." This is a striking example of decision-making involving imperfect alternatives (Komesar 1994) or to put it in the language of the chapter, ill-structured problems that do not admit of a single solution.

Chapter 4, "Expertise and Political Responsibility," examines a core example of the problem of aggregation as well as dependence on others—the *Columbia* shuttle disaster. In contrast to the official report on NASA decision-making, and to the influential "culture" thesis of Diane Vaughan, I emphasize the problems of organizing, assessing, and filtering expert input over roughly five thousand critical flight issues. What needed to be aggregated? Only the specialists had fully expert knowledge on these issues, and they were organized into teams which had within them distributed knowledge that needed to be put together. The administrators involved in these decisions relied on a system of information gathering that compelled the members of the responsible units to raise concerns, but also to back the concerns with data.

The NASA system of placing the burden of responsibility for flagging issues upon the engineering groups responsible for each issue, and filtering this through discussion and presentation groups, was and is a reasonable solution to a problem inherent in the fact that no group or decision-maker could possibly hope to be sufficiently expert to correctly judge all the claims made by the engineers charged with responsibility for each of these critical issues. Like any system for aggregation, this one had biases. In this case the bias excluded the considerations that would have led to a correct decision. But for the most part it was successful, and the reforms did nothing to deal with the intrinsic issues.

Chapter 5, "Balancing Expert Power," takes up two related issues. The first is the absence of knowledge considerations in standard accounts of high politics; these are cases where the descriptions are a matter of power with the knowledge left out. The decision to drop the A-bomb is a classic example of this kind of description. However, that decision was based on a complex process of aggregating expert opinion. The ultimate recommendation reflected a basic concern about the legitimacy of science—vast sums had been spent on the development of the bomb; failure to use it, with the attendant risk of lives lost during an invasion, would have radically undermined the credibility of science in the congressional inquiry into the decision that surely would have followed. This was, then, a decision made under the threat of democratic processes of scrutiny, and although it was an "expert" decision, it was sensitive to what democratic politics would have expected.

If this is a genuine case of expert authority subordinating itself to democracy, there is an alternative: the kind of self-proclaimed "democratic" use of expertise found in the ideology of Danish urban planners, expressed in the work of Bent Flyvbjerg in his analysis of the politics of the Aalborg city plan (1998). Flyvbjerg celebrates the struggle of the planners against "power," by which he means the people who believed they would be adversely affected by the plan and responded by opposing it politically rather than succumbing to bureaucratic coercion. This is simply an inversion of the idea of democracy and the misrepresentation of a form of expert power as democratic.

Flyvbjerg is against the use of democratic procedures to control bureaucrats, because he sees this as power opposed to rationality. But the case illustrates the use of political means to balance expert power. The A-bomb case illustrates something similar, but in the form of anticipation; when the experts were told that there would be a congressional inquiry into the decision if it went wrong, they responded by doing what they expected the public would want.

Chapter 6, "Quasi-Science and the State," looks at the processes of selecting and using experts in three distinct bureaucratic traditions. National administrative traditions are both extremely entrenched and quite different. The three traditions discussed in the chapter are the American pattern of imitating successful models in other states or cities, the British model of granting considerable discretion to experts in positions of power, and the

German model of stakeholders beholden to bureaucracies. Each produced very different responses to the great scourge of cholera. The British system produced an officialdom that clung to the miasma theory, but allowed for local discretion, which was used effectively to empower a private expert with a competing, and correct model.[2] The German model led to the disaster of the Hamburg cholera epidemic. The American model of distributed authority led, however slowly, to the adoption of best practices, those proven in other jurisdictions.

This case illustrates issues with Ulrich Beck's (1992) notion of the "demonopolization of expertise" and with "stakeholder" models generally. The issue is one of aggregation: stakeholders know something, as do experts. But compromise together with a failure to get the right experts can lead to disaster. The two alternative models relied on competition. Competition structured in ways that exposed the limitations of expertise, worked in the British case to produce the most important breakthrough in the history of cholera control; in the German case, the right expert was excluded by the stakeholders. Writers such as James Bryant Conant (1951) suggested ways to institutionalize this kind of competition in order to prevent the bad effects of expert monopolies, an important theme that recurs in other chapters.

Chapter 7, "The Pittsburgh Survey and the Survey Movement," considers a major social survey of the early twentieth century. The survey itself, and indeed the survey movement of which it was the crown jewel, were solutions to aggregation problems. The normal strategy of the survey movement was to bring together the local leaders concerned with particular social problems and develop an overview of these problems that emphasized the connections between them. The knowledge that was aggregated was the expert knowledge of the participants, who were experienced administrators familiar with the local issues.

But there was more to it. The survey was an attempt to enroll the public in an expert-led and defined political project of municipal transformation. Here the leaders were self-conscious about strategy. They believed that an enlightened public would be a progressive public, and democratically enthrone their particular form of expertise. This was a partial success in that the reformers won an election. But they were soon booted out, and the model itself never lived up to expectations, for reasons having to do with the contrast between what the rather paternalistic experts believed and what citizens knew and preferred.

PART III: EXPERT INSTITUTIONS

In the next section, I consider several developed or consciously theorized attempts at organizing expert knowledge for decision-making or application.

Chapter 8, "From Edification to Expertise" (with William Buxton), contrasts two models in the history of sociology: the public intellectual

14 *The Politics of Expertise*

or public sociology model, as exemplified by the early twentieth century American sociologist Charles Ellwood, and the model pioneered by the Rockefeller philanthropies. This model was first applied in medicine, which was reformed in accordance with the Flexner report. The model, as fully developed, was to improve training, promote professional societies, certify and institute forms of continuing education and connection with university medical schools, which were themselves improved and reformed, and so forth. The same professionalization strategy was then applied, with slight variations, to other fields, such as the professionalization of government work as "public administration." The chapter deals with the ways in which Harvard sociology benefitted from and adapted to this model, and to the new kind of expertise it allowed academics to assert.

Chapter 9, "Scientists as Agents," uses economic concepts from agency theory to make sense of the complex indirect system by which scientists warrant one another. It notes that scientists spend much of their time on evaluation. The sheer cost of this work is an indication of its importance. But what does it do? I suggest that science works on a complex and redundant system of bonding mechanisms, such as awards, rankings of university departments and journals, and so forth, which indirectly but effectively warrant trust in the results of science.

This, however, is an account of something like "classical" science or science other than the kind of science with a mission or policy orientation, such as that discussed in the final chapter, on post-normal science. In a sense this earlier form of science, which persists in some areas of science today, is a "liberal" model of science. It relies largely on indirect means, but it allows scientists to speak for science, an important aspect of expertise, without having any sort of official status. This model is valuable as a baseline to compare other forms of science and other forms of legitimacy.

Part I
Some Basic Theory

1 What Is the Problem with Experts?[1]

Discussions of expertise and expert power typically have "political implications," but the underlying political thinking that gives them these implications is rarely spelled out.[1] In what follows I will break down the problem of expertise to its elements in political theory. The first problem arises from social theory, and concerns democracy and equality. In the writings of persons concerned with the political threat to democracy posed by the existence of expert knowledge, expertise is treated as a kind of possession which privileges its possessors with powers that the people cannot successfully control, and cannot acquire or share in.

Understood in this way, expertise is a problem because it is a kind of violation of the conditions of rough equality presupposed by democratic accountability. Some activities, such as genetic engineering, are apparently out of the reach of democratic control (even when these activities, because of their dangerous character, ought to be subject to public scrutiny and regulation) precisely because of imbalances in knowledge, simply because "the public," as a public, cannot understand the issues. This is not to say that democratic actions cannot be taken against these activities, but they are necessarily actions beyond the genuine competence of those who are acting. So we are faced with the dilemma of capitulation to "rule by experts" or democratic rule which is "populist"—that is to say, that valorizes the wisdom of the people even when "the people" are ignorant and operate on the basis of fear and rumor.

The second problem arises from normative political theory. Regarding differences in knowledge as a problem of equality leads in some troubling directions. If we think of knowledge as a quantity, or a good to which some have access and others do not, the solution, admittedly one with practical limitations, is egalitarianization through difference-obliterating education or difference-obliterating access to expertise, for example through state subsidy of experts and the dissemination of their knowledge and advice.[2] But if the differences are better understood as differences in viewpoint rather than differences in quantities of knowledge, then we have another problem. Paul Feyerabend (1978: 73–76) insisted that a program of extensive public "science education" is merely a form of state propaganda for a faction, the faction of "experts." Thus it is a violation of the basic neutrality of the state, of the impartiality the liberal state must exhibit in the face of rival opinions in order to ensure the possibility of genuine, fair, and open discussion. This second issue may seem to be a marginal issue, of interest only to fanatics, but increasingly it has become a practical problem.

The abstract form of the problem is this: if the liberal state is supposed to be neutral with respect to opinions—in other words it neither promotes nor gives special regard to any particular beliefs, world views, sectarian positions, and so on—what about expert opinions? Do they have some sort of special properties that sectarian opinions lack? If not, why should the state give them special consideration, for example through the subsidization of science, or by treating expert opinions about environmental damage differently than the opinions of landowners or polluters? If they do have special status, what is it? The special status granted to religious opinion leads to its exclusion from the domain of state action. Religion is either not an acceptable subject of state action, or is granted a protected status of limited autonomy, as in the case of the established church in England, in exchange for the church's renunciation of politics. The status of religion has often been proposed as a model for the state's relation to science (Polanyi [1946] 1964: 59; Price 1965). But it is a peculiar analogy, because the state not only protects and subsidizes science, it attends to the opinions of science, which is to say it grants science a kind of authority, and reaffirms this authority by requiring that regulations be based on the findings of science or on scientific consensus, and by promoting the findings of science as fact.

With respect to religion, then, the state attempts some form of neutrality, if only by separating the two and delegating to churches authority over special topics or special rights. With science, and more generally with "expert" opinion, it is the opinions themselves that are treated as being "neutral." This special status becomes problematic when admittedly "sectarian" beliefs come into conflict with expert opinion and the non-sectarian neutral character of expert opinion is called into question. Problems of this sort have occurred, for example, in connection with the teaching of creationism throughout the twentieth century in the US. But the issues here are more easily ridiculed than solved. For problems like "is 'creation science' really 'science'?" there are no very convincing answers in principle, and no "principles" on which to rely that cannot themselves be attacked as ideological. Nor is the problem limited to sectarian beliefs. Research on the genetic background of criminals has been denounced as "racist" and government agencies have been intimidated into withdrawing support. Studies of race and intelligence, similarly, have been attacked as inherently racist, or "non-neutral." A letter writer to *Newsweek* wrote that "theories of intelligence, the test to measure it and the societal structures in which its predictions come true are all developed and controlled by well-off white males for their own benefit" (Jaffe 1994: 26). The idea that science itself, with its mania for quantification, prediction and control, is merely an intellectual manifestation of racism and sexism—that is to say, is non-neutral—is not only widespread, it is often treated in feminist theory as a given. There is a more general problem for liberalism that arises from this: if the liberal state is supposed to be ideologically neutral, how is it to decide what is and is not ideology as distinct from knowledge?

THE TWO ISSUES TOGETHER

If the two issues, equality and neutrality, are each taken on their own terms, they can be discussed in a mundane political way. The solution to the problem of experts uncontrolled by democracy is to devise controls such as the citizens councils on technology that have been started in Denmark; the solution to a public incapable of keeping up with the demands of the modern world is to educate it better, a traditional aim of scientists, economists and others, for whom "public understanding" is central. The problem with liberal democracy created by expert knowledge doesn't need a fancy solution; we can continue to do what we do now, which is to "muddle through." For example, we may just declare science to be non-sectarian and deal with oddities like creation science by judicial fiat, or decline to fund science, or to permit or reject technology that has controversial implications or arouses the antagonism of "public interest" groups on the basis of public opinion and political expedience. Taken together, however, the two problems raise a more difficult question: if experts are the source of the public's knowledge, and this knowledge is not essentially superior to unaided public opinion, not genuinely expert, then the "public" itself is presently not merely less competent than the experts, but is also more or less under the cultural or intellectual control of the experts.

This idea, inspired by Michel Foucault, is perhaps the dominant leitmotif in present "cultural studies," and informs its historiography: the ordinary consumer of culture is taken to be the product of mysterious forces that constrain them into thinking in racist, sexist and "classist" ways. These constraints are, so to speak, imbibed along with cultural products. In Donna Haraway's famous (but disputed) example, a person exposed to an "expert" representation of human evolution at a natural history museum, in which the more advanced people have features that resemble modern Europeans, becomes a racist and a sexist (Haraway 1984–85; Schudson 1997). It is now widely taken for granted that this kind of effect of expertise is the true realm of "politics," and that politics as traditionally understood is subordinate to—because it is conducted within the frame defined by—cultural givens, which themselves originate in part in the opinions of "experts" in the past, such as the presentations of museum dioramas. It is this general form of argument that I wish to examine here from the perspective of liberal political theory, for it is to liberal political theory, as opposed to liberal politics, that this cultural argument poses a challenge.

A standard view of liberalism, perhaps most pungently expressed by Carl Schmitt, takes it to be the product of the lessons of early modern Europe's wars of religion. Liberal politics developed, where it did develop, as the consequence of the adoption of a certain kind of convention: matters of religion were agreed to be outside of the domain of the political. The domain of the political was reduced, *de facto*, to the domain of opinions about which people could agree to disagree, to tolerate, and further agree to accept the results of parliamentary debate and voting in the face of disagreement. It was also implicitly understood that some matters, such as matters of fact, were not subject to "debate," but were the common possession of, and could be appealed to by, all sides in the course of public discussion. Schmitt made the point that parliamentary democracy depended on the possibility of "persuading one's opponents through argument of the truth or justice of something, or allowing oneself to be persuaded of something as true or just" ([1923] 1988: 5). Without some such appeal—if opinions were not amenable to change through discussion, and persuasion was simply a form of the negotiation of compromises between pre-established interests—parliamentary institutions would be meaningless shells. What Schmitt saw in the parliamentary politics of the Weimar era was that this assumption of parliamentarism no longer held. Rational persuasion with respect to what is true or just had ceased. The parties of Weimar politics, however, were more than mere interest parties. They were "totalizing" parties that construed the world ideologically, ordered the life experiences and social life of their members, and rejected the world-views of other parties and all the arguments that depended on these other world-views.

Schmitt believed that the former historical domain of parliamentary discussion, in which genuine argument was possible, had simply vanished. The world of totalitarianism, of the rule of totalizing parties, had begun. He didn't say that the liberal idea of parliamentary government, government by discussion, was wrong in principle. But there is a currently influential argument from principle that has the same conclusion. Stanley Fish has recently claimed that liberalism is "informed by a faith (a word deliberately chosen) in reason as a faculty that operates independently of any particular world view" (1994: 134). Fish denies that this can be anything more than a faith, and concludes that this means that liberalism doesn't exist. This is an argument, in effect, for undoing the central achievement of the modern state and unlearning the lessons of the wars of religion. But it is a curiously compelling argument nevertheless, especially if it is conjoined with the idea that the major products of the modern liberal state have been racial and gender inequity and injustice.

Expert knowledge is susceptible to a variant of this argument: expert knowledge masquerades as neutral fact, accessible to all sides of a debate; but it is merely another ideology. Jürgen Habermas makes this charge implicitly when he speaks of "expert cultures." Many other critics of past experts, influenced by Foucault, have substantiated this claim in great detail. Their point, typically, is that "expert" claims or presentations of reality by experts have produced discursive structures—"ideologies"—that were unwittingly accepted by ordinary people and politicians as fact, but were actually expressions of patriarchy, racism, and the like. Present-day "expertise" raises the same problems: the difference is that we lack the historical distance to see the deeper meaning of the claims of experts.

If it is true that expert knowledge is "ideology" taken as fact, the idea of liberal parliamentary discussion is, intellectually at least, a sham. The factual claims on the basis of which parliamentary discussion is possible are exposed as ideological. The true ideological basis of liberalism is thus hidden: it is really what is agreed to be fact, and what is agreed to be fact is, some of the time, the product not of open debate but of the authority of experts. The actual discussions in parliament and before the electorate are conducted within the narrow limits imposed by what is agreed to be fact, and therefore, indirectly, by expert opinion. To accept the authority of science or experts is thus to accept authoritative ideological pronouncements. So liberal regimes are no less ideological than other regimes; rather, the basis of liberal regimes in ideological authority is concealed under a layer of doctrinal self-deception.

These two problems—the problem of the character of expert knowledge, which undermines liberalism, and the problem of the inaccessibility of expert knowledge to democratic control—thus combine in a striking way. We are left with a picture of modern democratic regimes as shams, with a public whose culture and life-world are controlled or "steered" by experts whose doings are beyond public comprehension (and therefore beyond intelligent public discussion), but whose "expert" knowledge is nothing but ideology, ideology made more powerful by virtue of the fact that its character is concealed. This concealment is the central legacy of liberalism. The public, indeed, is its pitiful and ineffective victim.

Habermas gives a version of the social-theoretical argument that suggests why the usual solutions to these two problems, of neutrality and democracy, fail. The argument depends on a characterization of the viewpoint of ordinary people, which he calls "the internal perspective of the life-world." This perspective, he claims, is governed by three fictions: that actors are autonomous beings; that culture is independent of external restraints; and that communication is "transparent," by which he means that everyone can, in principle, understand everyone else (Habermas [1985] 1987: 149–50). But in fact, he argues, the life-world is the product, at least in part, of external controls, which he calls "steering mechanisms," operated by experts whose thinking is not comprehensible within the traditions that are part of, and help to constitute, the life-world. There is an unbridgeable cultural gap, in short, between the world of illusions under which the ordinary member of the public operates and the worlds of "expert cultures" (Habermas [1985] 1987: 397). The fictions of the life-world themselves prevent its denizens from grasping the manner in which it is controlled.

Robert Merton expresses a related point in a different way, with the notion that professionals and scientists possess "cognitive authority." Presumably Habermas has many of the same people in mind when he refers to "expert cultures," but there is an important difference in the way the two conceive of the problem. Habermas's experts don't exert their influence by persuasion, but rather by manipulating conditions of social existence (especially to manufacture a kind of unthinking satisfaction), which Habermas calls "colonizing the life-world." Merton's model, the relation of authority, is more familiar. Merton adds that this authority is experienced as a kind of alien power against which people sometimes rebel—the coexistence of acceptance and rebellion he calls "ambivalence" (Merton 1976: 26).

Authority is, in its most common form, a political concept, and it points to the problem posed by expertise for the theory of democracy. Experts are not democratically accountable, but they nevertheless exercise authority-like powers over questions of true belief. Habermas's picture is somewhat different: the experts he seems to be concerned with are not professionals whom we deal with often in a face-to-face way, but policymakers hidden behind a wall of bureaucracy. Whether this difference is significant is a question that I will leave open for the moment. But it points to some difficulties with the concept of expertise itself that need to be more fully explored.

Expertise thus is a more complicated affair than my original formulations supposed. Cognitive authority, whatever it is, seems to be open to resistance and submission, but not to the usual compromises of democratic politics. It is not an object that can be distributed, nor can it be simply granted—so that everyone can be treated as an "expert" for the sake of service on a committee evaluating risks, for example. To be sure, legal fictions of equality can be extended to such political creations as citizens' oversight committees, and legal fictions have non-fictive consequences that may be very powerful. But cognitive authority is likely to elude such bodies, for reasons pinpointed by Habermas: the limitations of the perspective of the life-world preclude communicative equality between expert and non-expert.

Construed in either way, expertise is trouble for liberalism. If experts possess Mertonian cognitive authority, they pose a problem for neutrality: can the state preserve its independent authority, its power to act as neutral judge, for example, in the face of the authoritative claims of experts? Or must it treat them as inherently non-sectarian or neutral? Experts in bureaucracies pose a somewhat different but no less troubling problem. If we think of the distinctively German contribution to liberalism as the idea that official discretionary powers ought to be limited as much as possible—the ideal of a state of laws, not of men—it is evident that "experts" have an apparently irreducible role precisely in those places in the state apparatus that discretionary power exists. Indeed, expertise and discretionary power are notions that are made for one another.

COGNITIVE AUTHORITY AND ITS LEGITIMACY

"Authority" is a peculiar concept to use in conjunction with "knowledge": in political theory one usually thinks of authority in contrast to truth, as for example Schmitt does when he paraphrases Hobbes as saying that authority, not truth, makes law. By authority Schmitt means the effective power to make and enforce decisions. Cognitive authority is, in these terms, an oxymoron. If you have knowledge, one need not have authority. But it is a nice analogue to "moral authority." And there is of course an earlier, and perhaps more fundamental, notion of *auctoritas* as authorship. The underlying thought is that the "authority" has at first hand something that others—subjects or listeners—get at second hand. And this is part of the notion of expertise as well: the basis on which experts believe in the facts or validity of knowledge claims of other experts of the same type they believe in is different from the basis on which non-experts believe in the experts. The facts of nuclear physics, for example, are "facts," in any real sense (facts that one can use effectively, for example), only to those who are technically trained in such a way as to recognize the facts as facts, and do something with them. The non-expert is not trained in such a way as to make much sense of them: accepting the predigested views of physicists as authoritative is basically all that even the most sophisticated untrained reader can do. The point may be made very simply in the terms given by Schmitt: it is the character of expertise that only other experts may be persuaded by argument of the truth of the claims of the expert; the rest of us must accept them as true on different grounds than other experts do.

The literature on the phenomenon of the cognitive authority of science (see Gieryn 1994; Gieryn and Figert 1986) focuses on the mechanisms of social control that scientists employ to preserve and protect their cognitive authority. The cognitive authority of scientists in relation to the public is, so to speak, corporate. Scientists possess their authority when they speak as representatives of science. And the public judgments of science are of science as a corporate phenomenon, of scientists speaking as scientists. So these social control mechanisms are as crucial to the cognitive authority of science, as they are to the professions, Merton's original subject. But what these literatures have generally ignored is the question that arises in connection with the political concept of authority, the problems of the origin of authority. How did cognitive authorities establish their authority in the first place? And how do they sustain it?

If we consider the paradigm case of physicists as cognitive authorities, the answers to these questions are relatively straightforward, and it is not surprising that the issue is seldom discussed as problematic. We all know (or have testimony that comes from users or recipients) about the efficacy of the products of physics, such as nuclear weapons, that we do accept, and we are told that these results derive from the principles of physics, that is to say the "knowledge" that physicists certify one another as possessing.

Consequently we do have grounds for accepting the claim of physicists to possess knowledge of these matters, and in this sense our "faith" in physics is not dependent on faith alone—though, it is important to add, these are not the grounds that physicists themselves use in assessing one another's cognitive claims, or are only a small part of the grounds.

If we take the model that is suggested by this discussion of cognitive authority in science, we have something like this. Expertise is a kind of possession, certified or uncertified, of knowledge that is testified to be efficacious and in which this testimony is widely accepted by the relevant audience. But if this were all there was to expertise, it is difficult to see why anyone would regard claims to expertise or the exercise of expert authority to be a threat to democracy. Authority conceived of as resting in some sense on widely accepted testimony (at least within the relevant audience) to the efficacy of the knowledge that experts correctly claim to possess is itself a kind of democratic authority, for this acceptance is a kind of democratic legitimation.

One might go on to suggest that these authority claims are themselves subject to the same kind of defects as those of democratic political authority generally. Public opinion may be wrong, and mistakenly accept authority that ought not to be accepted. One might cite the relation between theological authorities and audiences of believers as examples of the way in which spurious (or at least mysterious) assertions of special knowledge can come to be regarded as authoritative, and in which highly problematic esoteric knowledge is granted the same sort, or similar kind, of deference as is scientific knowledge. But in the case of theological knowledge we do see something that was perhaps not so clear in the case of the cognitive authority of science, namely that the audiences for authority claims may indeed be very specific, and may not correspond with the public as a whole. And claims made to, and accepted by, delimited audiences may themselves be in error, and subsequently be rejected by these same audiences or by their successors.

Thinking about the audiences of the expert—the audiences for whom the expert is legitimate and whose acceptance legitimates her claims to expertise—illuminates a puzzle in the discourse of the problem of expertise and democracy. Merton and Habermas, it appeared, were not talking about the same kinds of experts. For Merton, the paradigm case was the physician, whose expert advice, say, to cut down on high-fat foods, we receive with ambivalence (Merton 1976: 24–25). For Habermas, the "experts" who steer society from a point beyond the cultural horizon of the life-world, and do so in terms of their own expert cultures ([1985] 1987: 397), are themselves a kind of corporate body or audience which has no public legitimacy as expert, and indeed is largely hidden from the public. This model does not fit physics. If the account of the cognitive authority of science that I have given is more or less true, the authority of physics is itself more or less democratically acknowledged, and is thus legitimate in a way that the authority of hidden experts is not. Physics, in short, not only claimed authority, and embodied it in the corporate form of the community of physicists, but this corporate authority has achieved a particular kind of legitimation, legitimation not only beyond the sect of physicists, but acceptance that is more or less universal.

If we begin with this as a kind of ideal-type or paradigm case of a particular kind of legitimate cognitive authority, and call them "Type I Experts," we can come up with a list of other types in which the character of legitimacy is different. In this list we can include experts of the type discussed by Habermas, who seem not to possess the democratic legitimation of physicists. The easy distinctions may be made in terms of audience and legitimators. As I have suggested, the theologian is an expert with cognitive authority. Like the physicist, the authority of the theologian is legitimated by the acceptance of an audience—the audience is simply a restricted one, but a predetermined one. The cognitive authority of the theologian extends only to the specific audience of the sect. We may call these "restricted audience" experts "Type II Experts."

If the first two types of expert are experts for pre-established audiences, such as the community of physicists, or a predefined community of sectarian believers, a third, the "Type III Expert," is the expert who creates her own following. This type shades off into the category of persons who are paid for the successful performance of services. Massage therapists are paid for their knowledge or for their exercise, but payment depends on the judgment of the beneficiaries of that knowledge to the effect that the therapy worked. The testimony of the beneficiaries allows a claim of expertise to be established for a wider audience. But some people do not benefit by massage therapy, and do not find the promises of massage therapy to be fulfilled. So massage therapists have what is, so to speak, a created audience, a set of followers for whom they are expert because they have proven themselves to this audience by their actions. "Experts" who are considered experts because they have published best-selling books that do something for their audiences, such as Dr. Ruth (Westheimer), are experts in this sense as well: they have followings that they themselves created, but which are not general. They have *auctoritas* in the original sense.

Experts of three kinds—those whose cognitive authority is generally accepted, those whose cognitive authority is accepted by a sect, and those whose cognitive authority is accepted by some group of followers—each have a place in the scheme of liberal democracy. The expertise of the physicist is taken to be itself neutral; the state is neutral toward the other two, but in different ways. One can enter politics—Dr. Ruth might run for the senate, for example, or promote some political cause, such as sex education in elementary schools—but it is agreed that the other is to be excluded. The religious sectarian is excluded by way of the concept of the neutrality of the liberal state: the domain of politics is delimited, by agreement, to preclude the state, as the First Amendment puts it, from establishing a religion. But literally "establishing" religion and at the same time restricting it (on, for example, the model of the established churches of European states), can serve the same purpose of both separating religion from politics and assuring that the boundaries of the domain of the political are decided politically rather than by religious experts, thus delegating authority to Type II Experts. But this is a conscious and "public" choice.

There may, of course, be conflicts of a more or less transitory kind between the authority of physicists and political authority—King Canute may attempt to command the tides in the Wash against the advice of his physicists. Conflicts of a less transitory kind—between expert economists and economically inexpert political ideologues, such as those that concerned Joseph Schumpeter ([1942] 1950: 251–68)—might constitute a threat. This is because the economists' expertise is systematically relevant to policy, and that of the physicists is only transitorily so. But if the economists deserve legitimacy as experts with the general public it presumably is because, like Canute, the politicians who ignored their advice would fail to achieve their goals.

The incomplete legitimacy of economists points to a set of interesting issues. Claims to cognitive authority are not always accepted. Economists do agree among themselves, to a great extent, on what constitutes basic competence and competent analysis. There is a community of opinion, and some people who aren't members of the community—that is, the "public" of economics—accept the community's claims to expertise. But the discipline's claims to corporate authority–claims that would enable any economist to speak "for" economics on elementary issues, such as the benefits ceteris paribus of free trade, in the way that even a high school teacher can speak for physics—may be fragile. The sight of ads signed by several hundred economists is a kind of living demonstration of the distance between the claim to speak representatively found in physics and the claim in economics. In economics, agreement on the basics—long since assured within the community of professionals—still has to be demonstrated by the ancient collective ritual of signing a petition—itself among the most ancient of political documents. Even these near unanimous claims are not accepted as true: sectarians, textile interests, or a skeptical public may contest them.[3] Moreover, around every core of "expert" knowledge, is a penumbra, a domain in which core competence is helpful but not definitive, in which competent experts may disagree, and disagree because the questions in this domain cannot be decided in terms of the core issues that define competence. Establishing cognitive authority to a general audience is not easy: major achievements, like nuclear weaponry, antibiotics, new chemicals and new technology are the coin of the realm. Policy directives rarely have the clarity of these achievements, and policy failures are rarely as clear as Canute's tidal initiative.

TWO NOVEL TYPES OF EXPERT

Now consider the following type of "expert": those who are subsidized to speak as experts and claim expertise in the hope that the views they advance will convince a wider public and thus impel them into some sort of political action or choice. This is a type—the fourth on our list—that appears at the end of the nineteenth century in the US, and developed hand-in-hand with the development of philanthropic and charitable foundations. The fifth type, to be discussed below, is a variant of the fourth, or rather a historical development of the fourth. Where the effort to create and subsidize recognized "experts" failed—typically because their expertise was not as widely accepted or effective as the funders hoped—an effort was sometimes made to professionalize target occupations and to define professionalism in terms of acceptance of the cognitive authority of a particular group of experts. Both types exist nowadays, and in some fields there really is no clear distinction between the two. The difference is in the kind of audience, and in many cases, such as psychotherapists, perhaps, the "professional" audience is not so different from the public with respect to their actual sources of information and wisdom.

The history of social work provides a good example of a failed attempt to establish a claim of expertise that is further distinguished by the self-awareness of the process of claiming expert status. When the Russell Sage fortune was put to charitable purposes by Sage's widow, her advisors, themselves wealthy community activists, created an organization that attempted to persuade the public to adopt various reforms. The reforms ranged from the creation of playgrounds to the creation of policies for tenement housing and regional plans. Some of the participants were veterans of "commissions," such as the New York Tenement Commission, others were products of the Charity Organization Societies, still others came from social movements, such as the playground movement. What the foundation did was to subsidize departments with people employed as experts in these various domains. Some of them, such as Mary Richmond, had a great deal of experience, had written books, and were well known. Others were not well known, but learned on the job, and played the role of advisor to volunteer groups of various kinds—such as women attempting to promote the construction of playgrounds in their community, who needed advice on what to ask for.

The Russell Sage Foundation had a particular model of how to exert influence, a model that other foundations were to follow. They objected to "retail" philanthropy, and wished to influence others to commit their own resources to the cause. Playgrounds, for example, were not to be directly financed by the foundation, as Carnegie had financed libraries. The foundation offered expertise that local groups could use so as to assure that resources could be mobilized for the cause and used properly. At most, demonstration projects would be directly financed. The means of exerting influence were thus through the creation of public demands; this required means of reaching the public and, at the same time, persuading the public of the validity of the demands.

The foundation thought it had hit on the ideal device for doing this: the "Social Survey." Indeed, surveys were a powerful device, and literally hundreds of surveys—of sanitation, education, housing, race relations, child welfare, crime, juvenile crime, and so on—were done in the period between the turn of the twentieth century and the 1930s depression. The particular kind of survey the foundation was most enamored with was the comprehensive community survey. They had one great success with community surveying—the Pittsburgh Survey—and a few minor successes. What the Pittsburgh Survey did was to examine all of the aspects of community life that were of special concern to the nineteenth-century reform movements, and "publicize" them. To influence the building of better sewers and a better water system, for example, they included in their public exhibit to the community (one of their primary means of publicizing the results of the survey) a frieze around the top of the hall, which illustrated pictorially the number of deaths from typhus in Pittsburgh annually. Some of this effort worked; change did occur.

In the full flush of this success, the leading intellectual figure behind what he called "The Survey Idea," Paul Kellogg wrote extensively on the meaning of such surveys, and on the difficulty of persuading others of the expertise of "social workers," as they styled themselves. The foremost need was to persuade people to pay for expert knowledge. As Kellogg ([1912] 1985: 13) complained:

> while many of the more obvious social conditions can be brought to light by laymen, the reach of social surveying depends on those qualities that we associate with the expert in every profession; knowledge of the why of sanitary technique, for example, and of the how by which other cities have wrought out this reform and that. And townsmen who would think nothing of paying the county engineer a sizeable fee to run a line for a fence boundary must be educated up to the point where they will see the economy of investing in trained service in social and civic upbuilding.

Kellogg himself said that the task of persuasion would have been easier if there was an event like the Titanic disaster, which dramatized the need for lifeboats and confirmed the warnings of naval engineers. The survey and its publicity, however, were designed to serve the same purpose (Kellogg [1912] 1985: 17):

> To visualize needs which are not so spectacular but are no less real ... to bring them into human terms, and to put the operations of the government, of social institutions, and of industrial establishments to the test of individual lives, to bring the knowledge and inventions of

scientists and experts home to the common imagination, and to gain for their proposals the dynamic backing of a convinced democracy.

In the end, few communities were educated up to that point—at least to the acceptance of the generic kind of reform expertise that Kellogg and his peers claimed. But to an astonishing extent, the strategy worked, especially in such areas as playgrounds and juvenile justice. Major reforms were enacted on the basis of supposed expert knowledge that was based on little more than the highly developed opinions of the organized reformers themselves.

There is a sense in which this kind of expertise has proven to be a permanent feature of American politics, and now world politics, though in a somewhat different form. Organizations like the Sierra Club can support "experts" on policy matters, whose expertise is at best part of the penumbral regions of scientific expertise. These "experts" are not unlike those subsidized by the Russell Sage Foundation in its early years. Their role is both to persuade the public of their expertise and, of course, about matters of policy.

What distinguishes these two types of experts is the triad of support, audience, and legitimation that their role involves. Experts of the fourth kind, whose audience is the public, do not support themselves by persuading the public directly of the worthwhile character of their services or advice, as Dr. Ruth does, but by persuading potential subsidizers of the importance of getting their message out to the public and accepted as legitimately expert. So, like the economists who seek to be accepted by the public as experts, they too seek public recognition of their expertise. But the expertise they claim is inherently policy-oriented, rather than incidentally so. Kellogg, who played a leading role as a publicist for the survey movement, constantly likened the "social worker" to the engineer. But he rejected the idea that there was any need for a base for engineering knowledge in some sort of social science—the things the "social worker" engineer knew already about the right way to do things and the right standards to impose were amply sufficient to make public policy. The purpose of the survey was not to advance knowledge but to demonstrate to the public how far below standards their community was, and thus to spur it into action.

There is a kind of threat to discussion posed by these "experts" that results from the fact that they are subsidized, and are thus the preferred expert of some funder. The sources of the funding are typically concealed, as is the motivation behind the funding and the process by which the funding occurs. Concealment can serve to lend the claims of an expert a kind of spurious disinterestedness. But these are threats that liberal democracy is used to examining and indeed, in the case of the Russell Sage Foundation, the issue of interests was raised at the start, by no less a figure than Franklin H. Giddings, the leading figure of Columbia University sociology, and famously raised by congressmen at the time of the creation of the Rockefeller bequests. The problem, in short, became part of the public discussion, and foundations found ways to deal with the suspicions their activities aroused, not least by genuinely delegating a great deal of the control over the money to boards of notables.

The fifth type of expert is distinguished by a crucial difference in this triad: the fact that the primary audience is not the public, but individuals with discretionary power, usually in bureaucracies. The legitimacy of the cognitive authority exercised by these individuals is not a matter, ordinarily at least, of direct public discussion, because they deal with issues, such as administration, that are not discussed in newspapers until after they become institutional fact, and indeed are rarely understood by reporters, and may be subject to administrative secrecy of some kind. A paradigm case of this fifth kind of expertise is public administration, which contains the three distinctive elements of the type: a distinctive audience of "professionals"; experts whose legitimacy is a matter of acceptance by these professionals, but who are not accepted as experts by the public (and ordinarily are not even known to the public); and whose audience of "professionals" is itself not (or, at most, partially) recognized as possessing "expertise" by the public.

It would be useful to survey the major national administrative traditions to better understand the role of this kind of expert knowledge in each of them. Doing so, I suspect, would point to sharp differences with deep historical roots. But there are some commonalities as well, that result in part from the historical fact that public administration itself was the product of a strategy for the creation of expertise, which had American roots. In what follows I will simply describe the strategy and its origins, and consider the political meaning of the strategy in terms of the elementary political theory problems with which I began.

Public administration was a major target of the reformers of the early part of the twentieth century—corrupt and incompetent city officials, given jobs as part of a system of patronage appointments, were major obstacles to the correction of the conditions the reformers objected to. But political reformers—reform Mayors, for example—came and went, and the underlying problem of ineptitude and corruption remained. The movement for the professionalization of public administration, sponsored in large part by the Rockefellers (who had previously invested heavily in the professionalization of social work as well), changed this.

The professionalization strategy was rooted in the successful experience of Abraham Flexner in the reform of medical education, and in the Rockefeller efforts in creating a medical profession in China. It targeted practitioners and sought to turn them into an audience for expertise. One of the pillars of their form of medical education was to make it "scientific," and this meant in part the creation of a sharp distinction between medicine as a craft skill to be conveyed from one practitioner to another and medicine taught and validated by medical scientists, and the elimination of the former. One of the major goals of the reform of medical education was the elimination of part-time clinical faculty: this was made a condition of grants for improvement (R. Brown 1979: xv).

The professionalizing strategy employed by the Rockefeller philanthropists in this and other domains ignored, for the most part, the "general public," except to educate the general public in the differences between professional and non-professional workers. This education was supplemented by legal requirements and schemes of certification designed to drive non-professionals from occupations that had previously been weakly professionalized. The strategy, by the time it was applied to public administration, was well tested and mature, and the machinery for implementing it was already in the hands of the Rockefeller founders. The Rockefeller philanthropies already had a well-established relationship with the social sciences, particularly through such individuals as Robert Merriam and such organizations as the Social Science Research Council, as well as long-standing relationships with certain major universities—some of which were "major" largely as a consequence of Rockefeller largesse, and one of which, the University of Chicago, was a Rockefeller creation. During the 1930s, at a time when Rockefeller funding was being redirected away from "pure" social research—the professionalization of the social sciences themselves was a Rockefeller project of the 1920s, and social science institutions were still dependent on Rockefeller funds—and many universities were in dire financial straits, the Rockefeller philanthropists induced, through the use of their financial muscle, several key universities, such as the University of North Carolina, to establish training programs in public administration (Johnson and Johnson 1980: 111–12).

The 1930s saw the creation of a number of schools of public administration, of professional organizations of public administrators, and the gradual creation of a class of specially trained public administrators. The remnants of these original Rockefeller efforts still persist, in such forms as various schools of public administration and the professional associations of public administrators. The training, by experts, of municipal workers who had traditionally been "amateurs" and were appointed as political favors, led to the creation of a distinction between trained and untrained administrators, and between political and professional administrators. The expertise of the teachers of public administrators was no different than the expertise of municipal research bureau researchers. The institutional structures were novel and took the form not of training schools but of university departments, which eventually produced professional academic public administrators. These then became the experts, and their audience became the professional public administrators.

The striking feature of this development is that it solves the problem of the audience of the expert by creating an audience for the expert and assuring indirectly that this audience is in a position to compete successfully with amateurs. A similar kind of development took place during and after World War II with respect to foreign policy, area studies, and similar domains related to the postwar American imperium. Such organizations as the Russian Research Center at Harvard, for example, were the product of the same strategy, and involved some of the same players—previous recipients of Rockefeller funds. Later the newly created Ford Foundation played a significant role in the creation of foreign policy experts. In this case the primary consumer of professional employees was the federal government, often indirectly; the training of foreign service officers, military officers, and the like, was a major task of these experts. Indeed, the Harvard investment in regional studies began with contracts during World War II for the training of occupation army officers (Buxton and Turner 1992; Chapter 8 in this volume).

BUREAUCRATIC DISCRETION AND SECTARIAN EXPERTISE

It is with this step that the problem of democracy and expertise becomes salient. The experts whose expertise is employed are experts in the sense that they have an audience that recognizes their expertise by virtue of being trained by these experts. The audience, in a sense, is the creation of the experts. In this respect the expert more closely resembles the theologian whose expertise is recognized by the sect he successfully persuades of his theological expertise. In the case of theologians, however, liberal governments withdrew (or were based on the withdrawal of) public recognition of expertise from such sectarian "experts." In the case of the kinds of experts I have been discussing here, there is, in contrast, a discrepancy between the sectarian character of their audience and their role in relation to political authority. Since a great deal of political authority in modern democratic regimes resides in discretionary actions of bureaucrats, the control of the bureaucracy by a sect can amount to the denial of the original premises of liberal regimes.

Analogues to these "sects," as I have characterized them, exist in all modern bureaucratic traditions: the elite civil servant in Britain, the graduate of the *Grandes Écoles* in France, and in Germany the bureaucracy with its own distinctive internal culture. The German case perhaps does fit Habermas's category of "expert cultures." To the extent that these groups exercise power in terms of a distinctive "culture" that is neither understood nor accountable, they violate equality and neutrality. But one can also claim that there is a kind of tacit consent to their expertise.

In the case of physics, with which we began, there was a kind of generalized approbation and acceptance on the grounds of indirect evidence of the physicist's claim to expertise, and the claim to exercise powers of self-regulation and certification that should be honored by the public at large. In the case of professional bureaucrats and administrators there is perhaps something analogous. In the course of creating an audience for public administrators and area studies experts, there was indeed a moment in which the offer of "professionally trained" workers could have been resisted, and the amateurism of the past been allowed to persist. Similarly, there might have been, in the US, a strong civil service core that exercised some sort of generalized quasi-representative functions for the nation, as arguably is the case in, for example, France and Britain. There, professional administrators did displace "amateurs," and this occurred with democratic consent of a sort.

Professionalization was a mechanism of reform that was appealing to reformers who lacked a sufficient body of amateur political friends to fill the jobs that existed, or the needs for personnel that arose. War, here as elsewhere, was a significant catalyst of these changes, especially in the realm of foreign policy, where the need for occupation army expertise was soon followed by a need for expertise in dealing with foreign aid. It should be obvious that this kind of expertise more closely resembles sectarian expertise than the expertise of physics. The distinction is not that the pronouncements of ideologists and theologians are ideological, and those of physicists are not. The distinction is between what might best be described as generalized public validating audiences and specialized validating audiences that do not correspond with the general public. No foreign policy expert is obligated to demonstrate the validity of his views on foreign policy by producing an unambiguous success, like curing cancer or constructing atomic weaponry. Indeed, there has often been a large disparity between the views of experts and the kinds of facts upon which these views are alleged to be based, on the one hand, and, on the other, the views of politicians and the kinds of facts and results on which their acceptance or validation by the general public is based.[4]

In the case of foreign policy, opinions based on secret information gain a certain prestige, and a foreign policy analyst who does not have access to information that the public does not have is diminished in his credibility in the eyes of the target audience of the expert—namely, government officials who themselves operate on the basis of information that the general public does not possess. The implications of this discrepancy are obvious. Conflicts between democratic and expert opinion are inevitable, not so much because the expert invariably possesses secret information (though that may be the case with respect to foreign policy, and in practice is the case with respect to bureaucratic secrets generally), but is a simple consequence of the fact that the processes by which knowledge is validated by audiences are separate, just as the processes of validation of theological expertise by sect are distinct from the processes by which public validation is achieved.

Conflicts between expert knowledge of this special "sectarian" kind and democratic opinion are thus, if not inevitable, systematic and systematically produced by the very processes by which expertise itself is validated. The liberal ideal of a state that refuses to decide sectarian questions does not work very well when the sects are, so to speak, within the bureaucracy and their sectarian beliefs have their main effects on the discretionary activities of bureaucrats.[5] It is this peculiar combination of circumstances that allows for this kind of conflict, and it cannot be remedied by ordinary means. The whole process—of bureaucratic selection and training is the means by which this kind of influence is exercised: to root out sectarianism would involve rooting out the existing system of bureaucratic professionalization. Whether there is a practical alternative to this system of professional governance is a question I leave as an exercise to the reader. In specific cases, of course, government is "de-professionalized": professional diplomats are replaced by individuals from other backgrounds, formerly bureaucratic positions are made into "political appointments" or elected positions, government is run "like a business" by businessmen, and the like.

I have suggested here that the difficulties that have concerned theorists of democracy about the role of expert knowledge must be understood as arising not from the character of expert knowledge itself (and its supposed inaccessibility to the masses), but from the sectarian character of the kinds of expert knowledge that bear on bureaucratic decision-making.[6] There is, in the case of science, an important check on claims of expert knowledge that is lacking in the case of experts of the kind who threaten or compete with democratic decision processes: scientists need to legitimate themselves to the public at large. The expert who is a threat is the expert who exerts influence through the back door of training and validating the confidence of professionals, and whose advice is regarded as authoritative by other bureaucrats but not by the public at large. The authority of the expert whose expertise is not validated by public achievements is the authority that comes into conflict with democratic processes. Of course, there is, in a sense, a check: governments that fail to deliver on promises may earn the contempt of their citizenry. But this is not the same as the check on science, for it is quite indirect. If we know that the juvenile justice system is failing, this is not the same as knowing who in the system is to blame, or which of its various "professions" with claims to expertise ought not to be regarded as expert. The "public" may be dissatisfied, and find outlets for its dissatisfaction, but the very fact that the bureaucrats themselves are not directly elected and do not appeal to the general public for legitimation means that there is no direct relationship.

RECONCILING EXPERTISE AND LIBERAL DEMOCRACY

The discussion so far has distinguished five kinds of experts: experts who are members of groups whose expertise is generally acknowledged, such as physicists; experts whose personal expertise is tested and accepted by individuals, such as the authors of self-help books; members of groups whose expertise is accepted only by particular groups, like theologians whose authority is accepted only by their sect; experts whose audience is the public but who derive their support from subsidies from parties interested in the acceptance of their opinions as authoritative; and experts whose audience is bureaucrats with discretionary power, such as experts in public administration whose views are accepted as authoritative by public administrators. The first two do not present any real problem for either democracy or liberalism: physicists are experts by general consent, and their authority is legitimated by rational beliefs in the efficacy of the knowledge they possess. The expertise of self-help authors is private, and the state need not involve itself in the relation between sellers of advice and buyers. Theologians and public administrators present a different problem. Neutrality is the proper liberal state's stance toward theologians, because the audience that grants them legitimacy is sectarian. The state ought not to subsidize them or to give one sect preferential treatment over another. The fourth and fifth types present more serious problems. Both typically are indirectly subsidized by the state—foundations derive some of their money from tax expenditures. Had the Rockefeller fortune been taxed as an estate, there would have been no foundation, or if there were it would have been smaller.

What does this kind of laundry list establish? It makes no claims to completeness as a taxonomy of expertise. But it does contain all of the types of experts that figure in the problem as traditionally conceived. Habermas's shadowy expert cultures are there, but not in the same form: they appear not merely because there is expert consensus, but also because there are bureaucrats with discretionary powers who share in this consensus and are guided by it. Ian Hacking's classic paper on child abuse (1991) is an example of this kind of argument involving expertise in this sense: here the triumph of an expanded concept of child abuse is seen as the successful imposition of a definition that serves the interests of certain professional groups. The experts in question here are perfect embodiments of what I have called the fifth type of expertise. The political issue here is not expert knowledge as such, but discretionary power: the reason child abuse is a problematic category is because social workers and physicians acting in the name of the state employ this concept and operate in terms of a consensus about it.

If we reconsider the traditional problems—and the Fish/Foucault "cultural studies" form of the problem as well—in the light of the list, some of the difficulties vanish or are greatly modified, and some features of the problem stand out more sharply. Begin with the expert whose racist biases are passed off as science and become part of the culture through repetition and through presentations of "facts" in which the prejudices are concealed but nevertheless imposed on the public recipient. Two things become apparent about such experts: (a) that their expertise was not simply given, but somehow had to be earned or created—in the language of the present discussion, legitimated; and (b) that their expertise typically operates in the penumbral regions of science—that is to say, topics on which there is neither agreement on conclusions, on appropriate methods, or on whether the topic is itself entirely "scientific." To be sure many things may pass, in the eye of the public, for science. Scientific views, and scientific consensuses, may of course change, and the public may well legitimate and accept scientific communities whose views later appear to be wrong. The "public" is not merely the passive recipient of science and the prejudices and errors of scientists; it plays a role in their legitimation. The hard road that Darwinism had to acceptance should suffice to remind us that, although it may be easier to get public acceptance for views that flatter the self-image or prejudices of the public, the public is not a passive receptor. The legitimating done by the public may lag behind the legitimating done by the professional community by decades. And the public is not very adept at distinguishing the core of expert knowledge from the penumbra: this is a distinction made within the community of experts, and it may be erroneously made by them—in the sense that retrospectively the community may come to conclude that only a fragment of what was formerly held to be true was in fact true. So experts are fallible, and the public is fallible in judging claims to expertise. But this does not mean that the public is powerless to make judgments.

More importantly, however, "expert" claims of this sort do not permanently or inherently occupy the status of "scientific." When issues arise in which there are grounds for questioning the legitimacy of expert claims, they may, along with the legitimacy of the experts, come under public scrutiny and lose legitimacy. Indeed, this process, call it "politicization," is a normal fact of political life, and it goes both ways. That which is taken to be a matter of expert truth, or taken for granted as true by the public and therefore regarded by the liberal state as neutral, may cease to be taken as neutral truth. That which has hitherto seemed to be an appropriate matter for "politics," or for the negotiation of interest groups, or for "public" discussion, may come to be regarded as a "professional" matter that only experts certified by their appropriate communities have any real business discussing authoritatively. We do not regard legislators as experts on physics, and for one to oppose a particular physical theory or its teaching we would regard as an inappropriate act—as "politicization" of that toward which the state should be neutral.

This is typically an "academic" issue—academic in the pejorative sense. But sometimes it is not academic. Illiberal regimes, notoriously, do not accept these distinctions, leading to such things as Islamic science, Aryan physics, and socialist genetics, each sponsored by the state in opposition to expertise that has been defined as enemy ideology. But these are obviously very different cases than the ordinary expertise of, for example, physicians promoting CPR. It is nevertheless still common to collapse all of these cases of expertise, and the case of science itself, into the category of ideology. The term "ideology" itself is a good place to start with this issue, for it figures in Fish's attack on liberalism. Fish regards liberalism as a sham because it rests on a bogus notion of reason—that is on the assumption that there is such a thing as neutral "reason," which is reason that is outside of the battle between world-views (Fish 1994: 135). So Fish thinks of liberalism as

What Is the Problem with Experts? 37

founded on an ideology it takes for granted, an ideology that is not neutral, and thus, paradoxically, liberalism cannot exist, for the idea of liberalism as neutrality represents a kind of self-contradiction. It can exist only by hiding the untruth of its foundations.

There is bite to this criticism, bite that derives from the naturalism of the natural right thinking out of which liberalism historically grew. The liberalism of the American founding tended to regard the truths relevant to politics as immutable and self-evident, and accordingly could regard them as neutral facts. It seems that the same kinds of claims arise in connection with scientific expertise. It is at this point that science studies, particularly controversy studies and such topics as the law's construction of science, become relevant as well. One might read these studies to be making a point that is similar to Fish's: the self-descriptions of scientists are applications of an ideology of precisely the same kind, an ideology of neutral reason. A closer-grained description of the activities of science of the sort that science studies offers conflicts with these self-descriptions. Thus these studies undermine the distinction between politics and science by showing them to be constructed, historical, and so forth, meaning that science is really ideology.

Or does it mean this? To be sure, "controversy studies" in the literature on science studies have sometimes focused on the problem of expertise in order to problematize the claims of experts (e.g. Timmermans 1999, on CPR); to show that the public construction of science is wrong (e.g. Collins and Pinch 1993); or that the law's construction of science is wrong, or at least arbitrary and misguided (e.g. Jasanoff 1995: 60). But are the implications of these studies that expertise is ideological and therefore non-neutral? Or can they be taken differently?

When Collins and Pinch (1993: 145) discuss the contribution of science studies to citizenship, they wrestle inconclusively with the question of what is implied by their re-descriptions of science. Their message is that "scientists . . . are merely experts, like every expert on the political stage," like plumbers, as they put it, but experts who happen to have an immaculate conception of themselves, unlike plumbers. They suggest that both scientists and the public would be better off without this conception. The same point is made by Jasanoff with respect to judges. But in both cases it is not clear what the end game of this argument is. Professional ideologies of the sorts that scientists have and plumbers do not, can of course be exposed as false, or, to put the point in Schmittian terms, to be political or non-neutral. But there are at least two possible ways of reasoning from this kind of argument, which need to be carefully distinguished.

The differences between the two ways are parallel to the difference between the ways in which one might reason from Fish's account of liberalism as a faith which pretends it is neutral to faith. If we reason as Fish does, moving the givens of liberal theory into the category of faith (that is, outside the category of reason), we get a contradiction at the base of liberalism. Moving science and expertise generally from the category of neutral to ideological in the manner of Feyerabend begets a conflict with the practice of treating science as un-problematically a source of truth, or when the self-descriptions of scientists involve appeals which are absolute, such as the metaphysical claim that present science has succeeded in establishing the truth about the universe, or has a method for doing so—which I take it is part of what Collins and Pinch have in mind with the phrase "immaculate conception." But there is an alternative: we can take all of these presumptively absolute conceptions in a different way. Schmitt has a slogan that bears on this problem, the saying that what is political is a political question—NB, a political rather than a scientific or philosophical question, and for Schmitt this means a matter of decision, not truth. Terms like faith and reason, and also science, can be thought of as political in this sense as well, and indeed this is precisely how Schmitt thinks of such terms (Schmitt [1932] 1996: 31). But treating these terms as political at the "meta" level is not the same as discrediting them, eliminating them, or collapsing them into the category of "ideological." On the contrary, we can recognize them as political, recognize the foundations of liberalism as non-absolute, and still accept them in practice as a political necessity. To put this somewhat differently, consider the arguments made by Collins, Pinch, and Jasanoff. One end game is to treat such things as the law's construction of science as ideological; another is to treat both categories as themselves political. If calling something a matter of expertise is a political decision, so is calling something "ideological." None of these are, or need be, natural or absolute categories.

CONSTRUCTIONISM AS LIBERALISM

The answer to Fish is to treat the liberal principle of neutrality not as an absolute assertion about the nature of beliefs, but as a core rule, whose application varies historically, whose main point is to establish a means of organizing the discussion of political matters, that is to say the discussion of political decisions. We can apply this to the problem of expertise as follows: it is no surprise that, in order for there to be genuine discussion in Schmitt's sense, some things would be temporarily taken for fact, or, alternatively, some things would be left to the experts to settle. "politicizing" everything, making everything into the subject of political decision-making (or treating it as an analogue to political decision-making), would lose the advantages of the intellectual division of labor and make reasoned persuasion impossible. Some facts need to be taken for granted in order for there to be genuine political discussion, and some of the work of establishing the facts is, properly, delegated to experts. Indeed, to imagine a world in which such delegation did not occur would be to imagine a simpler society, at best a society of Jeffersonian yeomen, in which everyone knew pretty much what everyone else knew that was relevant to public decision-making.

To preserve the possibility of political discussion that such societies established, it is essential to delegate to experts and grant them cognitive authority. But granting them cognitive authority is not the same as granting them some sort of absolute and unquestionable power over us. The fact that expertise goes through a process of legitimation also means that legitimacy may be withdrawn and the cognitive authority of experts may collapse, and this suggests something quite different than the idea that liberalism is a kind of self-contradiction, and also something much more interesting. We, the non-experts, decide whether claims to cognitive authority, which in political terms are requests to have their conclusions treated as neutral fact, are to be honored. And we have, historically, changed our minds about who is "expert," and what is to be treated as neutral fact.

This is, so to speak, a "liberal" argument about expertise. It grants that cognitive authority and the acceptance of expertise, in modern conditions, is a condition of genuine public discourse. Liberalism, in the form of the principle of neutrality, is a means to the end of the creation of the conditions for public discourse. It is a means, however, that is not given by God, or the courts, or "reason," but lives in the political decisions we make to regard assertions as open to public discussion or not. Historically, liberalism established the space for public discussion by expelling religious sectarian "expertise." The challenge of the present is, in part, to deal with the claims of non-religious experts to cognitive authority. There is no formula for meeting this challenge. But there is a process of legitimation and delegitimation. And it should be no surprise that this process has come to occupy more of public discourse than ever before. But the very vigor of discussion, and the ability of the public to make decisions about what claims are legitimate, belies the image of the liberal public as victim.

Is this enough? Or is there a higher standard of proper public deliberation to which public acceptance of expert claims ought to be held? Antiliberals, following the arguments of Habermas and Foucault, have generally said that it is not enough. For them, it is precisely the point of the critique of expertise to show how our forms of reasoning in public deliberation are preconditioned by unchallenged and, practically speaking, unchallengeable forming assumptions that derive from experts.[7]

The kind of social constructionism that has been practiced in much of science studies is different in character, and has different implications, for it is concerned not with showing that some forms of discussion involve social construction and others do not, but with showing that even science has this character. As I have suggested, to the extent that it has been concerned with establishing the conventional and mutable character of many of the distinctions that philosophers of science have attempted to absolutize, that is to say to make scientists less immaculate and more like plumbers, social constructionism parallels a moment in liberal theory. The moment is the one at which it was recognized that the history of liberalism is a matter of "continuation by other means," in which the "foundations" of actual liberal democracies are conventions—custom, flexibly applied and typically somewhat vague "principles"—rather than rigid doctrines or acts of faith. A corollary recognition to this political realization is that despite being mutable and shifting, conventions have sufficed to preserve what Schmitt ([1923] 1988: 5) characterized as the real possibility of "persuading one's opponents through argument of the truth or justice of something, or allowing oneself to be persuaded of something as true or just."

The parallel claim that what counts as "expert" is conventional, mutable and shifting, and that people are persuaded of claims to expertise through mutable, shifting conventions does not make the decisions to accept or reject the authority of experts less than reasonable in the sense appropriate to liberal discussion. To grant a role to expert knowledge does not require us to accept the immaculate conception of expertise. The lesson of the second kind of social constructionism is that these conditions, the conditions of mutability—and not some sort of analogue to Habermas's ideal-speech situation—are the conditions under which scientific consensus itself occurs, and that there is no alternative. This is a negative message, but nevertheless an important one, in that it excludes a certain kind of utopianism about expertise and its "control" by some sort of higher reason. Excluding this kind of utopianism is a kind of answer to the issues with which we began. Expertise is a deep problem for liberal theory only if we imagine that there is some sort of standard of higher reason against which the banal process of judging experts as plumbers can be held, and if there is not, it is a deep problem for democratic theory only if this banal process is beyond the capacity of ordinary people.

2 Political Epistemology, Expertise, and the Aggregation of Knowledge

Begin with a bit of political theory, in this case the emblematic passage in the most consequential political theory text of the twentieth century, Carl Schmitt's *The Concept of the Political*:

> Words such as state, republic, society, class, as well as sovereignty, constitutional state, absolutism, dictatorship, economic planning, neutral or total state, and so on, are incomprehensible if one does not know exactly who is affected, combated, refuted, or negated by such terms. ([1932] 1996: 30–31)

What does this have to do with expertise? Plenty. Expert claims routinely "affect, combat, refute, and negate" someone or some faction or grouping of persons. When scientists proclaim the truth of Darwinism, they refute, negate, and whatnot the Christian view of the creation, and thus Christians. When research is done on racial differences, it affects, negates, and so on, those who are negatively characterized. This is why Phillip Kitcher argues that it should be banned (2001: 95). Some truths are too dangerous to ever inquire into, because, he reasons, even by inquiring we legitimate the negation that racial distinctions already carry. Expert claims also favor or disfavor policies or decisions that have factions or persons supporting them. When Robert Oppenheimer insisted on technical grounds that the H-bomb was unfeasible, his opinion disfavored, not to say negated and combated, the faction that supported the decision and favored the position of Stalin (cf. S. Turner 2003a). Claims about the human contribution to climate change favor the faction that believes in an extensive role of the state in regulating the economy. All these claims are "political."

But, one might ask, isn't there a fact of the matter in these cases? And aren't facts themselves non-political? According to this definition of the political, the answer is no. As Schmitt's famous slogan puts it: what is political is a political question. Making something scientific, or true, doesn't mean making it non-political. The political/non-political distinction, as Schmitt goes on to say, is itself political:

> Above all the polemical character determines the use of the word political regardless of whether the adversary is designated as nonpolitical (in the sense of harmless), or vice versa if one wants to disqualify or denounce him as political in order to portray oneself as nonpolitical (in the sense of purely scientific, purely moral, purely juristic, purely aesthetic, purely economic, or on the basis of similar purities) and thereby superior ([1932] 1996: 31–32).

The political/non-political distinction is thus political. But it typically comes in the form of a claim that something is non-political by virtue of being "purely" something else. The political enemies of Protestantism were one of the sources of the modern notion of politics, and liked to distinguish religious from political considerations, implicitly denigrating the political as compromising and holding themselves in the higher category of religious. Indeed, "politique was the preferred term of censure deployed by Catholic Leaguers to besmirch all those who would abandon religious truth and seek accommodation with known heretics and proven schismatics" (Saunders 2006: 155). This is the politics of fanaticism, of which our world provides many examples. And as it happens, the history of science politics provides many more examples: scientists who believe that the speech of other people should be suppressed, or that people who have the wrong ideas should swing from the lampposts, as Karl Pearson thought, are depressingly common. Scientists have often been compared to priests in the course of this history, in accordance with the idea that they possess some special truth and ought to be respected and believed because of it. And some of them have behaved like priests, for example by demanding, recently, that free speech about global warming be suppressed if it does not fit with "the scientific consensus."

This sort of intervention belies any notion that the relation between experts and democracy is unproblematic and benign. They are dangerous to democracy in the same sense that the Catholic Church was during its aggressive phases in the nineteenth and early twentieth century. The Taliban, the Mullahs in Iran, and so forth are dangers today for the same reason. But scientists don't in fact exercise such things as the power to suppress speech, as much as some of them might wish they did, so worrying about scientists in these terms sounds a bit crazy. This sense of craziness provides the motivation for Michael Schudson's essay in praise of experts and their contribution to democracy. For Schudson (2006: 492), experts are those people depicted by Walter Lippman eighty years ago, "who put aside their own interests and wishes when they examined the world," "people who cultivated the habit of discounting their own expectations," and were the saviors of democracy (which at the time was widely thought, because of the results of the use of mass intelligence testing by the army, among other things, to be threatened by stupidity of the masses). Lippman thought that, as Schudson puts it, "If journalists had experts to rely on, they could inform the citizenry responsibly" (2006: 492), and Schudson has similar views. He adds to this the sociological idea that scientists are professionals and that they would forfeit their professional existence if they strayed from the straight and narrow, giving various examples of economists who preferred to give the truth rather than succumb to political pressure (2006: 499–500). Experts, in short, are safe, because they police themselves—the same argument was made almost sixty years ago by Robert Merton, who compared the social control of science to that of a police state.

So experts are not a threat to democracy because they discipline one another, they are disinterested, and, more important, are modest; they discount their expectations. Aside from this last point, this is a characterization of expertise completely devoid of epistemic content—nothing about the truth of what they say follows from any of it. Indeed, the Taliban and the authorities of the Catholic Church also do these things. One needs an additional story to get to truth—an epistemology that makes the creation of truth under these conditions more likely than in some other way. Then there is the problem of relevant truth. "Truth in a structured discipline" is something different from "truth as such" and different again from "truth as relevant to a particular set of political decisions made in the here and now under conditions of complexity, contingency, and time constraint." Schudson and the historical enthusiasts for expertise—who typically have gone with the full logic of the argument for expert knowledge and opted for expert rule in place of democracy, rather than as an adjunct to democracy (a question Schudson doesn't answer is "who needs a public sphere?")—generally ignore these differences and without argument conclude that deference to the representatives of a structured discipline is all the truth that democracy needs, or the best solution to democracy's need for truth.

The assumptions of this account need to be examined. In fact, the account of expertise is (almost) completely wrong, and the wrongness is a sign of the huge gap between the public sphere literature, which Schudson has in mind, and the sociology of science, not to mention epistemic considerations proper. If the expert can say "I have paid a high price for membership in the club of (economists, physicists, surgeons, engineers, etc.) and would lose my reputation and membership in the club if I lied to you," then he or she is saying something relevant to trust, though not directly relevant to truth: this is the same kind of reasoning and institutional practice that governs collective enforcement of trust-establishing practices in stock-brokering, law, psychiatry, and other professions. This might be thought to operate in science in relation to fraud, and in some extreme cases this is perhaps true (though actual high-level cases, such as the David Baltimore affair, have turned out not to work in this way; actual cases of ruined careers are typically found among low-level contributors to large medical projects). But these examples, and the "discipline" of expertise itself, do not apply in any simple way to the domain of politically relevant truth. Consider Paul Ehrlich, whose every expert prediction in the policy-relevant domain proved to be wrong by a wide margin (a point gleefully made by his nemesis the economist Julian Simon). Not only was Ehrlich not expelled from the community of biologists, he was treated as a noble martyr to the cause of truth merely for suffering the indignity of having his claims questioned by non-biologists. In fact, ostracism is more likely to result from challenging conventional opinions in the community than from being wrong over and over again but conforming with the community. But there is more. One of the best-established findings of old-fashioned sociology of science was that making mistakes has virtually no career costs.

But there is a bigger issue. Professional communities are routinely, if not invariably, wrong. The inductive hypothesis in the philosophy of science, to the effect that our present scientific views can expect to be proven wrong because all past scientific views have been proven wrong, applies even more strongly to expert opinion, which seems to obey the pendular laws of fashion more often than the laws of scientific progress. To read an expert advice book from the early part of the last century is usually an exercise in the realm of the comic. Not infrequently, one sees the origins of the old wives' tales believed by one's grandparents. Yet, these were often based on data and reasoning as good as or better than the data and reasoning employed today. So skepticism about the truth of expert opinion is well warranted apart from questions of motive. And one reason they are so spectacularly wrong is precisely that the careers of experts tend to be bound up in a disciplining process that makes errors both inevitable and consensual, by punishing those who don't go along.

And there is an even more important issue. Experts typically make their reputations as real scientists, economists, or whatever. And they typically are careful to say nothing that conflicts with the rules of the game in their fields. Experts whose thing it is to speak for their field, and who are also professional apostates, are nonexistent. This is a role for the orthodox. But this does not mean that their pronouncements on policy conform to well-defined rules of the game. Far from it. Policy issues, including such policy issues as global warming, are partly based on facts, partly based on uncertain claims, on beliefs about human conduct and on other things, such as ideas about what is and is not natural about weather fluctuation, that are based on complex and uncertain inferences from data, or on guesses. They are epistemically different from what is ordinarily understood as science.

Moreover, experts routinely (contra Schudson) overreach, as the case of Paul Ehrlich shows. Is this the issue? Should they be more modest, as Lippman fantasized they were? Shouldn't "experts" just recuse themselves when they don't really have the facts to warrant a policy? The answer is not so simple. Consider an area in which expert claims have been made for decades, and invariably turned out to be not only false but deleterious to the objects of the expertise: development economics. Should development economists just shut up? They do know some things. But, realistically, they don't know how to produce vibrant economies in the Third World or lead

Political Epistemology, Expertise, and the Aggregation of Knowledge 45

millions out of poverty under the actual political and cultural conditions of impoverished nations. Does this mean they should they stop trying as experts to formulate policies and policy ideas? Probably not. Experts have no special expertise or meta-expertise that would allow them to know when their knowledge is partial and inadequate for particular purposes: this is something they learn by applying it. This is perhaps a domain in which the urgency is such that trying on the basis of very limited understanding is the only option. And urgency, or perceived urgency, is probably a reason biologists give Paul Ehrlich an ethical pass on his long list of false predictions.

What is a citizen to do in the face of a world of expert claims, many of which are dubious? There is a developing literature on the quality of public discourse that identifies the discussion of the decision to invade Iraq in the administration of George W. Bush as a failure. But there was no lack of discussion. C-SPAN ran an all night session of the U.S. Congress in which the issues were thoroughly aired. The public accepted the opinions of experts and an expert community. The experts were wrong despite producing all the right cues, establishing a consensus, and otherwise making themselves credible. Can the public be faulted for accepting their expertise? The question is a genuinely difficult one, and speaks to the whole question of democracy's capacity to deal with expert claims; a capacity tested equally by the case of the many claims of climate science.

In such cases, and indeed in all real world cases of any interest, meekly accepting the advice of experts is not good enough—it is bad public epistemology and an abdication of political responsibility. Simply delegating such questions to experts is, in any case, typically not possible. Experts may have opinions about policy questions, but these opinions don't have the authority of "science" in the sense intended—namely that they are part of something like a textbook consensus. Nothing in textbook science or for that matter economics is sufficient to settle any serious policy question. It is knowledge, but it is knowledge that needs to be put together with other people's knowledge to add up to a rational and epistemically sound decision. This is best understood, I will suggest in the next section, epistemically—as a problem in the aggregation of knowledge.

THE AGGREGATION PROBLEM: HOW TO THINK EPISTEMICALLY ABOUT EXPERTISE AND POLITICS

The problems that characteristically involve expertise have the following properties: decisions need to be made, for example about a policy; knowledge is "distributed," usually among many people and—this is crucial to what follows—unequally so; decision-makers, whether this means judges, the public, representative bodies, administrators, or commissions, must rely on or judge claims which they cannot epistemically fully own, that is to say other people's knowledge which they can only get second hand and can't judge as a peer. And there are political implications in Schmitt's sense—some faction loses, is devalued, etc. If the solution to this generic problem is neither simple "expert skepticism," nor affirming the importance and value to democracy of the experts and encouraging deference to them, what is? The issue is this: we are talking about comparatives here, and the comparison cases are unstated and untheorized. The contrast in this case should not be "doing without expert knowledge claims entirely," but something else. The question is "what else?"

I suggest that we see the problem of expertise, and the reliance on experts by democratic politics, as itself a solution, among other solutions, to a genuine epistemic problem, a problem of the aggregation of distributed knowledge for the purposes of making decisions: call this subject "political epistemology." Policy and politics happen in real time and in a world, as Schmitt himself famously said, in which a bad decision is often better than no decision at all. This is crucial to understanding the appeal of expert claims: in many cases people want guidance to solve problems that they consider important, and will embrace any credible expert who claims to have a solution, or even some facts relevant to the solution. But policy questions and the kinds of knowledge relevant to them is never a matter of "facts" of the sort that experts possess. The policy must always go beyond the facts, and is usually a complex mixture of "fact" and things that are the subject of considerable uncertainty. Among them are considerations about implementation, who is affected and how, what their wishes and preferences are, and practicalities of other kinds. Experts who know the facts in the narrow sense may feel that they have a special qualification for pronouncing on the things in this grey area, which relate to the facts in the narrow sense, but which are not, properly, the same sorts of epistemic objects. The long history of atomic scientists attempting to intervene in the weapons policies of their countries is an example of this. The truth of expert claims about complex mixtures of this kind is likely to be determined only in retrospect, so "truth in the long-run," which science purports to provide, is not a useful concept for distinguishing them in the here and now. The claims of science are part of what needs to be considered by decision-makers. But prudence broadly construed, and the prudent weighing and judging of expert claims, is the standard.

So what prudent alternatives are there to reliance on experts by the public? What is the comparison class? What are the other solutions to the problem of the aggregation of knowledge? I list a few below, with some references to my own attempts and those of others to make sense of this murky subject. In each of these cases my strategy is to "ask the knowledge question" about a particular institutional case.

1. Markets. For some problems, such as the aggregation of knowledge about individual preferences, the market is the best-known source of information. What will people pay? There is no good way to find this

out besides putting products in a market and watching them choose by paying particular prices and balancing these choices against others.
2. Families. This is Kitcher's model, and it is a solution to the problem of trust and conflict of interest and perspective between experts and the public. The idea is that the expert acts in a paternalistic (or maternalistic) way toward that which is theirs, including both their special knowledge and their family, and respects and accepts the concerns of the other members of the family. Knowledge is mostly, but not entirely, in the hands of the expert, and so is learning (cf. S. Turner 2003a).
3. Stakeholder models. This is another approach to the problem of melding knowledge and interests. If we attempt to make the people with both interests in and knowledge about something sit down and negotiate a consensual solution, we avoid the problem of inadvertently goring someone's ox, or of having their knowledge ignored. Since decisions are consensual, no one is forced to yield on the things they regard as most serious—either interests or beliefs—but they must sacrifice something less salient to them to achieve consensus, and make an ongoing choice, involving their knowledge, about the value of the consensual goal. Since these negotiations are typically secret or semi-secret, there is little learning, though the participants may learn a great deal, and have an incentive to learn, about matters involving their interests and beliefs, and those of other participants (cf. S. Turner 2004a, Chapter 6 in this volume).
4. Representative democracy. It may seem odd to think of this as a means of knowledge aggregation, but of course it is. Expert rule is usually understood as a rival to and improvement on representative democracy, with reliance on experts by democracy an improvement that avoids the bad normative implications of expert rule, though expert rule is something that many thinkers, such as J. D. Bernal and Karl Pearson, preferred. But there are some epistemic benefits to liberal democracy. Like the stakeholder model, legislative politics forces representatives and those they represent to choose—no consensus is required, but voting procedures produce decisions by compromise and horse-trading, the horses being interests and beliefs that are valued in the political market. In the US representatives know and look out for their constituents' interests; in Europe, interests are mediated through parties. Legislatures have long memories of their own precedents, and learn from them (S. Turner 2008a, Chapter 5 in this volume).
5. Self-regulating "expert responsibility" models. Consider the following problems of decision-making in the face of distributed knowledge: NASA's decisions to launch a shuttle, the dropping of the A-bomb, commissions reviewing policy issues and producing White Papers. In the case of NASA, there were approximately five thousand critical flight-threatening issues in every launch. No one could even list, much less make judgments about, all these technical issues, each of

which involved significant uncertainties. Those best able to judge how serious the problem was, i.e. the engineers in each relevant group, were given the responsibility to raise issues at a higher level, and held accountable. Surprisingly, they guessed wrong in ways that produced catastrophes only twice (cf. S. Turner 2005, Chapter 4 in this volume). The A-bomb decision involved a pyramid of technical committees tasked with specific issues, leading to a technical committee that weighed the options. Each committee had limited scope and responsibility. The final technical committee expected, by historical precedent, that their decision would be examined by Congress if something went wrong—as the alternative choice, the invasion of Japan could very easily have gone wrong (S. Turner 2008a, Chapter 5 in this volume).

6. Bureaucracy. This combines expertise, especially in the form of examinations and in-house knowledge, with elaborate consensus favoring career structures. Subject to what we may call, after Isaiah Berlin, "hedgehog error." Bureaucracies know one big thing, but they are often wrong, and there are few corrective feedback mechanisms, usually little transparency, and an internalization of knowledge or closure to the outside world, which produces knowledge claims that typically are not directly relevant to the internal knowledge production processes of the bureaucracy (cf. S. Turner 2004a, Chapter 6 in this volume; 2008a, Chapter 5 in this volume).
7. Direct expert commissions in a market-like atmosphere of conflicting or different expert claims. John Snow's demonstration of his correct understanding of the mechanism of cholera was a result of this kind of competition—the alternative was the wrong view of the British health bureaucracy and of the medical expert consensus (S. Turner 1997; 2004a, Chapter 6 in this volume).
8. Artificially created public/expert forums. These are mostly legitimation devices rather than means of aggregating knowledge, but through dialogue, concerns, beliefs, and preferences of the non-expert participants, knowledge that is typically not readily available in any other way.
9. Mechanical aggregation procedures. The model is guessing the number of beans in a jar. This approach avoids process problems, since the guesses are mathematically combined, for example, by taking the mean. It also minimizes interests, and therefore interest-related bias. But there is no learning, collectively or individually, and as a method it does not apply when there are issues that are not more or less quantifiable, for example, where there are conceptual incommensurabilities.
10. Deference to experts speaking as a community. Professional bodies, for example physicians, often produce collective advice, which relies on "professional" standards and control. It is subject to hedgehog error or group-think, as well as bias when professional selection or professional interests produce patterns of special interest. Learning

Political Epistemology, Expertise, and the Aggregation of Knowledge 49

depends on internal collective processes of consensus formation, which may be problematic in various ways.

11. Oracles. One might regard this as a joke. But flipping coins is a decision-procedure with some good properties, notably lack of bias. Weber regarded the specific form of the use of oracles by the ancient Jews as one of the keys to the origins of Western rationalism. Why? Because by making the answers come in a yes/no form, they forced the users to carefully construct and thus rationalize the questions (cf. S. Turner 2007b, Chapter 2 in this volume). One might even say that this was a collective, or expert, employment of knowledge, as it involved religious institutions. There is no learning, except with respect to the posing of questions.
12. Parties as expert bodies. The experiment with Communism managed to combine the epistemic traits of bureaucracies with political power, making truth and authority both a matter of the party line. This form elevates group-think and expert consensus, which is nominally independent of the state bureaucracy, into the core governing principles of the state (S. Turner 2006, Chapter 11 in this volume). Learning is done in conformity with party doctrine, and thus aspires to coherence at the cost of other epistemic values.
13. There is a sense in which "science" also aggregates knowledge, but not in the same sense. Science involves many decisions: to publish papers, to award grants, to give degrees, prizes, and so forth (S. Turner 2002, Chapter 9 in this volume). These are decisions only indirectly related to "truth" as such. The normal mode of "aggregation" is this: scientists speak "for science" as representatives, and this is accepted if it is not challenged. When scientists are forced to make epistemic decisions collectively, however, and to produce a consensus artificially, trouble—in the form of disagreement over what the "consensus" is—usually follows, as it has, for example, in relation to the consensus assertions of the Intergovernmental Panel on Climate Change.

One might extend this list indefinitely, and consider many other puzzling examples of expertise and knowledge aggregated into a whole that can serve as the basis for state action or public discussion. There is, for example, the knowledge of the dead of generations past, black-boxed into the technology and procedures we take for granted. But the list is sufficient to make the point that the democracy-expert relation is more complex than a matter of accepting the model of deference to experts or rejecting it. Rejecting it is usually understood as a matter of embracing an alternative—populism, or as Ségolène Royal put it, the expertise of the people, which she meant to contrast to that of the administrative class. Notice that this is not an alternative on this list, and for good reason. The reason is parallel to the reason "democratic legitimacy" is not on Weber's celebrated list of types of legitimacy. By itself, "democracy" is not a form of legitimation: it requires additional legitimating beliefs, such as the belief in the charisma or sacredness of the popular will, or in the procedures of democratic lawmaking. Similarly, popular expertise, participation, etc. are not in themselves methods of aggregating knowledge. Rather, they require some method to put all the knowledge in question into a means of decision-making. Royal had in mind the demonstrations against changes in youth employment policy—the aggregated wisdom of the mob, which bureaucrats were to respond to as a surrogate for a public opinion poll, a form, though a crude one, of aggregating knowledge.

At the end of the Enlightenment, Condorcet grasped with wonderful clarity that epistemic equality between citizens and scientists was an impossibility, and also understood that this had the effect of undermining the ideal of democratic rule. His immediate successors, Saint-Simon and Comte, took this a step further and renounced the ideal in favor of expert rule. This episode has been conveniently forgotten by today's enthusiasts for democratic deliberation and the public sphere (cf. S. Turner 2007a). What the democratic deliberation's and public sphere's literatures have studiously avoided grasping is the role of knowledge, as opposed to interests and identity politics, in the public sphere. But the reason is not that the problem has disappeared in the "knowledge society." It is rather that it has become so complex and pervasive that it is no longer visible as the option of expert rule. Our problem is to make it visible again. Revealing how knowledge actually flows, how it actually aggregates, and how aggregation fails, is a contribution that expertise studies can make to the public sphere and democratic deliberation literatures—a contribution that has the potential for transforming these literatures in a more realistic direction.

Part II
Aggregation

3 Truth and Decision

One of the great themes in Western thought is the contrast between science and other forms of knowing, believing, and thinking. Philosophers, historians, and pundits of all kinds have examined the contrast between science and common sense, between science and religion, between empirical science and speculative philosophy, and between universally valid science and localized "truths," such as those of law, custom, and social practice, among others. Each of these has helped to clarify the question of what is distinctive about scientific thinking and what is distinctively "better," more sure, or more valued about the conclusions scientists reach, although none of them has provided an entirely satisfactory answer. Even today, such ideas as "creation science" show the confusion surrounding the question of the character of science.

Many of the characterizations were originally intended by the philosophers who argued for them as criteria that distinguished or demarcated science from other forms of belief or cognition. These philosophers were aware that other forms of knowing shared some of the cognitive aims of science, such as consistency among relevant beliefs, so they were often concerned about identifying the special ingredient that made a belief "scientific." Despite its popularity, this strategy produced no unambiguously successful results. None of the supposed special ingredients has stood up to close scrutiny. A case in point is the familiar distinction between fact, which science was supposed to consist exclusively of, and values, which were supposed to be found, mixed with fact in religion, morals, ideology, and everyday belief. The historical study of the development of the ideas we call scientific methodology has shown that particular cognitive values, such as "observability" have a history in scientific practice. They arise in response to particular problems scientists face when choosing between theories, and they came to be criticized by scientists and to change in the face of other problems of theory choice (Laudan 1984). The insistence on observability as a criterion of valid scientific belief went by the wayside in the face of problems "in" physical theory that could not have been resolved without abandoning it—quarks and, for that matter, atoms could not have become part of the scientific universe had this value not changed. The presence of values is only one example of a failure in the "special ingredient" approach. Typically, there is a long history of criticisms showing that the particular feature used as a basis for distinguishing science is not always characteristic of science or is present in nonscientific forms of knowledge as well, or that the contrast is not as sharp as it appears to be.

In this chapter I will examine some dimensions of the contrast between scientific truth and decision. I will not search for a special ingredient but will try to develop some simple distinctions to help clarify the place of science in the kinds of decision-making in which managers and policy-makers engage.

SOME BASIC DISTINCTIONS

My strategy for drawing distinctions comes from the great theorist of military strategy himself, Carl von Clausewitz. In his classic book *On War* he faced an analogous problem: the important distinctions he wished to make could not be applied very precisely in practice; there were many considerations with which the main issues could be confused (and they had been by other writers), and the differences were matters of degree. His method was "first, to grasp in their extreme form the antitheses when they appear clearly, and then to go gradually from the pure to the borderline cases which in reality separate the two concepts or types" (Aron 1985: 67).

BELIEFS, DECISIONS, AND PROBLEM STRUCTURE

In characterizing scientific belief and decision in this Clausewitzian fashion, we can borrow from the literature on the philosophy of science and put to work in a different way some of its questionable attempts to characterize science definitively. For the most part, these various attempts rejected the cognitive values and intellectual successes of science during or slightly before the time in which the philosophers wrote. In the nineteenth century, science was dominated by the refinement of measurement and observation; consequently, the idea of empirical precision and the elimination of uncertainty in prediction appeared to many writers on science to be the hallmark of science. The important sciences of the day, such as observational astronomy, were occupied with particular practical methodological problems that reflected the science's level of instrumentation and theoretical development. For example, the idea that observations should be neutral from observer to observer was a highly important practical problem for nineteenth century astronomers, who had learned that astronomic observations were in fact not neutral but varied among individual observers. When these "errors" were examined, it was learned that each observer had a "personal equation," a systematic pattern to the errors each made, which could be reduced to a formula that could be used to correct for these errors (Stigler 1986: 240–41). Nineteenth century physicists, such as Ernst Mach, insisted that the laws of science were purely descriptive and suggested that the notion of causation itself was a theological or metaphysical residue, in part because of the difficulties the physicists had in reconciling conflicting physical models of what was known about the properties of light and sound. Philosophers and other commentators of the era reiterated these themes, and much writing on science today in introductory textbooks, and especially textbooks in psychology and the social sciences, reflects the image of science established in that period.

Developments in physics, especially the quantum revolution of the first half of the twentieth century, undermined many of these older images of science—for example, by accepting some theoretical limits to predictive and observational precision and by experimenting with explanations that avoided the traditional mechanical notion of causality. The highly theoretical character of quantum physics led philosophers of science to emphasize the problem of theory choice over the problems of observation and experiment that had dominated nineteenth century science. Once they had accommodated (with difficulty) the strange world of quantum theory to the traditional ideals of explanation and prediction, philosophers and historians of science became fascinated with the processes by which scientific concepts changed, coming to regard change not only as a permanent feature of science, but as the feature in which the distinctive cognitive properties of science—its "special ingredient"—could be found. They thought, in short, that what is distinctive about science is how scientific concepts and beliefs change.

The attempt to establish this claim, which was soon expressed in a number of versions, produced a great deal of illuminating thought about science. Karl Popper and his followers developed the idea that science proceeds by making daring hypotheses, refuting them, and, in the course of this, learning to make better ones. As Popper put it in one passage, he was rejecting the view that the development of "our knowledge of an orange rather than our knowledge of the cosmos" is the appropriate model for understanding change in scientific belief (Miller 1985: 227). An orange we can perhaps learn about in a routine way; the cosmos has always been the realm of speculation later corrected by observation. To Thomas Kuhn's famous book, *The Structure of Scientific Revolutions* ([1962] 1996), which provided much of the focus for discussion, we owe the notions that scientific concepts sometimes change in an abrupt fashion, in which contrasting frames of reference, and to some extent alternative criteria of "good science," succeed one another in dramatic ruptures, or "paradigm shifts," that are quite different from the routine replacement of bad results by good results characteristic of most science most of the time. But the idea that the way scientific concepts change is unique to science also proved to be illusory, or at least very much less straightforward than it first appeared.

The contrast between scientific knowledge and the kind of knowledge that goes into decision-making, either by public officials making policy or by managers, is one that is largely unilluminated by these assertions that science has such and such a special ingredient because good decisions and good science have so much in common. The ideal of objectivity, the preference for basing as much as possible on observable facts, even the distinction between changes that are routine corrections and those that are sharp shifts between disparate frames of reference are all to be found in decision-making contexts. Both science and decision-making are characterized by rationality, that is, by self-conscious reflection and analysis and by the idea that results should stand up to public scrutiny or criticism.

One might try to claim that the sense of these terms varies between decision-making and science—that, for example, what we mean by "the facts" is something different in the context of decision-making than in the context of science, or that scientific rationality is a distinctive kind of rationality. But to do this would require a heroic effort, for each of these terms—*facts*, *objectivity*, *public*, and the term *rationality* itself—has a shadowy history of dispute similar to that over the special ingredients that have been claimed to distinguish or demarcate science. The idea of the public character of science is illustrative (Ziman 1968). On examination, the "public" that vindicates scientific results, for example by replicating experiments or by repeating observations, turns out to be a very small group of competent specialists who share many ideas, experiences, values, and personal relations. The group of persons competent to discuss public policy decisions or the decisions of a business organization may be equally limited and may also share the same training and experience.

Another way of contrasting scientific beliefs and decision-making is apparently more straightforward. It depends not on our characterization of science but on our characterization of *decision*: a decision is an act; *believing* is a state of mind. The usual way to extend this thought is to say that the essence of *decision* is that it is oriented to purposes, or leads to actions that achieve ends, and that choosing ends essentially involves values or interests. In many public policy disputes, for example, the issues are not only factual but also matters of conflict between groups that have different interests or different values.

Convenient as this distinction appears to be, it is not without its own difficulties. As we have already noticed, science may be said to have its own values. Scientists form a kind of community, with its own interests, and particular scientists also have interests. Sometimes "scientific" disputes reflect differences corresponding to social differences among scientists, such as differences in background or institutional affiliations or in the sources of funds for research. A second difficulty is that many policy issues are not about values or purposes, which may already have been set by law or by some prior decision, but are primarily about "the facts," or are at least presented by the disputants as purely factual. Moreover, even where there are strong unsettled differences in values and interests that the lawmaker or policymaker must take into account, these differences may often be rationally assessed, and it may be evident what sorts of approaches are politically achievable in the face of the differences. The decision-makers may thus be said to be selecting the "scientifically" best course of action among those that respect political reality.

Yet in spite of these confusing mixed cases, at the extremes policy issues proceed in ways that differ from the ways pure science proceeds, and decisions made in organizations such as businesses also proceed differently. The contrast is visibly manifested in cases where science is ignored in decision-making or not given the weight that, from the scientist's point of view, it deserves. Later in this chapter we will examine an example of such a dispute. But to make any progress in understanding the contrast between scientific belief and decision itself, we must first consider a second contrast that is often confused with, and obscures the contrast between, scientific belief and decision: the contrast between well-structured and ill-structured problems. With this second contrast in mind, we can sort out some of the complications over the character of the contrast between science and decision-making.

In the extreme cases, the distinction between well-structured and ill-structured problems is fairly clear. Herbert Simon (1977) explains this distinction in the context of artificial intelligence by suggesting that problems are well structured when "a specific problem space has been selected" and when a "search space" of solutions—for example, solutions to a mathematical problem—can also be defined. Ill-structured problems include those in which there are alternative ways of defining the problem or problem space, where the problem changes over time, and where the information relevant to the solution also changes or can be defined in more than one way, thus changing the search space in which the solutions are to be found (Simon 1977: 238–40). It would be convenient if the contrast between scientific belief and decision could be reduced to this contrast—if *decision* always meant ill-structured problems, and *science* had only well-structured problems. Alas, this is not so. Popper's remark about studying oranges and studying cosmology is a protest against this kind of reduction; cosmology contains many ill-structured problems and is perhaps ill structured as a whole; many physicists, indeed, do not take it very seriously for that very reason. But by considering the cases where science is ill structured, we can get a better grip on the contrast between decision and scientific belief, which has turned out to be elusive.

DECISION AND ILL-STRUCTURED SCIENCE

The philosopher Bertrand Russell, writing in the wake of the Einsteinian revolution in physics, had a phrase, "the technique of the suspended judgment" ([1950] 2009: 27), which brings out the element of decision in certain moments in the history of even our most basic scientific beliefs about the world. For physicists living through the period in which relativity theory was transforming the basic understanding of the universe, the relativistic conception was something that they first had to make sense of as a hypothesis and then explore, while "suspending judgment" on the question of its ultimate validity. Once they had applied the hypothesis to problems in physics and had come to see the power of relativity theory as a way of thinking, they could accept it as true and teach it to the next generation of physicists as a given. For these students, there was no problem of deciding for or against relativity, as there was for their elders.[1]

Some hypotheses and ideas are simply accepted for the sake of argument or as a way to begin research on some confused problem area. In such cases, where the element of decision is strong and the element of belief is not; we do not accept the truth of the hypothesis or idea, much less take it for granted. To be sure, some researchers will believe very strongly in the fruitfulness of a given line of approach or that a given hypothesis will ultimately be vindicated, and these expectations may form the basis for their own decision to do research based on the hypothesis or, in their role as a member of the scientific community (for example, as a peer evaluator of a grant proposal, an administrator, or a lab chief) to approve the research and equipment expenditures needed to pursue these hypotheses. In these cases, the scientist is "acting" and "deciding," but his or her actions are no less a part of the cognitive business of science than are the scientific beliefs he or she teaches in a seminar or the assumptions inculcated in laboratory training. Indeed, the decisions depend largely on the same web of scientific beliefs and assumptions, on expertise, and on detailed knowledge of the relevant science.

With decisions of this kind, which also reflect, in part, considerations of immediate circumstances (which may change) and reflect uncertainties over how fruitful a particular path of experimental or theoretical work might turn out to be, we come within a step of the kind of policy decision that requires expertise and specialized scientific knowledge. With a few more steps, we arrive at the kind of decisions that policymakers, legislators, judges, and business people routinely face, in which the element of technical scientific knowledge is minimal, or serves merely as a constraint that leaves a wide range of choices, and in which the prospective element (particularly the expectation that the problem will remain the same or that circumstances will continue to justify a given "solution") looms large: the differences are a matter of degree.

Even with a simple decision about funding a grant proposal, the language of uncertainty and risk, costs and benefits, and investment begins to become appropriate. At each step in the direction of ordinary business or policy decisions, this terminology, which is appropriate to weighing considerations, becomes more appropriate, for the problems become problems in which one valid or possibly valid consideration balances out another. The logic of weighing is often obscure, but not because weighing factors and assessing uncertainties are inherently obscure. In some well-structured decision problems—such as a choice between investments in well-rated bonds with different rates of return or in decisions to issue life insurance policies—the considerations can be calculated precisely on the basis of very certain assumptions, so that superficially different decisions can be shown to be equivalent with respect to the balance of cost, risk, and benefit.

Many decisions involve considerations that are not public. In politics, what we pejoratively call "political" decisions are those in which the choice is dictated by the consideration that there is sufficiently intense opposition to the correct course of action that a particular decision-maker would be made ineffective in the long run if he or she chose that course of action. In the extreme case, where survival of a person's political career is staked against public consistency, the issues are often seen as matters of principle. Sometimes the "principle" producing the conflict is a matter of some long-standing commitment to a political aim, but sometimes the conflict involves the politician's refusal to recognize or accept publicly what is well established by science. The political necessity of lying, or ignoring established truths, undermines the public character of policy discussion because it undermines the expectations that factual considerations will equally constrain all participants in public discussion. In science, as in politics, however, vanity and excessive regard for one's own convenience and career are not unknown, and a certain amount of minor fraud, such as data fudging, probably occurs with some frequency. Politicians often think of their deceptions as serving higher purposes; perhaps some fraud in science is also justified in the minds of its perpetrators by a desire to give a hypothesis believed to be true a better chance for the consideration and funding it requires to be proven.

At the extremes, then, decision and scientific belief have sharply different properties. Scientific truth is fallible, which is to say that we must leave open the possibility that new evidence will undermine even those beliefs that are most firmly held—the demise of the Newtonian universe underscored this. Science waits for results in a given area of inquiry and need not accept or reject the full validity of any given idea at a given moment; competing theories, hypotheses, or approaches may continue to be entertained for some time without any resolution. But a particular kind of resolution, one that makes the facts everywhere the same, or reduces phenomena to a single general frame of reference, is a conscious goal in science, although it is always pursued with the recognition that it may be that the facts can be further reduced, that our information is incomplete, and that our best-founded beliefs about the basics may prove wrong. Scientific beliefs and practices are interdependent rather than discrete and separate from one another. Scientific "truths" also claim to be valid or true for everyone, although in practice this means valid to competent practitioners.

In contrast, decisions are forced choices, where not to decide is usually to decide—that is, to produce consequences that might have been avoided. Decisions are revisable only at a cost and are discrete or finite. They require a frame or definition of the situation that is more or less fixed, usually by taken-for-granted factual beliefs, by assumptions about the costs of improving these beliefs, by the personal limitations of the decision-makers, and by the limitations on their powers and other practical limitations. A "good" decision is good under the circumstances. Ordinarily, decisions must be justified to others, but to whom they must be justified and how they must be justified varies. The justification is provided in terms of consequences that may be anticipated and whose probabilities may be assessed—a decision may have good consequences, but if this is only because of luck, it was not a good decision.

With the basic contrast between scientific belief and decision in hand, we can further clarify the contrast by relating it to the contrast between well-structured and ill-structured problems. Some scientific problems, notably those involving basic assumptions and contrasting frames of reference, are ill structured, and it is not surprising that alternative concepts succeed one another differently than improvements in scientific conclusions about well-structured problems follow one another. Similarly for decision: ill-structured decision problems, most notably those involving alternative descriptions of the situation—some of which are congenial to certain strongly held beliefs or interests of particular groups of persons relevant to the decision, or reflect familiarity or experiences with different aspects or parts of the problem—proceed differently from decisions on well-structured problems, where the range of "solutions" is fixed and the grounds for choosing the "best" solutions are uncontroversial. What counts as "good" in a well-structured decision problem shares a great deal with what counts as a rational, or "true," solution to a well-structured scientific problem; similarly for ill-structured problems, except that in ill-structured problems the criteria of "good" and "rational" are themselves part of the problem, part of what is in dispute. A successful resolution of a fundamental dispute over basic assumptions or over ideals of adequacy in science will share some characteristics with a successful resolution of a dispute over an ill-structured policy problem. For example, both will produce such things as greater coherence in practice and should serve as the basis for further achievements or improvements.

One simplifying step in the face of ill-structured policy problems is to limit the choices to relatively well-understood options, with limited or understood error costs and a relatively strong information base, for which consequences can be monitored and corrections made (cf. Collingridge 1980). The result of such problem simplification is that changes are limited to incremental improvements. This strategy, which Lindblom (1979) calls "muddling through" and Etzioni (1967) calls "mixed scanning," is appropriate primarily in the noncompetitive situations found in public administration. In a competitive situation—such as international military competition, business competition, or, for that matter, competition between scientists—reliance on this strategy by one competitor creates opportunities for competitors who are willing to take greater risks and, in particular, to invest more heavily in a particular strategy that appears promising to them. In competitive situations, comparative advantage—that is, the advantage I have over you (resulting from my different resources, skills, information, and so on) in performing particular tasks or pursuing a particular strategy—becomes a major element in determining my choices because what is promising for me, as compared with you, will differ.

In science, for example, there may be the potential of great achievements in pursuing some topic or idea that the rest of the pack has neglected or in pursuing a strategy they have neglected because they lacked some special cognitive skills, resources, or information (Lugg 1978; S. Turner 1986). Similarly, entrepreneurs often prosper by following a strategy that takes advantage of opportunities their competitors have decided to forego. Entrepreneurs, however, often have opportunities for benefitting from comparative advantage that scientists do not because scientists must, for the most part, rely on the endorsement of other members of the scientific community to get a share of limited public resources, when entrepreneurs can seek capital from anyone who wishes to invest. (In practice, this possibility is purely theoretical for many strategies because the necessary sums and resources to support the strategy exist only in a few large organizations.)

THE REAL WORLD OF DECISION-MAKING

So far we have basically remained in the thin air of abstraction and necessarily so, for the concepts of decision and scientific truth, and, for that matter, the distinction between well- and ill-structured problems, are themselves composed of abstractions, some of which are difficult and confusing. Our fourfold distinction—between decision in ill-structured problem situations, scientific belief in ill-structured problem situations, decision in well-structured problem situations, and scientific belief in well-structured problem situations—is enough to get a start on understanding the complexities of real world policy problems with a scientific component.

In my discussion of these contrasts, I have hinted that the relations between science and decision-making, either managerial or political, are sometimes troubled. Despite the rise of the expert and the large role given to disembodied rationality in the modern understanding of the state and its bureaucracies (and of complex organizations generally), the full and satisfactory use of scientific knowledge remains a distant goal. News reports in which scientists issue warnings or take stands on public policy issues, and are then ignored reflect the reality that scientists continue, in many areas of decision-making about which they express "scientific" opinions, to be ineffective in influencing decisions (cf. Collingridge and Reeve 1986). Why should this be?

The history of science in actual US policy contains a particularly spectacular episode in the collision between science and policymaking—an episode that, more than a century later, still has important effects on American politics. This is perhaps a good example of the complex relations between science and policy and a good way, so to speak, to launch our fourfold distinction into the water. The clash was over irrigation in the American West, and its primary scientific protagonist was John Wesley Powell. On the other side were a variety of groups interested in development of one kind or another, primarily settlement.

JOHN WESLEY POWELL AND THE ARID LANDS

The Great Plains and, earlier, much of the present-day Midwest were settled through two governmental processes: homesteading, whereby the government gave 160 acres of land to farmers, who gained clear title to the land after farming it successfully for five years; and the sale of public land for nominal sums under particular rules designed to distribute land widely and to encourage agriculture and mining by pioneers. These practices had become such an important part of the American experience that one historian, Frederick Jackson Turner, considered the closing of the frontier to further pioneering as the great divide in American history and the great trauma in American self-image. He saw the American character, especially such traits as individualism, self-confidence, coarseness, pragmatism, and moral egalitarianism, as having derived from the frontier and pioneer life (F. Turner 1962).

By the 1880s, land matters had become considerably more complex than they had been in the early days following the Homestead Act of 1862. The land then being homesteaded, in places like Nebraska and the Dakotas, was short-grass prairie. The settlers were not always there to stay; many wished only to gain title by meeting the requirements for improving the land and surviving on it for five years and then to sell out and move on. This pattern of rapid population growth and the subsequent abandonment of homesteads (which were usually sold to create larger farms) had been established earlier in other regions; in hilly and rocky areas, the claims often simply did not include enough good land to support a family. The situation on the plains was similar, but the inadequacy of the land was not visible. Settlers might do well for a number of years, *if* the rains held. The 1880s marked a long wet cycle, and western agriculture boomed, producing an abundance of wheat at such a low price that there were major political repercussions in Europe, where traditional forms of production could not compete.

John Wesley Powell had gradually risen from director of a small mapping and geological survey in the Rocky Mountains, where he had made his reputation as the leader of a spectacular voyage down the Grand Canyon, and had expanded his horizons to become a competent geologist and an expert on the West's arid regions and the geological processes that formed them. He and his coworkers were the most expert students of the geological processes of the arid regions. Powell's work on the arid lands, published in 1878, had persuaded him that agriculture in the mode of the old Midwest was impossible in the uninhabited regions west of the 100th meridian and that as the pioneers reached the arid West their rights to land would be worthless, for the traditional allotment of land could not produce enough to support a farm family. He proposed a significant change in the homestead policy, a change that would have preserved the possibility of successful pioneer agriculture by changing the size of land allotments and the character of water rights.

In his Arid Lands report, Powell presented these ideas in the form of two model laws: one for irrigation districts, in which farms were limited to 80 acres, and one for grazing districts, with limits of 2,560 acres (Powell 1962). For irrigation districts, he proposed that land be allocated so that sufficient water rights were attached to the property. This was a rather tricky proposal, for an irrigation "right" would require new forms of collective authority to ensure its fulfillment, by controlling the distribution of available water and creating, maintaining, and controlling the means of distribution, a task requiring considerable capital as well as legal authority. Water corporations were already beginning to exercise the authority over water that Powell wished to bind to the land, selling it at high prices to farmers who did not have direct access to water and whose land was worthless without irrigation.

Yet Powell's proposals were not enacted, for various reasons. Attempts to close the frontier were politically suicidal, especially since many pioneers had been successful in the 1880s without help of irrigation, so there was little pressure to act immediately. Powell, however, knew from measurements taken by G. K. Gilbert of the level of the Great Salt Lake that these successes were temporary; the wet cycle would be followed by a dry cycle. Irrigation had long been necessary in some areas, and the technology was well understood. The idea that the West could be reclaimed by irrigation was becoming an influential policy concept. The promise of resolving the problem of aridity was not baseless—irrigation had, at least, a history of a few tangible successes.

Political interest in problems of irrigation began in earnest in 1888, with the return to the Senate of William Stewart of Nevada (Stegner 1962: 299). Powell, by now head of the US Geological Survey, cooperated with Stewart, who pushed through a law that provided for the release of lands once they had been classified as irrigable. Contained in the law was a provision for funding the US Geological Survey to survey the lands. The surveys were intended to become the basis of a land-classification system under which the arid regions would be opened to settlement. In part,

Powell's assent to the law was a political decision, for although he did not believe that irrigation could live up to the high expectations of the settlers and politicians, he understood that if he failed to participate, he would lose any chance to influence settlement policy. Powell's alliance with the promoters of irrigation did not last, however, in large part because there were basic factual disputes that were never resolved. For example, Powell gave a high estimate of the extent of irrigable land, consistent with the belief, shared with all competent commentators, that insufficient water was the problem, not the quality of the land, a large portion of which could have been successfully farmed if water for irrigation had been available. In contrast, the Public Lands Commission gave a low estimate, based on the literal reality that under any reasonable assumptions about irrigation, only a very limited number of adequately watered farms could be carved out of the western domain.

Opportunities for making decisions often do not take a convenient form. Here the issues came to a head as a result of a practical dispute over how fast land was to be released. The issue was the source of conflicts specific to the particular choices. Cattle interests wanted the public domain kept open for their own use and wanted settlement delayed. Corrupt land companies had in the past filed false claims and bought up settlers' claims and used them to create huge land empires; they wanted the lands to be given away quickly. Powell, who wanted democratically governed irrigation districts to be created beforehand with legal authority over rights to the use of water, wished to delay settlement until a policy had been enacted, but he needed the support of settler groups. Stewart, who had developed a personal antipathy to Powell, agitated for distributing the land rapidly. Settler groups were not yet politically organized, so even though they were supposed to benefit from these policies, they had no voice in the matter. When drought came in 1890, they organized an irrigation movement. The premises of the movement, however, were more optimistic than Powell's (Darrah 1951: 311–12). Perhaps in time Powell would have been able to persuade the settlers of the correctness of his views, but the pace of events precluded this.

By June 1889, one hundred fifty sites for possible reservoirs were certified by Powell, and an attempt was made to distribute these certifications widely so that congressmen could point to local results (Darrah 1951: 303). But no land had actually been released, so Powell appeared to be using his authority to block the process of land classification, of which selecting reservoir sites was only a part. The legal problem of who had authority over the larger process of classification was not entirely clear. When it became clear, it created more difficulties for Powell. The General Land Office, which had responsibility for recording and granting land claims, created a legal crisis by continuing to enter the claims of settlers ten months after the law passed. In 1889, William Howard Taft, President Benjamin Harrison's attorney general, ruled that these new claims, of which the Land Office estimated there were 134,000, were invalid because Powell had not designated the land for settlement (Darrah 1951: 306). The ruling in effect gave Powell authority over settlement and thus placed him in a grave political dilemma: he might have gone ahead and done quick "classification" surveys to speed settlement, but this was precisely what he thought was bad policy. For Powell, the classification policy was a whole. To classify lands as irrigable without answering questions of the collective organization of water rights made no sense because irrigable did not mean settleable; settlement demanded real water, and there was not enough water to irrigate all (or even many) of the "irrigable" lands. Powell believed that "it would be almost a criminal act to go on ... and allow thousands and hundreds of thousands of people to establish homes where they cannot maintain themselves" (quoted in Stegner 1962: 333).

There was no one to rescue Powell from his predicament. Without the legal machinery to achieve what he considered a rational land policy, faced with expectations of speeding settlement, and having only means he considered irresponsible, premature, and dangerous, Powell chose to construe the law narrowly, "not as authorizing construction of irrigation works but only as directing a comprehensive investigation of prevailing conditions" (quoted in Darrah 1951: 306) relating to the possibilities of irrigation. He spent much of the money allocated for irrigation studies on detailed topographical mapping. Maps took time, so this served reasonably well as a delaying tactic. But other persons in authority, notably the president, who had ultimate legal authority to release land, were content to leave Powell on the firing line. A movement in Congress did develop to change the law, but it had the aim of speeding settlement. This movement produced criticism of Powell, including questioning the legality of his using the bulk of the irrigation funds for topography rather than for site reconnaissance, an administrative decision to which his own staff had objections. Powell paid the price for his stand. Appropriations for the entire geological survey were sharply reduced, and he was forced to resign.

SOME LESSONS

Historians, especially at the time of the New Deal, made Powell a hero for his expansion of the role of the state (Stegner 1962: 334). Indeed, Powell's arid lands proposals did represent the spirit of state intervention, sharing the properties this often implies: static assumptions, antagonism to capitalism, rigidity, oversimplification, excessive optimism about the pliability of the individuals whose conduct was to be (to use a later phrase) socially engineered, and an inadequate respect for problems of implementation. The weaknesses are not merely failings of Powell's, but failings common to many policy proposals, so the case is a fair example of the difficulties of translating scientific knowledge into governmental action.

Powell had a very solid piece of scientific knowledge at the base of his proposals. He knew that the level of rainfall, together with a high level of evaporation, simply would not allow extensive irrigation and that the temporary successes of farmers in these regions were illusory, a result of cyclic variations. He correctly concluded from this that not only was traditional "wet" agriculture impossible in the West but that the schemes for western development outlined by other writers, boosters, and irrigation propagandists were over optimistic, and often absurdly so. The core of his position was a scientific result about rainfall that represented the solution to a well-structured scientific problem, namely the question of rainfall variations and their extent. The policy problem was an ill-structured problem, with no single problem frame, and it was also complex. Adequate policy solutions required combining policy, expectations, assumptions, and scientific knowledge into a coherent whole. Some of the subproblems in this complex whole were well structured or relatively well structured; some were not. Rainfall estimates were a well-structured part of the total problem, but they were only a part.

In subsequent historical commentary on this dispute, much has been made of the fact that some scientific writers of the period, and some boosters, accepted, or at least entertained, some form of a hypothesis propounded earlier by the British astronomer Herschel: that "rain follows the plow" or, in other words, that cultivating the soil actually influenced rainfall (Goetzmann 1966). Some people did take this idea seriously; on the non-scientific grounds that God had never intended that any part of the earth be perpetual desert (Worster 1979: 81–82). But even the most optimistic of these people also recognized that massive irrigation efforts were needed. The scientists who invoked the idea did not imagine that the effects of cultivation per se would be large, particularly in the arid plateau regions that remained largely unsettled. Like Powell, they believed that there was a radical difference between the arid regions and the East, and they took the view that the government must intervene and take "absolute control over the system of irrigation or keep a watchful eye over it" (quoted in Malin 1956: 195). Indeed, virtually every commentator, boosters and pessimists alike, sought government intervention and considered new forms of cooperation to be a sine qua non of effective irrigation (Malin 1956).

The pioneers, however, preferred the immediate exercise of a tangible right to one hundred sixty acres to the doubtful, delayed, and intangible benefits of collectively controlled water. The threat of delay and intervention doubtless intensified the preference. Politicians were found who could give voice to these preferences, denouncing Powell's scheme as "newfangled," "medieval," "utopian," "Russian," "patriarchal," "communal," and so forth (Manning 1967: 199). Behind the epithets was a basic political or cultural reality Powell had neglected: the pioneers' deep desire to own what was "theirs" without the ambiguity of untested collective controls. The pioneers' suspicions of public control were ultimately confirmed. When the second Homestead

Act was passed in 1909, it provided for bureaucratic control of government-subsidized irrigation schemes, and the federal bureaucracy exercising control proved to be arbitrary and sometimes incompetent (Worster 1985: 169–88). Powell had expected a more direct and democratic kind of irrigation control, but his ideas on the subject were fatally vague. The farmers lacked the technical expertise needed for large-scale irrigation, and they knew it. However dimly, they—and not Powell—had grasped the implications of dependence on a government organization in which the technical expertise and legal authority to irrigate would be concentrated.

Bureaucratization was virtually inevitable because of other miscalculations. Not only were the 1880s anomalous because of high rainfall; the decade was also anomalous because of high grain prices. Had these prices stayed high, irrigation might have been a paying proposition, and local irrigation districts might have been able to purchase expertise. Prices fell, however, and the irrigation program could only be pursued with enormous government subsidies. The need for subsidies produced demands for control and accountability on the part of the representatives of the taxpayers who paid the subsidies. Two bureaucracies that muddled through by seizing on a single strategy succeeded in justifying themselves and keeping their programs alive. They did so by creating alliances with developers, making over optimistic projections, and delivering a tangible product, namely, dams. The Bureau of Reclamation and the Army Corps of Engineers competed with each other to build dams and, in the course of this competition, squandered huge sums on dubious projects; this continues even today (Worster 1985; Reisner 1986).

That prices would remain high was one static assumption central to Powell's policy proposals that failed; the ideal of the family farm was another. The few farms produced by subsidized irrigation were not very appealing places—isolated, dust-blown, and unremunerative. The 1880s was also, coincidentally, the decade of the city; many of the cities in Europe and in the US doubled or tripled their populations during these years, and the increasing standard of urban living soon made pioneer life less attractive. By the time the bureaucratic machinery of irrigation was in place after 1910, there were few family takers for the farms they made possible.

The list of failings could go on. The point, for our purposes, is that policy is a complex combination of elements, of which the scientific is only one. A good scientist, as author and scientist C. P. Snow has observed, has a trace of the obsessional in his or her character and is often inclined, in decision-making situations, to become obsessed with pet ideas, data, arguments, and devices:

> The nearer he is to the physical presence of his own gadget, the worse his judgment is going to be. It is easy enough to understand. The gadget is there. It is one's own. One knows, no one can possibly know as well, all the bright ideas it contains, all the snags overcome. (1961: 69)

Powell was closest to certain problems, those of the geological aspects of water flow and evaporation, and was personally familiar with certain parts of the West. The engineers were most familiar with the technology of dam building, their "gadget." Each regarded his bit of knowledge as the basis of good policy. Other contemporary scientists, with different experiences and scientific backgrounds, had somewhat different perspectives, and as it happens, Powell's opponents had some solid scientific elements in their own policy ideas. The region varied significantly with respect to soil, which might have been made a means of classification (Malin 1956: 221). Alternative methods of tillage, fallowing, and planting were available or under development at the Agricultural Experiment Stations, altering the agricultural outlook, although not fundamentally, and introducing many more local differences than Powell's scheme envisaged. Powell was not expert on these subjects. Although Powell ignored the possibilities, no one really knew what could be done to diminish evaporation, for example, by planting trees on river banks, although it was well known that similar methods of water conservation were essential to the successful irrigation practices of certain agriculturalist Indian tribes in the region. In fact, some of these water-conserving ideas were later implemented on a large scale, for example, by planting a band of pine forests east of the Rockies during the 1930s.

Each of these bits of scientific knowledge might have been made the core of an alternative solution to the ill-structured policy problem of the western frontier. Once these alternatives had been fully fleshed out, with specific proposals for dealing with the questions of land ownership, collective control, and implementation, they would have been difficult to compare. Technical testimony might conceivably have been able to rule out all the science-based alternatives other than Powell's, but it is more likely that technical discussions would have had quite different effects. Powell dismissed the possible use of artesian wells for irrigation, and here the technical discussions only muddied the waters by showing that matters were perhaps more ambiguous than Powell said. Technical discussions of new forms of tillage would have helped Powell's case only if they were wholly negative. In any case, there were perfectly good reasons for rejecting Powell's scheme, apart from the scientific issues. The government did not guarantee that homestead claims were sufficient to support a family farm; indeed the process demanded the claimant prove the sufficiency of his claim by living from it for five years. Why not simply continue the policy and let the homesteaders decide when to give up?

The policy difficulties went very far beyond these. There were troubles over the legal character of water rights, issues over the number of settlers who could be accommodated, and questions over the real aim of the policy—whether it was development or the preservation of the possibility of pioneer family farming and the kind of small-scale democracy this implied. The complexities of these issues are discouraging for anyone who supposes that science can solve policy questions, because such complexities are characteristic, and not atypical, of important policy questions. Important policy questions are typically ill structured, and the scientific element, if it is itself well structured, is subordinate. If the scientific issues are themselves ill structured, as they often are, so much the worse. Often, of course, ill-structured scientific problems that engage our interest do so precisely because there is some pressing practical need for which science has inadequate answers.

THE DISTRIBUTION OF KNOWLEDGE

In cases where problems are ill structured and where the disputes, over time, come to take the form of disputes among approaches to the policy problem or the data, technical knowledge typically does not provide a decisive solution. Indeed, minor technical disputes, as we have seen in connection with Powell's problems over the extent of artesian water supplies and their potential in irrigation, often increase in seriousness and number the longer a debate continues. Such disputes may be unresolvable or very difficult to resolve because they are either scientifically ill structured or because they arise between specialists in different fields who are relying on different data sources, different analytic skills, and a different range of prior practical experiences. Some observers have concluded from this that science has no place in policy and that the claim to expertise, so often followed by a parade of conflicting and contradictory "expert" testimony, is a spurious one (Collingridge and Reeve 1986). The modest truth to be found in this large claim is that in decision-making, demands made on science and on highly specialized scientists are often not appropriate.

Even in apparently simple issues involving expert opinion, such as the testimony of physicians in court cases over the physical abuse of children, there is typically a mismatch between what the physician can honestly say on a scientific basis about the probability that a given injury was an accident and what the court needs to know to make decisions of great seriousness, such as removing a child from a family or depriving a parent of his or her freedom. From the law's point of view, the problem is well structured: particular kinds of evidence of particular kinds of actions and intentions are required. For the physician, the problem is also well structured: the probabilities that particular patterns of injuries were accidental are small. But the two problems are different enough that lawyers and physicians typically emerge frustrated from their encounters with each other. What holds for child abuse holds more strongly for such practical problems as informed consent, assessments of mental competence, and the like, which are often less well structured, both scientifically and legally.

Scientists are often guilty, as Powell was, of overestimating the importance of the scientific facts they know best. This is an instance of a more general phenomenon in the distribution of knowledge, illustrated in the parable of the elephant and the six blind men, each of whom, on the basis of their solid tactile knowledge about one part of the elephant, mistakenly generalized to different images of the whole. Scientists, policymakers, and citizens each know things that the others know less well. In a famous passage on rulership, Aristotle compares the ruler to the cobbler and asks whether the cobbler, who is the expert on shoes, should make decisions about shoe making, or whether the person who must wear the shoes should. His point is that only the wearer knows if the shoes fit, but this is not enough knowledge to make the shoes. The citizen knows his or her own desires and feelings, whether the shoes pinch, as it were. Scientists have specialized or limited areas of familiarity or competence, and this means that they are often especially unsuited to addressing complex questions of practical administration or application or, for that matter, to speaking in the name of science as a whole, much less for society as a whole. But the knowledge and particular cognitive skills scientists possess are often essential to decision-making in complex and ill-structured situations. No political procedure can substitute for this knowledge or eliminate the difficulties inherent in the narrow distribution of essential knowledge and cognitive skills.

4 Expertise and Political Responsibility
The *Columbia* Shuttle Catastrophe

One of the major conflicts between the principles of democratic politics and the practical reality of expertise in public decision-making takes place in connection with responsibility. The basic principles of democracy include some notion of political responsibility, usually understood to take a bidirectional form, in which the relation between ruler and ruled takes the form of representation and the relation in which the ruled control the ruler takes the form of accountability. The means by which the people assure that the persons who politically represent them are responsible to them vary among democratic regimes. Even within the general framework of representative liberal democracy the character of political responsibility varies considerably, both within a particular regime and between political regimes. Moreover, typically a modem state employs many devices apart from simple parliamentary representation, and very often these devices, such as juries, commissions, independent judges, law lords, and the like predate (or are based on models that predate) parliamentary government. Yet they involve their own notions of responsibility that resolve, ultimately, into a form of political responsibility.

Expert opinion has traditionally played an ambiguous role in basic constitutional arrangements, falling neither into the ruler nor the people side of this structure. Mill, in his classic constitutional text *Representative Government* (1861), was exceptional in that he was careful to discuss what he called "council" as a part of representative government. But he was vague about how council relates to responsibility, and for good reason. There are some very striking differences between the kind of responsibility that can be assigned to decision-makers and the kind that can be assigned to experts, either in making decisions which are the products of expertise or expert opinion or simply expressing expert opinion in the context of a process leading to decisions. In this chapter I will explore these ambiguities in terms of a case study: the *Columbia* Shuttle catastrophe of 2003.

RESPONSIBILITY: THE *COLUMBIA* SHUTTLE

In its sharpest form, the contrast between the personal character of decision-making, which leads to the notion of personal political responsibility, and the liability for the decisions made, is represented in Max Weber's famous colloquy with Erich Ludendorff, in which the people are given the ultimate power to judge the actions of their leader and to send him to the gallows if he fails.

Max Weber: In a democracy the people choose a leader whom they trust. Then the chosen man says, "Now shut your mouths and obey me. The people and the parties are no longer free to interfere in the leader's business."
Ludendorff: "I could like such a democracy!"
Max Weber: "Later the people can sit in judgment. If the leader has made mistakes, to the gallows with him." (Marianne Weber 1975: 653)

Expert opinion, by definition, can never be judged in this way. Characteristically, expert opinion is not even formulated in the first person. Nor are individuals thought to be personally liable for opinions competently formulated within the limits of professional standards of expert knowledge. Put more simply, expert knowledge is impersonal knowledge expressed or formulated by individuals, while political responsibility is personal and judged by collective processes.

The reality beyond these abstractions, however, is more complex. The individuals who express technical opinions do so as persons, and the expression itself is governed by a kind of ethic. Speaking for science has a form that resembles representation, though the representation is of the science community and its opinions (see S. Turner 2002, Chapter 9 in this volume). But a personal element remains. The somewhat paradoxical notion of unbiased technical opinion, which is to say a technical opinion that is genuinely impersonal and therefore genuinely purely technical, is exemplary of the problem: if an opinion were purely technical, it is difficult to see what sort of question of bias could arise. The term itself implies that technical opinions are inherently impure, a mix of the personal and the technical, and that one can be held responsible for technical errors and biases, but not for one's unbiased opinions (Thorpe 2002). Unbiasing one's expressions of opinion, however, serves to obscure or eliminate one's personal responsibility for them, and thus shifts responsibility to decision-makers.

When something goes wrong in a situation that involves matters that are primarily technical and include political responsibility, these abstract paradoxes about the relation between technical expertise and responsibility turn into real administrative and political issues, and bureaucratic distinctions between council or expert opinion and participation in decision-making break down. The *Columbia* shuttle catastrophe of 2003 is an example of this transformation and concretization of the problem of responsibility. The catastrophe itself immediately led to the creation of a classic pre-democratic council mechanism for delegating technical questions to experts, namely a commission. The commission was given a task which drew on a specific and highly developed political tradition of boards of inquiry designed to assign responsibility for particular outcomes in complex events. What is striking about the *Columbia* case, which embodies the paradoxes of political impersonality, is that technical advice itself appears to have been responsible for the decision. This means that the board had to evaluate expert opinion and decision-making made on the basis of the technical advice. I will suggest that the phenomenon of expert knowledge here, as elsewhere, presents pervasive challenges to the notions of political responsibilities that underlie democratic theory, which can be highlighted by asking the Schmittian questions of "Who decides?" and "Who exercises unquestionable discretion" (Schmitt [1922] 1985: 32–3). The answer here appears to be that no one can be assigned responsibility—an anomalous result for democratic theory.

In general, the production of expert knowledge is controlled through the indirect means of professional certification and recognition, as well as the concentration and control of opinion through methods of peer review and evaluation that typically do not directly assess the truth or validity of expert claims, just their minimal professional adequacy, but which nevertheless, through a series of complex redundant and overlapping mechanisms, generate consistent expert conclusions that fall within a small range. Thus responsibility for expert opinion is diffused by the very mechanisms that create the phenomenon itself, though as we will see there are some important exceptions to this. For the most part, however, the political power experts exercise over one another is limited, episodic, and indirect. Journal editors, board certifiers, and degree granters exercise discretion, but their powers are indirect: they do not determine truth, but evaluate competence, admissibility of claims, and the application of standards. This is the personal substructure of the impersonality of expertise. The wide distribution, indirectness, and uncontroversial character of personal decision-making allow for the illusion of impersonality. Political decision-making, in contrast, involves direct mechanisms of command and control as well as direct mechanisms of punishment for failure, which enforce responsibility. The impersonality of expert claims, in contrast, removes the possibility of assessing responsibility, and even expert error itself becomes something that only experts themselves are in a position to assess. One intriguing aspect of the *Columbia* case is that the commission was used precisely for this purpose: as a means of using expert opinion to evaluate the actions of an expert bureaucracy, NASA.

The *Columbia* case provides a quite stark example of the transformation and evanescence of the concepts of representation and accountability in the face of expertise. In the immediate aftermath of the catastrophe, in numerous newspaper editorials and statements by congressmen there was a call for blame to be assessed and the blame-worthy punished. For the public, holding individuals responsible was an essential aim, and their representatives took this as part of their own political responsibility. The expressions of the desire to hold individuals responsible were typified by those of Senator Ernest Hollings, who observed that this was "an avoidable accident" (a condition of responsibility), and noted that "in similar circumstances a Navy ship captain would be 'cashiered'" (*St. Petersburg Times* 2003).

In response to the widespread public desire for accountability NASA's administration, anticipating an external investigation, immediately appointed an internal review committee, which was assigned the task of investigation. The committee was promptly dismissed by the press as an inside job, in spite of the care that NASA had taken to include persons who were not directly involved in the decision-making. An additional board of outsiders and former NASA officials was also appointed under the title of the *Columbia* Accident Investigation Board (CAIB) (Lytle 2003). The CAIB chose to mimic the aircraft accident investigation boards. In this case, two hundred investigators were put to work producing a report that cost nearly a half billion dollars.

The CAIB was advised not only by technical experts but also by top line management theorists and social studies of science scholars. It came to conclusions that were contrary to the those of interested outsiders and citizens as well as Congressmen, many of whom rejected implicitly the CAIB account in favor of one that emphasized responsibility. The board and the managers responsible for the shuttle also took opposing views of the problem of responsibility. The differences point to fundamental issues over the aggregation of expert opinions and over the assignment of responsibility for errors and incompetence that bear directly on the fundamentals of liberal democratic theory. In what follows, I will show why these are intrinsic to the problem of expertise.

ENDING THE PROBLEM OF RESPONSIBILITY: NASA AND THE CAIB

Among the first acts of the commission was to choose a model for their inquiry, namely aircraft accident boards, that enabled them to avoid the task of assigning personal responsibility. The ostensible reason for this was that it would be impossible to expect candid testimony to a commission which was inquisitorial and judicial at the same time. But the choice also reflected generic and important difficulties with applying judicial and quasi-judicial concepts to expert inquiries. One problem was this: the board was compelled to rely for its judgments not only on the testimony of the potentially guilty, which would be an ordinary situation in criminal cases, but on their claims as experts—in which bias would inevitably be an issue. Although the reasoning behind particular decisions, the differences of opinion about these technical decisions, and so forth, were more or less accessible to the members of the commission, who functioned as near-experts, and were accessible to the advisers to the commission as even nearer experts, neither the commission nor its advisers could reasonably hope to develop a completely independent understanding of these issues on their own. So the testimony was a curious combination of exculpation and expert witnessing of a kind that no ordinary court would have permitted as testimony.

Public discussion of the inquiry continued to use the phrase "smoking gun," which is to say the language of criminal accountability, and, despite the board's self-limitations, the reality that the findings of the board would be translated into some sort of punitive action was never far from either the public discussion or the thinking of the participants in the process, both on the Board and among the NASA employees. Because technical causes implied prior administrative choices, there was good reason to believe that some sort of personal accountability would result.

Public speculation about causes, and particularly about damage produced by the large chunks of foam that had shed from the fuel tanks at liftoff, began immediately after the event. The release of internal NASA e-mails involving a frantic discussion among engineers of the possible consequences of foam shedding added to the speculation. The e-mails included a characterization of a potentially catastrophic scenario which proved to be an eerily accurate prediction. The puzzle then became the question of why nothing was done, even after a plausible professional opinion within the NASA team had made this prediction.

The initial reaction of the NASA bureaucracy to foam speculation was to attack its credibility. The NASA director Sean O'Keefe, a manager with science studies management background rather than a physicist, disparaged what he called "foamologists" and characterized the effect of the foam on the *Columbia* as similar to the effect of a styrofoam container on hitting the front of a pickup truck. To call the adherents to the foam explanation "foamologists" implied that there was no form of technical expertise at its base—foamology is a parodic name for a nonexistent technical discipline. Presumably these comments reflected what O'Keefe had been told by senior technical managers. As it turned out, he was relying on technical opinions that turned out to be grossly in error.

The magnitude of the error became apparent in the middle of the inquiry when an experiment was conducted by the CAIB simulating the kind of high speed foam hits that the orbiter had actually been subject to. It was clear that the foam was more than sufficient to do the kind of damage that would have doomed the orbiter—and that the foamologists were right. But there was a crucial ambiguity about the results that bore on responsibility: the discussions within NASA during the flight involved the heat tiles that protected the orbiter during re-entry, which were assumed to be the weakest link, while the actual damage, as the CAIB reconstructed the evidence, was to the leading edge of the wing, made of reinforced carbon-carbon (RCC) (CAIB/NASA 2003)

THE SHUTTLE MANAGER'S DEFENSE

In the middle of the investigation, after it had begun to be clear that the technical cause of the catastrophe was foam, the mission managers, those responsible for the decision about what to do about possible foam damage, held an extraordinary press conference to get their side of the story into the media. This side of the story was part of the evolving NASA response to the events, which is itself revealing as a confirmation of the claims about the nontechnical causes of the event that form a large part of the CAIB report. In this interview the NASA managers centrally involved in the decision-making retreated to a second line of defense, which for our purposes poses the critical issue because it so neatly encapsulates the core problem of expertise in relation to fundamental concepts of responsibility and representation.

The actions that came into question were taken by Mission Manager Linda Ham, her deputy, and their senior technical advisor, in response to an informal request by the debris team for satellite imagery of the bottom of the orbiter to see if it was possible to identify holes or damage to the tiles of the kind that would have resulted from a foam strike. This request was made shortly after the launch itself, after a frantic e-mail discussion within the team about the videotape of the launch, where extensive foam shedding had been observed. There is some question about the exact nature of the discussions between the various advisors concerned to have an image of the tiles and the flight management team, but the response of the management team was extremely interesting. The management team not only declined to entertain their request, but declined to do so on procedural grounds, because the request had not come through proper channels, or to put it in the peculiar bureaucratic language of Ham herself:

> We have read news reports that the mission management team had declined a request for outside assistance and if you read through the transcripts, you'll note that the mission management team never addressed a request for outside assistance because it never came up in any of the meetings. It never came up to me personally. (Harwood 2003a)

There was some confusion over what amounted to a proper channel for such a request, but the request was discussed at length not only with Ham's assistant but with her technical advisor, and Ham herself intervened and "killed the request," according to reports (Cabbage 2003) because the "possible request" had failed to come through proper channels, and thus was not a bureaucratically genuine request, or in the language of NASA, a "requirement" (Langewiesche 2003: 81).[1] But to track down the source of the request, as Ham put it:

> I began to research who was asking, and what I wanted to do was find out who that person was and what exactly they wanted to look at, so

that we could get the proper people from the ops team together with this people or group of people, sit down and make sure that when we made the request we really knew what we were trying to get out of it. (Harwood 2003a)

This statement was widely interpreted as indicating that she was trying to identify the source of the request in order to punish and intimidate the requester, a desire that becomes more relevant in the context of some other remarks by Ham about the model of decision-making for the process.

Ham, in the interview, argued explicitly against holding anyone responsible, on the grounds that "we do operate and we communicate, and everything that we do, we do it as a team," commenting that "if the system fell down, we will fix the system, but it is really difficult for me to attribute blame to individual personalities or people" (Harwood 2003a). Ham had good reason to attempt to deflect responsibility, as she had made the critical problematic decision. In her capacity as manager, she had decided that the problem was something that the team could not and would not have done anything about until after the mission anyway. But she did so with the public assent of relevant technical officers. Formally, what she said was true: This was a collective decision, though a collective decision made through a process that, as she herself observed, might have been flawed.

Part of the problem of Ham's responsibility arose through issues of intent. She appeared to have been motivated by managerial considerations (that in retrospect seemed trivial and inappropriate) about the cost of getting the images and about the inconvenience and cost to other elements of the mission of maneuvering the orbiter into a position such that photographs could be taken. Moreover, Ham raised questions about the adequacy of the paperwork and rationale for dismissing foam events on previous flights, and indeed, because there had been such a large number of these events, the problem was one of which she was at least minimally aware. But here again her motivation appeared to be simply to construct an adequate rationale for dismissing the event which could be based on the precedent of previous rationales for dismissing it; "appeared to be" because if she had taken the possibility of damage seriously she would have opened a full scale inquiry while the flight was still going on. Her concern with the paperwork on previous flights seems to have included no interest in or willingness to actually do anything with the paperwork, such as reading it or having it re-examined for its relevance. And her bureaucratic approach to the problem of foam shedding seemed, in retrospect, also to be inappropriate and callous. Her interest in citing it appeared to be to use it as bureaucratic authority for her own actions. Her comment that she hoped the paperwork was good, in the context of her failure to address the question of whether it was, indicated that she had no interest in the question, despite the fact that she had to be aware, as her comments indicate, that these rationales were often not especially good.

Because it would have at least been possible to consider strategies to save the orbiter at this point, this decision would have been in a similar context, such as military context, culpable, and intent would have been relevant. But she employed an Eichmann-like defense of "following procedures." And the top administrators of NASA seemed not only willing but eager to treat this as not only acceptable but competent managerial action. As O'Keefe later said, she was an excellent manager and other divisions of NASA would be eagerly competing for her managerial services. In the military context, she would likely be court-martialed, as Senator Hollings observed, though in those contexts as well the reliance on procedure would have been at least partly exculpatory.

Why did this apparently strange acceptance of the "procedural" defense seem normal within NASA? One answer is this: NASA was tracking 5,396 individual hazards that could cause major system failures in flight, and about 4,222 of those could either threaten mission success or cause the loss of the crew. Waivers had been granted on 3,223 of those known problems (Halvorsen 2003). Thus, there were many possibly catastrophic unsolved problems with the shuttle with similar paperwork histories. Foam shedding was a case in which the paperwork was extensive, the problem had been experienced repeatedly before, progress had been made in dealing with it, and in no case had the damage been severe enough to cause the loss of the orbiter. So there was a substantial rational probabilistic ground for thinking that the problem would not arise in the case of this foam strike either, and Ham herself noted in the key meeting that "the flight rationale [for going ahead with launching after the foam strike in October was] that the material properties and density of the foam wouldn't do any damage," and suggested looking at the data from a 1997 flight where there had been debris damage (Sawyer 2003). In the face of "paperwork" of this kind, the reliance on procedure becomes less puzzling. No manager could hope to assess five thousand hazards on their merits: that was the task of engineering teams that had the formal responsibility to speak up, through channels, if they believed the issue needed to be addressed. Ham relied on those procedures because there was no practical alternative to doing so.

The second line of defense opened by Ham pointed to some reasons why this would have been a defensible action purely on grounds of the NASA model of handling expert opinion. As one NASA official was quoted, "she did the best she could do given the information she had. She talked to people she trusted, she listened to the analysis" (Harwood 2003a). This in itself is a peculiarly ambiguous formulation, but it is nevertheless, from the point of view of responsibility, an interesting one.

As it happens, the technical advice, which seems to have decisively sealed the fate of the requests for imagery, was from Dan McCormack, a senior structural engineer, who told the team that the analysis of possible tile damage by the contractually responsible Boeing team showed no serious threat, and that the RCC wing edge might show some coating damage, but no "issue" (Sawyer 2003). At this meeting another engineer spoke up to agree with him. The Houston-based NASA engineer, Alan Rodney Rocha, who had expressed strong concern, backed down after this analysis.

What should we make of these errors? In a model of decision-making in which there is a well-developed division of labor such that particular technical decisions and particular competencies match perfectly, there is no problem in assigning responsibility. If a particular cable breaks, the person whose job it is to make decisions about the cable and to be expert about everything relating to the cable is responsible. But a complex system typically cannot be understood in this way and new systems contain novel unknowns that cannot be understood in this way.

The technological division of labor (and expert knowledge) that works for automobiles or aircraft carriers, which are well-understood technologies, will not work for a poorly understood technology because the relations between the parts that correspond to the division of labor may be different than expected. In this case at a certain very simple level there was a part with a problem tile, and therefore a corresponding body of "expertise." This primary level of expertise did not fail: no one was proved wrong with respect to anything that they properly gave a technical opinion on. The tiles, as far as the CAIB could tell, were *not* the cause of the catastrophe (James et al. 2004: 9). The error was in taking this legitimate piece of expertise and interpreting it to have significance it could not bear. This is a problem of aggregating technical opinion or deciding what to make of it.

The NASA method for aggregating expert opinion involved two key elements: to rely on an elaborated division of labor involving teams responsible for specific engineering systems used in the orbiter and the launch system, as well as teams for specific problems, such as debris. Each of these teams reported to higher level mission teams which operated in a similar way: they had a managerial hierarchy, with persons who were formally responsible, but operated, with respect to technical issues and to a large extent also with respect to managerial issues, as a team which required consensus. Technical disagreements were taken seriously, and a strong rule of procedure was to insist on data-based discussion. Both of these elements of procedure worked against minority opinion, a point to which I will return, but also created a situation that made the zone of relevance of particular kinds of expertise ambiguous. So that a person participating in a consensus decision who was not genuinely expert in some area could overreach and deliver a strong message that could affect the consensus.

Among other things that need to be said about consensus in the context of large bureaucracies is that the consensus that occurs in the face of unequal, and indeed hierarchical relations between those participating in decisions, is not necessarily "representative" of expertise in the same sense as consensus that emerges among equals. Even in the case of a consensus among formal equals, it is typically necessary to reach agreement through the artificial means of specifying what counts as agreement, such as through voting, because a genuine consensus is so difficult to actually achieve. In the case of hierarchical bureaucracy, "consensus" is easier to achieve because it is typically only consent, not overwhelming agreement between independent experts. People on the bottom tend to go along with strong judgments made at the top out of fear for their careers; there is a strong selective bias in any bureaucratic career structure that punishes those who reject prevalent ideas.

But even in the case of genuine consensuses of independent experts, there is a question of domains of expert competence. And this is a conundrum that is central to the problem of the political significance of expert knowledge. Ham was caught in the following paradox of authority. She was not herself an expert on the issue in question, and was compelled to rely on expert judgment. But because she was not an expert, she could not independently determine who was genuinely expert. To put this in another way, there is a paradox of managerial omniscience: if the manager is sufficiently omniscient to determine who is in fact expert, she will be virtually as expert as the expert herself, and indeed, this would be the limiting case; so the closer one approaches to the limiting case, the less there is any need for expertise, counsel, and expert advice in the first place. Not surprisingly, she relied on "the system." In this case she relied on senior technical advisors, who screened and evaluated technical advice and comments from engineering teams, and on data-driven presentations at meetings in which quite large numbers of managers and engineers, representing different teams, participated.

AGGREGATING EXPERT OPINION: THE ROLE OF META-EXPERTISE

Some method of aggregating expert opinion was necessary, simply as a result of the complexity of the system. But a subtle and important change in the character of the expertise in question occurs as the technical issues move up to the highest level of decision-making, and a related change occurs in the meaning of consensus. If we ask who was responsible for the fact that the team went wrong in arriving at a consensus, the greatest responsibility falls on the people who influenced the consensus. The culpable figure in the story now becomes the expert who overreached his competence with bad but persuasive advice. One could imagine constructing from this an appropriate, enforceable ethic of expert opinion that made this kind of error culpable. But this cannot be a workable procedure, as it would have the effect of chilling discussion, which should consist in sharing information and mutual persuasion. Ham was accused, perhaps correctly, of creating an atmosphere in which engineers were intimidated and afraid to speak out. But Ham relied on the fact that the relevant technical advisors had a formal responsibility to raise concerns. It was Ham's zeal to hold them responsible for raising questions that chilled the atmosphere and prevented discussion.

So a method of limiting this kind of discussion by making people responsible for the consequences of presenting an opinion to a group would have a predictable effect of restricting the content of the discussion further.

It is evident that assigning responsibility for expressions of technical opinion is a peculiarly difficult matter.[2] The engineers who invented the scenario that correctly predicted the course of events once the orbiter was damaged made a great point to the newspapers that their predictions were only speculative, absolving themselves from responsibility for not pushing their arguments harder, which was their clear formal responsibility, on the solid grounds that their scenario was only speculative, that is, not a technical opinion in the engineering sense, grounded on known principles and data. One of the key figures, Bob Daugherty, who did the damage assessment that indicated "what would happen to the shuttle's left tires if extra heat got inside the landing gear department because tiles were damaged" (Dakss 2009: np) and sent a series of e-mails about this, indicating his frustration with the lack of response, was later to insist that "his messages have been grossly misinterpreted and were neither warnings nor concerns, but "just engineers talking" (Cabbage 2003: np), an interpretation that the investigators rejected.

The distinction between "just talking" and something else is nevertheless interesting, for the something else would have to be "taking managerial responsibility." The "team" structure of NASA's consensus system for employing expert opinion requires engineers to take this dual role, and thus, in effect, to police themselves with respect to the expression of their opinions, which has the effect of requiring them to distinguish between offstage technical speculation and opinions for which they are accountable as members of a management team. One might say that it was this part of the "system" that failed, because a whole series of engineers who expressed doubts in the course of "just talking" failed to take the next step of invoking formal procedures that would have made those doubts into managerial actions (Cabbage 2003).

Their actions were thus defensible: they lacked confidence in their own predictions. So, however, were Ham's. Ham pointed to some reasons this would have been a defensible action purely on grounds of the NASA model of handling expert opinion. Ham argued that she relied on the best technical advice available. The advice that she received clearly was not correct, nor was it in fact the advice that the most appropriate and competent experts even in NASA itself would have given her. Nevertheless, in another significant sense, it was the best advice. It represented the assessment made by her own senior technical advisors of the technical advice given by the debris team and the advice given by other technical specialists, through a formal process involving responsibility, however burdensome, in the case of the lower level engineers, those responsibilities were. Only in retrospect could she have known that this heavily vetted advice was wrong.

What these various "bests" in the category of advice indicate is what is perhaps the fundamental problem in understanding technical advice in terms of these familiar bureaucratic and democratic concepts: accountability is difficult. The potential role of an aggressive advocate of a technical opinion raises some other interesting questions. Terms like "consensus" and "team" have a formal meaning as well as an informal reality. The formal reality is that particular group dynamics, groupthink, submission to a dominant or stubborn minority, a general reluctance to make waves, and the sense of safety of apparent majority opinion, may be the operative determinants of outcomes. The formalistic idea that expertise can be pooled through discussion ignores these processes. It also conceals an important change in the nature of the expertise that is supposed to be collectively produced. We might call the expertise of the competent practitioner operating in an understood domain of practice "primary" expertise. What these bodies are designed to produce, however, is expertise about expertise: meta-expertise. The errors of the *Columbia* management team were caused by failures to be expert about expertise—errors in judging the relevance, probative character, and implications of "primary" expertise claims about tile damage and about debris damage that arguably was literally correct. The Boeing analysis, for example, included caveats that had to be ignored or judged irrelevant to make the report useable in the decision process. With this we enter into the interesting zone of ambiguity.

THE ETHICS OF SPEAKING AS AN EXPERT

The effect of these considerations is not to eliminate notions of responsibility so much as shift them to experts functioning as councilors. But the problem of "responsibility" for council is a difficult one, especially since the distinction between council and representation itself seems to imply that the responsibility falls on the recipient of the council who holds actual decision-making responsibility. Nevertheless, with respect to the concepts of scientific expertise and engineering expertise the traditions contain very strong notions of responsible expression of opinion, and yet another, even more revealing model, is to be found in medical expertise. In the case of scientific expertise, it takes the form of an expectation to observe the distinction between what is known to science, that is, what is accepted as knowledge that is genuinely scientific by at least a virtual or presumptive consensus of scientists, and "speculation" or opinion. Scientists learn to speak in both ways and to distinguish the two and routinely criticize one another for crossing the line between the two. In engineering, the tradition is to draw a distinction between that which can be fully and predictably calculated according to known formulas and which results in predictable outcomes, and that which cannot. One of the interesting examples of drawing this line occurs in connection with the concept of "software engineering." The claim has been made that software engineering is a misnomer because the sheer complexities of software result in bugs and problems that cannot be fully predicted or reduced to formula, and therefore cannot be, in the full sense of word, "engineered." Medical expertise is governed by a different set of imperatives in which "speaking for" the medical consensus is not as central, because a balance needs to be struck between the need to respond, even in the absence of complete knowledge, to suffering and the Hippocratic admonition of "do no harm." This leads toward a greater emphasis on responsible speculation. Some years ago the chemist Linus Pauling suggested that vitamin C might be a response to cancer. Within the limits of chemists' notions of responsibility for utterances, Pauling could reasonably say that this was a plausible hypothesis. But from the point of view of medical expertise, it was insufficiently plausible to justify the potential suffering it could cause for those who, predictably, over-optimistically took this advice and failed to avail themselves of more effective treatments, and was, therefore, denounced as irresponsible. Yet physicians themselves are commonly willing to try treatments that are not sanctioned by any medical consensus if they work for the individual or appear to work in other empirical cases even though the underlying mechanisms are not known. For many drugs, for example, most of the prescriptions written are "off-label," meaning they are written for conditions other than those they were tested to treat. But this is justified by the physician's own assessments, for which she can be held responsible, of the potential benefits and risks of the uses, which typically are based on experience—"empirical" in medical parlance—rather than a full understanding of the relevant mechanisms and disease processes.

This more conservative ethic bears directly on the *Challenger* and *Columbia* cases, because each situation involved the assessment of data which either could not be, or had not yet been, reduced to the level at which it could be "engineered," but which nevertheless could justify a certain judgment about the relevance of the facts and their importance and epistemic weight. The problem with *Challenger* was a seal on a joint that was known from prior post-flight examination to have behaved in an anomalous way, but which had also successfully functioned under the exact stresses that the joint was being engineered to function under. Here, understanding and empirical knowledge did not match, just as empirical knowledge and medical science often do not match. In the face of uncertainties of this kind, it is common to employ heuristics based on the "empirical" successes of the past. The fact that some theoretical consideration had failed to accurately predict a problem in the past was a reasonable ground for ignoring it, or if not for completely ignoring it, giving it a smaller weight in decision-making. In the case of *Challenger*, some engineers *were* concerned about the problem, but in the end a specific kind of consensus process within a managerial system, which we will discuss in the next section, overrode those concerns, and even those who voiced the concerns went along with the consensus. It is this process that many commentators pointed to as eerily reminiscent of the *Columbia* catastrophe and indeed it involved the same kinds of discrepancies between data and actual past experience: foam had not, despite hitting the orbiter fifty-seven times, done sufficient damage to threaten a flight (*Columbia* Accident Investigation Board 2003; Kelly 2003).

In the case of *Columbia*, there was an additional problem involving the data and its presentation that resulted from the way in which NASA routinely responded to this kind of issue. As I have mentioned, NASA discourse operated on a principle of accepting only data-based claims, yet was reluctant to spend the money and effort required to collect the relevant data when, empirically, things were working. The difficulty with data thus took on the following structure. A concerned engineer or engineering group would seek authorization to conduct the relevant engineering study, have this request denied, and then be told that its concerns were not backed by data and therefore could not be considered. Typically this response came from two sides of the communication system. On the management side, decisions were made to prioritize the relevant requests for research; on the expert advice side, claims made by lower level engineers were routinely dismissed for not being sufficiently data driven. Not surprisingly, in this information poor environment, it was difficult to persuade either consensus groups or higher-ups of positions involving any concern, and the overriding desire of groups to be seen as problem-free discouraged arriving at a consensus that would have placed them in conflict with the announced goals of both mission management and the agency itself. This meant that, in addition to the usual mechanisms that served to punish employees for failing to act in accordance with consensus, there was also a mechanism that had the effect of threatening to punish the groups who formed the consensuses.

Should experts restrict their claims to those matters about which they are truly expert? There is a complex issue here. At the close of World War II, James Bryant Conant, reflecting on his experience, was very direct about his sense that experts, particularly scientists, routinely had hobbyhorses; this implied that they routinely overreached their technical competence in advancing their own views. He also recognized that the consensuses of scientists were often in error, even with respect to their most fundamental beliefs. It was this aspect of Conant's thought that is amplified in his protégé Thomas Kuhn's *The Structure of Scientific Revolutions* ([1962] 1996), where conformity to the paradigm was taken to be characteristic of normal science. Conant's suspicion of the overreaching expert is particularly relevant here. Who is the best judge of the limits of expertise? The question seems to lead us to exactly the problem of expert omniscience with which we ended our discussion of managerial responsibility.

If experts are genuinely the best judge of the limits of their own expertise, it would seem that expertise in effect has no limits, or to put it differently, that they are not only experts in the primary sense but meta-experts, at least in relation to everything involving their primary expertise. They would have to have the kind of birds-eye view of the domains of expertise that their own expertise relates to, which permits them to say what they are expert about and what they are not. In practice, experts often must apply the tools of their own expertise to situations that are outside of the core of their expertise, and for the scientist, this is simply the means of producing scientific results and scientific progress. For the engineer, it may be the necessary element in engineering creativity, which obviously cannot consist merely in the application of known formulas to previously solved problems, but may involve the discovery of new applications that can be then reduced to formula, or the making of novel applications. In the case of the expert who dismissed the foam problem and those experts who were above him and took his opinion as their own, backed by the "consensus" of experts at the lower level, one wonders whether this was merely, so to speak, a "normal error" of expertise rather than something genuinely culpable. Without the kind of expert knowledge possessed by others, would this expert have known that his particular extension of his knowledge was simply erroneous? Without what we might call omniscience about expertise, omniscience about what the limits of expertise are in particular cases of expert knowledge, we would not be able to make these judgments. And there is no reason to think that this particular expert possessed this particular kind of second order omniscience.

There is also a problem relating to the use of consensus and the conflict between a refined division of labor and the pooling of expertise to produce a consensus. If the point of consensus is not merely to diffuse responsibility and produce what I have elsewhere called fact-surrogates (S. Turner 2003b: 41–43) for managers to operate with, but is to actually facilitate and improve expertise or improve consensuses that are in some sense better than the limited expert knowledge within particular expert domains in the division of expert labor, there must be some discursive process that allows for the dialectical evolution of this improved consensus. And whatever else the discursive ethic of this form of discussion might be thought to consist in, it does seem that the familiar considerations of Mill's *On Liberty* ([1859] 1975), of collective fallibilism and willingness to tolerate dissent and indeed even to encourage it, must be part of the ethic.

The problem, however, is that this particular model, and even its elaborated and modernized version as promoted by Habermas under the title of "the ideal-speech situation," in which second-order considerations about the assumptions and interests of the parties involved is made open to discussion in order to facilitate the rationality of the discussion, is undermined and fundamentally transformed by the asymmetries of knowledge that are intrinsic to the situation of expert knowledge itself. The participants are not equal and all the relevant issues are not fully accessible to all the participants. Typically they are fully accessible to none of the participants. As an expert, one participates in these discussions with a command of a particular limited range of techniques of analysis, experience, tacit knowledge, practical understanding, and so forth, and the considerations that one can bring to bear on the questions to which the consensus is addressed are necessarily limited to those considerations that one not only understands best, but understands the grounds for best. In the setting of discussions with other experts with different domains of expertise, it is impossible to completely eliminate these asymmetries through discussion—Habermas's model. Discussions, however prolonged, will not produce the same tacit knowledge, practical experience, theoretical understanding, and so forth in all of the participants in the discussion. So the discourse must be of a kind that relies on trust in the expert claims of others, and also in at least some of their meta-expert claims. And this means that participants must rely on, or at least make judgments of, the self-discipline of the other participants—particularly of their observance of the distinction between expertise proper and meta-expertise, questions involving the limits, relevance, and character of the participants' own expertise.

This means that the kinds of considerations that motivated Mill, namely that free and open discussion would allow the formation of a consensus in which the participants understood one another, cannot fully occur. There is an ineliminable role for meta-expertise, judgments about the competence of others to make the claims they make, and this adds an ineliminable limit to any given participant's capacity to inquire into the grounds for claims made by others. Put differently, the condition of omniscience about expertise—perfect meta-expertise—cannot be obtained.

Necessarily then, this means that the notion of responsibility for assent to a consensus is no longer readily applicable. One necessarily assents to things that one does not fully understand. But one cannot be held responsible for that which is beyond one's powers. One can scarcely be said to be responsible for an outcome about which one necessarily relies on others and on one's inevitably limited non-omniscient judgment of their capacity to make those judgments. But since every participant in the dialog is in this situation, in effect no one is responsible. Moreover, any stringent ethic of self-limitation in discussion would defeat the purpose of open discussion entirely and simply amount to delegating the decision or elements of the decision to those people who claimed to have relevant expertise or were assumed by the division of labor of expertise to possess that expertise. This suggests that we really have no usable model of consensus here and that these consensus processes are a kind of black box, which we can relate to as consumers in terms of their reliability, but not in any reasonably full sense understand, much less assign individual responsibility for.

NASA, MANAGERIAL RESPONSIBILITY, AND CONSENSUS

I have introduced this rather odd concept of meta-expertise, expertise about expertise, not because I think there could be expertise about expertise, but because there would need to be such a thing in order for many of the common claims about experts to make sense. It was an interesting feature of the *Columbia* inquiry that there was a significant amount of speculation, for example web pages about the competence of the NASA managers, especially Linda Ham. The suggestion was made that anyone with elementary knowledge of physics would have realized that foam could have caused significant damage, and it was implied that the lack of this knowledge explained her mistaken actions. A more sophisticated variant of this argument was made by Hugh Pennington, who argued that,

> when the known weakness in the design of the solid rocket boosters was discussed at the *Challenger* pre-launch conference, one senior manager was unhappy. He was told to "take off his engineering hat and put on his management hat." He did, and the launch proceeded to catastrophe. With *Columbia*, the team examining the effects of the insulating foam that had peeled off the enormous external fuel tank and hit the shuttle at 500 mph (creating a hole in the wing that led to the craft's destruction on re-entry) made numerous requests for imagery to be obtained to check for damage. Managers were not interested; such strikes had happened many times before and were classified as not posing a critical threat. Imagery requests were denied. When asked why the team had not pressed their requests harder, the engineers "opined that by raising contrary points of view about shuttle mission safety, they would be singled out for possible ridicule by their peers and managers." (Pennington 2003)

Put into practical organizational terms, this reasoning would suggest that there should be a complete separation between the expression of expert opinion and decision-making that no expert should be forced to put on a "management hat." It further suggests that sanctions for expressions of opinion—even informal sanctions such as "possible ridicule"—should be forbidden. This gives us a theoretical model for the aggregating of expert opinion for decision-making: experts express opinions for which they are not accountable, even informally, to their peers; decision-makers decide what to do with these opinions, and they are the only participants to have any responsibility. Needless to say, this is a piece of utopianism.

Having the expert put on the managerial hat makes them accountable for their opinions. It explicitly makes them accountable not merely for their technical opinions, but for something more—weighing the importance, evidential base, risks, and consequences of having their opinion taken seriously, which is to say it holds them responsible for meta-expertise about their own expertise. Is this also utopian? One view might be that the answer to the question of who is a better meta-expert about a given area of technical knowledge than the expert in this area is "no one," and that ordinarily, experts should be managed by experts of the same kind, and define their own scope of decision-making competence as well as their expertise. This was certainly the position of the atomic scientists in the

West during the two decades after the bomb. They believed, because they were technical experts about nuclear weapons, that they were uniquely and even solely qualified to make judgments about nuclear disarmament, about which weapons programs should be pursued, and about nuclear strategy. Eventually, however, a vast array of other kinds of experts staked a claim to expertise on these topics, and a body of informal meta-expertise guided both decision-making and the use and assessment of expert claims.

The atomic scientists, however, sought managerial power and responsibility, and complained about the inability of the decision-makers to understand them or respect their claim to special expertise with respect to these meta-expert topics. This model is another piece of utopianism, at least when it conflates the distinctions between technical knowledge and what I have been calling meta-expertise of how to assess the claims of experts in decision-making. It implies that experts should simply be delegated managerial authority in those domains about which they are expert, and that their own claims about the significance and relevance of their expertise should be accepted, even where the political consequences, about which they are not expert, are enormously significant.

The NASA system was an attempt to deal with expertise in a practical way by holding those who expressed opinions responsible for their opinions, as they bore upon decisions. "Just engineers talking" was not discouraged, and obviously, in this case, occurred. But there clearly was a problem of aggregating opinions in public discussion, which was shown in the many comments that participants in the decision-making process made about the risks of expressing concerns. There was a gap in perceptions between the underlings and the top mission managers about the quality of the atmosphere for discussion. From the point of view of the underlings, there was a sense that anything that was raised with managers had to be sugar-coated, that messengers with bad news would be punished, and so forth. The managers, in contrast, placed faith in the formal procedures, which obliged many people to raise these concerns if, in their professional opinion, the concerns were valid. They also placed faith in reliance on hard data while failing to provide adequately for the collection of relevant data. And they seem to have been exceptionally blind to the ways in which pressures to perform and to conform to the consensus not only imposed responsibility for expressions of opinions but effectively prevented opinions from being aired. The CAIB investigators interviewing the mission managers identified this as a serious failing. In the course of the CAIB inquiry, Ham was asked,

> "As a manager, how do you seek out dissenting opinion?" According to him [the investigator], she answered, "Well when I hear about them . . ." He interrupted, "Linda, by their very nature you may not hear about them." "Well, when somebody comes forward and tells me about them." "But Linda, what techniques do you use to *get* them?" She had no answer. (Langewiesche 2003: 82)

One answer she could have given was that it was the formal responsibility of her subordinates to raise these questions. She chose not to blame others, however, and appealed to the idea that, because the mission workers were a team, no one should be held responsible. But the failure to "speak to the opposition" and otherwise maintain an appropriately open kind of discussion points, as the CAIB investigator intuited, to a deeper issue with meta-expertise. Part of the point of the discursive processes of a large technical project of this kind, without the kind of stable division of knowledge spheres characteristic of well-developed technologies, such as the automobile, is to provide a collective surrogate for the necessary meta-expertise. Discussion, sharing perspectives and concerns, is the means of constructing the meta-expertise necessary for decision-making, but also, in a situation in which experts are responsible for meta-expertise about their own areas, provides the expanded understanding necessary for participants to grasp how their own domains of responsibility relate to that of others.

As important as this domain is, it is also, necessarily, the least accountable of all. The point of discussion is to arrive at a meta-expert climate of opinion. But the content of this climate of opinion itself is no one's responsibility, nor is the content a matter of expertise proper. At most, issues of *process* such as those the CAIB investigator raised with Ham, can be treated as matters of responsibility. So the inclusion of managerial responsibility in this fashion has an ironic consequence. It makes the manager-councilors more circumspect about their claims, but at the same time frees them from responsibility for outcomes. The outcomes are the products of consensus for which no one is formally responsible.

CONCLUSION

What happened to the call to hold NASA officials responsible? There are four answers to this, and a coda which suggests that all of the discussions were misguided. The first is the answer given by the CAIB, which, in addition to its discussion of the technical causes, blamed the NASA "culture." The second is the response of NASA employees and former employees, which was curiously mixed. A number of different persons were identified as culpable, but perhaps the strongest reaction was that Linda Ham was a scapegoat. The third is the response of the politicians, who eventually gave up on the question of responsibility. The fourth is that of NASA management, which professed acceptance of the conclusions of the CAIB, but did what was in effect, the opposite. The coda is this: the newest understanding of the cause of the foam shedding and the foam hit itself suggests that this particular foam-shedding event was significantly outside any past experience.

One of the oddities of the CAIB report and the administration of NASA is that the board relied very heavily on social science knowledge, including the work of Karl Weick, the revered organizational social psychologist and former editor of *Administrative Science Quarterly*, and Diane Vaughan, the author of an influential book on the *Challenger* (1996). The report appealed, as Vaughan did in her book, to the organizational sociologist Charles Perrow's classic book on normal accidents (1984). The advisors to the board included Harry Lambright, who was a longtime professor in the Syracuse Science and Technology Administration program. Sean O'Keefe, the head of NASA, was both a student and a professor in the same program. So the participants were steeped not only in social science lore but in the STS tradition as it pertained to these kinds of decision-making processes.

What these participants shared was a commitment to a body of organizational behavior theory that itself served to shift issues of responsibility from individual managers to managerial processes and structures. The origins of modern managerial thinking in "scientific management" had been based on an attack on "the pressure system" and argued for the theory that there was a "one best way" for performing tasks that workers themselves could not discover and hence should not be held accountable for. The Human Relations approach that followed shifted responsibility for such things as workers' feelings to managers, who came to be thought of almost as therapists. So the appeal to an organizational level of analysis already implies the diminution of the notion of responsibility and perhaps even its relegation to the medieval torture chambers of premodern organization practice.

When the CAIB dealt with the problem of responsibility, it did two things. It pointed its finger at fundamental problems in the way in which NASA was managed that were not problems that could be assigned to any single past or present administrator or administrative action. The issues were matters of process, and then "culture," a more recent organizational behavior concept. The notion of culture served as a useful stand-in for the guilty party, but since cultures cannot be held responsible, it had the effect of eliminating the notion of responsibility entirely.

So it is perhaps useful to close with a brief discussion of the culture argument and its implications and validity. One of the peculiarities of Vaughan's book on the *Challenger* was that the culture concept was applied to a body of decision-making practices that on another approach would have simply seemed rational. Engineers working with advanced and complex technologies, especially with technologies that are not mass produced, are routinely faced with the problem of understanding how parts fail while operating with relatively limited data. The best analogy here, perhaps, is the work of the engineers and mechanics of race cars. This is a technology in which one routinely tries to get more out of the machinery than other people have, and thus is always straining at the limits of the machinery, which routinely breaks. The failures provide data for strengthening, fixing, and redesigning parts. Safety is of course a concern, but technical decision-making relies, necessarily, on heuristics applied to actual experience. Every decision Vaughan attributed to "culture" in the book would just as plausibly be attributed to the reliance on these heuristics,[3] and, as I have argued here, reliance on meta-expert judgments is ineliminable. The use of the heuristics or pragmatic justifications is only a part of meta-expertise, but, in any complex system with uncertainties, it is a necessary part.

The "culture" explanation had practical implications, and here the NASA response becomes relevant. On the one hand, O'Keefe took public responsibility for the task of changing the culture. On the other, he rejected the means of changing the culture that best fit the situation. Some background here is relevant. In the early 1990s, when culture became a managerial concept, there was a spectacular and largely successful attempt to change the manufacturing culture at Ford Motor Company, in order to get managers to emphasize quality over productivity, as manufacturing quality had been a long-standing Ford problem. Some managers, particularly the head of a major New Jersey manufacturing plant, resisted or ignored the newly imposed "culture." As an important part of the strategy of cultural change, he was fired, and the reasons for his firing were widely circulated. Public execution, in short, is a major device for culture change. The other devices, such as charismatic "change-agent" leadership, are more problematic, and less relevant to the NASA situation. O'Keefe, however, insisted that there was no need for a "public execution" (Cabbage and Shaw 2003), and did precisely the opposite of what Ford did: he reassigned staff members implicated in the report and allowed others to retire, but praised others, including Ham, and never circulated or even publically acknowledged the reasons for these personnel actions. Even the CAIB members accepted this. As one of them put it, "Do you want their heads on a fence someplace?" and added, "Rather than listen to what he says, watch what he does" (Leusner et al. 2004).

The predictable result of this, as Aneil Mishra, a Wake Forest professor who studies organizational change put it, would be this:

> People will read between the lines and make up their own stories and sentences and paragraphs. And they will either be wrong, distorted or they may be right. He went on to say, Sean O'Keefe needs to be telling people why those 14 or 15 people were replaced, who replaced them and why. He predicted that "if he doesn't start doing that, the culture will change, but it will be for the worse." (Leusner et al. 2004)

Barry Render, a NASA consultant and business school professor, made a similar point:

> The message [from O'Keefe] is that the old system is still in place. Clearly, someone had to take blame, but they just got a lateral transfer [or] were due for retirement anyway, so that's not a big deal. (Leusner et al. 2004)

When Admiral Harold Gehman, the head of the CAIB, responded to senators pressing him on the question of accountability, he had said that, "if someone—the administrator of NASA or the head of this committee, wants to find out whose performance was not up to standard, it's all in the report." O'Keefe himself said there would be "no ambiguity on the question of accountability at all" (Cabbage and Shaw 2003). But NASA employed a routine organizational ritual that deflected the problem of responsibility further. As Robert Hotz, who had been on the *Challenger* review board put it, "you hang it on the procedures and the organization. The manager is automatically removed" (Leusner 2003). Because this would have happened anyway, as a sacrificial propitiation, it meant nothing.

Eventually a large body of opinion formed in support of the idea, as Barry Render put it, "There isn't one person to blame" (Leusner 2003). Ultimately even the politicians, who were most adamant about holding individuals responsible, such as Representative Dana Rohrabacher of California, a member of the Congressional supervising committee, in the end were persuaded that this was extremely difficult, perhaps impossible, to do. Those who persisted found the "culture" analysis of the CAIB to be an obstacle. "I'm trying to get past this 'culture' finding and fix responsibility," Senator Hollings said (Pianin 2003). But he could not.

The debate about responsibility continues online as I write this, a year after the event. The discussion is strikingly complex and inconclusive. A significant body of NASA opinion has concluded that Ham was a scapegoat, but also accepted that formal responsibility had to be taken by decision-makers to satisfy the demand to blame and punish someone, however ritualistically. A new finding by NASA explains why this foam incident was in fact unlike previous foam incidents, in which the foam had "shed" or peeled off in small pieces and fallen down along the tank and largely missed the shuttle. This time, according to the new analysis, a suitcase-sized chunk, propelled with explosive force by liquefied air that collected beneath the foam, struck the orbiter, apparently causing a large gash in the wing. If this analysis is correct, the event was genuinely anomalous, and even more firmly beyond the assignment of responsibility.

5 Balancing Expert Power
Two Models for the Future of Politics

The puzzle of the political significance of expert knowledge has many dimensions, and in this chapter I plan to explore a simple Oakeshottian question in relation to it. To what extent is the present role of expert knowledge similar to that envisioned by the "planners" of the 1940s who were the inspiration for Oakeshott's essay, "Rationalism in Politics" ([1947–48] 1962)? This role, as Oakeshott and many of its enthusiasts portrayed it, was to replace politics as hitherto practiced with something different. Rationalism thus depended on a theory of the "politics" it sought to supplant, though it rarely attempted to articulate this theory. In the context of the time, there was no need. In the 1930s, economic depression and the inability of party politicians in the British parliament to agree on measures to deal with the economic situation provided endless negative examples of "politics" standing in the way of action, and a sharp contrast with the state activism of Hitler, Mussolini, and Stalin. In the postwar period, the planners had their chance, and the modem British welfare state was born. Much of what this state did applied ideas of Fabian Socialism, which had presented itself as objective, rational, and expert. But as an administrative fact, the welfare state had no need of the ideology of planning, and the discussion faded. The question I wish to address here is this: expertise forms a much larger part of governance than it did in the time of the "rationalism" of the planning movement; does this mean that rationalism has arrived by stealth, that is to say in practice, without appealing to the overt ideology of rationalistic planning? This is a question of the place of expertise in our politics, and thus a political question.

In its original form, planning was an attempt to replace politics, which it understood as irrational, with the rationality of planning. This ideology died, but the importance of technology, technical decisions, expertise, and science in relation to what formerly were thought of as political matters increased enormously. So did the role of discussion of such issues in politics itself. One can discern two basic patterns of political response to the enlargement of expertise. One involves the proactive management of expert knowledge by legislative bodies: the other is more reactive, and involves popular protest against decisions and initiatives that arise primarily from experts in state bureaucracies. These patterns are not well understood, and are closely linked to specific national political traditions. But they are important as prefigurations of the future of politics: expertise will play a larger and larger role in political life, and the response to it will provide more and more of the drama.

I will consider two very different cases, one which conforms to the saying, extant since the 1930s, "experts on tap, not on top," and one which exemplifies the expert on top, but in a world with political limitations. The cases vary on many dimensions: one is European, the other American; one relates to high politics and to a rare historical moment of stark, consequential decision, the other to an application of planning; one involves a strong tradition of political accountability, the other a tradition of bureaucratic independence from politics. The political outcomes differ as well. In the first case, the experts attempt to assert control and are rebuffed; in the second, they are forced to compromise. My aim is to better understand the conditions of these responses, and the deeper political significance of the difference between the two patterns, a significance, I will suggest, that is in accordance with a more traditional understanding of the stable political orders of the past in terms of balances of power.

FOUR KINDS OF POLITICS

Let me simplify the discussion of politics by introducing some simple ideal-typical distinctions. "High politics" is the politics of leaders. It involves agonistic decision-making, and, more generally, decision-making in the face of inadequacies of comprehension, typically, it is decision-making in the face of opponents whose actions create uncertainty as the product of a lack of reliable information or sources. This can be distinguished from politics in the sense of the politics of representation, and especially democratic representation, the politics of formal or informal roles of speaking and acting for some particular group or, as is ordinarily the case, a faction or subgroup of a group. Complaints about the intrusion of politics into policymaking often refer to the intrusion of this kind of politics of factional representation. A third kind of politics is bureaucratic: this is the use of bureaucratic discretion by state officials, which may be for idealistic goals, to enhance their own power, protect turf, serve the interests of some constituency, encourage cooperation or agreement among stakeholders, or to protect themselves from popular protest or political interference by elected officials. A fourth kind involves protest and disruption, typically by formal or informal NGOs focused on a single issue or decision.

High politics is the place where the familiar language of "the political" is least prone to obliteration. Yet it is also a setting that places particular, and extraordinary, demands on knowledge. Leaders typically act in situations of uncertainty and incomplete information, typically of conflict, when the intentions of their enemies and the reality of the situation are unknown, and in which, and this is perhaps the most important feature, there is relevant information, for example, secret information, which is open to question with respect to its reliability. In these cases, the leaders must necessarily rely on their assessments of the knowledge claims of others and of their veracity, competence, and the adequacy of their understanding of the situation. High politics, in short, is about situations of conflict or of seriously consequential decision-making in which the participants have neither the leisure nor the capacity to wait before acting, necessarily involving epistemic judgments of the knowledge at hand. High politics in this sense is not restricted to the classical situations of warfare and diplomatic strategy. But these are good places to begin.

From the point of view of politics, the epistemic side of these issues has traditionally been invisible. Experts, in particular, have usually played a small role in the kinds of political and biographical narratives that traditionally serve as a basis for our understanding of the nature of politics. Discussions of the decision-making of leaders themselves have typically focused on the agonistic aspects of politics, the calculations that leaders make in relation to adversaries and rivals. This is understandable. The choices and tactical and strategic decisions of adversaries and rivals are the largest of the uncertainty with which decision-makers in politics are compelled to cope. Experts have not played a starring role in these narratives, or been treated as adversaries, simply because, though there are interesting exceptions, they usually are not themselves rivals to power nor do they possess means of altering the contingencies faced by the leader. To paraphrase Napoleon's famous remark on the Pope, they have no battalions. Experts traditionally have played an opposite and less dramatic role. The reliance on experts by politicians is designed to reduce uncertainties or answer questions about what possibilities are open to the adversaries and to the political figure, leaving the decision-making to the leaders themselves.

This invisibility is continued on the side of writings on expertise itself. Narratives on the side of experts typically involve stories to the effect that the correct advice of an expert was not taken. To a great extent then, expert stories are histories written by losers, or people who believe that outcomes would have been better if past decisions had been made differently. The narratives of successful experts are peculiarly non-triumphalist in character, consistent with the pose of expertise itself to be merely offering the facts and not to be engaged in manipulation or agonistic struggle with rivals. The expert's story is commonly one of a struggle to speak truth to power through the fog of committees, bureaucratic resistance, and, in some cases, over the voices of expert rivals who are motivated by erroneous views, hobbyhorses, professional jealousy, and so forth.

In consequence, writing about high politics is normally writing with the expertise left out, while writing about the effects of expertise on politics is writing about failures to be listened to. The successful influence of expertise on politics, that is to say cases where expert opinion actually alters the decision-making process, are typically invisible because they are treated as part of the normal activity of politicians seeking to determine the facts of the matter before making decisions which are interesting as decisions because they relate to contingencies rather than fact. Perhaps the most interesting and most fully elaborated example of this complicated relationship is the case of Churchill's science advisors during World War II. This is especially interesting because it was the subject of a set of Harvard lectures by C. P. Snow who was highly critical of Churchill's preferences for a particular science advisor, Lord Cherwell, over the figure whom the science establishment most closely supported—Henry Tizard, known as "Tizard the Wizard"—along with his complaints about the consequences for the war effort of Churchill's reliance on Cherwell. The issue is almost completely invisible in the many elaborate histories of Churchill's conduct of the war. These accounts nicely exemplify the narrative problems I have mentioned here, but the absence of the topic nevertheless points us to some very fundamental issues about the nature of politicians' reliance on expertise and the conditions under which that reliance occurs. There are, however, cases where we can reconstruct the role of experts, and learn something about the ways in which expertise constrains and fails to constrain politics.

DROPPING THE ATOMIC BOMB: EXPERTISE AS HIGH POLITICS

The atomic bomb decision was one of great secrecy and it involved a relatively small number of persons who produced a report, which led to the decision to drop the bomb. This committee, known as the interim committee, included a number of high-level scientists and military officials, each of whom brought both some kind of expertise to the committee and a great deal of experience in making decisions. The committee was not "political," it was advisory, but it would be wrong to see these activities as somehow free from ordinary considerations of political responsibility. The main player in this decision, James S. Byrnes, was later secretary of state, however, in the course of this decision process, he was actually a private citizen with no powers of command at all. Byrnes nevertheless operated in terms of a very well-developed historical tradition of political responsibility. At the end of World War I, Congress had instituted a wide ranging committee of inquiry into the conduct of the war. Byrnes not only believed this inquiry could be repeated, but that it was likely to be repeated, as he constantly reminded the other members of the committee of scientists and military men who were charged with making advisory recommendations. According to the memoirs of one of them, James Bryant Conant, this was not among the considerations that had entered into the discussion before it reached the level of the committee (Robertson 1994; cf. Hershberg 1993: 232).

If we focus on this committee and its actions, we can see it as engaged in high politics and as a location within which high politics occurs. The participants in the committee operated under the constraints of the information available to them and the form in which this information was available to them. In their possession were a series of reports that were the collective products of other bodies, largely analogous to their own but more specialized in character. There were reports from the scientists and military reports that were estimates, for example, of casualties likely to be suffered in an invasion of Japan.

The peculiarities of expertise narratives become clear when one considers the status of these reports in the eyes of the members of this committee. The reports were not taken as fact, or as truth spoken to power. The committee members understood that the documents in front of them were themselves political products in the sense that they were the results of negotiations designed to produce agreements about the content. They knew that there was a tendency to indirectly exclude certain opinions from consideration by the very process by which particular groups of experts were constituted, so that the product in all likelihood did not represent the full range of reasonable opinion. They knew that individuals suppressed their disagreements within committees for various reasons such as producing consensus leading to a kind of blandness or mediocrity in the final product. They knew also that groups of experts have particular known, as well as unknown, biases and that the reports were likely to reflect those biases. Documents of the kind that they were dealing with were, after all, written for their effect, written to be used, and written in the light of their potential uses. One could often discern in them, and adjust for, the document's biases in support of a particular outcome desired, though not stated as desired, by the committee authors. Their attitude toward these reports was nicely put by George W. Bush when asked about the government report on global warming. Bush replied that yes, he had seen the report put out by the bureaucracy, which is to say a report that he treated as motivated by a particular identifiable set of interests and biases.

In the case of the bomb decision, and indeed in the usual cases of high politics, nominal supreme power is invested in some individual, and this sets the general tone of the process. Decision-making operates in terms of specialized advice relating to particular decisions or plans that are, more or less by the definition of high politics, not a matter of open public knowledge or discussion. This is not to say that advisors, leaders, and decision-makers are not attentive to public discussion, but that they operate in situations removed from immediate public discussion and typically can expect informed public scrutiny or investigation only long after the fact and after the outcomes of the decisions have become known.

Trust plays a role in the politics of advice that differs from its role in the politics of election campaigns and legislative politics. The individuals involved in high politics are preselected for their trustworthiness and the identifiability of their biases. Unpredictable people generally do not rise to high levels of responsibility or high advisory roles for precisely this reason. Persons with strong known positions often do, especially if they are capable of departing from a doctrinaire position in the face of new facts, so that in a peculiar way their agreement carries special weight. A considerable amount of competition for power consists in competition to advise, to define the framework of decision, to have control over the sources of expert information presented, and so forth.

When one begins to think of the environment within which the committee operated, it is evident that it involved the elements that I have identified as characteristic of high politics. There were enemies about whose behavior there was a significant degree of uncertainty. In this case there were two main uncertainties, one of which involved the bomb itself and the other involved the question of the consequences of other courses of action, notably the choices between the uncertain effects of either dropping the bomb without warning, dropping a demonstration bomb with a warning and a demand for surrender, or not dropping the bomb at all and opting for an invasion.

The historical controversy over the decision has focused mostly on the existence of casualty estimates associated with the fourth option, and particularly a report which claimed that casualties would be relatively modest, thus making the dropping of the bomb itself unnecessary. This particular report is worth considering as a typical case of the kind of material with which such decisions are made. The report was itself the product of a more or less well-understood process with more or less well-understood biases. It obviously could not be taken as a certain prediction, nevertheless the very existence of the report posed problems from the point of view of the consideration of political responsibility. Byrnes, and as a consequence the members of his committee, anticipated the possibility of a systematic Congressional review of the relevant decisions after the war, which would have included the existence of this report.

One of the contested topics of this historiography of the bomb is the fact that the more optimistic parts of the expert committee work that were submitted to the interim committee, notably these low estimates of the expected casualties in an invasion, which might have led to the bomb not being used, were ignored. Yet in light of the consideration of the expectation of review, the dismissal of those estimates takes on a somewhat different meaning. Decisions, in wartime, to expend the lives of even this number of expected casualties when these casualties could be avoided would, at least to many people, seem to be not an act of peace but an act of culpable stupidity. If the bomb had never been dropped at all and remained as a speculative threat, or if the bomb was dropped only for the purposes of demonstration rather than actually employed in combat, and the Japanese had ignored the demonstration and resisted an invasion at great cost in lives, a decision to give a demonstration would have been culpable. In any case, it was the responsibility of the committee to assess such reports. Evidently the low estimate of potential casualties in an invasion was dismissed because the estimates of minimal enemy resistance were starkly in conflict with new facts on the ground in Okinawa, where very stiff resistance was being put up by the Japanese—stiffer resistance because Okinawa was understood by the Japanese not merely as a holding but as a physical part of Japan. The committee members might reasonably have concluded that there was a significant probability that casualties would be far higher. This is a typical example of lay knowledge being used to evaluate and correct expert claims in light of purposes and issues about which experts were not expert. The committee also needed to ask whether the technology would work.

Both bombs worked perfectly. The committee was not faced with this fact, but it was with the possibility of failure, a possibility not unknown in warfare and one which the technical experts on the committee were highly cognizant of. Byrnes himself, of course, was not a technical expert, and in any case the scientists who were so confident about the powers of the bomb were expected to be biased in favor of confidence about the effectiveness of the bomb and their opinions were reasonably discountable by men of experience. Some things that were "known" were unknown to the committee. For example, the possibility of the severe radiation sickness on the part of the people not killed by the direct blast. This was "known" in the sense that someone had actually made this prediction, but it was not part of any of the material available to the committee, so the committee had no ground for considering it.

This committee was a paradigm case of a successful extension of a pre-existing tradition of democratically responsible high politics. The committee ignored the attempt by scientists to determine the decision. One of Byrnes's concerns especially was to justify the huge cost of the Manhattan Project to Congress. He anticipated that serious questions would be raised about this expenditure had the bomb not been used, or its use withheld. And these would indeed have been serious questions. The first responsibility of a liberal democracy ought to be toward the lives and well-being of its own citizens, especially those it compels to risk death on the battlefield. Every penny that went for the bomb was a penny not spent on some other weapon that would have saved the lives of Americans. The scientists never asked this question—they had no sense of political responsibility to the population, which had already paid for the bomb in casualties that would have been prevented had the money and effort been spent on other weapons. That the committee chose differently from the scientists is a sign of their recognition of their political responsibilities; that they knew what these responsibilities were, and had confidence that their advice would be judged retrospectively to be correct, is evidence of a predictable system of democratic political accountability. They knew the precedents, could anticipate the questions, and acted accordingly. And this predictable character made their advice and role invisible—where the expert becomes visible, something has gone wrong. Not surprisingly, historians largely ignore such advice. In a sense, this is appropriate. The committee did not exert power so much as correctly anticipate the considerations that would have been central to a congressional inquiry, which itself would have been motivated by an anticipated congressional, and thus public, debate. So, here the locus of power is public debate, to which the committee deferred by anticipating its likely content.

The committee calculated correctly about the problem of a congressional inquiry: the success of the bomb in ending the war precluded the questions that failure would have produced. This was the dog that didn't bark—but it was very much part of the story. Byrnes anticipated the kind of congressional inquiry that might have followed a decision to hold the bomb in reserve and chance an invasion. A large and highly motivated group of families of the troops who would have perished in the invasion would have asked whether the decision-makers had the blood of these soldiers and marines on their hands. The risk of very high casualties was impossible to rule out. If the families of the dead were told that the decision had been made because a group of scientists involved in the development of the bomb were squeamish about its use, or that they were willing to use it against Hitler, but not Japan, the political consequences would have been enormous. The question "who lost China?" poisoned political debate for a generation, and it was a large part of Lyndon Johnson's motivation in the Vietnam War to avoid a similar question. The "political consequences" were, moreover, "democratic." The leadership knew that their representatives had the power to hold them responsible: the fallout that they wished to avoid was from their own citizens, and from the elected representatives who would be sure to exploit the inevitable questions to advance their own careers. Thus the decision was a paradigm case of democratic accountability.

Yet the decision produced a remarkable result in the fourth kind of politics: the "Scientists' Movement," which included the creation of a variety of organizations that attempted to influence policy and claim special expertise about atomic matters or to serve as a forum for discussions of weapons policy and science policy. This is, of course, a well-documented episode. In terms of the ideal-type classification of politics presented above, it is an example of a protest movement that claimed expertise, a claim bolstered by the fact that its leading participants were contributors to the development of the bomb itself. The political effect of the scientists' movement was substantial, though unintended. Byrnes's reaction, that the scientists were political idiots intruding on matters that were not their domain, was institutionalized. People such as Oppenheimer were suspected of subordinating their scientific advice to political purposes, and removed from positions of influence.[1] Politicians were alerted to the anti-democratic potential of scientists' movements, especially when scientists were in a position to use their claims to special expertise to bring about policy results that suited their ideology. The response served to assure that scientists' claims would get special scrutiny, and provided, surprisingly, a new model for relations between science and politics, in which the scientists' claims to expertise, which were extensive and continued to be extensive for decades, were marginalized by the construction of bureaucratic systems that formalized, and limited, roles for scientists in relation to policy, and assured that military bureaucracies had their own expertise. Many naval officers, for example, were sent for training in nuclear physics.

Eventually the scientists' movement petered out, though it survives in such organizations as the Union of Concerned Scientists. But the movement continued not as a pure scientists' movement, but as an adjunct to the extreme Left. It drew force from a popular Ban the Bomb movement that was especially strong in the UK. In the US, some scientists continued to speak out and make apocalyptic pronouncements about the nuclear threat and the need to disarm, a posture welcomed by the Soviet Union and in one case rewarded with the Lenin Peace Prize. As a coda to this discussion, it should perhaps be observed that this was a case in which the democratic process was "right" and the scientists in the movement were "wrong." According to the conventional wisdom of international relations thinkers today, the scientists were wrong on every important count. The possession of even a small number of nuclear weapons by a country proved to be a successful deterrent: not only to nuclear warfare as such, but to any kind of warfare between states with nuclear weapons. The results of nuclear weaponry, on this view, have been unambiguously pacific, producing a sixty-year peace among major powers that stands in sharp contrast to the first forty-five nuclear-free years of the twentieth century, in which great power conflict, punctuated by ineffective arms restrictions treaties, were the norm. Nuclear weapons and the threat of deterrence made the treaties of the post-1945 period meaningful because they were backed by force, rather than threats that were known by the relevant belligerents to be idle.

BUREAUCRATIC RATIONALITY MEETS "POWER"

Much of the literature on experts has focused on very different kinds of decisions, on what is, in effect, municipal decision-making on controversial technologies or public works, or regulatory decision-making, which is part of bureaucratic politics. One issue is how the different kinds of situations of decision-making compare and relate to one another. Many of the studies of decision-making involving expert knowledge and the actions of representative governments at the municipal level have concluded that expert knowledge has little or no effect on the decisions that are made; experts are powerless and politically inconsequential (Collingridge and Reeve 1986). On the face of it this is a somewhat puzzling thesis given that, in the course of making domestic policy, municipalities and national governments are

102   *The Politics of Expertise*

characteristically surrounded by experts, commission reports by experts, and employ experts in the course of implementing decisions. The role of experts in these settings is obviously far greater today than it was even in the most recent past. Before 1940 in Britain, for example, there was an extensive discussion of the problems of using experts to make decisions about the siting of telephone lines, a problem that resulted from the technical limitations of "long-line" telecommunications service. The puzzle, which vexed the civil service for decades, was this: could a lower ranking technical expert override or dictate a decision by a higher ranking civil servant who had no technical competence? The issue could take this form only because of the extreme rarity of reliance on technical experts. Today this situation is completely different in all modern countries. Even such a mundane decision as locating a road commonly requires feasibility studies, impact statements, and so forth, all legislatively mandated and all produced by experts. Yet it is also the case that the decisions that are ultimately made are not always those that the expert advises.

Another novelty that relates to these decisions is that there is now a process, sometimes formalized, of public participation which includes negotiations with stakeholders and not infrequently involves public protest that influences decisions made either by elected officials or bureaucrats responsible to elected officials. Sometimes this process produces street politics, protests, or activist movements which seek to close down the projects. The ubiquity of this kind of political response is relevant to understanding the deeper political significance of the notion of public participation. Not infrequently, these protests and movements succeed, and governments and bureaucracies withdraw proposals or modify them, sometimes in order to survive politically.

The relationship between bureaucratic politics and protest politics is not accidental, as we shall see shortly. But to understand the relationship we need to go beyond the imaginary defined by rationalism, which took as its implicit target the politics of representative democracy, routinely targeted in the 1930s—especially by scientists on the Left who were attracted by the idea of planning—for its inability to come to decisions, implicitly as a result of being driven by interests and paralyzed by conflicting interests.

In 1994, Bent Flyvbjerg published a study of a city planning effort in the Danish regional center of Aalborg. The book has been praised as equivalent to the writings of Machiavelli in its depiction of contemporary politics. The case is interesting as an example of a particular kind of expert politics. But it is also interesting, and exemplary, as the expression of a residual form of the rationalism rejected by Oakeshott, and its continued presence in academic writing, as well as representing a strong articulation of the working ideology of the Danish city planning bureaucracy and, by extension, the ideology of urban planning generally.

The Aalborg city planning story begins with a collaborative effort by a number of bureaucrats in different bureaucracies, each of which had both significant regulatory and funding power in the city of Aalborg. They produced an agreement on an ambitious plan of urban transformation which was pushed through the political process, and in the view of its protagonist, and indeed of Flyvbjerg himself, was undermined and transformed beyond recognition, and *derationalized*, in the course of its implementation. The story, as Flyvbjerg tells it, is one in which power trumps rationality. His theory is this: Rationality is weak and power is strong, but rationality under particular kinds of conditions can break through and become the basis not only of decision-making but the full implementation of the rational decisions themselves. These rationality permitting conditions can be readily disrupted by those who have power and are in a position to undermine rational outcomes for their own irrational "reasons," meaning "interests."

The protagonists of reason in this case are Aalborg city planning bureaucrats whose primary concern in the initial stake for this project was with the key element of removing private vehicles from the city center and supplanting them with more rational, meaning collective, forms of transportation. This involved creating a central bus terminal facility in the center of the city, and through a complex process a particular city square called Nytorv was transformed. The theory behind this transformation was that people would give up car use if convenient bus service existed. Convenience was in large part defined as a short wait between transfers. A strong effort was also made to facilitate access for bicyclists. The cyclists' association was, although a weak political player, one of the strongest supporters of this plan, and implicitly served as Flyvbjerg's model of rational agreement with the plan.

One can ask, and indeed Flyvbjerg does ask, what political tradition operated in this decision process. The answer Flyvbjerg does not give is one that I will give now, simply to explain the situation. Danish bureaucracies, and indeed Scandinavian expert bureaucracies generally, resemble German bureaucracies in that they are only loosely supervised by elected officials, hold many discretionary powers, and are expected to (and do in fact) play a leading role in the creation of cartel-like relationships of cooperation between various stakeholders in relation to particular decision-making processes. The "stakeholder model" much discussed by Tony Blair, in this particular tradition is a model characterized by long-term flexible relations of mutual dependence. Bureaucracies have the power to punish and disrupt the activities of non-cooperators through regulation. So it is this asymmetric power of the bureaucracy, rather than straight bargaining, that is the basic power relation.

Put more straightforwardly, the "stakeholders" not only have a stake in their own aspirations and desires, but are dependent on the bureaucracies that have discretionary power over them, strive to preserve working relationships with them and, indeed, see the interventions of the bureaucracies favorable to their interests as important strategic means. The bureaucracies not only strive to generate, in a cartel-like fashion, commonalities of interest, but are themselves the embodiment and subject of long-term relationships that are in the interests of those who are governed by them.

These bureaucracies, especially in their regulative and subsidy-granting mode, are expertized bureaucracies; they possess distinctive technical training, usually of a kind not shared by the stakeholders themselves, for example in city planning or transportation analysis. Even where this expert knowledge is not a monopoly it predominates and is supposed to be the basis of the discretionary actions of the bureaucracies, which are not understood to be despotic and tyrannical power holders but rather experts who are professionals constrained by the canons of professionalism and technical competence. Expertise predominates in the soft discipline of a bureaucratic system of career advancement in which success is, practically speaking, success in accordance with the expectations of one's professional peers in the planning bureaucracy. There are, for example, awards for planning successes, and the Aalborg plans received the European award in city planning.

The city of Aalborg also has an ordinary political process, a case of the politics of representation, including a mayor and several aldermen who were not only formal decision-makers, but who were often in a position to either facilitate the activities of the bureaucracy or, in some cases, impose their own particular preferences on the planning process. In this case, there was a socialist mayor, who for some years was known as the "bus mayor" because of his devotion to public transportation. This mayor, like other politicians, sought to leave as his monument a vastly expanded system of public transportation. The party system, as it operated in Aalborg, involved representation by various parties and operated in a generally consensual way, not surprisingly, given the predominant political role and power of the various expert bureaucracies.

The villain of Flyvbjerg's piece is the chamber of commerce, which ordinarily operated in a cooperative way in the system of long-term relations of mutual dependence described here, but which objected to various features of the proposed plan, supported others, and worked in various ways to modify the plan, correct aspects of the plan, and insist on emergency alterations to the plan. Its main aim was to protect its members against the perceived risk of excluding private automobile traffic from the city center. The chamber of commerce issued various reports, the arguments and claims of which repeatedly changed, but each was designed to show that downtown merchants would suffer considerable losses if cars were restricted in the fashion envisioned by the plan. In the end, they proved to be the most rational of agents—they succeeded in weakening these provisions so significantly that they got what was for them the best of both worlds: an expanded public transportation system that increased commercial traffic from bus travelers, though at great cost to the municipality, and the accommodation of the private automobile so that no significant losses of business occurred.

The original plan, however, was left in shambles, so that this result could be understood not so much as the successful outcome of a process of stakeholder politics but as the simple irrational destruction of a rational and progressive exercise in comprehensive city planning. This is Flyvbjerg's interpretation, and he characterizes the outcome as the result of an underlying political tradition of several centuries in which merchants and merchant associations exert ultimate power in towns. In the case of the city plan, Flyvbjerg argues, the merchants once again forced the city politicians and city administrators as well the planning bureaucracies to serve their interests; in this case, not only at the great expense of the cost of the transport plan and the construction involved in it, but also at the cost of the lost elements of the original plan: ideas in the areas of housing and about the creation of bicycle paths that were ultimately not implemented. These more ambitious elements were disrupted and abandoned or modified because they no longer fit the revised plan.

RATIONALITY OR BUREAUCRATIC POWER?

Flyvbjerg draws a series of Nietzschian aphorisms from this result, which bear repeating here.

1. Power defines reality.
2. Rationality is context-dependent, the context of rationality is power, and power blurs the dividing line between rationality and rationalization.
3. Rationalization presented as rationality is a principal strategy in the exercise of power.
4. The greater the power, the less the rationality.
5. Stable power relations are more typical of politics, administration, and planning than antagonistic confrontations.
6. Power relations are constantly being produced and reproduced.
7. The rationality of power has deeper historical roots than the power of rationality.
8. In open confrontation, rationality yields to power.
9. Rationality-power relations are more characteristic of stable power relations than of confrontations.
10. The power of rationality is embedded in stable power relations rather than in confrontations (1998: 227–37).

These maxims express the weakness of rationality in the face of power. For Flyvbjerg, this weakness is a threat to democracy that can only be overcome by "more participation, more transparency, and more civic reciprocity in public decision-making" (1998: 235).

One is struck by some peculiarities in this treatment and this conclusion. Begin with the obvious point—that Flyvbjerg seems not to expect that the problem of democratic participation is the responsibility of the elected representatives involved in the decision. For him, their proper role is to cooperate with one another and with bureaucrats. "Democracy" is identified not with an open, conflictual, representative politics, but rather with the public interest as defined through the bureaucratically dominated stakeholder model. "Participation" is something to be produced through the stakeholder model by involving larger numbers of groups in the cooperative effort supporting the project. "Civic reciprocity" is Flyvbjerg's code term for cooperation in projects which are mutually beneficial but in which each side potentially gives something up for the greater rationality of the project itself. The bicycle club, which was coopted into the supporting stakeholders for the project by the promise of an extensive network of bicycle paths, on this reading, is cooperative, in that it exchanged public support for the project for the beneficial outcome the project would produce for its members. The chamber of commerce, in contrast, failed to live up to the code of civic reciprocity, because it opposed the project once it decided that its benefits were insufficient. One might think that cooperation goes both ways, and that it was the fault of the bureaucrats that the deal seemed insufficiently tempting for the usually cooperative chamber of commerce. From the point of view of the politics of representation, the very fact of their opposition and the public character of the battle they waged against the plan, especially in the newspapers, is a paradigm example of successful public participation. But Flyvbjerg does not see it this way, in part because he understands the plan to be rational and opposition therefore to be irrational, in part because for him the "public" is by definition opposed to the "private" interests of the chamber.

Flyvbjerg is thus no devotee of explanatory symmetry. He supposes that there is such a thing as a rational city plan, and that this is the sort of thing that a city planning bureaucrat with the requisite technical skills, acting in his competence as a planner, could produce; that other people's rationalities (the pursuit of their own private interests, for example) or the alternative conceptions of the public interest, are, because they fail to accord with this plan, by definition irrational. Because they are irrational they are explicable, to the extent that they are explicable, as a matter of error and the insistence of the agents in this political process on their own ideas and their own ideas of their own interests. Thus it follows that the insertion of these erroneous ideas into the process is an expression of power. The insertion of the ideas of the bicyclists, in contrast, conforms to reason, and thus is not an expression of power.

At no point does Flyvbjerg consider that bureaucracies are themselves in the business of power, and at no point does he consider their activities, such as the creation of a plan and attempt at inducing cooperation among others, as an exercise of power. Without saying so, he identifies reason with the collective reason or social reason represented by the planners, and private reason with unreason. To be sure, he spends a great deal of effort showing the inconsistencies and self-servingness of the claims of the merchants' association and their misuses of research. He also identifies failings in the decision-making processes, inadequate uses of research by the planning bureaucrats themselves, and their failures to deal effectively with their merchant enemies. But the treatment is asymmetric: the bureaucrats fail to live up to the high calling of rationality; the merchants are knaves.

The asymmetric treatment of the main players in this drama, namely the planning authority and the merchants, means that the rationality of the plan is never dissected, its ideology is never analyzed and no consideration is given to the possibility that the outcome was perhaps better than the outcome intended by the planners, which would imply that the political process here worked in a quite prosaic way to successfully accommodate different viewpoints and different claims to expertise, however messy these claims may have been. So we get a strange silence about the validity of the claim that the experts embody reason and, at the same time, an implicit acceptance of their own claim that the plans that they recommend are strictly and essentially the product of their expertise as planners and not a matter of, as Weber uses the term, their "ideal interests" or their ideological commitment to a planning strategy that others do not necessarily acknowledge as wholly legitimate or disinterested.

The fact that the questions aren't asked means the conclusion, that reason is only able to triumph in stable relations between political players, follows because by definition relations become "unstable" in the face of conflicts about beliefs and interests in which the two parties decide that it is more in their interest to destabilize the relationship than to continue it. This is the moment when politics breaks out, even in the setting of the middle-sized municipality, such as Aalborg. In this classic bureaucracy-dominated political system, the costs of destabilization are high if one is engaged in ongoing relationships of dependence with the bureaucracy, and less costly if one is not. Protestors taking to the street in a "manifestation" of public opposition is an attempt to destabilize, but one in which the protestors typically have no continuing relation of dependence to protect or risk. The chamber of commerce did have such a relation, and the risks of non-cooperation were significant.

This is the usual relationship of the Germanic and Scandinavian expert bureaucracy to their citizens and, although Flyvbjerg naturally does not say so, it is a relationship deeply rooted in the predemocratic past of these societies that was essentially unchanged by the transformation of authoritarian politics into formal democracy. That, say, the royal authorities and the merchants of a city like Aalborg traditionally worked out a relationship of mutual accommodation in light of their recognizable and unmysterious mutual dependence seems hardly to be a novel or problematic claim; that their interests sometimes conflicted, that they took different views of particular problems, and that they worked this out in a sense does amount to a political tradition, though not a democratic one. The fact that the bureaucratic powers later acquired the ideology of planning and "rationality" does nothing to change the fact that they possessed, and continued to exercise, the prerogatives of the older order of state bureaucracy.

DEMOCRACY WITHOUT POLITICS

The central distinctions on which Flyvbjerg's arguments rest are variants on the familiar thematic ideas that Oakeshott called "rationalism"—that decisions made "normally" do not require antagonism, the clash of interests, or differences of opinion and belief, but can be handled best by a bureaucracy with a "democratic" bias, open to the desires of citizens and with their "participation." What does participation mean in this context? The same formulae were employed in Oakeshott's time, for example by Barbara Wootton, who held that a better way to make decisions than politics within the British tradition was a new form of consultation with advisory committees, namely tribunals, "through which the ordinary person can make known where the planned shoe pinches; through this machinery he can often stop the pinching" (1945: 175). Implicitly, of course, in these tribunals the bureaucrats hold all the cards—they have the expertise, and they take the advice that they deem it reasonable to take. And this is true whether the ideology behind it is the elaborated one of "planning" or merely the ordinary retail rationalism of expertise. And it is assumed that ordinary representative politics, which was not sufficiently expert to produce or even intelligently supervise "planning," was irrelevant to the kind of public participation that was relevant.

One may ask the Sherlock Holmes question here: why did the dog, in this case the elected representatives, not bark? Wouldn't it have made more sense, and perhaps led to a more rational result, if the plan had been contested politically from the outset, that the stakes and interests of the stakeholders had been made clear in the course of political discussion, and some sort of workable compromise been hammered out? Why didn't the real politicians ensure that this happened? Wouldn't this have been real public participation? This is an "American" question, in that it assumes that the normal place for making decisions of this kind is in elected bodies, not bureaucracies. And the difference points to some deep differences in the way in which European politics works, questions that reflect different conceptions of politics, but also some fundamental institutional differences in the role of political parties. The "American" view of liberal democracy is this: the rough rationality of liberal democracy comes out of playing the political game, the game of legislation, with stakes. Political horse-trading is a crude market test—it reveals what one's stakes really are, and how strongly one believes what one believes, and at the same time allows the participants to learn the stakes, theories, and theories of others about who benefits, and who desires. Political discussion is a kind of epistemic leveler: everyone needs to make their case to the same audience of representatives, whose actions in turn are scrutinized by the press and the voters, and everyone has something at stake. But everyone also decides for themselves whether what they profess to believe is sufficiently well-grounded to fight and commit scarce horse-trading resources to: thus it is common, and often taken as a sign of hypocrisy, for political leaders to pay lip service to ideas that they do not believe in sufficiently strongly to commit resources to them. The realm of issues in which there are extensive and conflicting expert claims happens to be one in which this kind of discrepancy between what is professed and what is done politically is typically large. A good test of whether a politician believes in the pronouncements that are made about energy policy or global warming is the extent to which the politician will sacrifice other goals. The appearance of inaction is often the result of unvoiced skepticism. Thus what the epistemic market decides, as it operates in the context of horse-trading in representative democracy, will very often be systematically at variance with the pronouncements both of experts and representatives.

Continental critics of American democracy have typically been appalled at this process as it operates in the US. They liked the idea of rational persuasion, but not the deal-making and interest-serving that was intertwined with it, and which they tended to see as venal and vulgar, and as a degeneration from the kind of aristocratic English liberalism of the early nineteenth century, which they admired.[2] In any case, their own experience of parliamentary democracy was quite different. The obvious differences were in political form, between a parliamentary system and a strong presidency, and between a weak bureaucracy and a strong one, but a basic difference involved the role and character of political parties. European parties were class or ideological parties, with a strong degree of party discipline and party control of participation, enforced by party slate-making. "Representation" involved party first, for the party was in control of political careers.

In theory, parliamentary government was inherently more effective than the model of separation of powers in the US. It avoided the possibility of conflict between the executive and the legislature by making parliament determine the leader. But in practice the organization of politics in terms of parties led to political paralysis. Party politicians had no incentive to compromise, or, in some cases, even to rule. They depended on their base, which was loyal not because the party delivered the goods but because it expressed their ideological or class position. This produced its own form of hypocrisy. Parliamentary discussion was often largely performative. There was little creative competition for votes because there were few voters whose allegiances were up for grabs and whose beliefs were unknown or malleable. Parties were ideological. Stability, of the sort that Flyvbjerg regarded as a condition of rationality, was, in a practical sense, a result of this situation. Scandinavian politics in particular was characterized by long periods of party dominance and trivial party differences. Intense political contestation of the "American" kind was unheard of, in part because contestation that was unauthorized by parties had no place in parliament, and the range of issues parties chose to contest was small. In these circumstances bureaucratic solutions to political problems could be pursued uncontested as well, insulated by the double layers of party politics and parliamentary quiescence. But there was another sort of *statis* that parliamentary party politics produced: the endless collapse and recreation of parliamentary coalitions. The strong presidency created by de Gaulle's constitution of 1959 was designed to overcome the limitations of this kind of parliamentary politics. In that case, it purchased stability and effectiveness by elevating the leader above parliament.

Politics could be conducted in this way because there was an alternative to this kind of politics that was congenial to it. The state bureaucracy could function as problem solver, but also as—in a way nicely exemplified by Flyvbjerg's account—a largely autonomous power, negotiating with stakeholders, creating mutual interests, and testing, through the process of negotiation, the seriousness of beliefs and the centrality of interests. The state, in short, through its negotiations with stakeholders, supplants "politics." This is politics by other means, bureaucratic politics, a form that avoids the ordinary kind of political accountability. "Participation" without accountability comes to mean something essentially therapeutic—to participate is to have the satisfaction of expressing opinions without any direct effect. It provides the same kind of moral satisfaction as protest demonstrations, but in a prophylactic forum which creates the illusion of power without the substance that political conflict would give it.

The differences in the development of the "Left" response to nuclear weaponry in the US and Britain (whose politics, with respect to the issues discussed here is a kind of half-way house between the US and the Continent) exemplify the differences. Each country had an active scientific Left in the 1930s which supplied scientists to the war effort, and each produced strong opponents to nuclear weapons. But in the US, these movements converted into attempts to use the authority of science to influence policy by issuing expert opinions on various technical issues in the public eye, or into attempts to influence congress and public opinion. In Britain, in contrast, the grand figures of science who objected to nuclear weapons spoke out in protests or wrote books presenting their personal views against nuclear weapons, and supported the mass protest movement for nuclear disarmament. None of this ever stood a realistic chance of becoming party policy, and as time went on, the forms of protest themselves became more extreme and self-marginalizing. When Lord Russell denounced Kennedy and Macmillan as the greatest monsters in history, the distance between this movement and the give and take of liberal democratic political discussion was obvious. Yet the campaign for nuclear disarmament did affect policy. Successive governments sought to mollify the sentiments it was based on, and remove the ancillary issues on which it traded, such as formal control of the button. It was, as its supporters believed, a form of politics. But its effects were primarily on the utterances of politicians, not their actions. Few people were convinced.

Demonstrations against genetically modified food, rationalized agricultural policy, and the like are also a form of politics. But the presence of this kind of politics is a sign of the unavailability of political accountability of the rough kind represented by horse-trading liberalism, with its implicit epistemic market. Instead there is a "yes" or "no" at the public level, as with the Aalborg plan. It is an open question whether the rationality of horse-trading liberal democracy is to be preferred to a bureaucratically dominated rationality punctuated by protests and operating under the threat of protests. Both use expertise, but in different ways. In the bureaucratically dominated stakeholder model, negotiation with a strongly epistemic component is a large part of stakeholder process. And these negotiations provide a forum for discussion in which degrees of belief matter. The outcomes may well mimic what a more market-like political process would produce. But they are typically more consensus oriented and less procedural.

The ubiquity of protests is closely paired with the substitution of bureaucratic politics for the political market. But just as the market resists bureaucratic rationalization by resistance in the form of shortages and surpluses, the bureaucratic rationalization of politics, and the substitution of "participation" for accountability, produces the politics of protest. The promise of rationality given by Flyvbjerg is conditional on "stability." The successful management of potential conflict by means of bureaucratically led negotiation is thus always done under a shadow, the shadow of the threat that politics, in the form of protests, will break out, and even in those societies most terrified by fear of politics, it breaks out regularly.

Rationalism promised to overcome the ills of the political marketplace of liberal democratic politics. But it produced its own nemesis in the form of protest politics. The attainment of "rationality" always occurs under the shadow of the possibility of disharmony, of popular manifestations of hostility, which are perceived as irrational and often are, in the sense that they involve suspicion, negation, and a kind of political irresponsibility available only to those who know that the consequences of their actions are only very indirectly related to what policy will actually be implemented. To protest is not to choose to accept the consequences of a choice, as in politics proper, but to protest the choice. These are the moral pleasures of political impotence. The long history of these pleasures on the Left and Right, and the fear that those who indulge in them will actually have power, defines this politics.

ADMINISTRATIVE TRADITIONS AND POLITICAL TRADITIONS

Oakeshott's comments in "Rationalism in Politics" ([1947–48] 1962) that the Germans do not have a political tradition, by which he is perhaps best read as meaning that they did not have a political tradition for representative rule or high politics outside of the practice of parliamentary party competition. The Germans certainly had a state tradition, and a tradition of professional governance that still has a strong hold not only in Germany but in Scandinavia, the tradition of *Staatswissenschaft*, which is the lineal source of the present "policy sciences" in the US. It was intentionally imported by the Burgess in the course of founding the faculty of political science at Columbia in the 1870s and instilled in its students, who brought it to the rest of American academic life. A related "professionalization" project was promoted by the Rockefeller philanthropies. Bureaucratic traditions do compete with representative government, by leaving political traditions with less to do, and therefore few occasions for learning, establishing precedents, and applying itself to new circumstances. But the motivation for professionalizing and expertizing is reform—reform to correct the ills of "politics"—meaning the ills of interest based manipulation of decision processes, amateurism, and corruption, as well as incompetence.

We have become accustomed, through Foucault, to thinking of power/knowledge projects beginning in hegemonic intellectual constructions, such as Bentham's model of punishment, and becoming an unseen and unnoticed part of the fabric of everyday administration, in this case in the modern disciplinary order. One could certainly tell this story about what Oakeshott calls rationalism. There was, in his time, no shortage of intellectual constructions promising to replace the political by the technical, including the grasp for power of the atomic scientists themselves, and as the example of Flyvbjerg shows, there are still ideologists of expert power with thinly veiled hegemonic ambitions. And in one respect rationalism was right: the sheer ubiquity of expertise in modern political life. It is also true, as Foucault would expect, that there are efforts to stigmatize the opponents of experts as irrational and retrograde. "Rationalism by stealth" would fit the Foucault model. It would occur where the line between the political and the expert is repeatedly redrawn in favor of the expert, and the moments in which a political tradition of accountability that applies to experts is exhibited and sustained are gradually diminished to a narrow few, and those who objected to this regime would be despised and ignored, but continue to resist. But things seem to be turning out differently. Expert power has produced its own nemesis, or rather revived the political forms in which other kinds of knowledge are constructed.

The older view of the Left and of the bureaucracy was that democracy meant rule on behalf of and in favor of the people, by reliance on expertise. The French Socialist leader Ségolène Royal was recently quoted as endorsing "the expertise of the people" against the expertise of the bureaucratic state. The occasion, the success of the protest movements in forcing the government to back down on a law allowing a new employment contract designed to reduce joblessness, an attempt at "structural reform," is exemplary. The use of the term "expertise" to characterize this expression of popular conviction is telling. Its appearance in this context is as though the internal dialogues of the obscure discipline of science studies have burst onto the center stage of contemporary politics. The origins of Royal's use of the term are doubtless more mundane. But its use in the context of party politics in a rigidly partisan parliamentary system and strongly bureaucratically dominated state such as France signifies that the "stealth" aspect of expertise no longer exists. Political traditions are evolving to respond to and counter expertise, and to bring issues about expert claims, in which the quality of expert claims and the validity of the assumption of their disinterestedness are raised, into the heart of political life. That the response, even in the most state-centered political orders, such as France, is no longer confined to protest movements, is significant. The rationalist dream was to abolish politics in favor of expertise; its result has been a new birth of politics.

The great stable political orders of the past operated in a state of tension or evolving balance, or stasis. The partners were typically groups or institutions which depended on one another but had different interests, and who could shift the balance of power between them without undermining the interests they had together. Flyvbjerg's example of the royal bureaucracy and the merchants is a case in point, as is the relationship between nobles and royals that made up the European order of the last millennium. Expert knowledge and its alternatives—the knowledge of the protesters and of legislators in the political marketplace—also have the potential to be analogous to this kind of balance. Expertise typically knows something about a problem, but not enough to successfully turn it into a technical matter: global warming, economic development, and the other great problems of the present have this character. The hegemonic ambitions of the expert in these cases are frustrated not only by their ignorant opponents (who are not so much ignorant as in possession of knowledge from different epistemic pools or modes) but by the facts themselves and the failures of expertise the facts produce. Protest and the political horse-trading of liberal democracy provide not merely a reminder of the limits of expertise, but are balancers, which provide not merely a check but a dynamic partner to expertise. If we take what was right about rationalism, its sense of the knowledge intensity of future politics, and combine it with a recognition of the epistemic character of this balance, we have the rudiments of a new model of the future of politics.

6 Quasi-Science and the State
"Governing Science" in Comparative Perspective

Open discussion is a political ideal that today stands atop the hierarchy of the common political values of the West and of the world at large. Its nineteenth century origins are to be found in James Mill, who took it from the physiocrats of the century before. As John Stuart Mill put it in his autobiography, "so complete was my father's reliance on the influence of reason over the minds of mankind, whenever it is allowed to reach them, that he felt as if all would be gained if the whole population were taught to read, if all sorts of opinions were allowed to be addressed to them by word and in writing, and if by means of the suffrage they could nominate a legislature to give effect to the opinions they adopted" (cited in Dicey [1914] 1962: 161–62). As John Austin said, the elder Mill "held, with the French *Economistes*, that the real security of good government is in a *peuple eclaire*" (quoted in Dicey [1914] 1962: 163). The language reappears in Habermas, as does the sentiment (1973: 282).

Is a *"peuple eclaire"* a meaningful ideal today in the face of the complexity of expert knowledge? In *Risk Society*, Ulrich Beck (1992) applies it to the problem of experts, but modifies it in a significant way. Beck gave voice to a demand for "forums of consensus-building cooperation among industry, politics, science, and the populace" (1992: 29). This amounts to a rejection of the conventional electoral legislative representation mentioned by Mill. Subjecting experts to the discipline of consensus-building is a form of governance, and it is perhaps trivially true that even science is always governed through some sort of consensual, negotiated cooperation between these elements. But it is also true that the notions of cooperation and consensus could be specified in a number of divergent ways. Beck has a maximalist view of the nature of the appropriate consensus; he argues that this demand can only be met if certain conditions are satisfied:

> First, people must say farewell to the notion that administrations and experts always know exactly, or at least better, what is right and good for everyone: demonopolization of expertise.
>
> Second, the circle of groups to be allowed to participate can no longer be closed according to considerations internal to specialists, but must instead be opened up according to social standards of relevance: informalization of jurisdiction.

Third, all participants must be aware that the decisions have not already been made and now need only to be "sold" or implemented externally: opening the structure of decision-making.

Fourth, negotiating between experts and decision-makers behind closed doors must be transferred to and transformed into a public dialogue between the broadest variety of agents, with the result of additional uncontrollability: creation of a partial publicity.

Fifth, norms for this process-modes of discussion, protocols, debates, evaluations of interviews, forms of voting and approving-must be agreed on and sanctioned: self-legislation and self-obligation. (Beck 1992: 29–30)

This list points to a model of governance: stakeholders meeting in negotiation forums. Beck says that there is no assurance that these measures would work: "negotiation forums are not consensus production techniques with a guarantee of success." However, they can "urge prevention and precaution and work towards a symmetry of unavoidable sacrifices" (1992: 30).

Can any institutional framework of the sort implied by Beck's "demand" solve the underlying problem with experts: that expert knowledge is simply inaccessible to non-experts, who are forced, like it or not, to accept the authority of experts? Is the problem one of institutional form, or is the problem the nature of the knowledge in question? The problem of "the governance of science" in the narrow sense, the problem of the intelligent exercise of popular control over science, is a simulacrum of this larger problem. If those who are empowered to make decisions about science cannot understand the science they are making decisions about, or perhaps even meaningfully communicate about it, is the intelligent exercise of popular control over science possible?

As a matter of political theory, the problem is fundamental to democracy. It was not a left-wing ruler, but Harry Truman who affirmed the following, in his vetoing of the original bill to establish the National Science Foundation:

This bill contains provisions which represent such a marked departure from sound principles for the administration of public affairs that I cannot give it my approval. It would, in effect, vest the determination of vital national policies, the expenditure of large public funds, and the administration of important governmental functions in a group of individuals who would be essentially private citizens. The proposed National Science Foundation would be divorced from control by the people to an extent that implies a distinct lack of faith in democratic processes. (Penick 1965: 135)

There is a problem of "governance" of science because science is not self-funded. Ordinarily it must rely on "governmental" mechanisms' real states, or state-based authorities, and the money of the populace and the industries from which taxes are extracted. And this enables us to specify the problem more clearly. Democracies require accountability, and as a practical matter, the problem of accountability requires a bureaucratic solution or authority that can be held responsible.

Bureaucratic solutions, like constitutions, do not travel well, and cannot be simply transplanted into a new setting. Thus the problem of national bureaucratic and governmental traditions is closely related to the problem of the governance of science in the sense of accountability: Traditions serve both to define the form of politics about expertise, and to determine what forms of "governance of science" are practically feasible in a given national political tradition. So what I will have to say here will have a great deal to do with a comparative problem. And what I will argue is that different national administrative traditions have led to different forms of the governance of science.

For convenience we can restrict our discussion to liberal democracies. But it is important to see that the problem is one that arises in a particular form as a result of the transition from non-democratic to democratic orders. Beck's maximalist solution to the problem of expert knowledge is to bring it to the level of bargaining between stakeholders. Traditionally, science has occupied a different category, and as Beck sees it a privileged or monopolistic category. Yet it would be a mistake to think that the creation and acceptance of such a status is inherently "anti-democratic." It would of course be possible to have a democratic consensus that agreed to assign the task of supporting and controlling science to the category of national security, and locate control in the military, which is traditionally exempt, or largely so, from political control, as it was formally in the Wilhelmine period in Germany. The military, indeed, represents a traditional form of expertise, together with a form of accountability. Military control was a model that the US (and also of course Germany and the United Kingdom) operated with in connection with atomic research during the war and, in the case of the US, well into the Cold War. But this model was thought to be a temporary expedient, inconsistent with the requirements of science itself, namely its requirements of open discussion, and thus inapplicable to other areas of science and, in the long run, to nuclear research itself. But it signals that there are radically different possible solutions to the problem of accountability, and to the problem of what administrative structures are appropriate for "governing" science in the external sense. But while the form of delegation is equally appropriate to monarchs or democratic regimes, a specific problem arises with the delegation of powers in democracies, and Beck's discussion allows us to pinpoint it.

DELEGATION

The standard solutions to the problem of governance in the external sense recognize the inability of public discussion of the sort "demanded" by Beck to deal effectively with science. This places the problem of science in a larger class of problems for which it is recognized that public discussion is inadequate, and for which it is reasonable as a matter of efficiency, justice, expedience, or some other consideration to delegate the task to others. Delegation often occurs when there are strong public passions of one sort or another that legislatures do not wish to take responsibility for or believe simply to be misguided. Monetary policy, for example, in most countries, is delegated to specialists who are positionally neutral, such as governors of reserve banks. These figures are also selected because of their expertise. But the tasks that they perform are not "scientific" economic tasks, though they may well act on the basis of economic evidence and accepted economic principles. Their task is essentially a political one—and one granted because the task cannot be trusted to ordinary legislative representative politics (similarly for judges). And, in a more complex way, bureaucracies are forms of delegation—forms that have traditionally fit very problematically with democracy, in part because of their historical origins as delegations of royal powers, and as an executive extension of the royal staff.

Presumably Beck—who is of course not a libertarian—has some notion of delegation, to the executive powers of the state and its bureaucracies. So the issue is not whether to delegate, but what to delegate and how to delegate. If one is going to argue that the present modes of delegation are inappropriate political models for dealing with technical decisions, one must deal with the problems that these techniques are designed to solve: the necessity of at least minimal technical competence and specialized knowledge on the part of the decision-makers, something ordinarily not shared with representatives to parliament or with ordinary generalist civil servants. One must also question whether the quality of the decisions would be worse if they were subject to ordinary politics. It is, so to speak, a constitutional question as to whom a given decision ought to be entrusted—to representatives directly, to "the people," to a "cooperative" arrangement, or to a specialized body.

In legal contexts, we are perfectly comfortable with the notion that considerations of legal guilt and innocence ought not to be simply the province of representatives of the people. The history of the tribunes in the Roman legal system and the failings of lynch law are ordinarily understood to be good grounds for creating an insulated specialist judiciary, and in addition, in the Anglo-Saxon tradition, the practice of delegating the tasks of fact-finding as distinct from matters of law to juries selected from the people. The legal analogy is intriguing, because it poses the problem quite directly. Who is to decide what is a question of fact and what is a question of law? One might imagine a system in which juries decided what their own competence was, and could ask judges at their discretion for advice about matters of law. But the system is one in which judges decide what is a matter of law and what is not.

FORMS OF DELEGATION

The relevance of these examples is this: there are many ways of delegating limited powers of the state, or of dividing up discussions, decision-making powers, advisory roles, and so forth. Other forms of expertise, closer to that of science proper, have a long history of delegation as well, notably in the medical sphere, where state authority was used to deal with epidemics. In addition, there are procedures for licensing and certifying professionals. The ubiquity of these procedures raises an important point. Even Beck presumably would not advocate the abandonment of professional licensure. And there seems to be no argument to the effect that delegation as such in relation to technical questions is a bad thing, nor does it seem that there is a conflict in principle with either the principles of liberal "government by discussion" or democracy with a (democratic liberal) decision to delegate powers to an expert or mixed body. But these all represent forms of the governance of science. There are issues of conflict of interest and particular problems of trust that arise in connection with particular forms of delegation. Nevertheless, there does seem to be a tendency, evident in Beck, to idealize some sort of participation or participatory democracy as the appropriate solution to problems with experts. The difficulty with this solution, as I have hinted, is that there seems to be no coherent type of discourse that could be engaged in by members of the public as such communicating and arguing directly with "experts." Indeed, most of the commentators on these issues are loath to suggest that conventional forms of democracy be granted special powers over experts, or to seize responsibility for technical decisions or technical controversies in general. Indeed, one of the reductio ad absurdum arguments against state control of science in the late 1930s and early 1940s in Britain pointed to the possibility that the choice of reagents in a chemistry lab would be subject to popular vote. What is ordinarily called for is something else: some novel kind of forum in which experts could be in some sense held accountable or forced to legitimate themselves. Beck's demands of course go beyond this, but in the same direction, toward some sort of popular control of science.

Accountability and legitimacy are terms of political theory that refer to different mechanisms of popular control. Accountability ordinarily means that there is a greater degree of supervision, usually based on numerical targets and procedural guidelines. Legitimacy is the idea that the actions of political leaders or institutions are accepted as valid. One of the oddities of the discussion of these issues in Beck and Brian Wynne (1996) is their apparent assumption that these processes of legitimation and response to the public are not in fact ongoing, and that there is some special crisis of legitimacy that is in particular associated with "experts," as distinct from problems of accountability. Discussions of "legitimation crisis" of course have long been a staple of critical theory and the idea that the political regimes of the West are constantly skating at the edge of delegitimation is an important part of the imagery employed by these writers. But legitimacy in this sense is extraordinarily hard to assess.

The issue of legitimacy, or some analogue to it like "trust in the claims of experts," arises routinely in American liability cases; in that context commentators routinely argue that "junk science" is given too much credibility and that the motives and conflicts of interest of experts and claimants are given too much weight. Indeed Sheila Jasanoff seems to endorse this claim in her commentary on the courts (1995). The distrust takes a conventional form in these cases. Large corporations are considered to be able to pay (and are criticized if they don't pay), and not only capable of lying, but eager and willing to lie, and also able to hire "experts" who will lie on their behalf. This certainly does not speak to any sort of problem of experts being taken too seriously. And indeed scientists commenting on the role of junk science in the courtroom routinely complain that jurors and judges are not adequately cognizant of the importance of the reputation for institutions such as universities, and the unlikelihood that expert witness research done by them would be tainted by the fact that it is paid for by large corporations in the midst of bitter disputes.

The issues here are complex, and so many interrelated issues arise in each given court case that it is difficult to say what role expert witnesses play. Nevertheless, jurors are clearly capable of discounting expert claims on the grounds of what, for them, amount to conflicts of interest arising from the fact that they make their living as expert witnesses. This skepticism is entirely justified by the incredibly seamy practices of attorneys using expert witnesses. Expert witnessing is a business with an active market and active marketing. Any personal injury lawyer in the US is deluged with advertisements from "expert witnesses" seeking work. These witnesses are clearly concerned about the marketability of their particular strengths, such as apparent candor and sincerity, and so are the lawyers who hire them. In an adversary system this presumably is the way it should be. But, plaintiff lawyers are also successfully tapping into an enormous amount of suspicion of the motives and credibility of large corporations and of the scientists they employ, however apparently independent they might be. This suggests that the whole issue of the credibility and power of experts, as much as the literature wishes to separate it, cannot be separated from the particular institutions in which expert witnessing or expertise plays a role and the general experiences and attitudes of particular audiences with these institutions. But negative experiences with institutions of delegated powers are common, and not restricted to science.

In the US, for example, many people have negative experiences with the federal government and federal agencies, which they perceive as arrogant, irrational, punitive, and self-serving. It would be astonishing if scientists employed by these same agencies were thought to be credible, honest, and truth telling, and indeed they are not. The different configurations of expert distrust in European countries almost certainly reflect the distinctive experiences of citizens of those countries with their own civil service bureaucrats, politicians, regulators—in the case of Britain, a special civil service dominated by generalists, and in the case of Germany, a bureaucracy dominated by secrecy and hidden discretion. The political decision to grant discretionary powers to these kinds of agencies is subject to the consequence that each bureaucratic form creates its own suspicions. In the US, the suspicion that government agencies are attempting to make work for themselves often undermines their credibility, as does the fact that people experience the arbitrariness of government bureaucrats enforcing unintelligible regulations in an irrational way.

To be sure, citizens ordinarily do not grasp the details of organizational structure that motivates particular forms of bureaucratic behavior. Nevertheless they get a general impression about the variety and motivation of bureaucrats and act accordingly. The same holds in continental and British contexts, though the distribution of authority is significantly different and the forms that distrust take are accordingly also different. If we looked at the responses of the public as rational responses to the kind of information that they acquire in ordinary context about these institutions and about experts, we would see a learning process by which citizens change their views of the utterances of bureaucrats, especially on such subjects as risk when these utterances are confounded by events.

If we consider the problem of delegation in its earlier contexts—and this is oddly preserved in the enlightenment conception of the public—the delegation of the powers of the king are delegations of his own powers, powers that he could exercise if he was so inclined. Military powers are the paradigm of this—kings were warriors, like their vassals. By the time that Bismarck could tell Moltke that "the king has a great military mind—you," this was a dated illusion, but nevertheless not an incredible one. The idea that a king was a supreme legal authority died slowly, carried on in legal theory as the fiction that the law represented the will of the sovereign. But in the case of science, the illusion could not survive the first moments of the scientific revolution—that the king was the greatest of scientists is an absurdity not even the most convinced of monarchists could have voiced (it remained to the admirers of Stalin to do so). But for the democratic liberal successors to royal power, the problem was more acute. The claim that the public was "the great scientist" or the ultimate arbiter of scientific truth was too difficult to state (although Hobbes and the Enlightenment each did so with peculiar qualifications; Peters 1956: 57). And even in the age of kings there was a specific form of delegation that recognized the special character of scientific knowledge, and created appropriate forms for it—Royal Academies and prizes, such as the Nobel, which is awarded by a "royal" rather than a "parliamentary" body. The persistence of these monarchical forms is revealing—tension between the democratic and the scientific has not disappeared.

THE FRAGILITY OF EXPERTISE

The radical change in public opinion following the Three Mile Island nuclear disaster reflected new information. To understand this process of learning however it is quite useless to focus on the discrepancies between expert and public opinions on various subjects and hold them out as evidence of the irrationality of public opinion. Public opinion can of course be misled about risks and indeed *is* misled when the media report heavily on minor risks.

Nevertheless the number of media reports and their apparent significance are data for the public, and it is this data that the public operates on, in conjunction with a great deal of other information, such as the information they derive from experience in dealing with government agencies about the motivations and competence of these agencies.

That experts are constantly having their acceptance as experts, their legitimacy, tested and questioned is a central feature of the notion of expertise and the phenomenon of delegated powers. The history of particular forms of expertise, such as the expertise of agricultural science, shows quite clearly that establishing credibility is difficult. Consumers are perfectly capable of rejecting the excuses given by experts. Selling expert knowledge is an extremely difficult matter, and conspicuous public successes are an important part of the process of gaining acceptance. A few snippets of this history will suffice to make this point. When Justus von Leibig first introduced commercial chemical fertilizers with the backing of "science," the fertilizers had various unexpected and unintended side effects that harmed farmers—this was among the first of the science-made environmental disasters. When the farmers were harmed they became extremely suspicious of the claims of fertilizer companies. Out of this came the demand for improved expertise, particularly with respect to soil chemistry, and state geologists eagerly stepped into the breach to provide improved information and means of testing soil chemistry.

Some farmers simply resisted change and ignored the blandishments of experts. These farmers became the focus of a lengthy public effort to improve agricultural practices and thus improve the lives of those farmers. The history of this enormous undertaking, chronicled in *The Reluctant Farmer* (Scott 1970), led to the creation of the Cooperative Extension Service in the US, which sponsored such things as high school tomato growing contests, cooking contests, and the like in a more or less successful attempt to both involve poor farmers in the broader community and to get them to think more effectively about improvements in agricultural technique and the use of the results of agricultural science.

The interesting thing about this process is the incredible difficulty and fragility of expertise. The whole notion of an experimental farm subsidized by the state was for many farmers itself risible, and the fact that experimental farms required subsidies seemed to them to prove that the farms were bad farms. It was only through a wide variety of public efforts, such as the exhibition of prize animals, that schools of agriculture in the nineteenth century were able to impress upon farmers that agricultural scientists indeed did know something more that would be useful to them. But in most cases it was only the role of scientists in dealing with animal epidemics that really established the credibility of state university agricultural science. The results in these cases were visible, immediate, and economically significant. To save a herd of cattle or a flock of sheep by relying on the advice or medicine of the agricultural scientist of the state university was to be seduced by experts. But it should not be thought that the experts had an easy time of time of this seduction or that farmers or anyone else were initially impressed by the claims of agricultural scientists.

What needs to be remembered is that the road to expertise and professionalization goes both ways. Groups can establish themselves as possessing expertise on the basis of either exemplary achievements or apparent successes in dealing with problems regarded as intractable, as was the case with the expertise of the various social movements of the late nineteenth century concerned with reform of prisons, juvenile justice, the treatment of fallen women, and the like. But the public can become dissatisfied with the results of this expertise and can decide to rely on other forms of action. The increase in juvenile crime, for example, has served to undermine the credibility of expert juvenile crime specialists who administer a juvenile justice system that was reformed in the early twentieth century on the basis of expert claims by various judges and reformers. The task of the juvenile detention halls and the like has in some cases been handed over to groups operating military-style boot camps and in other cases even to groups attempting to teach such things as Aristotelian ethics to juvenile prisoners. The message in these cases is simple. There are alternatives to professionalization and the "public" is perfectly capable of exerting pressure on political institutions to employ these alternatives.

Focusing on the example of science and its expertise is in fact somewhat narrow and misleading about the universe of expertise claims as a whole. Science and medical science earned an enormous amount of trust on the basis of such exemplary achievements as the discovery of penicillin, the polio vaccine, and the atomic bomb. But there is no reason in principle or in practice that this trust may not be dissipated, or that attempts to extend or use the authoritative influence of science in support of the tobacco lobby or extreme environmental regulation will not lead to the rejection of these forms of expertise.

WHAT IS THE GOVERNANCE OF SCIENCE?

These cases yield complex lessons, but one lesson stands out. Powerful bureaucracies are, almost necessarily, conformist with respect to the expert opinions that they develop. Bureaucracies are not debating societies. They operate efficiently only when commands are followed according to rules and in accordance with limited discretionary power and in which career advancement depends on conformity to the culture of the bureaucracy.

Bureaucracies are not prone to entertaining a diversity of viewpoints. Indeed, to delegate decision-making power or to delegate implementation of a policy to a large and powerful bureaucracy is almost necessarily to accept the particular expert opinions to which the bureaucracy conforms. This is not inconsistent with the doing of science, and indeed there is a great deal of bureaucratically organized science. But bureaucratic organization within science is a different matter from the bureaucratic organization of science itself.

Science, in contrast to bureaucracy, *is* a debating society. But even debating societies need to be governed, and to make decisions. If we consider the problem of decision-making in the domain of quasi-science as a separate and distinct problem, we can begin to ask some questions about how governance ought to be organized, especially to deal with questions of what sort of models of the organization of discourse and decision-making are available. Even the most cursory inquiry into this topic will show that science and quasi-science are already largely subject to various forms of "governance," including forms of self-governance. In science, as with other debating societies, governance characteristically begins with the problem of membership and the problem of regulating participation in discussion. It is obviously necessary to understand these governance structures, and the many more complex governance structures that depend on them, before asking questions about the redesign of the governance of science. Beck's model of discussion ignores these questions for a simple reason. His aim is to obliterate inequalities in status in discussions of this sort, which is precisely what most of the means of governance are designed to either establish or recognize.

The fault here is simple—this takes an abstract principle and treats it as an organizational directive. Like Hobbes's insistence that the king is the final arbiter of truth—something that makes sense in a specifically religious context as a part of the "more fundamental" task of the king to secure peace—it makes little sense in the practical light of existing complex institutions of delegation that have grown and established themselves through testing. Some of these means are so commonplace and ubiquitous as to escape notice.

To take a particularly obvious example, consider the licensing of new professionals in medicine, which is the largest "scientific" activity. Physicians are characteristically subject to at least three major forms of governance. The obtaining of medical qualifications is itself done through procedures at least partially controlled by qualified physicians, for example in the granting of medical degrees, qualifications that may in turn be subject to state control, as when the state regulates the granting of degrees, and in a federal system, where the national government either controls the accreditation of universities, of degrees, or accrediting agencies, as is the case in the US. The state also may directly act to license physicians. And finally, the state traditionally exercises, among its police powers, powers over public health, particularly in the face of epidemic disease, and employs physicians as experts, for example, in involuntary commitment proceedings for the mentally ill.

Similar minimal combinations of these three governance roles or variations on them occur in many other expert and particularly scientific professions. If one thinks of a few of the relevant examples, such as the role of clinical psychologists in advising the state with respect to treatment of the mentally ill and the similar role of the social worker with respect to the care of children, one can see how these mechanisms have developed over time and indeed substantially expanded. One might even argue that the rise of these professions in particular and the learned professions generally is closely bound up with the phenomena of their governance, especially in those cases in which the professional exercises delegated powers of the state. Yet these professions are also partly, and in some cases largely, marketized. Patients may choose physicians, or, as is more common, institutions choose to employ physicians, social workers, and psychologists, who compete for positions. This competition is itself a form of control. So a large part of the "cooperation" between the populace, industry, and so forth that Beck is concerned with occurs through the mechanism of the market, but a market that is itself regulated in various ways, such as licensure.

With respect to science itself, the primary issue has traditionally been one form of the delegation of state power, the spending of the state's money to pursue the goals of science. This delegation of state power seems peculiarly benign compared with the exercise of police authority discussed above, but it nevertheless may have very substantial implications and consequences. The "governance," however, is characteristically indirect, and aspects of it are marketized. By "indirect" I mean what in political theory is known as the liberal preference for indirect forms of rule: forms of rule other than command and control. Beck's model implicitly relies on a scheme of command in the last instance—it involves *forced* cooperation, forced by the state acting as the agent of the populace, to control and replace the uncontrolled "cooperation" of the market. In science, it is a market that is already substantially governed by indirect means, and in which there is already competition for research funds.

The liberal preference for indirect means is a preference for non-coercive means, and the Left has traditionally criticized this preference as insufficient to bring about the results the state ought to be bringing about. But there is a deep problem with this critique: it rests on a questionable notion of the capacity of the state to bring about good results. The questions that are ordinarily raised are not merely a matter of liberal and Left, however. They reflect national experiences with particular means. The preference for marketizing, cooperative, or more direct forms, such as "planning," reflects experiences with each of these modes. The degree of federalization, the devolvement of powers to lower levels of government that can enter the market as buyers of science, or academic talent, varies as well.

We will shortly return to these issues by considering the example of cholera in the nineteenth century. But there is a generic issue that needs to be addressed, that relates especially to science, over the character of decision-making and the existence of conflicts of interest, that arise from the fact that they *are* governed, however indirectly, or to put it differently, incompletely marketized.

The problem we face with decision-making in this domain is that it is quasi-scientific, in a particular sense: competent decision-making requires scientific knowledge, but scientific knowledge is not sufficient to make the decisions. The problem of conflict of interest arises because scientists are used to making decisions, or to giving advice to those who make decisions. Scientists are, to some extent at least, independent agents with career strategies independent of the state who may greatly benefit by acting for their own interest and against state interest, for example, by spending money on projects that advance their careers without advancing state purposes on which the state planned to spend the money. So decision-making must either be organized in such a way that conflicts of interest are avoided, or the risks of conflicts of interest ignored. The problem can be put most starkly by considering the most extreme model of the centralization of state scientific authority—one individual having the power to grant all of the positions that would enable a scientist to pursue research. Could this individual be trusted? It is questionable that any individual could be competent to exercise such powers, even if self-governed to be the very model impersonal meritocrat. Partiality of knowledge would itself produce biases. So it is questionable whether science could ever be governed impartially by an individual, and whether individuals can ever be fully free of partiality. These may seem to be wholly academic questions, but in understanding the partly marketized forms of current science governance, it is important to realize that they arose out of, and as reforms of, systems that looked very much like this. John Wesley Powell, the head of the US Geological Survey, the largest scientific organization of the nineteenth century, served as the decision-maker on whose desk, in Truman's famous expression, the buck stopped. In Germany, Friedrich Althoff, the creator of what Max Weber criticized as the Althoff system, exercised similar powers over the whole university system, determining the courses of the careers of academics by determining what positions they would be offered.[1]

The usual solution to the problem of partiality and the problem of conflict of interest is to collectivize decision-making and base it on a consensus of the competent. If the government hands money over to scientists organized in a collective body, who use such mechanisms as peer review to fund those projects that scientists agree to be the most worthy, the government has a mechanism of distribution, a means of assuring some degree of accountability (through the threat of withdrawing funding if scientists acting collectively do not live up to their collective responsibilities). This form of delegation is arguably the most efficient means of reaching at least some state goals, notably the advances of science. When we consider the problem of governing science, what we ordinarily mean is to impose some form of governance that is more restrictive and directive than this sort of governance. This was the solution that in practice took hold in the twentieth century, against which Beck rebels, and which Truman rejected in theory but accepted in practice by the National Science Foundation of the US, as a simple consequence of the impracticality of doing anything different. The actual legislation as it was approved created a presidential board of governors of the foundation that was not self-governed. Opinions differ over whether in practice this amounts to little more than a fiction, but it is an interesting fiction since it brings the National Science Foundation itself into line with a long historical tradition of similar bodies that take the form of commissions. One may then ask why the commission form seems to have such an natural affinity to quasi-science decision-making processes, and go on to think through the significance of "commissions" in a "knowledge society" (which is to say, in the terms I have used here, a society in which quasi-science, decisions requiring science but not settled by science, plays an increasingly large role). I will return later to the problem that concerns Beck, which we can now restate: the concern that experts have *collective* interests or collective biases or partialities that conflict with the interests of those they purport to serve.

TWO KINDS OF CONSENSUS

Collectivizing decisions, even by such modest means as using peer review to create artificial competitive situations for the granting of research funds, involves a special use of the concept of "consensus," a use that goes to the heart of the distinction I have made here between quasi-science and science. The core distinction is between consensus on the corpus of basic scientific knowledge, that is to say what scientists agree to be scientifically true, and consensuses of other kinds that require scientific knowledge, but for which science is not sufficient. A simple example of this is to be found in grant applications. Scientists predict results from their work, predict outcomes, and predict potential benefits from their work, and also predict historical outcomes of decisions to fund or not to fund their research (cf. S. Turner 1999d). Decision-making seeks a consensus, or rests on a consensus achieved through procedures of voting or scoring.

From a political point of view these differences are best understood in terms of the difference between the *consensus of scientists and scientific consensus*. Scientists themselves distinguish what is and is not a genuine scientific fact.[2] Speaking as *scientists* they may also attempt to construct a consensus of competent scientific peers, not merely with respect to their opinions about the truth of a model but with respect to their opinions about the sufficiency of the evidence and the adequacy of their explanation. With this we are already in a domain of quasi-science, where "science is required but not sufficient." The "meta"-judgments about sufficiency of evidence are unlike those made within science about candidates for the corpus of scientific knowledge itself. And it is these judgments that most closely resemble those involved in the governance of science.

Many problems other than funding, of course, are subject to discussions among scientists and attempts are made to establish a consensus with respect to the relevant facts. In attempting to identify a scientific consensus with respect to given problems, the National Institutes of Health regularly hold meetings that include experts of various kinds who are asked to evaluate the existing research, fit it together, iron out, and evaluate inconsistencies, and arrive at a policy relevant to scientific conclusions. These are in effect status reports, reports on the state of the evidence with respect to a particular question and of the areas in which the evidence more or less strongly supports some policy relevant conclusion. Which are these: scientific consensuses or consensuses of scientists? Clearly the latter. The consensus that these reports represent is a forced consensus in the sense that it asks for an assessment of the evidence at a particular point in time and with respect to a particular evidential situation.

Judgments about the status of something as an accepted scientific fact, of the candidates for addition to the corpus of scientific knowledge, are different in intent. They are not understood to be time-relevant or evidential situation-relevant, though it may well turn out that the evidential situation changes in an anticipated way that undermines the previous consensus. It is perfectly reasonable to complain that the two kinds of consensus are illegitimately run together in discussions of science as it relates to policy questions, and indeed the distinction is frequently intentionally observed. Attempts to employ standards appropriate to science, such as peer review, to judgments about policy-relevant issues, such as global warming, for example, run together the two kinds of issues, typically without explanation or argument. The fact that claims made about global warming are subjected to "peer review," for example, does not make them into facts like those of core science, even if the reviewers and the review process are the same. Peer review is a procedure of evaluation, a decision-making device.

There is no need here to construct an artificial, "principled" distinction between core science and quasi-science, for it is a distinction in the world—a distinction made within science, by scientists, on a continuous basis. Roughly, core science consists of the results that are accepted as fact, as belonging in textbooks, as permanent (however differently it might be construed in the future), and accepted or deserving of acceptance as such by, in principle, all scientists. "Peer review" has an elective affinity to the notion of acceptance in "accepted scientific fact," but not a close one. Papers that are accepted for publication by peer review are not, as outsiders wrongly think, "bullet-proofed" by the process, but rather merely accepted as legitimate subjects of discussion—interesting and not obviously false or inadequately supported by experiment.

Peer panels can produce many other things as well, and do, especially in the governance of science: decisions regarding the funding of research or the awarding of prizes, fellowships, graduate student support, and so forth. And they can also be used to produce, or simply legitimate, claims in quasi-science, such as claims about global warming or adolescent pregnancy. These are topics in which methods of modeling are controversial and where there are "facts" that are accepted as scientific, but where these facts alone are far from sufficient to warrant strong predictions, especially about the effects of policy. Typically, they are subject to the infirmity discussed previously in relation to cholera. They do not concern closed systems, in which all parameters are known and all relevant causes included. They represent good guesses, and typically the topics themselves are such that good guesses are the best knowledge that one can have.

In the case of adolescent pregnancy, to choose a behavioral science example, it will never be true that all variables will be known, or that an isolatable basic process will be identified that is subject to control. But policy requires "knowledge." So it is not unreasonable to do what in fact was done: to bring together the main researchers, with their data, for a discussion that was designed to determine what consensus existed, both on the problem and on the state of the evidence. This is a paradigm case of quasi-science.

There may well be perfectly good *political* grounds for adopting such a strategy for obtaining a "consensus of scientists," and it may be perfectly appropriate to apply them in these cases. And there may be good political reasons for making other choices. Standard-setting and regulatory decisions are often made by committees that reflect both the representatives of interested parties, scientists familiar generally with what is known about the causal processes and scientific knowledge about the relevant chemicals or disease processes as well as the relevant technologies.

The political question to ask about such committees, and the discourse that occurs within them, is somewhat different from, but not entirely independent of the epistemic question of what it is that these committees know that justifies their decisions. Granting a committee the right or responsibility to set standards, for example, for the concentration of some particular chemical in drinking water, is a political act. It presumes that a committee of a particular kind is in some sense a better way of making a decision than other available options, and "better" may mean a great many things. It may simply be more convenient to delegate such decisions when legislatures feel that they are either not competent to make the decisions or if, for more Machiavellian reasons, they consider it useful to shift the blame for decisions onto another body. Or it may simply be that it is more convenient for representative bodies being lobbied by special-interest groups to remove from their own consideration decisions that cannot be made in ways that these groups regard as beneficial.

THE CHOLERA CASE: NINETEENTH-CENTURY EXPERTISE AND ITS POLITICAL ABSORPTION

So far I have strayed very far from the problem with which I began: the place of expert opinion in liberal democracy. But we are now in a position to see in the abstract what sort of problem this is. The state is in the business of organizing discussion as the basis of state action, and in the business of acting itself. "The State," however, is an abstraction. In practice, the state delegates its executive authority to civil servants, or bureaucracies, and delegates much of the "discussion" as well, to bodies of various kinds, or to civil servants in bureaucracies, who use their discretionary powers to regulate and control, or to induce cooperation. There are strong national differences in the patterns of delegation.

Beck's formulation of the problem of expertise as a problem of cooperation, as I have suggested, is "German," and it recalls the strategies of cartelization and government support that were the basis of the industrial development of Germany in the nineteenth century, and a prominent part of the German *Sonderweg*. The same must be said of the patterns of science funding: The German method involved industrial support for academic laboratories in which industry was induced to "cooperate" by bureaucrats with various broad discretionary powers. These strategies of delegation and organization repeat themselves throughout the history of German science. Such strategies are not imitable where appropriate bureaucratic traditions do not support them. When the US sought to do so, imitating Japan with DARPA in the 1990s, the results were not impressive. But something can be said about the differences in regimes of handling expertise apart from the lesson that solutions do not travel well, illuminating the problem of governance of science.

In what follows I will consider the example of cholera. In recent writings on cholera in the nineteenth century, scholars have exposed the extent to which the "right" experts were ignored, the distinctiveness and contingency of the situations in which they were, and the extent to which politics, and especially bureaucratic politics, played a significant role in the failure to both receive new ideas about cholera and implement the necessary measures, particularly in the creation of sanitation processes and water filtration. The story of the Hamburg epidemic of 1892 is emblematic of expertise gone wrong. The reactions of the St. James Parish Board (London), which was persuaded by a commission that included John Snow to remove the handle of the Broad Street pump (1854), is emblematic of right decision-making. The actions of the sanitary commission of the city of New York also stand out as a success: but so does the complex background to the creation of this board, relevant here because it is a classic "commission." The actions in Britain of the General Health Board, which operated with a bad theory of cholera that was only slowly abandoned, and that out of bureaucratic self-regard, once accepted, was claimed credit for, are examples of partial success. London was spared an epidemic like Hamburg's as a result of their efforts.

Richard Evans's classic text on the Hamburg cholera epidemic of 1892 comes to the following conclusion:

> Hamburg experienced a major cholera epidemic in 1892 for three basic reasons. Last in order of importance, and coming into operation only when the other two factors had had their effect, was the chronic overcrowding, poverty, and malnutrition which ... existed in virtually all the poorer areas of the city, above all after the new harbor construction of the 1880s. This acted as a "multiplier" of the disease by facilitating its rapid spread from person to person. It could only come into action because the disease was carried to virtually every household in the city by mains water. The failure of the Senate and the Citizens' Assembly to agree on a proper filtration system for the water-supply until it was too late, and the failure to implement a comprehensive system of sewage disposal and treatment, must be accounted the principal reasons for the epidemic proportions reached by the disease.... Most important of all was the Hamburg authorities' policy of concealment and delay. (Evans 1987: 304)

This is a good point to begin the comparisons, because this was a case in which expert knowledge-science was catastrophically misgoverned.

The misrule occurred through a combination of the inability of "public dialogue between the broadest variety of agents"—to use Beck's phrase—to reach agreement, and a powerful official bureaucratic apparatus able to keep secrets. So we may take it not only as a test of Beck's model but as a test of a certain model of governance of science: one in which powerful bureaucracies are directed and controlled by public discussion that is itself governed by elaborate procedures. The alternatives to this model are those in which intermediate bodies—what David Guston calls boundary organizations, or what I have called here "commissions," operate to provide facts or conclusions that can be made the subject of public discussion.[3]

Beck, curiously, says little about the prosaic sociological problems of the organization of implementation. But one must assume that he has in mind powerful bureaucracies with strongly coercive power: the kinds of regulative powers he wishes to grant to "cooperative" discussion require it. Cooperation presupposes a distribution of powers among those who are doing the cooperating, or requires an agency to enforce the cooperative arrangements. What Beck seems to imagine is even more invasive, and incidentally, characteristically German—a situation in which the function of the bureaucracies is to induce cooperation, its power is to a large extent to grant permission to act, and in which the power to withhold permission is decisive and final, not subject to judicial review or much direct legislative control. Envisioning such instruments in the governance of science is difficult as we shall see—science, as Michael Polanyi ([1951] 1980) stressed a half century ago, characteristically involves competition and risk-taking and choice under competitive conditions. So understanding how powerful bureaucracies and their alternatives, such as boundary organizations, have actually functioned in domains that involve science, areas of "quasi-science," is one of the few ways we have of envisioning alternative possibilities for the governance of science.

In Hamburg there had been, prior to the epidemic of 1892, a long political discussion over the problem of drinking water, of precisely the inconclusive kind that Beck supposes should be an expected outcome of what we may call "expert-egalitarian" discussion, by which we may mean "discussions in which everyone is treated as undifferentiated with respect to their expertise." A political decision needed to be made for filtration and clean water, which was costly but, according to the theories accepted elsewhere, essential to avoiding cholera spread through the water supply. The decision was blocked through disagreement over how to charge for it, as well as over skepticism about the need. The *popular* opinion that the available river water was especially pure was an important reason that the political discussion failed to produce agreement. Yet the Hamburg politicians *did* consider expert advice from their local bureaucrats and the local medical community: the two were closely entwined, and supported a theory of cholera derived from Max von Pettenkofer (Rosenberg 1962: 194–97, 199–200).

The board acted in accordance with a process in which they were constrained not by the views of other experts, which might have forced them to consider alternatives to their own view, but were directly controlled only by the Hamburg senate and lower house, politicians and notables who provided the sole form of official public discussion. Hamburg also had commissions, but public discussion in these commissions conformed rather closely to Beck's ideal, and the commission was ignored (Evans 1987: 158). There was no delegation of decision-making power to expert bodies, no "monopolization," which is what Beck in principle rejects. Delay and nondecision were the consequence.

The inadequacy of the advice of the Hamburg medical community reflects a more general phenomenon. One of the features of bureaucracies is that career advancement is heavily dependent on conformity. Strong bureaucracies penetrate into the professional or expert community, affecting the climate of opinion within them. The effect of a powerful bureaucracy in this case was to assure conformity with what turned out to be a mistaken theory of cholera. But powerful bureaucracies of this sort succeeded elsewhere. In Berlin, the same kind of bureaucratic power produced conformity with what turned out to be the right theory, and Berlin was spared. But Koch's powers, as described by Evans, are the fullest realization of the intertwining of bureaucratic power and control of opinion through the control of careers:

> Koch could ... be assured ... of vigorous backing from the Imperial government in imposing his views on cholera prevention on medical authority throughout the Empire. Already in June 1884 he was made a member of the Prussian Privy Council (*Staatsrat*) and co-opted onto the Cholera Commission for the German Empire. This had hitherto been controlled by Pettenkofer. Koch became the dominant force. In the same year he organized a course of the diagnosis and prevention of cholera, in which 146 doctors took part, including 97 civilian (i.e., non-military) doctors from all parts of Germany and 20 other countries. In 1885 he became full professor (*Ordinarius*) of Hygiene at the University of Berlin, and was appointed Director of a specially created Institute for Infectious Diseases in 1891. These positions enabled him to influence large numbers of pupils in favor of his ideas and methods. His influence was further spread by his senior pupils.... Koch founded a journal for the propagation of his ideas, the *Zeitschrift für Infektions-karnkheiten*. Thus Koch and his pupils were rapidly taking over the field of hygiene. (Evans 1987: 266–67)

So the expert advice that the politicians dealt with was in each case essentially monolithic, but different. The expert with authority in Berlin was Koch. But Koch had no direct authority over Hamburg, whose physicians were influenced by Pettenkofer, a Munich physician. Pettenkofer took the view that the cholera bacterium alone could not produce the disease—and in a famous demonstration, he drank a beaker of infected water, to no ill effect—which he thought required other conditions, including "fermentation" in the ground, which implied different public health measures.

If we consider two other cases with different structures, the results are revealing. In London, there was a national bureaucracy, the General Health Board, headed by a statistician and sanitary reformer named William Farr. Farr was wrong about cholera—he was a miasmatist, who had produced an impressive curve fit to data on cholera deaths in London, which he published, based on the idea that elevation decreased the number of cholera deaths in an epidemic. He also produced a vast quantity of research relating to other variables, especially social variables, water quality, and so forth, none of which produced the startling consistency of the elevation data. The bureaucracy headed by Farr was never powerful as a regulatory body. Decisions about water, for example, were local. Moreover, the career structure of London medicine was such that no bureaucracy had much ability to assure the conformity of the local medical community. Farr's office had a monopoly on the official publications it produced about cholera, but these were not binding on local authorities. Nor was there any particular career benefit to conformity to the position of the General Health Board. And this led to a different outcome.

Beginning with the political achievement, only now being acknowledged, of the St. James Parish committee: it was persuaded to remove the handle of the Broad Street pump, now one of the most celebrated episodes in the history of medicine (Brody et al. 1999). The means by which this political act occurred are partly known. The Parish committee, faced with a local outbreak of cholera, what we would now call a "cluster," appointed John Snow and Henry Whitehead, a clergyman, to a special cholera inquiry committee to deal with an outbreak of cholera near Golden Square. He applied the spot map technique and found that seventy-three of the eighty-three cases were near the Broad Street pump, which Snow reasoned was the source. Whitehead was skeptical of this explanation at first, but was soon convinced. Some who drank the water escaped cholera; others who didn't drink it contracted the disease. But the proportions were overwhelmingly in support of the pump hypothesis. The Parish committee asked Snow to write the report up, and Whitehead himself figured out what had contaminated the pump water—a leaky cesspool three feet from the pump. The material came from the washing of the diapers of an infant who had died and for whom the cause of death was listed as diarrhea. The discovery led the Parish committee to excavate the pump area, which revealed that the brick linings of both the well and the cesspool had decayed, allowing seepage. The pump's handle was removed, and the outbreak subsided. This was an act of a small political body faced with an emergency, but in a position to create its own commission, listen to its conclusions, and act independently on them—or decline to act.

This dramatic episode was only a small part of the story, however. Snow's own efforts began long before this episode, and the absorption of his views continued long after. The medical background was complex. Cholera was the most researched disease of the century, and many correlations, as well as many well-attested cases, were part of its large literature. Snow, a private physician, was struck by the many remarkable cases in which cholera spread over vast distances, apparently carried by individuals, strange cases in which cholera attacked one group, such as the passengers of a particular ship, and spared those who had left from the same port at the same time, and cases where one company of soldiers passing a water hole and drinking from it left healthy, and the next one became deathly ill. These cases were difficult to square with any sort of miasmatic or "fermentation" account. He hypothesized, as it turned out correctly, that the real cause was minute material in the evacuations of the victims that got into the water supply or was otherwise ingested. In an era in which proportionality of cause and effect was a standard methodological rule, and before the microbe account of disease was accepted, this was a radical idea. It was also easy to regard it not as radical, but as old news. Even Farr's research office agreed in some respects with the basic idea: Bad water was one of the many variables they found to be associated with cholera. But bad water was poorly defined, and not defined in a way that was readily amenable to policies that allowed epidemics to be stopped or prevented. In the long run, this was the loophole through which the bureaucracy grudgingly accepted Snow's arguments—as though they had been their own all along. But it was an important loophole, for it allowed for the institution of reforms that had the desired result.

Snow's hypothesis was startlingly reconfirmed as a result of a natural experiment in which a mysterious outbreak of cholera occurred after changes had been made in the water supply, but only among the customers of one water company. This appeared to refute Snow. It was then discovered that the company had been illegally drawing water from a source that was "impure." What is striking about this story is, on the one hand, the obduracy of the bureaucratic experts, though they did eventually concede that Snow was right, and on the other hand the ability of Snow—and the motivation—to persuade the Parish committee, which promptly created a "commission" rather than attempting to make the decision on its own, to act on his ideas, and the openness of the committee to being persuaded. The result was that London did not have another cholera epidemic after the changes in the water supply were fully effected.

The American version of this story is equally interesting, largely because it represents a different combination of politics, expertise, and bureaucratic structures. In the US, public health matters in the nineteenth century were for the most part controlled by municipalities, which were, in the case of New York and other major cities, democratic in a particular sense, dominated by the "spoils system."[4] The major device for dealing with the threat of cholera was sanitation, and sanitation contracts were a political plum. Boards of health, in a typical arrangement that applies to many boards even today, were composed of elected officials who were stakeholders of various kinds who sat as the board of health and used its special powers when circumstances required. The politicians—Democrats, in this case—preferred to conduct business as usual. But they were vulnerable to reformers, and in the manner that they were defeated the deep roots of national political and bureaucratic traditions become visible.

De Tocqueville, writing a few decades before, had observed that,

> A single Englishman will often carry through some great undertaking, whereas Americans form associations for no matter how small a matter. Clearly the former regard association as a power means of action, but the latter seem to think of it as the only one. ([1835] 1969: 514)

This is precisely how cholera was attacked. As Charles Rosenberg notes in his history of the American response to cholera, "it is hardly surprising that New York's Citizens' Association (an informal group of respectable—and predominantly Republican—Gothamites organized early in the 1860's to promote 'honest government') should sponsor a subsidiary Council of

Hygiene and Public Health" (1962: 187). This "council"—a case of a Tocquevillian association—surveyed the sanitation arrangements of the city, and reported the dismal results of the sanitary regime in place. Another arm of the Citizens' Association was at work on reforming the political structure that produced it, proposing a bill in the state legislature to create a board of health that did not operate on the spoils system, and had experts rather than politicians on it. This was a lesson drawn from the examples of Paris and London, but also from Providence, Rhode Island, and Philadelphia. The bill required that the board consist of medical men trained especially for public health work (Rosenberg 1962: 188–91).

The state of knowledge in 1866 was expressed by the New York Academy of Medicine, yet another Tocquevillian association, which advised the medical profession to,

> for all practical purposes, act and advise in accordance with the hypothesis (or the fact) that the cholera diarrhoea [sic] and "rice-water discharges" of cholera patients are capable in connection with well-known localizing conditions, of propagating the cholera poison, and that rigidly enforced precautions should be taken in every case to disinfect or destroy these ejected fluids. (quoted in Rosenberg 1962: 195)

The resolution reflected some medical politicking—the "local conditions" clause assured unanimity, though few doubted that the discharges alone were the cause. But it also reflected the internationalization of expertise on the topic, and the rapidity of "conversions" to the "Snow-Pettenkofer" account of the disease (which in practice was the Snow account) was impressive. The New York Sanitary Commission, which had been granted enormous power by the legislature, acted accordingly: "the bedding, pillows, old clothing, and utensils—anything that might 'retain or transmit evacuations of the patient'—were piled in an open area and burned" (Rosenberg 1962: 205). New York City escaped cholera, other states copied the legislation (1962: 211), and the contained "epidemic" of 1866 was the last serious cholera threat in the US.

The politics of opposition are worth noting, especially in light of Beck's demands. The commission was imposed by the state legislature, which was dominated by Republicans; the Democrats, Catholics, and immigrants of New York City opposed it as the creation of rural lawyers that favored the rich at their expense (Rosenberg 1962: 208). The New York Sanitary Commission was composed of experts, but "public" experts, rather than individuals who were the creation of consensus producing career structure in a powerful bureaucracy. They were accountable professionally but also accountable as public figures for their actions, in the sense that their reputations were closely tied to the outcomes of very public decisions. And there were associations, such as the Citizens' Association and the New York Academy of Medicine, that were independent watchdogs, with an eye on the practices of other governments and on international expertise. A member of such a board was highly constrained by these bodies—someone who did not wish to jeopardize a carefully built-up reputation both as an individual and as an expert would be obliged to resign or protest bad decisions.

Beck's model contrasts with this rather sharply, because in a situation of expert egalitarianism, reputation is unimportant or equalized, as is responsibility for the outcome: rather than being held responsible, a person can behave irresponsibly without consequences or act in terms of self-interest without consequences. Indeed, this is a major part of the Hamburg story. The issue of taxation that was entirely a matter of political interest prevented the reaching of a resolution, exactly as Beck says is a permissible outcome, consequently filtration devices were not built until after the epidemic had taught the public lesson that they were necessary. To be sure, of course, had Hamburg been as fortunate as Berlin and had the right leading figures in its bureaucracy, bureaucratic power and the consensus it favored would have produced the right decision. But the issue of "governance" is not eliminated by the existence of powerful bureaucracies. Someone needs to pick the powerful bureaucrats and to judge the bureaucracy. The Hamburg notables and politicians, who were closely related to the medical community, proved incapable of doing so. Thus the combination of interest group democracy and powerful bureaucracy in this case proved fatal, and more generally is prone to the same very particular kind of error.

GOVERNING SCIENCE

Germany had the best science at the time—Koch won a Nobel Prize for identifying the cholera bacterium. Yet it had the worst cholera epidemic of Europe, long after other countries had solved their cholera problem. Is it too much to compare this to the situation in German physics during WWII? There again, Germany had the best scientist, Heisenberg, and the best intellectual resource base. The customary view of this episode is that authoritarianism led to failure. Heisenberg, uncorrected by vigorous debate from his subordinates, made a key error and failed to see the solution to the problem of fusion. But in a larger perspective, the problem may be one of the organization of scientific activity: The bureaucratic structure of the research effort led, as it led in the Hamburg medical community, to a consensus that turned out to be false. And it is difficult to imagine a powerfully bureaucratic mode of the governance of science that would not be systematically prone to this kind of error.

James Bryant Conant, writing after WWII, described the following model for presenting expert opinions to decision-making bodies (1951: 337–38). To avoid what he took to be the central problem of scientists promoting their own hobbyhorses, he suggested that even a good idea ought to be able to withstand criticism and that opponents be selected to play the role of the devil's advocate. These opponents would promote alternative proposals so that the decision-makers would be given a genuine choice; the experts would be forced to articulate arguments not merely persuasive to nonexperts but tested against the proposal of the expert opponent. This left judging in the hands of nonexperts, but gave experts their due as pleaders of cases. There is a sense in which this model is the one that most closely represents the situation in St. James Parish, and in the commission that the Parish committee created when it joined Snow with a skeptical clergyman. Snow obviously was arguing against something and it should have been known to everyone, as it certainly was known to Snow, that this was not only a minority view but a view opposed by the official bureaucracy. Snow nevertheless prevailed, producing perhaps the single best decision in the whole cholera affair.

The New York model is also revealing: expertise constrained by expert scrutiny, where the "outside" experts are genuinely independent, and the reputations of the experts exercising authority are, in effect, marketized, so that they would suffer for their obduracy, constrains experts very effectively, while at the same time producing decisive results—the New York methods were highly effective and easy to imitate. Whether this is a model that can be used in other political traditions, such as the German, in which "cooperation" is the working norm, is open to question. But in each case there is some means of protection against the error-prone combination of bureaucratic power and the quasi-scientific "consensus of scientists."

Liberal democracy does not require the leveling of expertise, as Beck assumes. Decisions and fact-finding on matters of quasi-science can be delegated, and delegation, in the form of commissions, is a standard device. But it does require that the consensuses produced by these delegated discussions are reasonably free from conflicts of interest and partiality—something effectively precluded by powerful bureaucracies that create climates of opinion.

7 The Pittsburgh Survey and the Survey Movement
An Episode in the History of Expertise*

The Pittsburgh Survey was part of the survey movement. The movement was characterized in three key documents of self-interpretation: the first, an article by Paul U. Kellogg, Shelby Harrison, and George Palmer in the *Proceedings of the Academy of Political Science* in 1912; the second, a paper by Kellogg and Neva Deardorff presented to an international social work convention in 1928; and the third, Shelby Harrison's introductory essay to the catalogue of surveys constructed by Allen Eaton in 1930. Ordinarily, such documents provide the beginning of historical analysis and are critically revised by later historians. However, there has been relatively little written about the surveys and the survey movement since it expired (the exception is the volume edited by Bulmer et al. 1991). So these texts give shape to a kind of dim memory of a movement to promote social reform through sociological research, which, for mysterious reasons, disappeared.

The Pittsburgh Survey is recalled by social scientists and historians in the light of this memory. Yet each document of self-interpretation on which this historical memory is based was a deeply polemical construction. This chapter reconsiders the viewpoint and aims of the surveyors themselves by locating the Pittsburgh Survey in a history of expertise. The Pittsburgh Survey had a special place in the self-conception of the leaders of the survey movement, and this is reflected in these texts. It seemed to the surveyors to be the harbinger of a major new form of social change in which a new kind of expert would play a central role. In fact, the Pittsburgh Survey was the high water mark of the movement.

Paul Kellogg was part of a circle of reformers and philanthropists associated with the New York City Charity Organization Society (COS). One particular philanthropic organization closely associated with the New York COS, the Russell Sage Foundation (RSF), supplied the funding, some of the personnel, and the guiding ideas of the Pittsburgh Survey. This New York–based foundation was not the only organization active in reform research. The New York Bureau of Municipal Research, which was copied in other cities such as Philadelphia, was an especially successful institution. The bureaus made some parallel claims to expertise. But they supported different reforms (for the most part, reforms in financial controls and municipal management) and were supported by different segments of the community and various philanthropists, notably Carnegie and Rockefeller (Schiesl 1977). Eventually, through the efforts of the Rockefeller Foundation in the 1930s, public administration became a profession, and the reforms originally proposed by the bureaus of municipal research were carried out by municipal administrators who were, increasingly, trained professionals. Each model of research-based reform had its own successes and failures and its own historical trajectory. This chapter tells a parallel story with a different ending. The survey movement model made perhaps the most ambitious claims to expertise. But social work as conceived by Kellogg was supplanted by a different model, a model of individual treatment, and it became a profession on this basis a change greatly aided, incidentally, by the Rockefeller philanthropies (See Abbott 1988; see also Lubove 1965). The conclusion will explain why the survey movement took this trajectory.

WHAT DID SURVEY MEAN?

Surveys, in some sense of the word, had long been a method of producing change. In reform contexts, the term sometimes meant no more than a systematic cataloging of conditions. By 1905 canvassing had become a widespread activity of reform organizations. When Paul Kellogg wrote in 1912 that he had discerned a great movement in the direction of surveys like the Pittsburgh project, he had a particular idea of what the Pittsburgh Survey represented and exemplified. What did he have in mind? The specific examples he listed in "The Spread of the Survey Idea" included "surveys" of conditions in Buffalo's Polish section, in Newark, in Sag Harbor, and in Kentucky; Presbyterian church surveys in rural Illinois, Missouri, and Pennsylvania; and federal immigration studies of localities, such as mill and mining towns (Kellogg 1912: 1).

Why did Kellogg include these surveys? What did he exclude? He specifically distinguishes these "surveys" from several of the most famous reform-oriented surveys of the era, such as Rowntree's survey of York and The Hull House Maps and Papers. These surveys, he wrote, share some elements of the survey idea but are "not identified with the more or less crystallized movement which to-day engages our attention" (Kellogg 1912: 2).

The first entry on the Kellogg's "A" list, the survey of Kentucky conducted by the ladies' clubs, is revealing. In Kellogg's own view, this report fits his criteria more closely than Rowntree's studies. This "survey" seems to have been an example of a local organization seeking expert help from outside the community and paying for it out of its own resources. But it was not a survey in the sense that it collected data and analyzed it. This suggests that what Kellogg had in mind by the "survey idea" had little to do with the methodology of data collection and analysis and much to do with the question of who sponsored the survey and whether the sponsor employed and recognized a particular kind of social work expertise. Indeed, Kellogg eagerly pointed out communities that commissioned surveys from their own funds, involved leading citizens of the community, and used volunteer help from the community, led by professional "surveyors" (Kellogg 1912: 8, 15).[1]

SOCIAL WORK EXPERTISE: THE ENGINEERING MODEL

The professional surveyors Kellogg had in mind were expert social workers (see Brooks [1918] 1969). But he had a special notion of social work and a distinct idea about social work expertise. Whereas *social work* was often applied indiscriminately to charity and reform activities, such as Social Gospel–oriented religious work, and implied no special training, Kellogg used the term to mean comprehensive community reform and conceived of the social worker as an engineer (Kellogg 1912: 4; Harrison 1930: xviii, xxiv).[2] His justification was that the cities he studied were *made* environments that could be remade. The fact that no single person had made these environments, built the buildings, designed the streets, constructed the factories, organized the social and charitable institutions, or invented the form of municipal government did not make these social institutions any less "made." The task of the social worker as engineer was to identify the problems in the community machinery and recommend steps to take to fix or improve it. Social research was an investigation of the structural elements of the community.

The concept of structural elements suggests, in addition to the analogy it draws between the social worker and the engineer, a theory of society—a theory of its structure and its elements. But what was the theory that informed the social engineer's thinking? There was no explicit theory. The topics of the Pittsburgh Survey largely reproduced the organizational division of labor at the Russell Sage Foundation (RSF), which itself reproduced, with some omissions, the standard list of reform movements and agenda. The RSF was organized around particular reform topics, such as playgrounds, child hygiene, and women's work. It relied on highly specialized experts in these areas with strong connections to the activists. This model was a quite effective action tool. The individuals who headed Russell Sage departments, such as Mary Van Kleeck who headed the Committee on Women's Work, Mary Richmond who headed the Charity Organizations Department, Leonard Ayres the education specialist, and other less well-known figures such as Clarence Perry who became the head of the Playgrounds Department, helped to professionalize workers in their fields.[3] All of these topics had a place in the Pittsburgh Survey; each had a long history of reform activism.

But the idea of "structural elements" suggests the one innovative idea the Pittsburgh Survey embodied: putting reform experts together with community activists to study one particular locality "comprehensive." The major result of their efforts at bringing together experts on various subjects, according to Kellogg and Deardorff's 1928 retrospective, was that they could now see the impact of one problem on many facets of community life.

> The long neglected hazard of work accidents was found at the first staff conferences ramifying in so many directions that practically every member was faced with one phase or another of it. It bore upon the relief funds of the labor unions, the multitudinous benefits societies of the immigrant races, and the relief plans of corporations; it had led to the organization of employers' liability associations and employees' liability associations; it was bringing pensioners to the charitable societies and inmates to the children's institutions; it was a dominating factor in the local system of state subsidies to charitable institutions; it was the concern of the coroner's office, the office of foreign consuls and the health bureau, where it was one of the two causes which gave Pittsburgh its high general death rate; it had to do in a minute degree with the discipline, intelligence, grit, and moral backbone of the working force in the mills; in the courts it harked back to the fundamental issues of public policy and freedom of contract; and in its effect on income on the standard of living of workingmen's families it set its stamp on the next generation. (Kellogg and Deardorff 1928: 791)

The discovery was retrospectively presented by Kellogg as the major fruit of the distinctive approach of the survey.[4] It is perhaps no surprise that he was attracted to the model of the social worker as an engineer fitting together the parts of a large problem.

As Kellogg conceived it, the basic task of the survey was to consult with local experts, such as directors of orphanages and other eleemosynary institutions, notables of the community who were involved in its philanthropic, religious, and charitable institutions, as well as, to a more modest extent, owners of business and property. The idea was that these individuals, especially the leading professionals of the community, such as doctors and educators, were experts in their own domain and as such were already aware of certain community problems. What these individuals were likely to be less aware of, and in any case could not deal with, were problems that arose outside their own special domains and over which they had no practical control. Thus, a physician concerned with the high rate of tuberculosis in a community might be aware of environmental or workplace causes but would be unable to prevent these health hazards. Similarly, if industrial accidents caused impoverishment in a community, the director of the poorhouse or other charitable institutions could not improve working conditions in dangerous industries.

The Pittsburgh Survey team viewed the social worker as facilitating and directing community leaders in reaching a consensus on reforms. Commitment was crucial to the whole survey idea. The survey needed local initiative and sponsorship because local notables were one of the target audiences for the survey's results. According to the model Kellogg elaborated, the circle of participants was to expand and various community leaders would air their views before the surveyors. Naturally, this stage of the survey required a certain delicacy. But it assured that the results of the survey would not simply be dismissed.

PUBLICITY AND COMMITMENT

Consensus building involved more than enlisting local leaders. The Pittsburgh Survey, like the similar Springfield Survey later directed by Harrison (the only survey truly comparable to the Pittsburgh Survey in scope, but done in a middle-sized town), devoted considerable effort to publicizing the survey results to a wide public. For example, the surveys built models and held exhibits. The official title of the Russell Sage Foundation section devoted to surveys, the Surveys and Exhibit Unit, reflected the centrality of public presentation to this conception of a survey.

The public exhibit of the Pittsburgh Survey findings was carefully constructed and considered a triumph by the surveyors. Frank E. Wing, an associate director of the survey and director of exhibits, described it: "One startling and convincing feature of the Pittsburgh Civic exhibit in November, 1908 . . . [was] a frieze of small silhouettes three inches apart stretching in line around both ends and one side of the large hall in the Carnegie Institute in which the exhibit of the Pittsburgh Survey was installed" (Wing [1914] 1974). The silhouettes, a sign explained, represented the death toll from typhoid fever in the previous year. The exhibit was well attended, and the lessons learned were used in the Springfield Survey, which went even farther in attempting to rouse civic consciousness by participatory publicity devices.

THE FATE OF THE SURVEY AS A MODEL

What was the fate of this ideal? The short answer to this question is simple. It was a dead end. Kellogg's "survey idea" did not spread; although nongovernmental surveys did proliferate, few resembled the Pittsburgh Survey. But in the late 1920s, Shelby Harrison, in his preface to Eaton's bibliography, attempted to salvage the ideal of the Pittsburgh Survey and to substantiate the historical claim that there was a survey movement. He did this by reinterpreting the proliferation of surveys. Harrison identifies three more or less paradigmatic surveys—the Pittsburgh Survey, the Springfield

Survey, and the Syracuse Survey—and uses this list as proof of the existence of a survey movement with the Pittsburgh-style survey at its core. But Eaton's bibliography and Kellogg's account of the survey idea seem to conflict. Harrison tried to resolve this glaring conflict in his introduction. He explained,

> The first surveys covered a broad range of subjects; they were general studies of entire communities, these communities ranging in size and form all the way from the local neighborhood or parish, city ward, town, and city up to counties and states. . . . [But soon] a tendency set in . . . toward employing the survey to appraise one major phase of community life, such as health and sanitation, public education, housing, recreation, employment and industrial relations, child welfare, dependency and charitable effort to reduce or relieve it, and delinquency and correction. (1930: xxvi)

This is an accurate description of what occurred. The survey movement did not develop in the direction favored by Harrison and predicted by Kellogg. The Pittsburgh and Springfield Surveys date from the earlier part of the period covered by the bibliography. The later surveys in the bibliography were specialized. The trend toward specialization without synthesis through the efforts of the social work "engineer" was exactly the opposite of what Kellogg had envisioned. What went wrong?

Harrison tried to put the best face on this outcome. If we start with an engineering conception of social work and the notion that the various institutions in a community fit together in a way that could be "engineered", we can think of the kinds of surveys involving these specialized institutions, such as school surveys, church surveys, sanitation surveys, or health surveys as elements of the social survey conception in its full form. So the Eaton bibliography included many studies that were not directly connected to social work at all, such as research motivated by the efficiency movement in primary and secondary education.

The idea that such subjects as school efficiency, sometimes involving such picayune matters as the proper time to cut and water grass at schools and maintenance schedules for school buildings, were part of social work is strange only if one has in mind present notions of social work. For Kellogg and Harrison, the engineer was concerned with all parts of the machine. The problem for Kellogg and Harrison was that the very idea that justified all these concerns as part of the same movement, the engineering conception, was itself a failure.

To put it a little differently, the issue is this: for Kellogg and Harrison, the true social survey was distinguished by the central place it accorded to social work "engineering." This notion had lost favor by the time the Eaton bibliography was compiled. The bibliography is, in effect, an apologia, written after the survey idea had expired. But Harrison reports only a "trend." Why did the survey model fail to develop as Kellogg had originally hoped?

SOCIAL WORKERS AS EXPERTS

Kellogg's model makes the social worker "engineer" central. He presents the social worker as an expert with the kind of diagnostic powers that a physician acquires through the study of other cases and applies to each new case. As he says in "The Spread of the Survey Idea," "The survey takes from the physician his art of applying to the problems at hand standards and experience worked out elsewhere" (Kellogg 1912: 4). The expertise is by its very nature external to local situations—that is to say, not normally possessed by persons within a given community and not even obtainable by analyzing local conditions without help from the outside expert. But it is quite different from the expertise claimed by the scientist, and the investigations Kellogg envisioned had a quite different starting point from that of "pure science."

"To illustrate," Kellogg wrote, "if your pure scientist were studying the housing situation in a given town, he would start out perhaps without any hypotheses, tabulate every salient fact as to every house, cast up long columns of figures, and make careful deductions, which might and might not be worth the paper they were written on." This was obviously not the procedure he recommended. He proposed research that applied the standards worked out elsewhere. "Your housing reformer and your surveyor ought to know at the start what good ventilation is, and what cellar dwellings are. These things have been studied elsewhere, just as the medical profession has been studying hearts and lungs until they know the signals which tell whether a man's organs are working right or not, and what to look for in making a diagnosis" (Kellogg 1912: 4).

Part of the expertise of the social worker, then, is the possession of standards. Over and over again in the field of social concern, says Kellogg, the right standards conflict with popular taste and the desires of commerce. In other domains, conflicts between correct standards and popular taste or commerce occur as well; the failure to resolve them in favor of standards known to experts, results in such events as the Titanic disaster. "Compare the commercial demand for speed and capacity in ocean liners with the commercial demand for butter fat. Compare the blind popular demand for luxuries in cabins with the blind popular demand for a thick collar of cream. Life boats are like clean milk." In the case of the Titanic, the experts knew, "but their judgments have fallen on deaf ears." After the disaster, "the average man at last sees; and (in high rage) he is calling for a change. Those responsible for ocean vessels are charged to make safety keep pace with the great structural changes in the shipping industry; to apply science to human well-being, as well as to speed" (Kellogg 1912: 16). Just as the naval expert possessed expert knowledge of the need for lifeboats on the Titanic, the social worker, Kellogg thought, possesses expert knowledge of human needs.

Kellogg had no doubts about the ability of social work experts to establish standards, but he says nothing about how the standards are to be established and what "science" should be "applied" to social problems. He is more concerned with publicity, with the conditions under which the public becomes aware of the need to impose standards.

> In many of these deep-seated social needs, apparently some great disaster has to overtake us, and smite us, before as a people we are aroused to them, and half-blindly often wholly unthinking of our own responsibility, demand immediate reform. This is so whether it is a dam which gives way like Austin; or a theater which burns like the Iroquois; or a blazing schoolhouse full of children like that at Cleveland; or a loft building like the Triangle. (Kellogg 1912: 16)

The survey commended itself as a method of publicity that emblazons these needs upon the public consciousness without the occurrence of a catastrophe. The journalistic means of bringing these real needs to human terms was the case study method. As Harrison later wrote, "The survey takes from the charity organization movement its case-work method of bringing problems down to human terms; by figures, for example, of the household cost of sickness—not in sweeping generalizations but in what Mr. Woods called 'piled-up actualities'" (Harrison 1912: 5). The aim is to enable people to act without a catastrophe,

> to visualize needs which are not so spectacular but are no less real ... to bring them to human terms, to put the operations of the government, of social institutions and of industrial establishments to the test of individual lives, to bring the knowledge and interventions of scientists and experts home to the common imagination, and to gain for their proposals the dynamic backing of a convinced democracy. (Kellogg 1912: 17)

The survey, Kellogg believed in 1912, need not do this unaided. "Two strong movements—one towards greater efficiency; the other towards greater democracy" had, he believed, created the conditions in which experts and an aroused public could work together for reform.

The first movement is reflected nationally by the President's Commission on Efficiency and Economy; the second finds expression in the Western Insurgent Movement which through the initiative, referendum and recall, seeks to bring the legislative "say" back to the people. If we were to personify the first movement, it would be to give it the character of the expert; the second, the character of the average citizen. And in the general trend, we have the expert and the average man coming together and jointly challenging the frontage, which existing institutions, professions, and organized forces bear toward the needs of the time (Kellogg 1912: 14–15).

The social worker is the expert in the social realm, an expert on human need and the engineering of community institutions to bring about the satisfaction of basic human needs. The survey is a particularly powerful means of creating a bond between the expert and the public. "The public interest it creates comes harder but has better staying qualities. In so far as it must lay a framework for setting forth the wide range of needs and opportunities which fall within its field, so it has inherent the prospect of a more sustained and organic accomplishment." Kellogg thus supposed that the "common man" could be brought around to accepting the expert ministrations of the social worker by the techniques of publicity and persuasion exhibited in the Pittsburgh Survey. This enabled him to believe that the survey was itself a kind of democratic force, and he envisioned the average citizen and the expert "coming together" and "jointly challenging the frontage which existing institutions, professions, and organized forces bear toward the needs of the time" (Kellogg 1912: 14–15, 17).

THE AFTERMATH

This optimistic vision, needless to say, was never realized. The "pure scientist," upon whom Kellogg heaped such scorn in 1912, became in the 1920s the beneficiary of massive support by the Laura Spelman Rockefeller Memorial (LSRM). Research of the sort that Kellogg advocated, involving the "expert" evaluative assessments of "social workers," disappeared entirely. Research on questions of social policy and on the effectiveness of social programs came to more closely resemble the research done by "pure scientists." Kellogg was bitterly jealous of the beneficiaries of this change in climate and protested vigorously against it. He ascribed it to the foundations' fear of being accused of "the heinous crime of 'propaganda'" (Kellogg and Deardorff 1928: 827). There was some truth in this accusation: the foundations were subject to congressional investigations that threatened the revocation of their tax-exempt status and were cautious about such accusations. The Rockefeller philanthropists were especially sensitive after a formative incident in which it appeared that philanthropic funding was used to support propaganda that benefitted the interests of Rockefeller businesses—a serious misuse of the charitable exemption. After this episode, a number of changes were made to let "the objectivity of research be established beyond cavil" (Fosdick 1952: 26–27). Kellogg complained that the effect of this effort was "to declass as recipients for grants some types of organizations that have a penchant for bringing things about," resulting in "affluent research bodies and poverty stricken agencies which are endeavoring to effect results" (Kellogg and Deardorff 1928: 822).

But this was an oversimplification. When the Laura Spelman Rockefeller Memorial decided to fund the social sciences in 1923, the aim was just as "practical" as the smaller Russell Sage Foundation's. But its young director, Beardsley Ruml, was deeply skeptical about the knowledge base for social action. He wrote in 1922, "All who work toward the general end of social welfare are embarrassed by the lack of that knowledge which the social sciences must provide. It is as though engineers were at work without an adequate development of physics and chemistry, or as though physicians were practicing in the absence of the medical sciences" (quoted in Fosdick 1952: 194). Kellogg, with his rhetoric about engineering and medical practice, embodied precisely the kind of embarrassment Ruml had in mind. (Fosdick 1952: 194, 199)

Ruml was not alone. The validity of the kind of approach to social problems that the Russell Sage Foundation had adopted was being called into question, even within the RSF, and the question of the role and purpose of research was a source of ongoing friction. Robert W. DeForest, one of the founding fathers of the Russell Sage Foundation and a close personal friend of Olivia Sage, the donor, wrote in 1920 to the director, John Glenn, "Any expenditure for research or investigations should clearly be directed toward some practical end to be obtained as a result of such expenditures; ... where we already know enough for purposes of practical action I think further knowledge is unnecessary." Glenn, himself an activist, replied by saying, "I agree that research should be 'directed toward some practical end.' There is, however, a question as to what ends are practical."[5] Most of the research done by action agencies was not motivated by an interest in such questions. Mary E. Richmond, head of Russell Sage's Charity Organizations Department, in an internal memo about the research uses of Charity Organization Society data, observed in 1915, "The social reformers wanted us to begin to gather the data they needed in order to interest people in measures already decided upon." The research "was prompted not so much by a spirit of discovery as by a desire to gather more publicity material."[6] Propaganda of exactly this kind, of course, was at the heart of Kellogg's strategy in Pittsburgh, a strategy continued and refined by Harrison in Springfield.

Kellogg, like DeForest, believed that enough was known to proceed with "getting things done." He defended to the last the expansive claims for the expertise of social workers that he had made in 1912. The notion came, however, to an ignominious end in a "research" effort that attempted to assess the effects of Prohibition. In the 1928 paper written with Neva Deardorff, he complained that though "our Federal prohibition amendment was the most sweeping piece of social legislation that ever attempted to regulate the manners and morals of a whole people.... It has gone for ten years without any comprehensive inquiry." This, for him, was an example of the failure of the "scientific approach" and an opportunity to demonstrate the notion of social work expertise. The Social Science Research Council, funded by the Rockefeller philanthropies to support social science, had a committee on the subject that issued a report showing the lack of data and the difficulties of gauging results. But the settlement houses, "with their slender resources but essential dynamic . . . had the initiative to gather testimony as to the social consequences of our half-enforced prohibition" (Kellogg and Deardorff 1928: 823). The report, *Does Prohibition Work?* (1927) written by Martha Bensley Bruere (under the auspices of a committee that included Kellogg himself and various important settlement house heads, such as Jane Addams) is even more explicit than Kellogg in its hostility to social science as supported by the Laura Spelman Rockefeller Memorial.

The foreword, written by Lillian Wald of the Henry Street Settlement in New York, explicitly dissociated the book from attempts "to prove or disprove the value of prohibition by statistics"; which had "been extensively undertaken by both sides of the controversy and with criticism equally destructive to both" (1927: ix). Bruere made a similar comment: "I hope this material will be used for some good purpose and not just more statistics" (1927: xiii). Instead, the book collected the impressions of 193 settlement house workers and social workers all over the country. A questionnaire was given out, with the following instructions:

> This questionnaire does not call for "yes" or "no" answers, but for detailed, descriptive information as accurate as you can make it and graphic enough to make the reader understand the kind of people you are talking about and the conditions under which they live. Whenever possible make your answers the records of individual experiences and realistic pictures of family life as it has been affected by drink—or the lack of it—since the passage of the Eighteenth Amendment. (Bruere 1927: 182, 305)[7]

The compilation was thus, according to Bruere, "not a statistical report but an authentic document of professional opinion couched in the language in which it came to me. Not one statement in it but was made by some social expert who was asked to contribute to the study; not one fact that we do not believe we have verified; not one quotation that is not from a signed report now on file in the office." When her respondents offered statistics, she said, "I have covertly discouraged them—have indeed, opened the way to their redoing their statistical material back into the human elements it is composed of" (1927: viii–ix, 303, 305).[8] The study concluded "that all of the things hoped for by the advocates of prohibition are being realized in some places and that even where the law is least observed, some of them have come true" (1927: 304). This expert judgment was at variance with that of the electorate, which shortly after repealed the Eighteenth Amendment. It was also at variance with the emerging ideas of "professionalizing" social workers. Kellogg and his peers thought that there are various "root causes" for social problems that could be identified and eliminated.

The causes were individual causes, like drink or workplace accidents, that could be eliminated by regulation or by the provision of the appropriate goods and social services. The intellectual model for this reasoning was built into the forms that COS workers used to deal with cases. The COS form listed standard reasons for family problems, such as drink, which tempted social workers to think that abolishing drink would abolish the problems that alcohol "caused." This assumption had been under assault for two decades by the time this book was written. With the rise of professional social work, it became passé.

Mary E. Richmond, in an internal memo in 1916, went to the heart of the problem with this reasoning, which is of course central to the Pittsburgh Survey, a discussion of the notion of "the causes of poverty." In the case of a certain drunkard under treatment, she asks,

> Is drink the cause of poverty here, or is it merely the outcropping of certain personal and environmental characteristics? I think the latter, but at one stage or another, this man's poverty and that of his family might have figured in statistics as "caused" by any one of half a dozen favorite labels, whereas all we could truthfully say was that, at successive stages of treatment, these and these and these conditions appeared along with poverty in his family and helped to complicate its treatment.[9]

Intellectual considerations like these would not alone have discredited the "root causes" model. But Richmond's point about the causes of poverty fit with the practical experience of caseworkers and was a better basis for the training of caseworkers. Individual therapy, rather than community reform, became the dominant model in social work as it was "professionalized" in the 1920s. Professionalization, tied to therapeutic expertise, solved a problem that Kellogg's notion of the social worker as community engineer could not solve. For Kellogg's model of the survey as a vehicle for expert-directed reform to work, it was necessary for the public to accept "social work" expertise on a retail basis, so to speak, issue by issue, rather than wholesale, by accepting the value of the agencies that employ case workers. The public, or at least community leaders, had to be persuaded, because the public had to finance surveys, and then not only to accept the results but also to support the politicians who were to put the recommendations into effect.

The idea that communities should supply the bulk of support and participation for their own surveys collided with several political realities, notably the reality that communities did not wish to be portrayed in an unflattering way—a problem faced by other forms of social research as well. The problem with the comprehensive community survey was that the public relations consequences of such a survey were likely to be negative. As Leonard Ayres, director of the Education Division of the RSF, shrewdly observed, "People who have their photographs taken usually feel, upon seeing the negative, that it should be retouched."[10] Ayres was a successful promoter of school surveys. But he presented school surveys as a means of assessing public spending on schools and concentrated on such high-consensus issues as the full utilization of school buildings. This gave the education survey a base of support and an interested audience.

Kellogg never found an analogous base of support and audience for comprehensive community surveys. He gamely argued that "a survey is 'good business' in the long run from the standpoint of a city's prosperity." But the argument is not very convincing. Community leaders, who might accept or encourage school reform, would be less inclined to support a community survey that would be negative, much less one that would "challenge the existing frontage which existing institutions, professions, and organized forces bear toward the needs of time" (Kellogg 1912: 15). The survey, when it records municipal successes, is perhaps good advertising and these are the cases that Kellogg points to. Rural sociologists learned that bland descriptions of communities praising the friendliness of its citizens were acceptable, whereas seriously critical surveys with statistical evidence, together with photographs, were likely to be suppressed and cost the researchers their jobs (see Nelson 1969: 179). But in most cases, the bulk of what would be documented would be the unmet needs of a community, journalistically enhanced for maximum impact. A progressive elite might find various ways to use such a survey against entrenched institutions and politicians. Nevertheless, the number of cases in which a survey of the sort done in Pittsburgh would be attractive must have been very small.[11]

The surveyors' strategy, in short, was intrinsically flawed. The strategy of the Rockefeller philanthropies was more successful. They sought, on the one hand, to promote what they called realistic knowledge and, on the other, to professionalize the relevant workers by strengthening the system of professional training. The expert is understood in this model to speak primarily to the professionalized worker rather than the citizen. The tactical role of subsidy obviously changed in this model. "Expert knowledge" that was useful to the professional was subsidized through outright support of the production of expert knowledge constructed for these useful purposes, through subsidized training, and especially through subsidized publication—the key element in the creation of the modern "expert" (cf. Buxton and Turner 1992, Chapter 8 in this volume). The model was extremely successful in the case of medicine and public health, and later in the case of public administration. The LSRM helped social work to become professionalized by its support of several key graduate schools of social work in the 1920s and '30s.

The success of this expert-to-professional relationship reflected the more realistic match between the kinds of knowledge that experts could reasonably claim to possess and the needs and career structures of professional social workers. Like public administrators or public health officials and physicians, social workers became a "professional" community structured in such a way that the reliance on expert guidance was integral to the identity and structure of the profession itself. The specific role of the expert and the professional are made for one another. The relationship is limited and therefore not subject to the full range of conflicts with public opinion that arise in the case of the more grandiose vision of social work backed by an aroused citizenry advanced by Kellogg. It is difficult, in the light of this history, to see the "failure" of the Pittsburgh model as anything but inevitable—a grasp for authority that exceeded the reach of "social work." It was the path not taken, but only because it was a path that led nowhere.

Part III
Expert Institutions

8 From Edification to Expertise
Sociology as a "Profession"

The earliest exponents of "sociology" in the US used the term to mean both "systematic knowledge of society" and "systematic reform teachings." Only in the 1890s did they feel a strong need to distinguish between the two. The first large body of empirical research on "sociological" topics was performed by bureaus of labor statistics, agencies created by the state to collect data and opinions on matters relating to the life of the laboring classes. This research was specifically understood to be an instrument of reform: the bureaus were a political concession to labor, and most of their research, which involved the first large-scale voluntary questionnaire studies undertaken in the US, was designed to demonstrate the factual validity of the reform arguments made by the labor movement and to publicize these facts to the citizenry at large. The advocates of "social science" who formed the American Social Science Association believed that the teaching of "social science" was the main aim of social science, and the main means of reform.[1] The founder of American sociology, Lester F. Ward, wrote his systematic treatise as a demonstration of the possibility of constructing a teachable scientific doctrine of reform (Foskett 1949).

We would find these self-conceptions oddly inverted today: for us, "sociology" is a body of knowledge that, incidentally, is taught; for them, it was a public teaching that, incidentally, was a body of knowledge. They thought of this body of knowledge as "scientific," but they had in mind no special theory of science. To the extent that, for example, Ward discusses the topic of the epistemic status of social science at all, it is primarily the distinction between rational and religious or traditional, or more simply between the contrast of the self-conscious, or thought-through, with the unreflective or prejudiced.

In this chapter, our concern will be with the transformation of this idea and its variants to the present conception of sociology as contained in such phrases as "policy science" and "knowledge utilization." The transition took place over many years and remnants of the older model were present within sociology, and to an even greater extent in the public image of sociology, at the beginnings of the post–World War II era. We will concentrate on the background to the attempt, during the early postwar years, to construct a new conceptual model of the place of sociology in relation to the state and public life,[2] and examine in some detail the Harvard background to Talcott Parsons' conception of sociology as a "profession"—it is a ghost that haunts present sociology, which has largely failed to become a legitimate profession and has, in addition, lost most of its older audience. One might treat this topic entirely as a history of ideals, unrealized ideals, for most of the thinking that went into the creation of a new role for sociology went unactualized, or only partly actualized. The model proved far more difficult to institutionalize and finance than their advocates expected. But Parsons' model had some interesting organizational successes, and gained significant support from foundations. Moreover, the model contributed an essential element to the larger model of sociology that had emerged by Parsons' illuminating report on the profession of 1959, on the eve of the great expansion of sociology. The successes were impermanent nevertheless. To understand the reasons for this, one needs to understand the weaknesses that were there from the start, and to understand them one needs to understand what problems the model initially solved.

EDIFYING SOCIOLOGY: THE ORIGINAL AMERICAN SOCIOLOGY AND ITS AUDIENCES

The older kind of sociology promoted careers in which the tasks of edification, the means of propagating the results of research, the means by which the research was supported, and the theory of educability went together. The careers are illustrative. Ward was a government scientist, a protégé of one of the great political talents in the history of science, John Wesley Powell, whose greatest achievement was to fashion a politically popular and useful geological survey (S. Turner 1987). Ward began his career as an edifying reformer by serving as the editor of a freethinking journal called *The Iconoclast*. Ward had trouble finding an audience, but he was read in reformist circles and was a member of a coterie of government scientists in Washington that was itself oriented to the public and the public uses of science rather than to disciplinary or academic science. Franklin H. Giddings, a member of the next generation of sociologists, the son of a congregational minister, was a working journalist before his economic writings in the public press and his work for the Massachusetts Bureau of Labor Statistics and in the Cooperative Movement led to an academic position. Throughout his life as an academic, Giddings wrote as a journalist, contributing frequent editorials to the *Independent*, many of which were small gems of sociological reasoning. He also served on boards of settlement houses and related agencies, gave talks at New York public gatherings, and, during World War I, served as a propagandist by giving a series of lectures in the south. Giddings even had a political career, serving on the New York School Board and entertaining aspirations for the position of mayor. E. A. Ross, one of the other founders of the American Sociological Society, wrote almost exclusively for "popular audiences." One of the first Chicago PhDs in sociology, Charles A. Ellwood, had himself been introduced to the idea of social science by reading R. T. Ely's Chautauqua volume; throughout his life he was a success with the heirs to this audience, including Protestant ministers, as an opponent of fundamentalism. Ellwood's books were on several occasions "book-of-the-month" selections or alternates for major book clubs, and several of them were translated into many languages (1923a, 1923b, 1929, 1938).

In each of these cases the writers were bound to the nonacademic public in crucial and direct ways. The common trait is this: in each case, most or all of the financial support of the activities came from the audiences for the activities. Reform-minded citizens supported and attended lectures and bought the books written by sociologists. Before the emergence of a textbook market in the 1920s, if writers such as Giddings, Ross, or Ellwood could not communicate to a nonacademic public, they would not have been able to publish their books. This closely dependent relationship with their audience was clearly understood and accepted by the early sociologists themselves. In his editorial preface in the first volume of the *American Journal of Sociology* (AJS), Albion Small described the demand for sociology and the purposes it was to serve in terms that derived from his mentor, Ely. An "undisciplined social self-consciousness" in the larger public, articulated in "popular philosophies of human association," had been produced by the increasing social interaction of the age (1895: 2). A social "movement" that was a counterpart to these philosophies, "fostered by reflection on contemporary social conditions" (1895: 2), had emerged. These "popular attempts to explain present forms of society, and to get favorably placed for effecting change in social conditions," not "schools," were the primal and continuing source for sociology.

> It is a very callow sociologist who imagines that he and his collaborators are inventing the subject matter of a new science: They are trying to perfect means of answering obtrusive questions which the ordinary man is proposing every hour. They are not creating but representing popular curiosity. Life is so much more real to the people than to the schools that the people are no sooner possessed of some of the tools of thought, and some means of observation, than they proceed to grapple with more vital questions than the scholars had raised. Hence social philosophies, popular in source, partial in content, but potent in political effect, get vogue before scholars know the terms of the conditions which these rule of thumb philosophies claim to explain. The doctrines of professional sociologists are attempts to substitute revised second thought for the hasty first thoughts composing the popular sociologies in which busy men outside the schools utter their impressions. (1895: 6)

Popular intellectualizing about society, produced by the press of changed social circumstances, thus creates "a strenuous demand for authentic social philosophy" that constitutes "a summons to unique forms of service" for the academic sociologist.

The relationship between sociology and its public, in short, was defined in the first instance by the actions and intellectual needs of this public. Moreover, the verdict of men of affairs with respect to the value of its "revised second thought" of sociologists is the ultimate source of "authority" in the relevant sense, the sense of possessing power to produce practical effects in social action. To have this power, sociology needed to sustain the interest of this public by speaking its language, responding to the problems the public articulated first.[3] This conception was embodied in the way "empirical research" in early sociology was financed. In the case of the survey movement and the rural surveys done by university-based rural sociologists, the work was done largely through the donation of time and money by persons in the community in which the survey was being performed, and the persons participating in the survey both as questioners and respondents were the primary audience for the survey results. The creation of appropriate exhibitions and the recruitment of competent local professionals for help in the survey and advice as to what sorts of inquiries would be most useful or meaningful were major features of the survey movement.

The idea of a community survey is given as an exercise in Small and Vincent's Chautauqua textbook of 1894. The point of such a study is for the members of the community themselves to come to appreciate the character of their social relations. In rural sociology this was developed in special ways that involved the voluntary help of school children, who would produce a map for a county fair that would visually display the bonds between town and country, precisely the lesson the rural sociologists wished to teach as a means of beginning the improvement of rural life through the "socialization"—by which they meant bringing into the social life of the community—of the poor "hoe-farmer" and his family (Galpin 1920: 315–55).

There were often additional sources of funds for research of this kind. *The Polish Peasant*, for example, was financed by a woman with reformist aims who wished to publicize the problems of Polish immigrants. The Russell Sage Foundation contributed heavily to community surveys. Yet these were cases where the audience for the survey and the financial sponsors overlapped. Mrs. Ethel Dummer, W. I. Thomas's angel, was a person like the person she hoped the books would enlighten on the question of Polish immigration. "Defining the situation" was understood by her as a means of reform, and a better means than the methods of traditional charity, which had in this case proven inadequate.[4] The Russell Sage leadership was composed of reform-minded civic leaders, the top crust of the class of persons who the social surveys, such as the Pittsburgh survey, were intended to stir community action. The practice in performing these surveys was to rely on the local knowledge of members of the professional classes in the expectation that they would be affected by the survey and support the reforms it suggested. The state Bureaus of Labor Statistics of the late nineteenth century, which were the precursors to the social survey movement, provided material for the labor leaders and reformist audience that supported them politically in the state legislatures.

Such relationships were not without their constraints, some of which were hard to bear. Writers such as Ward found it difficult to find an audience for, or get much of a living out of, his sociology, and did paleobotanical work for money even after his formal retirement from the Geological Survey. Thorstein Veblen's books were all published under a commonly used device by which the author guaranteed a minimum of sales: only one of his books passed the minimum. At the academic salaries of the day, these were difficult burdens. Textbook writing was a financially viable compromise, and especially in the '20s and '30s it was the primary publication outlet for sociologists. Nevertheless, this was also a form supported by its audiences (albeit the captive audiences of students in the classes that were assigned the texts), which had its own constraints, namely, the constraints of the demands of the professorial audience that selected the textbooks for use, selections themselves constrained by considerations of what the student market could bear.

These constraints were felt acutely by social scientists, many of whom, by the 1920s, did not bow to them as cheerfully as Small had done. The reasons for this are not hard to discover. The ideal of sociology as a pure science had entered into the self-conception of sociologists with Giddings and his students, who did not, in fact, abandon the older task and the older audiences (and who in several cases, such as Howard Odum, were extremely effective in dealing with the larger public), but rather drew increasingly sharp lines between scientific (meaning for them quantitative) knowledge and other kinds of writing. The 1922 report of the American Political Science Association that led to the creation of the Social Science Research Council had listed five needs: time for research, clerical support for research, funds for "field work," "adequate provision . . . for the publication of results of scientific research of a type that do not possess immediate commercial value" (i.e., publication subsidies), and the education of university authorities and the public in "the necessities of political science" (Social Science Research Council 1933:1). From this point on, sociology came to be dominated by researchers whose publications and the routine research work that went into the publications were heavily subsidized, freeing them from the demands of reformer audiences.

This produced a social division that turned brutal in the late 1920s and '30s. Many sociologists had retained a wider audience. Charles Ellwood, Pitrim Sorokin, and Harry Elmer Barnes were each successful "public intellectuals," to use Jacoby's term (1987), and had been as or more successful at it than his own favorite example, C. Wright Mills, ever became. They lost their struggle for the profession. The sociologists who were subsidized and wrote primarily for the narrow audience of professional sociologists wound up dominating professional sociology, and the public intellectuals, including each of these three, died as professional outcasts. But they saw that the freedom from the constraints of the older kind of relation with the public carried an intellectual and moral price—dependence on the foundations and on the networks of favor-granting and information that enabled them to gain subsidies—and they were unwilling to pay this price.[5]

THE ROCKEFELLER ERA

The standard image of the history of American sociology reduces these changes in audience to incidents in the story of the "professionalization" of the discipline; the sociologists who lost are stigmatized as inadequately professional. The image is misleading, especially with respect to the lessons of the past for the present dilemmas of academic sociology. The continuities between the early edifying era to the present are important. In the first place, the public audience was a significant concern for many sociologists until well into the post–World War II period, and the authors who were involved with such organizations as the Social Science Research Council in its first decade did not abandon it entirely; nor did they intend to abandon it, as the effort that went into such works as *Recent Social Trends* indicated. Two of the more prominent "edifying" ideas (of social research as a mirror for society,[6] and of the need to replace ordinary ways of political and social thinking with more "scientific" modes of thought) also had a central role in the post–World War II period.[7] Only after the War was a campaign mounted against "popular" sociological writing, notably by sociologists who were foundation officials and who were concerned that too much credit was given by universities to sociologists who wrote textbooks and popular works. In the second place, the transition to a "professional" audience was itself in large part made possible by the existence of alternative means of financial support. Support, of course, was not given without strings: the demands of audiences were replaced by the demands of grantors.

In the interwar years, the subsidies that replaced the hard work of selling books and lecturing to paying audiences and summer schools derived almost entirely from Rockefeller sources, channeled through the Institute of Social and Religious Research (ISRR) in the case of Robert Lynd and such statistically oriented sociologists as Luther Fry. The Social Science Research Council (SSRC) was the source in the case of Ogburn, Rice, Lynd, and others. Park and the Chicago School depended primarily on the Local Community Research Committee of the University of Chicago (Bulmer 1984: 129–50). The sums invested in the subsidization of the work of these scholars were staggering, and it is perhaps useful to bear some of these cruder realities of finance in mind. That the transition to a professional style of empirical sociology could not have taken place without this financial support is perhaps obvious: to subsidize the efforts of research workers, particularly the persons who performed the calculations of partial and multiple regression by machine, the data collectors, or the field researchers, took professional rather than volunteer help, and this cost a great deal of money, as did the subsidization of the publication of books that the general public would not buy.

Sociologists gained this support because the persons who financed social science, in this case the Rockefeller officials, saw the social sciences as an instrument for other purposes: as useful or potentially useful. What took place in the interwar years was a long and fitful process of mutual testing and social invention in which the social sciences devised various projects and administrative devices that were presented to the foundations for their support, and the foundations selectively financed proposals and evolved new expectations based on the successes and failures of past efforts. Social scientists did not know how to satisfy the vague ideas of the foundation leadership, but they did know that some progress could be made in certain established directions, such as statistical practice, and that statistical analysis could be performed on trends or phenomena publicly regarded as problematic: the labor statisticians had taken up virtually all the same problems in the nineteenth century, and they could be taken up again with the new methods of partialling and multiple regression. Many of the changes that took place in this period were incremental changes of this sort, and were increases in scale, rather than intellectual innovations.

Despite their desire to make the social sciences "realistic," the Rockefeller officials had no interest in the "scientistic" ambitions that informed the enterprise that developed. In the early 1930s they cut back drastically on funding. Many products of SSRC subsidization, such as F. Stuart Chapin's *Social Science Abstracts*, ceased to exist. The SSRC itself began to look for other ideas that would raise funds, and found Rockefeller support for the professionalization of public administration. Conventional scientistic statistical sociology had no other place to go for funding that could fully replace what the Rockefeller philanthropic efforts had provided, and over the next ten years they struggled to conceive an appropriate role. The models of funding that were eventually developed owed something both to the experience of the flush years of the late 1920s and the efforts of the lean years of the late 1930s. Most notable in this regard was Paul Lazarsfeld. Although he never considered himself to be a sociologist, he developed a model of social, psychologically oriented survey research that served as proprietary research for business interests.[8]

In what follows we will be concerned with a model of much broader influence, namely, that of "professional formation" developed at Harvard in the 1930s under the rubric of the "Industrial Hazards Project." The interest of this model is in its effects: it was later refined and systematized by Talcott

Parsons (another nonsociologist), and became the basis for the ideal image of the social role of the sociologist, especially in relation to the public, to financial sponsors, and to other professions.[9] As with Lazarsfeld's model of the professional survey researcher, the solution had its origins outside of sociology in the efforts of the Harvard professional schools to address the problems of the professions in dealing with a changing industrial order. In spite of its arcane origins, the idea behind Parsons' model of sociology as a profession spread or was independently arrived at and supported by others. It became a major plank in the program for sociology established in the postwar period.

THE HENDERSON MODEL: SOCIAL SCIENCE AS A HELPER TO THE PROFESSIONS

From 1924 to 1929, the Laura Spelman Rockefeller Memorial dispensed some $21 million for social-scientific research. The Bulmers estimated this amount to be the equivalent of $112 million in 1980 dollars (Bulmer and Bulmer 1981: 385–86). In 1930, in the twilight of the era of its most generous support for the social sciences, the Rockefeller Foundation approved a grant of $875,000 to Harvard University in support, over a seven-year period, of "a comprehensive program in industrial hazards."[10] The project was centered in the work of Elton Mayo on the "personnel problems of industry" and in that of Lawrence J. Henderson and his collaborators on "the nature and consequences of fatigue." The grant was to be administered by a newly formed "Committee on Industrial Physiology," consisting of Mayo, Henderson, biologist William Morton Wheeler, Wallace Donham, and David Edsall (deans of the business and medical schools respectively). Edsall initially served as chair, after having negotiated intensively with foundation officials to have the proposal approved.[11]

Even by the heady standards of social-scientific support established by the LSRM in the previous decade, the grant was exceedingly generous.[12] Moreover, the terms of the grant allowed for a good deal of discretion and flexibility in its deployment. Not only could the budgets of Mayo and Henderson be increased as the committee saw fit, but the available balance of the grant (around $25,000 to $35,000 a year) could be considered as a "fluid research fund" and allocated to "such projects within the general program as may promise most important results."[13] Rockefeller officials and committee members had reached an understanding that this portion of the grant would be used to support Henry Murray's work in psychopathology, McFie Campbell's research on psychiatry (both as they related to Mayo's study), and for PhD students in engineering working with Philip and Cecil Drinker in the area of industrial hygiene (Pearce 1929: 2).[14]

Given that none of its central participants were directly linked to recognized social science disciplines, why was the Industrial Hazards Project supported by the Rockefeller Foundation under the purview of its newly formed social science division?[15] Examined against the backdrop of foundation policy at the beginning of the 1930s, their enthusiasm for the Harvard proposal can be easily understood. In some sense, it was to the Harvard group's advantage that its work was not connected to recognizable fields of social science. From the early days of Rockefeller intervention in the social sciences, including such enterprises as the Chicago Local Community Research Committee and the SSRC itself, the aim of Rockefeller officials was to break down the boundaries between the social scientific disciplines as institutionalized in American universities. By encouraging the pursuit of knowledge for its own sake—largely through individual scholarly initiative—the disciplines were an obstacle to the engaged and problem-oriented but "realistic" research the Rockefeller officials favored. While the foundation had been, and was still willing to, support so-called basic social scientific research, this support was instrumental, aimed at increasing the "realism" of the academic social sciences. The Rockefeller strategists, however, never lost sight of their firmly held creed that the "advancement of knowledge" was not "an end in itself" but a means "to promote the well-being of mankind throughout the world."[16]

With the formation of a new social science division in 1929 (under the direction of Edmund E. Day), Rockefeller social science funding went into a period of transition in emphasis, though not fundamental change. The earlier concern to build up the foundations of social scientific inquiry was displaced by "direct support of specific research projects and programs" relevant to problems of social control.[17] The only such "recognized field of inquiry" to receive support in 1930 was "the field of hazards of economic enterprise, particularly as these relate to . . . issues of general economic stability."[18]

By virtue of its inherently practical orientation, the Industrial Hazards Project accorded well with the foundation's interest in "the processes by which the results of research are given practical effectiveness."[19] Moreover, with its concern for the problems of industrial life, the scope of the Industrial Hazards Project was consistent with the Rockefeller Foundation's long-standing interest in the area of industrial relations (Geiger 1986). Yet the project was not approved solely because it accorded with foundation priorities. Elton Mayo's work had been continuously supported by various Rockefeller entities since 1923, and had been almost uniformly praised by foundation officials. Thus, his ongoing research undoubtedly provided some of the impetus for the formation of a wide-scale program in industrial hazards, rather than the other way around. This work, among all the projects that Rockefeller support had made possible during the 1920s, most closely fit the original premises of Rockefeller social science support.[20] Mayo's work came to the attention of Donham and some of his colleagues, who were able to make arrangements for Mayo to come to Harvard in 1926.[21] His interests in industrial psychology fit with a number of initiatives already underway at Harvard. Upon becoming dean of the Business School in 1919, Wallace Donham began to actively transform its approach to teaching and research by putting particular emphasis upon the "case method,"[22] whereby students would learn from simulated experiences with real business situations. He also came to the view that capitalism was in a crisis (see Donham 1931), which demanded better knowledge of the relations at the workplace. While Edsall had a nominal interest in workers' health and safety,[23] his standpoint in relation to occupational health was that of the corporate manager. "Hazards of industry" were not only of concern because they damage health. As Edsall affirmed in a press release, they could cause industry "very grave financial loss" and threaten its stability.[24] Edsall's concern with the threat to the stability of industry posed by industrial illness was in accord with the notions of Mayo and Donham about how psychological states affected worker morale and productivity.[25]

In the mid-1920s, Donham and Mayo began to realize the relevance of medical and physiological research to their efforts, and drew in a biologist and Harvard doyen, L. J. Henderson, to explore matters of common concern. Henderson was enthusiastic about Mayo's proposed work in the area of "human problems of administration," and established the fatigue laboratory at the school (as well as moving his office there) so that he could work more closely with him, in what proved to be an "important, happy, and mutually stimulating association" (Donham quoted in Cannon 1945). As Mayo began to merge his efforts with those of Henderson, Donham, Edsall, and others, he came to see their work as providing the nucleus for a major research initiative in the area of industrial relations. Along similar lines, Donham attested that the part of the business school in the project represented an extension of Mayo's work. Nevertheless, Mayo's efforts required the support of both a greater "physiological background," provided by Henderson and the medical school, as well as "industrial and social background," to be provided through the Business School.[26]

The Industrial Hazards Project was an effort to demonstrate how a "collaborate [sic] attack"[27] of this kind could be put into practice. Their commitment to this approach was strengthened when it was realized that the foundation would be supportive of collective research. As Edsall reported to Mayo, upon learning (in a conversation with Edsall) of the collective approach that the Harvard group had in mind, E. E. Day "seemed very much interested in the large general scheme." Edsall went on to suggest that Day would look much more favorably upon the work of Mayo and Henderson if their contributions were "building stones in the general scheme" rather than "individual things." Accordingly, Edsall had given Day the "picture . . . of a large scheme, into which your [Mayo's] work and Henderson's fitted."[28] In the proposal he submitted to the Rockefeller Foundation the following September, Edsall took great pains to stress how the various Harvard ventures fit into a shared "general scheme." As he described his strategy in the proposal to Stanley Cobb (in an effort to explain to Cobb why he and his collaborators had not been included in the application): "I of course have to . . . stress those [areas] that I think that R. F. people will take an interest in. It has been the most difficult job I ever undertook anyway to prepare that memo. In such form as to make things hold together as an intelligent general scheme that they would think rational."[29]

Edsall's efforts were successful. Following his visit to Harvard in October of 1929, foundation officer Raymond Pearce maintained that the "combination of work under Drinker, Mayo and Henderson properly represents as wise and complete an approach to the solution of industrial hazards as could be worked out."[30] Similar sentiments were revealed in the foundation resolution to allocate funding for the project: "The general program, dealing as it does with all phases of industrial hazards, is essentially unique and gives promise of highly significant contributions in a field in which scientific contributions are greatly to be desired. Liberal support of the program seems desirable until the work has passed well beyond its present experimental stages."[31]

The diffusion of knowledge into realms of life where it could be acted upon by professionals was an established Rockefeller method. Its earlier successes in reforming the medical profession and medical training were always present in the minds of Rockefeller officials. Supporting "social technology—or social engineering" as practiced in "schools of professional training," that is, as they embodied the "well-recognized divisions of business, law, public administration and social work," continued this idea.

Social science could have the practical effects that the Rockefeller officials wanted it to have through "professional" schools that "seek to translate the findings of the social sciences into practical techniques" and "bridge the gap between scientific research and the situations of practical life," thus helping to bring about "changes in our social institutions and social practices." In particular, these schools were thought to be of "great importance in training those who later control our economic, political and social affairs."[32] The conditions at Harvard were especially favorable for training of this kind, because so many professional schools and academic departments could be potentially involved.[33] In particular, the integration of the project's work with the Business School meant that it could potentially influence the training of future corporate leaders. Moreover, through extension activities operating through a variety of channels, business practitioners could be influenced directly.[34]

While the Industrial Hazards Project was funded by the division of social sciences, conventional social scientific research, as it had developed in American universities, was largely absent from the project. The core of the project was Mayo's work on applied industrial psychology, supplemented by the Fatigue Lab's physiological research and insights from medicine. However, these on their own were insufficient to address the broader problems of how labor management could be brought to bear on human adjustment in industry. This task, according to Donham, "required not only Mayo's expertise in philosophy, but an economic and sociological background."[35] But the conventional social sciences were largely dismissed by Henderson and his colleagues. "Unlike the Departments of Economics, Government, and Social Science," Henderson claimed, "we make every effort to base our work on experimental investigations and upon what is the equivalent of the clinical experience of physicians, but that, on the other hand, we aim to include that minimum of carefully constructed and cautiously limited theoretical analysis that appears to be necessary whenever men are taught by a method that is not simply apprenticeship."[36] Henderson believed that the goal of social science education should be "the formation of social scientists, like the best physicians, skillful in both theory and practice."[37] To this end, Henderson organized two courses that were offered under the auspices of the Department of Sociology (of which he was an outside "member") in which those involved with the various professional initiatives were encouraged to participate. One of these, the Pareto Seminar, was first offered in 1931–1932. Henderson was attracted to Pareto's conception of "residues" (sentiments or values) and "derivations" (beliefs functioning as ideologies). From the standpoint of the framework provided by clinical medicine, it would be possible to diagnose these forms of nonlogical action, thereby contributing to society's equilibrating processes.[38] According to Henderson, the professional practitioner was to act in relation to the social order in the same way that a physician dealt with illness. The human organism was believed to have natural healing processes that, if left to themselves, would restore the body to a state of equilibrium. In some circumstances, interventions would be needed to assist these natural healing processes. His Paretan-inspired conceptual scheme allowed one to make a diagnosis (as a prelude to intervention).[39]

Another course, Sociology 23, "Methods and Results of Certain Sociological Methods," was taught beginning in 1936–1937. In this course Henderson undertook to apply the Paretan-derived schema to concrete reality. Known informally as "concrete sociology," the course consisted of a series of lectures given by persons with concrete experience of the real world. More specifically, as he later explained, "the plan of Sociology 23 contemplates the professional formation in the use of theory of all sorts of men,— social scientists of every kind as well as men of affairs."[40] At the beginning of the course, Henderson outlined a conceptual framework that was supposed to provide an orientation to the concrete cases that were examined. Henderson eventually hoped to publish the introduction and the lectures, along with an appendix on various "residues" in history, as a textbook of concrete sociology. The reception of this idea by publishers was lukewarm, and the project never saw print.

The failure of Henderson to find a publisher was symptomatic. Although the aim of the program was, in a sense, to edify, the audience to be edified was small, and an audience of professionals. The Cabot weekends or the case study method helped to secure reciprocity with this special audience.

However, the "reciprocity" could not, realistically, include the financial support of this audience: this was necessarily subsidized edification. The conditions for such a relation between experts and the limited audience of "professionals" thus included substantial financial support. The new model was subsidized, specialized edification for audiences that could not be impressed with what Brinton described as the "preacher's tricks" (1939) of the older kind of edifying sociologist. From this we may derive a working definition of "expertise": it is edification in which the hearers are not the primary payers. The SSRC sociologists of the 1920s and '30s had subsidies, but they had failed to do what Henderson did: establish a reciprocal bond with a valued audience. The successful "expert" must find a valued audience and secure subsidies, direct or indirect: the subsidies are needed because the audiences cannot support the "expert" through lecture fees, royalties, or similar means.

Despite Henderson's ambition and substantial Rockefeller support, the work of the Industrial Hazards Project did not have the immediate impact upon professional and academic practice envisaged by its proponents.[41] By extension, the goals of the project (mirroring Rockefeller Foundation concerns) to bring about social control and understanding in the public sphere by way of influencing professional schools and professional training were not realized. This failure was rooted in the insularity of the project. While it pointed the way toward greater cooperation among like-minded professionals, it offered little sense of how these insights could be expressed organizationally so that foundation and state support could be routinized. Moreover, it failed to provide an ongoing basis for the mediation of its ideas to the professional strata and to the general public, with a view to generating social control. What the project lacked was a theory of how the practice of professionals could be socially organized. It fell to Henderson's most influential protégé, Talcott Parsons, to translate the thought and activities of the Industrial Hazards Project into a full-scale program of social-scientific institutionalization.

PARSONS AS A HENDERSON PROTÉGÉ

Parsons not only participated in the Pareto Seminar and presented case studies in Sociology 23, but was invited by Henderson to discuss the work of Pareto with him at length, after Henderson had read a draft of *Structure of Social Action*.[42] That Henderson regarded the *Structure* as legitimating his own efforts is evident in a statement he sent to Rockefeller Foundation director Raymond Fosdick:

> the learned study of Talcott Parsons shows that there is a clearly marked convergence of the conclusions of theorists from Hobbes to Marshall, Durkheim, Max Weber, and Pareto, upon a certain set of abstractions,

concepts, or variables which seem to be adequate for the construction of a simple, modest frame of thought that can be acquired without great difficulty and used to good purpose.[43]

He went on to say that "My introductory lectures for Sociology 23 are intended to expound this conceptual scheme. I know that it can work because I have seen it work effectively for some forty persons."

In developing this scheme, Parsons was indebted to Henderson.[44] In one of the papers that he presented to Sociology 23, Parsons observed that "a profession has not only a tradition and skills, it has a 'function'. Its members perform services which are called for, having a relation to practical problems confronting other individuals in the society. Thus a function in turn implies a 'situation' to which the function is oriented. The medical function may be defined . . . as the maintenance and restoration of 'health'."[45] Hence, medical practice may be oriented to "the restoration of health by dealing with a given disturbance of . . . equilibrium." Along the same lines, "the sick person may be regarded as one who is out of adjustment with his normal routine of functioning."[46] Parson's conception of the relationship between the medical practitioner and the wellbeing of patients was virtually identical to that of Mayo and Henderson. From this foundation, Parsons began to develop an account of how institutionalized social control could be developed. Fundamental to the process of institutionalization was the "modern half" of the pattern variables (disinterestedness, universalism, functional specificity, and affective neutrality). They not only defined the patterns that controlled social action, but also served as guidelines to professional practice. In effect, by virtue of performing according to these patterns, the professions would also be contributing to the exercise of social control.[47]

PARSONS' MODEL: THE "NATIONAL MORALE" PHASE

Wartime circumstances provided the impetus for the consolidation of this approach. Parsons was active in a number of different ventures whose intent was to contribute to the war effort.[48] He used the Henderson/Mayo schema as the basis for expanding the diagnostic skills of social analysis. The industrial morale that had been the concern of the industrial hazards researchers became embodied in "national morale"—the focal point for the initial work of Parsons and his circle of Harvard colleagues. As part of the Harvard chapter of "American Defense," a committee concerned with issues of national morale was formed. Parsons became involved in the group during the summer of 1940 upon hearing a radio address by the chairman for Massachusetts of the national committee, Harvard president James B. Conant. He agreed to serve as the vice-chairman of the Committee on National Morale, whose members included Gordon Allport, Carl

Friedrich, Edward Hartshorne, and Henry Murray. Parsons described the mandate of the group as

> doing intellectual work which might be useful for clarification of thinking and policy on problems in the field of national morale, interpreted broadly as the morale of any country involved in the present crisis. We decided that this could best be done in the form of discussion groups which would survey the field, one nation at a time, . . . and attempt in the end to formulate the results in rather comprehensive memoranda, the material of which could be put to various uses.[49]

After initiating discussion groups on Germany and Japan, the committee hoped to turn its attention to France and the US.

In exploring what factors made for morale, or conversely, the conditions that placed morale in jeopardy, Parsons elaborated the Hippocratic standpoint developed by Henderson. This was particularly evident in his reflections on how a propaganda policy could be most effectively developed and implemented (Parsons [1942] 1964). He noted that "it would be surprising if the fundamental structural and functional aspects of it [institutionalization] should be confined to the one relatively narrow functional sphere of medical practice" ([1942] 1964: 160). On this basis, he likened the social system to a functioning organism, whose natural tendencies to heal itself could be assisted by professional intervention. In this case, the role of the Hippocratic clinician was to be played by a form of "social psychotherapy":

> Just as deliberate psychotherapy in the medical relationship is in a sense simply an extension of functional elements inherent in the structure of the role of physician, so, on the social level, the propaganda of reinforcement would be simply an extension of many of the automatic but latent functions of existing institutional patterns. ([1942] 1964: 173)

In the same way that "conscious psychotherapy takes advantage of the patterning of the physician's role" to control the patient, Parsons argued, "influence on the social structure might be exerted by deliberately working 'along with' existing control mechanisms" ([1942] 1964: 171).

The role of the physician was taken to be the appropriate model for the application of propaganda, for "to treat propaganda policy as a kind of 'social psychotherapy' is to act directly in accordance with the essential nature of the social system" ([1942] 1964: 174). By affirming the presence of shared cultural norms, in a manner akin to a psychiatrist, the social scientist could thereby help integrate dissonant tendencies into the social order. It was for this reason that the proposed propaganda agency, under the tutelage of social scientists, was to be modeled upon psychotherapy ([1942] 1964: 174).

Parsons understood very well that this kind of propaganda was directly descended from the edifying efforts of traditional social science in the US, for he emphasized that "the social sciences . . . have been particularly important in the diagnosis of the situation of society, the meanings of various phases of its history and of tendencies to change" ([1942] 1964: 165). The relationship to this traditional public was conceived in a way that inverted Small's formulation: the public was now a patient to be treated therapeutically. The role of helping the professional propagandist also provided an answer to one of the puzzles about sociology as a profession: the "functionally specific" contribution of the sociologist to the division of labor in the social sciences could include the giving of advice to propaganda agencies on the subject of sociology's special knowledge, namely, the value-orientations and norms that serve the essential well-being of the social system. Propaganda agencies were only one of the potential audiences Parsons envisioned for sociology, however, for he thought that this knowledge would be useful to other policy makers and "professionals."

These goals of sociology were to be realized in collaboration with anthropology and social psychology. The division of labor coalesced within the Committee on National Morale. The problem of morale was considered to be global, demanding a comparative analysis of how individual motivations intersected with social institutions. Given the need to determine the factors making for national morale in each particular country, the appeal of cultural anthropology was obvious. Moreover, Parsons' concern that the Committee help build national morale led him to draw on social psychology—in its applied psychotherapeutic form—for its insights into how social control could be more effectively exercised. Wartime exigencies, in this sense, provided an opportunity to use sociological analysis in such a way as to redefine the situation in terms of a more realistic and less distorted version of the liberal democratic view. What "we can 'do' about it" is, "with the backing of the defense group, to state our views and contribute our bit to getting across an acceptable definition of the situation."[50] Parsons' views on morale, propaganda, and social control complemented the activities of other members of the Committee on National Morale during its early years. In addition to offering a seminar in "morale research," Gordon Allport and Henry Murray produced a volume entitled *Worksheets on Morale* (Allport 1968: 396). Allport also collaborated on a long article surveying the contributions of social psychology to the war effort, particularly in relation to the building of morale (Allport and Veltfort 1943). Edward Hartshorne wrote on the role of youth culture in National Socialism (1941). The committee members did not limit their efforts to academic publication per se, but rather engaged in what Parsons described to President Conant as "a set of activities and plans in the field of the application of some aspects of social science to the war situation." The aim was to bring to bear "our own sociological knowledge of and approach to the social situation in those countries in order to clarify some of the principal factors which must underlie any intelligent practical policy." Such a "broad understanding of the 'state of the social system'" was "of great importance in such practical fields as propaganda policy, the rather general orientation of foreign policy, and perhaps most of all, the problems of post-war settlement."[51] As Parsons stressed to Conant, "this initiative has already born at least indirect fruit." His junior colleague and codirector of the Committee on National Morale, Edward Hartshorne, had in September 1941 joined the Psychology Division within the Office of the Coordinator of Information. As part of a shift towards the use of "comparative sociology" to provide a "general background analysis of different countries," the Psychology Division enlisted the expertise of the Harvard group on two occasions. "These two studies," according to Parsons, "have already gone far to demonstrate the possible fruitfulness of sociological and other social science techniques in an applied field in which they have not previously been utilized to any significant extent." He optimistically noted the interest of the Coordinator's Office in work of this kind.[52]

Closely related to this initiative, in the fall of 1941, Parsons had been approached by Dr. Bartholomew Landheer of the Netherlands Information Bureau in New York. He proposed to Parsons that "a series of sociological studies of the social situation in some of the occupied countries of Europe be initiated." Subsequently, a meeting was held, attended by a group of sociologists and representatives of governments in exile from occupied countries (the Netherlands, Poland, Czechoslovakia, and France). It was agreed that a study of the preoccupation social structures of the four countries would be undertaken, to be followed by an investigation of the "social effects of military occupation." The coordinator's office, Parsons noted, was also very interested in these proposed studies.

Parsons did not view this as mere application or as consulting work. He emphasized to Conant that it was urgent that these initiatives be integrated into the academic structure of Harvard. While faculty and students could take part in such activities on an informal basis, "if . . . funds and official status were available a very much higher order of accomplishment would clearly be possible." Parsons thought that the Rockefeller Foundation could possibly grant funding for the Occupied Countries study, if official university status for the project could be arranged, and raised the question with Conant of whether "there might not be a possibility of attempting to get a foundation grant to promote studies of this sort more generally at Harvard."

> It should be clear that I am thinking of this whole problem in terms of the potential development and usefulness of some of the newer work which centers in parts of the fields of sociology, anthropology, and psychology, as distinguished from much of the traditional work done in such fields as economics and government. In addition to its potentiality of immediate usefulness in relation to the war the situation I have outlined would seem to present a favorable opportunity for promoting the development and recognition of this type of work. If an

experiment along these lines were successful it might have far-reaching ramifications in academic social science. I think Harvard has here an opportunity to do some pioneering work which might well have great importance for the future of the social sciences both here and in the country at large.[53]

Despite Parsons' concerted efforts, the Rockefeller Foundation ultimately declined to support the kind of university-based research initiative that he had proposed. Nevertheless, support from a different quarter suddenly materialized. Harvard was chosen as one of the sites for the Civic Affairs Training Program, which was to begin operation in 1943. Its purpose was to prepare officers "for military government service in occupied territory," through the provision of instruction in military government policies and practice, the teaching of foreign languages, instruction about "certain foreign peoples," and training about how to use one's skills and knowledge effectively in foreign countries (Hyneman 1944: 342).

Parsons was selected as one of the instructors in the program at Harvard, which had been designated to focus on China and the Mediterranean. According to Parsons, the training program held out the prospect for undertaking research projects along the lines he had been advocating. "Once in something like that," he confided to his former student, Kingsley Davis, "the chances for further opportunities opening up are very much better than they are in attempting to do anything from the outside."[54] While Parsons' task as an instructor was to impart material of relevance to the task of military administrators, he used the program as an opportunity to further refine the "comparative analysis of institutional structure," which he held to be "of great importance in fields like general foreign policy and propaganda," and "central to any proposal to administer foreign areas with a minimum of friction with the local populations."[55] More generally, Parsons saw the "army program in area and language work" as providing "a great boost to the field of comparative institutions in the future." The responsibility of training "for highly practical purposes ... ought to go quite a long way toward giving some parts of sociology a far more mature attitude and standing."[56]

In addition to administering and contributing to the army training program, Parsons continued his involvement in issues related to the morale problem in Germany. In particular, he turned his attention to how German society could be transformed into a liberal democracy in the postwar period. With his emphasis upon situations as the basis for attitudes and actions, Parsons contended that one could not simply induce desired social transformations by changing the character structures of the individual members of German society. Parsons encountered this position at a "Conference on Germany After the War," where the "psychoanalytically oriented psychiatrists" in attendance suggested that if "psychiatrically oriented 'teams'" would "educate German parents to change their ways, so as to produce nonauthoritarian personalities in their children," German society would be transformed (Parsons 1969: 63). Consistent with his views on how the emergent social order would develop, he suggested that the most effective way to transcend National Socialism was through a "dynamic change in institutions . . . those patterns which define the essentials of the legitimately expected behavior of persons insofar as they perform structurally important roles in the social system" ([1945] 1964: 239). A stable institutional structure would, in turn, ensure "the interlocking of so many motivational elements in support of the same goals and standards" ([1945] 1964: 240).

The implied interdependence between character structure and institutions meant that "any permanent and far-reaching change in the orientation of the German people probably cannot rest on a change of character structure alone, but must also involve institutional change; otherwise institutional conditions would continue to breed the same type of character structure in new generations" ([1945] 1964: 238). In effect, Parsons' recommendations for the postwar treatment of Germany drew on the insights yielded by the fusion of institutional sociology, psychotherapy, and cultural anthropology that he and his coworkers at Harvard had established.

The wartime experience of cooperation between the three fields set the stage for the formation of the Department of Social Relations in the postwar period. Parsons' strategy was complex. First, he established a functionally specific place for sociology in the division of labor in the social sciences, as exemplified in his advice on reconstruction in postwar Germany: on such matters as the systemic relations between institutional, characterological, and cultural aspects of a situation in which intervention was needed, sociology could say something distinctive about the institutional level and the interrelations between levels. Second, Parsons established a set of scholarly relationships, which mimicked the older Henderson network, between scholars in the area of social relations, and he worked to define the cognitive problems of these disciplines in relation to one another. Third, he connected this work to purposes that promised permanent subsidization. Area Studies, from which the Russian Research Center benefitted, proved to be one of the major funding success stories of the next twenty years, with the SSRC administering major programs, the Ford Foundation contributing massive amounts of money, and, ultimately, the federal government supporting the work. Area Studies is, indeed, the archetypical domain of the "expert": virtually every expert is subsidized, and the audience is small, but highly valued—persons who must make decisions relating to the national interest. Parsons had a considerable role in the governance of the Russian Research Center, and his conceptual scheme was influential among the scholars who worked in it (see Moore [1954] 1966: 181). This was precisely the relationship Parsons believed should hold between pure theory and the intellectualizations of specific professional domains.

In the postwar period, the foundations proved to be highly receptive to this model. The Russell Sage Foundation trustees "declared their faith in 'experimentation and demonstration designed to bring about a closer and more effective relationship between the professions concerned with social welfare, health, and related fields, and those engaged in advancing knowledge of human behavior,'" and secured funds from the Carnegie Corporation and Ford Foundation to advance those aims (Lansing 1956: 43). The "Gaither Report," commissioned for the new Ford Foundation, concluded that support under the heading of "Individual Behavior and Human Relations" should be directed toward "increasing the use of the knowledge of human behavior in medicine, education, law, and other professions, and by planners, administrators, and policy makers in government, business, and community affairs" (Gaither 1949: 91).[57]

Funding of this kind and, later, federal funding enabled sociologists to establish themselves in medical schools. This bond with the professions, which was alien to the SSRC mode of scientization of the social sciences as practiced in the late '20s and early '30s, was the source of a great deal of federal funding for sociology in the '50s and '60s. The sales pitch was that subsidizing sociology was an indirect subsidy to the causes that sociologists served as experts. Medical sociology research, sociologists in medical schools (and basic sociology, especially methodology that served medical social research indirectly) could thus be made the beneficiary of the desire to improve professional practice.

THE PROGRAM REALIZED

If we leap ahead to Parsons' 1959 report on the discipline, one can see that Parsons described the professionalization of sociology in terms that were virtually identical to those that he had used in the '30s. He reiterated the key idea that the audience of sociology was not the public directly, but professionals, stressing that "it is of the highest importance to the development of sociology that its relation to a whole series of applied functions be *mediated* through the professional schools which train practitioners in these functions and which form centers for 'action research' aimed at yielding directly practical results" (1959: 557).

One can also see through this text how many problems remained with the program of the professionalization of the discipline. The successes he reported were substantial: "within the last generation sociology has risen substantially in relative prestige" (1959: 553). Parsons attributed this to the professionalization of the discipline in general, and specifically to the increasing differentiation of sociology from "non-scientific aspects of the general culture, such as philosophy, religion, literature and the arts" (which is to say, differentiation from activities with a large public audience that reciprocally supports them); the differentiation of sociology as a science from "practice" and the emergence of a "proper relation" to applied fields; the differentiation of sociology from other fields in the social sciences; and the "extent to which the canons of scientific adequacy and objectivity have come to be established as the working code of the profession" (1959: 547).

The phrasing barely conceals an anxiety that is expressed elsewhere in the report. The anxiety is that, after all, the basis of sociology's success continues to be the concerns of the old edifying sociologists (the concern with the solution of the traditional social problems, and with what Parsons considers the "ideological" aspects of sociology), and that the successes of sociology with the wider public continue to overshadow the achievements of "professional" sociology.[58] He conceded that the strengthening of sociology's position in the university and "in the world of practical affairs" corresponded temporally to an increased importance of sociology as contributor "to our society's ideological 'definition of the situation'" (1959: 553). Parsons sensed, as did Mills in *The Sociological Imagination*, published the same year, that sociology was becoming fashionable, and said that "perhaps we may say that, ideologically, a 'sociological era' has begun to emerge, following an 'economic' and, more recently, a 'psychological one'" (Parsons 1959: 553). He grasped that some sociological writers had successfully tapped into the "broad ideological preoccupation" with what he called "the conformity problem," and he understood that the popularity of the discipline as an undergraduate major had little to do with, and was perhaps inimical to, its "technical" pretensions (1959: 554).

The vocabulary Parsons uses in discussing these issues is what Mary Douglas calls the language of purity and danger. "The emergence of sociology into a central position in the focus of ideological preoccupation means that it must serve as a primary guardian of the scientific tradition, counteracting the many tendencies to introduce biases and distortions" (Parsons 1959: 555). Parsons was also practical enough to recognize that the confusion between sociology and social reform, which he treats as a problem of incomplete differentiation (1959: 548), not only continued to be an essential condition for the success of sociology but was taking on ever more threatening implications as a result of its potential for breaking down the achievements of professionalism (1959: 555). Keeping the interest of undergraduate students, he saw, depended on making some concessions to their unfortunately confused expectations and "ideological" concerns. The concessions he had in mind were, however, designed to separate the activity of teaching undergraduates from the profession by creating more rigid lines between types of careers in academic sociology (1959: 554)—a strategy long discussed in SSRC circles.[59]

Today, when these pressures, and the undergraduate audience that produced them, have largely disappeared, we may more calmly begin to reflect on the coherence of the strategy of treating sociology as a "profession," and on the idea of the "mediation" of sociology's contributions through the professional schools. It is evident today that, despite Parsons' brave talk of

1959, the idea that sociologists had taken a permanent place in the medical schools "in an organizational status parallel to that of physiologists, biochemists, biophysicists, bacteriologists, and so on" (1959: 556) was in error. Sociology is in retreat in the schools of medicine and public health in which it briefly flourished, and the role of sociology in mental health, the area of the first and most successful inroads, is under assault even by the patients. However, sociologists are increasingly to be found in schools of business, but this is because organizational studies have increasingly become simply an alternative and largely autonomous specialization within management studies. We may take these two cases as alternative outcomes of a similar process.

Medical sociology was the product of grants; the "experts" it produced needed to establish a stable relationship with an audience of professional practitioners. This never happened, at least to the extent that was originally envisioned, and, as a consequence, funding ultimately diminished. The reasons physicians never took sociology seriously are many, but one that is of general significance in connection with the "professional" model is this: the methodologies and explanatory paradigms that proved so successful in establishing a domain for sociology in medicine, for example, by showing that certain medical outcomes were statistically associated with "social" variables, proved to be poorly adapted to the policy problems they revealed. The research paradigm of demonstrating a statistical relationship between some social attribute or socially distributed condition and some undesirable outcome, such as infant mortality, rarely pointed unambiguously to solutions. The solutions tried by well-meaning physicians and public health officials possessing this knowledge rarely were very effective: not only were the correlations between policy-mandated inputs and demonstrable outcomes often very low, but the character of the failures raised questions about the validity of the implicit causal reasoning that had motivated the policies. In most cases, there was a great deal of redundancy or over-determination built into the "social problems" that policies sought to eliminate: eliminating one "cause" simply meant that a different "cause" would produce the same outcome. Sociologists never overcame this deficiency or successfully adapted their methods to the practical demands of the audience, and it is unclear how they could have done so—in any case, the bond between the "experts" who were created by the grants to medical sociologists and their putative audience never gelled.

Other cases are somewhat different. Sociological ideas and methods of various kinds have entered the thinking of teachers of management, and sociology has influenced the legal profession, from the "sociological jurisprudence" of the turn of the century to the critical legal studies movement of the present. The lawyers and management thinkers who were inspired by sociology kept the audiences that these ideas gained them; the kind of continuing dependence characteristic of the relation between medicine and biochemistry was not established.

The edifying impulse has not entirely disappeared in American academic sociology. But the "public" audiences that formerly supported sociologists by buying books and attending lectures, such as the Chautauqua reading groups and liberal Protestants, have changed or disappeared. The older themes of the edifiers are now subject to programs of the welfare state that produce interested "professionals" of a different kind. A few books reach a wider public—but none of them reach a public as large as the one David Riesman reached in the 1950s or the potboilers of Father Greeley reach today. The themes of the works that do succeed, such as Robert Bellah's *Habits of the Heart* (1985) or the work of William J. Wilson, are the evergreen themes of race and poverty—Myrdal's topic—and the ills of American individualism, which are the same themes, with minor variations, that Riesman and the Lynds took up, and that had been stressed by Giddings and Ely, veterans of the cooperative movement, and by C. J. Galpin, seeker of rural community. But the trained incapacities of disciplinary sociologists to communicate to wider audiences means that successes of this kind will become less frequent, and much less relevant to the "mainstream" of the discipline. In any case, the demand for literature of this type is not sufficient to sustain an academic discipline.

Despite the endless and intermittently successful attempt to link the "behavioral sciences" to such causes as national security, the most consistent support for the creation of a professional sociology has historically come from persons who shared the social concerns of the edifiers. The primary backers of the incorporation of the social sciences into the National Science Foundation, from Harley Kilgore to Hubert Humphrey (England 1982: 54, 271), were liberal reformers.[60] So there is a sense in which professional sociology was established using the moral capital that edifying sociology had accumulated. This capital is now gone, and the path to recouping it is closed; the great venture of the creation of a professional sociology was a failure, except in the realm of conventional disciplinary politics. One aim of the "professional" model was to find a way to sustain a scientific sociology, to provide it with a secure base from which to make claims for subsidies. To the extent that mainstream sociology has "succeeded" without securing this alternative base, its successes are Pyrrhic.

"Success" is obviously not an unproblematic concept. Even so, some simple reflections on the readership and patronage of sociology will suffice to show how serious the constraints on any "solution" to the problems of the discipline are, and how fragile the "institutionalization" of the discipline has been. Albion Small's journal never did what he hoped it would: despite a content that emphasized reform authors and Christian Socialists, it remained a publication with a small and also narrow readership. Odum's *Social Forces*, made possible by the massive Rockefeller support of his institute, did better with respect to the narrowness of its audience in the '20s, when it served as a sociology journal and as a journal of opinion for and about the south, earning the approbation of such literary figures as Mencken and coming under attack by the fundamentalist ministers of North Carolina. From this point on, subsidies were essential. Even the most famous literary successes of sociology, *Middletown* (Lynd and Lynd 1929) and *The Lonely Crowd* (Reisman et al. 1950), were supported by John D. Rockefeller Jr. and the Carnegie Corporation, respectively. The necessity for direct publication subsidies waned with the academic revolution of the 1950s and '60s and the consequent expansion of library sales, which constituted an indirect subsidy for books that would not have been publishable had they been dependent on individual purchasers. Nevertheless, the increased costs of publication, the flood of published works, and the reduced ability of libraries to acquire have diminished this indirect subsidy. In a simple way, this underlines the dependence of sociology, as presently constituted, on patronage. The alternatives to this dependence are few.

A return to the public of an Ellwood is not feasible: the public of socially concerned liberal Protestants is no longer there, or is no longer capable of supporting the kinds of books Ellwood wrote. The conditions under which sociology must operate as an academic discipline in a modern university preclude this. The gap between what is accepted in the university as scholarship and what is accepted by the modern equivalents of Small's "men of affairs" is sufficiently large that few sociologists can successfully satisfy both,[61] and, in addition, satisfy the expectations and needs of increasingly disencultured undergraduate and graduate students.

9 Scientists as Agents*

A large proportion of the time and effort of scientists is spent in activities that have no obvious place in the traditional model of "basic science discovery leading to application in a marketable product." Some of this time is spent on basic science that does not lead to application in a marketable product; this can be assimilated, though very problematically, to the traditional model by regarding it as failed effort or the production of a different kind of good, such as generally available scientific knowledge that can be seen as a "public good." But an overwhelming proportion of the time and effort of scientists is spent on a series of activities that fit neither the core model nor its variations: writing grant proposals, negotiating revisions of proposals, evaluating proposals; evaluating other scientists for promotions or appointments, writing and reading letters on their behalf; evaluating students and postdocs, in ways ranging from grading students in classes to making admissions and funding decisions about them; reading (as a peer-reviewer) articles, notes, abstracts, and the like submitted for publication or to conferences, and evaluating (as an editor) the comments made by referees; evaluating other scientists for prizes or awards, membership in honorific bodies; serving as a consultant and evaluating proposals, scientists, or ideas for firms; performing site visits on behalf of funding agencies, accreditation agencies, and the like.

These evaluative activities are tremendously expensive. If one calculated the time that scientists spend on them at the same rate as consulting fees, the costs would be astronomical. But they are inseparable from the way science is presently conducted. Although obviously some of these activities can be internalized to firms, and costs reduced, it is not clear if it would be possible for there to be "science" anything like the science we are familiar with if all of these activities were internalized to firms producing for the market. Firms, indeed, rely on the existence of these activities in many ways, from obtaining financing to gaining acceptance for their products, and this has been the case at least since the era in the middle of the nineteenth century in which chemical fertilizers were introduced.

In this chapter I will attempt to say something about the economic character of the "evaluative" part of science, the part that is almost completely hidden by usual accounting methods. Yet despite the fact that the costs are hidden, there is no question that these activities involve transactions.

The transaction that occurs when a scientist agrees to spend an afternoon evaluating the work of a colleague at another university who is applying for promotion is sometimes a cash transaction—some universities pay a small honorarium for this service. Scientists are also paid consulting fees by firms for professional opinions of various evaluative kinds, which are substantively identical to those that they give within a university as part of their job, for "free" in connection with colleagues, as part of their membership on an editorial board, as a journal reviewer, or for a nominal fee as part of a grant-reviewing team. So for the most part the "payments" are implicit. We lack a coherent understanding of what goes on in these transactions: Why they exist at all? What are the larger functions they serve? What sorts of choices, markets, and competition are involved in them. These transactions markets and competitions are the subject of this chapter.

GETTING A GRIP ON THE ECONOMICS OF EVALUATION

The costs of the these "evaluative" activities are borne in peculiar ways that have the effect of hiding them: it costs about $50,000 to value evaluate and editorially prepare an article for a major medical journal, including the costs of editing and the operation of the editorial office, but not including the cost in time of peer reviewing. These costs are paid through journal revenues, which are largely the result of sales to libraries, and partly through advertising and sometimes membership dues of professional associations. So libraries contribute to the support of this expensive machinery, as do peers, who donate their valuable time, which is in turn paid for by universities and research institutions. If the journal is subscribed to by practitioners, costs are borne ultimately by customers; in this case patients and the third parties that pay on the behalf of patients. The time of scientist professors is paid for by universities, and the journals are paid for out of library budgets. These costs are in turn borne by funding agencies in the form of indirect costs, by students in the form of tuition, and so forth. So the payments are indirect and much of what makes the journal valuable—the contributions of the authors, editorial board, and peer reviewers—are part of a system of implicit payments whose character is difficult to grasp in terms of standard economic models, but nevertheless is quantitatively enormous if we consider the time and effort that these activities involve.

The peculiarly indirect and complex structure of actual payments involving science makes it very difficult for economic analysis to deal directly with flows, transactions, and choices. And since science is paid for in significant part by a complex system of state subsidies, it is difficult to value it. It is even difficult to say what the portion is. The difficulties are evident in the structure of expenditures of the universities themselves, which operate through an elaborate system of cross-subsidies. Tuition is paid at one price for undergraduates and for large categories, such as graduate students, without regard for differentials in actual costs of instruction. There are consequently huge cross-subsidies, most of which cannot be determined from an examination of university budgets. The internal economy of universities is itself complex and often purposely mysterious. For example, university managers construct elaborate strategies to deal with the fact that there are restrictions on different kinds of funds, and that much of the management of funds consists in using funds collected under one pretext for other purposes. Donations from aged alumni, for example, rarely support daily operations and are often for things that the university could do without. But there are ways of making prior assets acquired with restrictions, such as buildings, produce funds that the university can employ for other purposes. Thus a dormitory donated by an alumnus can be used to extract fees that can then be used for other purposes. Similarly, of course, for tuition fees.

One of these means has a great deal to do with science: "indirect cost" payments for grants are for the most part payments for assets the university not only owns but in many cases can raise funds (and thus double bill for), such as buildings, library assets, and so on (S. Turner 1999c). So universities can construct strategies or simply benefit from past donations in the form of money that is unrestricted in its uses and only very indirectly connected to present costs. Indeed, in some universities, particularly state universities where there are legislative restrictions on the use of particular funds, there is more or less open trading in types of funds, such as funds that can be spent on alcoholic beverages, whose exchange value varies in the way that exchange rates of different currencies vary. Needless to say, these strategies are not reflected in the "books" in any easily accessible way, and it is even very difficult to ask such apparently simple questions of accounting as "which departments do we make money on and which do we lose money on?"[1] This means that it is also very difficult to estimate the total expenditures that universities make on science, and indeed the total cost of science itself. If we are to include costs of evaluation, the subsidization of scientific publications by library budgets, and so forth, the picture would certainly look different.

There are other ways in which the economic processes in this domain can be approached. One can begin piecemeal with studies of such things as the value of a Nobel Prize in raising money for a biotechnology venture, for example, and such studies certainly point to the profound economic significance of evaluations in science. But because of the peculiar history of science studies, there is another option: one can reinterpret prior findings and theoretical efforts from other fields, notably sociology, in economic terms, in order to get a general understanding of the processes, an understanding that can subsequently be tested against piecemeal studies. Within this strategy there are a number of different possible options, and the approach I will take here reflects a set of choices in the face of these difficulties that needs to be explained in advance.

The first choice is theoretical. There is no question of simply "applying" market models to the activities I will consider. But I do not propose, or see the need for, market analogies, such as the notion of a marketplace of ideas or such notions as public goods. The main difficulty with studying and conceptualizing the vast body of activity I have described above results from the weakness of conventional models in cases in which the usual simplifications cannot be matched up with economically measurable quantities. The activities themselves, however, are not merely analogous to markets. They are genuinely economic activities, which have real (if almost always implicit and indirect) costs and consequences, and they are engaged both rationally and self-consciously strategically in a setting in which choices are made that have direct consequences for who gets what and how. Choices are made by agencies that dispense and receive real funds and sign real contracts. The choices that are made greatly affect the decisions of the scientist participants in these activities about how to choose what to do, and what to invest time and effort in.

This approach contrasts sharply with some other approaches. Uskali Mäki (1997) in a recent paper comments on his disappointment with Ronald Coase's (1974) paper on the marketplace of ideas, which, Mäki observes, is actually about publications such as newspapers (and their costs) rather than about ideas and knowledge.[2] As my comments suggest, I think that basic facts about the costs of activities in science such as the costs of journal articles have been ignored, perhaps because of the difficulties of understanding the web of implicit and indirect transactions involved. And I suspect that the basic facts about the costs of tangible and tangibly economic activities provide a necessary, and perhaps sufficient, place to start. I leave the construction of marketplace analogies and the kinds of analogies needed to apply notions like "public goods" to others, but my bias is that they are unneeded and, in the case of the evaluative activities I will consider here, actually serve to obscure the way in which scientists and the evaluative institutions of science create value. And in the end I think an answer to this question suggests a transformation of the way in which science has been understood, both by economists and by the community of science studies scholars.

My second choice has already been alluded to. My approach to the economic structure of these evaluative activities will itself be somewhat indirect. The activities can be interpreted in noneconomic terms, but the noneconomic terms point to and illuminate their economic structure. My core argument will be that there is a clear and important element that can be understood in terms of, and resonates with, though it does not precisely match, some familiar economic conceptions associated with principal-agent theory. Some of the similarities are obvious. Clearly scientists act and use science and have their science used in chronic situations of information asymmetry, or to put it somewhat differently, in situations where the users are at best only partly competent to judge the validity of the science that they use, and are also characteristically not even competent to fully understand the science that they use. This situation of chronic lack of ability to fully understand makes the notion of "information" (i.e., something that might not be known by one party to a transaction would be transparently understandable to them) of very problematic applicability in these settings. Nevertheless, asymmetries are obviously central to the activity of evaluation in science, and so is overcoming them.

The application of these concepts is obviously not easy even in the paradigm cases of principal-agent theory, and is substantially more difficult in the complex system of mutual monitoring and agency risk spreading that I will discuss. Thus while the general similarity between the problem of principal-agent theory and the problematic of monitoring in science is undeniable, because of the implicit character of transactions in science, there is no straightforward way to "apply" these notions. But there are both actual transactions and implicit transactions with significant actual costs and detectable price-like variations throughout this system. For example, in some respects the incredibly expensive and time consuming processes of evaluation discussed above are surrogates for the kinds of monitoring expenses employed in the regulation and approval of drugs by regulatory agencies, which require expensive research conducted according to standardized protocols. But in another sense, these monitoring processes are inseparable from the evaluation system of science and dependent upon it: the research must be conducted by qualified researchers, i.e., those who have subjected themselves to many of the monitoring activities discussed above by becoming PhD scientists. In addition, drug companies are eager to have peer reviewed researchers publish material related to drug testing.

To ask why this should be so is to enter directly into the complexities of concern to this chapter. A simple, but central, issue is the obsessive concern by the participants in science over pecking orders, particularly with respect to such arcane questions as the value of publishing in one journal over another or the much more extreme difference of, say, an abstract published in an obscure proceedings of a meeting and distributed and printed by a drug company. Are these obsessions irrational? The facts of science—the "informational contents"—are literally the same in each case: nothing about the "application of basic science" or the public goods model distinguishes the kinds of publication. But drug companies and researchers invest very heavily in these distinctions, with real money and costly time and effort. Are they irrational? Or do these approaches to the economics of science simply fail to understand what these activities and choices are about?

NORMS AND COUNTERNORMS: A TYPICAL PRINCIPAL-AGENT STRUCTURE

We may begin with a simple observation. In one of the most famous papers ever written on science, "A Note on Science and Democracy," Robert

Merton described four "norms" of modern science: universalism, disinterestedness, "communism," and organized skepticism. Merton inferred these norms, we are told, from the practice of scientists (1942; cf. 1973b). Three of the four relate directly to evaluative processes, and the fourth, "communism," turns out to be even more directly relevant to the concerns of this paper.

Merton's analysis has been controversial, but the controversy is itself revealing. One of Merton's critics, Ian Mitroff, argued that the "norms of science" as formulated by Merton were essentially backwards (1974). What scientists actually valued was exactly the opposite of, for example, disinterestedness. They valued passionate dedication to the goals of a project and fervent beliefs in the ideas that were being developed or the methods that were being used. Something similar could be said about the other norms. Yet Merton anticipated much of this criticism, and noted especially that, despite the norm of community possession of knowledge, there were intense priority disputes, and argued that the peculiarity of priority disputes is that they were not matters of egoism alone, but were themselves normative in character. The signpost of their normative character is the fact that disinterested observers often enter into the discussion of priority disputes to secure the norm (Merton 1973b: 292). Michael Mulkay (1976) treated the Mertonian norms as an "ideology" in the pejorative sense of a story told to the public (though he conceded that this was also a story that could be employed within science by scientists, i.e., a political mythology), but also argued that, in fact, there are no strongly institutionalized norms of this sort in science. The mythological character of the "norms" turns out to be a useful clue.

All norms exist to restrain impulses of some sort, so there would be no "norms" unless there was something valued, desired, or sought for them to be "counter" to. However, there is a special class of human relationships in which self-denying norms are especially prevalent, and it is this class of relationships that is the subject of principal-agent theory. The theory concentrates on those relationships in which we rely on someone whose interests conflict with ours, and on the costs of dealing with the problem of conflicts of interest. A good paradigm case of this is the relationship between a client and a lawyer. The client trusts the lawyer to exert himself on behalf of the client. However, the client not being a lawyer, is not in a position to effectively judge whether the lawyer is properly representing the client or giving the client adequate legal counsel and advice. This is why trust is required in this relationship. Not only is the client suffering from a deficiency in information or inability to make judgments, but the lawyer is a person with interests as well which the lawyer can advance, potentially, by cheating the client. Another case of an agency relationship is the relationship between a client and a stockbroker. The stockbroker benefits, as the lawyer might, by doing commission work for the client. The stockbroker also advises the client on what work needs to be done. Similarly the lawyer advises a client not only about what legal steps to take but benefits from the client's decision to take those legal steps that are necessarily costly to the client and beneficial to the lawyer who is paid for carrying out those steps.

The term "trust" has a certain seductiveness, but it is a seductiveness born of the illusion that something is being explained by it. Unfortunately, in the writings of more than a few commentators, trust functions as an unmoved mover, or as a kind of mystery that produces results without having a cause. Although principal-agent theory is not the only approach to trust, it deals with the costs of routine systems of trust that are impersonal and rely on the existence of, or beliefs about, the incentives under which people operate. Incentives means tangible, if sometimes indirect and difficult to measure, costs. Just as love is free, but roses are not, the cognitive respect we give science is not purchased by science directly, but is maintained through activities that do have costs.

In the cases of lawyers and stockbrokers, matters are simple: the self-denying normative structure of the codes and rules that these two professions operate under is clear. A stockbroker should be aggressive and motivated by money. A stockbroker who is not would be unlikely to do what he needed to do to keep your business. Similarly, a lawyer needs to be aggressive and motivated by money in order to do anything on your behalf. Yet, at the same time, both lawyer and stockbroker must substitute the client's interest for their own interests. The "norms" of legal representation and stockbroking are characteristically statements of the absolute subordination of the stockbroker's and lawyers interests to the client's interests. The "counter-norm" is that the stockbroker and lawyer should be tenacious and highly motivated, and motivated by the fact that someone is paying them for these services. Even lawyers, when they hire other lawyers, want the shark to be an entirely altruistic shark who puts their interests before the shark's own interests in every respect. And we know that there are some mechanisms for punishing a lawyer who violates the rules, and that indeed the bar association disbars people, uses its dues to support actions involving the punishment of lawyers, and so forth.

At first glance this seems to have little to do with science. Sharks in science are not sharks on behalf of the interests of a client. But science is also about ambition, score keeping, playing by particular rules of the game, and being a shark in debunking false claims. Scientists do all of these things in the context of a large and complex set of institutions, a large number of which are devoted to regulation, which in one fashion or another involve people acting authoritatively on behalf of science. Science is thus "political" in a mundane sense. As I have suggested, scientists make authoritative decisions in the name of others, such as decisions on behalf of organizations or collective bodies or in the name of science itself, and have such decisions made about them. Many of these are "gatekeeping" decisions, and indeed the business of gatekeeping is perhaps the primary means of exercising authority in science.

The making of evaluative decisions and the exercise of authority or advisory authority is a pervasive fact of scientific life: in directing the work of subordinates, in asking funding bodies for resources, and the like. But this political "decision-making" character of science is also a largely undiscussed fact—whether by commentators on science, philosophers of science, or sociologists of science.[3] The reason for this neglect, in part, is that these decisions occur under a particular theory or ideology: the idea that the scientists making the decisions are operating neutrally or meritocratically, and that the public role of science itself is neutral. Science is thus mundanely political, but its overtly political features are conceived to be unpolitical. This line of reasoning has the false implication that the activities are somehow inessential to science, or that it is transparent that there are merely administrative, and that they work so effectively because scientists do in fact always agree on merit.

The problem of concern to me in the rest of this discussion is the problem of what this "regulatory" activity means. My concern is not to debunk the "meritocracy" argument so much as to explain the mystery that it produces—the mystery of why, if merit is so transparent, there are so many and such expensive mechanisms for assuring it. There is a sociological literature, to be discussed below, that treats it as a matter of the maintenance of "cognitive authority," and this is certainly part of the story. But reading institutions politically is not the same as explaining why they exist, how they came to exist, and why they take the form they do. The fact of decision-making on behalf of "science" is the feature of these institutions that is the topic of the norm-counternorm structure, and it is this activity—judging and evaluating—that produces many costs and incentives, such as the incentive of publication in a prestigious journal or winning a Nobel Prize, which is the proximate goal of many scientists' efforts. But the activity itself deserves some consideration, for it is unusual, especially when compared to the usual subjects of principal-agent theory.

REPRESENTATION, BONDING, AND MEMBERSHIP

All collective or political activities depend on some model—an "ideology," in the nonpejorative sense—of representation (Pitkin 1989). As I have noted, one peculiarity of decision-making in science is the idea that any scientist, or at least the most accomplished scientists, can truly represent or speak for "science" as a judging or evaluative body, without being elected or otherwise "chosen." Thus scientists engaged in peer review are understood to represent not their personal or economic interests but to be impartial judges evaluating from the point of view of scientific opinion at its best. Although in practice it is accepted that scientists who have made accepted research contributions to a particular area are the most competent to judge new work in that area, it is also believed that they "speak for science" rather than for themselves when acting as a representative.

Why do these arrangements exist at all? As we have seen, this is an ambiguous question, in that one might choose to interpret decision-making processes in accordance with the political mythology of science and say that they are part of the administration of things rather than the governance of people. Some scarce resources—jobs, research opportunities, and so forth—do exist, and allocating these requires some administrative expense. It might be thought that mere administration—at least if the mythology were true—would be a matter whose costs could be minimized, delegated to scientists who function essentially as clerks, leaving talented scientists for more important work. Obviously that is not how these processes work. And as difficult as it might be to estimate the costs, it is clear that the costs go very far beyond administrative expense, and even the administrative expenses are largely connected with a degree of evaluative scrutiny that occurs in these cases. So the problem of the economic function of these expensive activities is intact. Why are they performed in the way they are?

Central to what follows is the relation between who evaluates and the value of the evaluation—something that the "transparent merit" model necessarily denies, and that conflicts with at least some understandings of Merton's "norm" of universality. It is obvious that some evaluations are more valuable than others because the evaluators are more valuable as evaluators, the distinction is more competitive, or the journal more prestigious. The pursuit of more valuable evaluations or certifications has real costs—the costs of investing the time and effort to publish in an especially competitive journal, for example. My thesis here is that there is a market for evaluators and evaluations, and that the existence of this market is critical to understanding science. The market is bilateral; that is to say the evaluators compete with one another—how and why will become clear shortly—and the scientists who are being evaluated compete as well, but also make complex market choices between the forms of evaluation available to them. The market is competitive on both sides. But there are also potential problems with these markets that can make them seriously defective, and it is a matter of policy interest, and interest to scientists, to consider the effects of the workings of these markets, and to alter institutional arrangements in response to these defects.

The markets are about agency relationships, and to understand them it is necessary to understand something about the complexities of the agency structures that occur in science. When scientists exert discipline, reward, exclude, and accept, they act as "agents" or representatives, and when it is done on behalf of a journal or professional society, the society itself is the political embodiment of a collectivity. The simplest agency structure is "representation." The decision-maker is an agent of a collectivity, either an actual one, such as the American College of Obstetrics and Gynecology, which is in the business of certification (quite literally) for practitioners, has a publication, and selects scientific articles through the actions of editors who act as representatives, or a hypothetical one, such as the "scientific community" or "science" itself. The agency relationship has costs for the members and for the agents, though the costs may be difficult to estimate and the transactions themselves may be implicit.

Science differs from medical practice in a decisive way. In medical settings (similar to law and stockbroking) there are typically single certifiers, such as the American College of Obstetrics and Gynecology, or the bar association. In these monopolistic cases, there are costs, benefits, enforcement, and so forth, but no markets in which certifying organizations compete. In science, matters are considerably more complex. The basic logic of the relationship is nevertheless the same: getting a PhD or submitting a paper to a journal is a transaction in which someone pays for a form of certification. The difference is this: in medicine or law one either passes one's exams and is certified or one fails. In science, the individual pursuing a career can choose between different forms of certification, add different forms of certification to one's CV, pay different prices for different forms of certification and thus develop and act on a strategy for accumulating forms of certification. These certifications are then valued in various market-like transactions—such as employment decisions—by buyers who themselves can think and act strategically about the market of certifications.

What function does this system of agency relations perform? There are various possible ways to answer this question, but the most straightforward and obvious one is this. The agents or evaluators by the act of evaluation assume risks. The economic function of the activity is to spread risks that arise from wrong answers, scientific error, bad scientists, and so forth. The process here has many imperfect analogues in more familiar economic activities, such as cosigning for a loan, bonding, signaling, and so forth. My preference is for the notion of bonding: an act in which an agent pays for an assurance (in this case an assurance by other scientists) that the agent will act in accordance with a principal's interests in a situation of information asymmetry (cf. Jensen and Meckling 1976). But the analogy is imperfect in several respects. The asymmetry is not simply a matter of "information" and the assurances take various forms, such as assurances about minimal competence as a scientist, or minimal adequacy sufficient for publication in the case of a journal article. In each case—for example when an academic program awards a degree or a journal accepts an article, the program or journal assumes a risk that its assurances of adequacy will be found out to be false, and the consequence of error is damage to "reputation," which translates into a loss of the value of future assurances of the same type. This feature is central—and for this reason, and for convenience, I will retain the term "bonding."

The term seems merely to be about reputation. Reputation is a deceptively simple notion, however. There is a sense in which reputation is contrasted with reality, and thus that there is some sort of falsity or illusoriness of reputation. But in the case of the bonding that happens in science, this is potentially misleading, for it suggests that no real value is created by the activities of evaluation. Something like this suggestion appears in what Merton called the Matthew effect (1973b), by which scientists whose achievements are recognized in various ways "accumulate advantage" so that a scientist who has gone to the right schools, published in the right journals, and won the right prizes is more likely to have his achievements cited. The implied distinction is between the intrinsic value of the science done by the scientist and the increased impact that results from advantage. But if we think of the process of accumulating advantage in terms of bonding, it becomes clear that at each point of accumulation something has actively been done, at a cost, to create value through reducing risks, specifically by distributing risks to people other than the scientist accumulating the advantages. So the total value of the "product" in question, the science, is not only the ideas, the intrinsic value, but the guarantees that come along with it, in the form of risk bearing actions taken by editors, hiring departments, and prize givers, each of whom has put the value of their journal, department, or prize at risk by their actions. The accumulation of advantage is thus like the accumulation of cosigners to a loan. So where Merton, operating in terms of notions about merit, and concerned to make the argument that science proceeds successfully and without external interference in terms of merit, finds it puzzling and problematic that advantage accumulates, the "bonding" approach finds it understandable.

Why is there so much "bonding" in science? One of the concerns of principal-agent theory is the problem of adverse selection, and there is a sense in which one can see the web of evaluation activities that is so important to science itself as a means of avoiding a large number of potential adverse selection problems. Scientists themselves need to select ideas to pursue, to believe, and to take seriously. Academic departments and businesses employing scientists need to make hiring decisions. These decisions are almost always made in the face of asymmetries, and where there are risks of making bad choices. "Bonders" provide ways of spreading these risks. To put this very simply, because in science only a few can seriously evaluate an idea, the rest must rely on their certifications of the idea, and thus certification takes on a massively important role.

A somewhat more puzzling question is why are there so many forms of bonding in science. The system, incarnated in the CV, is one in which single distinctions do not suffice. Not only does a scientist seek many kinds of certifications, they are sought from, and available from, a wide variety of sources. Understood as a total market or system, it is complex in the following ways: most of the certifications are indirect with respect to matters of truth. What is judged is the minimal adequacy or interest of a journal article or PhD dissertation. The effect is that a scientist acquires various "certifications" from a variety of sources, and these certifications overlap, sometimes involving the personal quality of the scientist, sometimes of a particular article, sometimes, as in the case of prizes, for a "discovery" or "contribution" that spans many years and consists of many items. The fact that they overlap amounts to the building in of redundancy. An established scientist will have passed through many tests, of which the CV is the archaeological record. The existence of all this redundancy is a relatively recent phenomenon in the history of science, and it deserves its own discussion, which I will provide shortly. It must suffice to say that there is obviously a market here, with both demand for bonding and an incentive to supply it. So far I have focused on the demand side of this relationship. I now turn to supply.

BONDING AND VALUE

What I have said here about bonding suggests that assuming risks is a major activity of science, that one might expect that it will show up in the form of transactions, and points out that it does, for example the phenomenon of accumulated advantage. But this account assumes that there is something of value already there for the transactions to be about, and in a sense this is the central puzzle of the economics of science: what is the value of knowledge? Several points ought to be made about scientific knowledge that bear on this question. First, scientific knowledge is "embodied knowledge," in the sense that it has little or no value as pure information. One needs to know what to do with it and this requires an investment in scientific education.

This simple fact is critical to understanding the way that scientists solve the problem that any possessor of embodied knowledge faces: how to convert one's knowledge into money. One way is to employ it in the production of things that can be bought and sold—this is the model around which much discussion of science has revolved, and it produces the familiar puzzle of the value of basic science, and such solutions as the idea of science as a "public good." Patent law is a kind of extension of the notion of product that creates an artificial right to produce something that can itself be bought and sold but is valuable only if it either produces something or prevents something from being produced. But much of science cannot be converted into such a right simply because there are no products with sufficiently high market value that patenting makes any sense and the patent process is limited to things that it makes sense to create rights about. But there are other options for scientists to convert their embodied knowledge into money.[4] One widely employed option is consulting. Here there is no mystery about the existence of a market, the existence of competition, and the existence of market pricing processes.

A primary way in which knowledge can be converted into money is through the transmission of that knowledge to others, at a price. Teaching is a primary source of income, or a large source of income, for the possessors of many kinds of knowledge, such as musicians. Musicians are also paid for performances, and this is a useful model for understanding the value of scientific performances. Musicians are not, for the most part, their own judges. There is a public audience for music. Science, however, is different. There is a public audience for science, to be sure, but it is an audience that assesses science in very general ways, and through its products, but does little to distinguish among scientists, and to the extent that it does, is inclined to grant much greater credit to the kinds of scientists who write for the public than scientists themselves do.

If we invert the usual way of thinking about the relationship between these performances and judging and think of them on the analogy of the kind of music teacher who charges, and raises, tuition on the basis of successful performances, we have a model for the role of scientific publication, as well as a very good explanation for scientists' concerns about having their successes credited to them. Performances, or discoveries, are a source of demand for the other things that the scientist can do, such as teach and make judgments. This close link suggests an alternative view of Merton's norm of "communism." There is no need for musicians to have an "ethic" of public performance, since performance is, in effect, a condition of their making money through tuition. One can of course, as a musical non-expert, judge the products of musical tuition, so the link is not so close. Still, performing demonstrates one's possession of the embodied knowledge that one charges tuition to transmit to students.

In science, unlike art, production and assessment are closely related, and indeed, since developing hypotheses and testing them almost invariably have implications for the validity of previous hypotheses, there is a sense in which all science is authentication. Yet the activity of criticism and production is separated in various ways, in that there is a moment of pure thought, so to speak, in which hypotheses are formulated; and other moments when hypotheses are, sometimes very expensively, tested; and another when scientists assess the work of other scientists by means such as peer review or simply reading and criticizing the works of other scientists. Finally, with art, there is an object whose value is increased by the efforts of art historians. In science, matters are much more obscure. People are bonded; ideas are bonded; some bonding, such as degree granting, is the sort of thing one pays for, some, such as publication in a famous journal, is not.

One might say, however, that this pattern is characteristic of the old economics of science, in which a particular kind of competition for talent, between university departments of physics, chemistry, and the like, was central. Whether there has been, or might be, a radical change as a result of present changes, such as the corporatization of bioscience is a question I will take up in the conclusion.

THE MARKET FOR BONDERS

The problem of judgment of peers is that these judgments themselves require bonding because there are known conflicts of interest that arise in judgments of competitors and judgments of work in the same specialty. Evaluators may be biased in judging the general significance of work in a particular area that resembles theirs, and, if they are competing for fame and fortune, they have a general interest in seeing work that cites and, thus, extends their being funded. By the same token, they may have an interest in impeding the research of a competitor. Competition of exactly the same kind exists between "bonders" as such. Journals compete, prizes compete, and departmental programs and universities compete. Departments compete with corporations in the hiring of scientists. And there are various incentives to the creation of novel bonding mechanisms, such as official journals and scientific societies.

The potential risk, from the point of view of the journal or the department, is the risk of bonding too much, or the wrong things, so that credibility as a bonder (and consequently the value of implicit "certification") is diminished. The more demanding the standards, the more prestigious the certification might be. But if the standards are different in such a way that there are well recognized achievements that fail according to these standards then the value of certification is likely to diminish generally, for the users of certification will be unable to say when the certification is useful and when it is not. Overly generous certification obviously risks the same effect, especially if it is potentially biased, for example in the direction of allowing dangerous or useless therapies. The market, in short, demands a certain uniformity and punishes those who deviate from it, though the uniformity is in effect a moving equilibrium. But the "market" is not closed: the rise of new forms of scientific activity may make previously important certifications peripheral or worthless.

Central to what I have argued here is that there are different kinds of bonding—from journal gatekeeping, to grant giving, to degree granting, and award giving—that are redundant and overlapping. By this I mean that no single mechanism is sovereign or final. It must be noted that it is part of the founding mythology of modern science that no person is authoritative in science. The experience of the prosecution of Galileo by the church was formative: scientific bodies were generally reluctant to certify scientific truths, to avoid the risks of error. If we recognize the lack of sovereignty in the agency activities of scientists as bonding representatives, it becomes obvious that under normal historical circumstances—that is to say circumstances of polyarchy rather than a Stalinist uniformity—there will always be a variety of overlapping communities, consumer groups, and forms of certification that will sometimes agree and sometimes fail to agree, sometimes produce equivalent bonding results and sometimes not.[5]

The model I have constructed here points toward some way of characterizing the intentions of the parties to at least some of these processes. Buyers of science have various purposes, such as being cured or annihilating their enemies by the use of nuclear weapons. The consumers have a need for certified knowledge because it is cheaper for them to accept certification than to find out for themselves. But there may be competing certifiers or bonders. In the simplest case there is a kind of equilibrium of bonding. The "results" of science are thus standardized so that one can choose between the scientifically bonded and the unbonded. In situations of scientific change, the situation will typically be more complex. Users may be buying, and happy with the results of, scientific work that is not universally certified or bonded by scientists, but only by some small faction. This may persist indefinitely, though to retain the credibility of bonding as such, scientists have an interest in giving some sort of final judgment on particular claims, especially if those claims have market appeal and are bonded by competing bonders. To fail to recognize a genuine new achievement is to become less valuable as a bonder. And it is perhaps for this reason that bonding agencies seldom subject themselves to the risk of making direct and unqualified endorsements of scientific claims. In the end, the majority does not rule, but rather the credibility market and its demands rule.

It is this market that produces the distinctive norms of science described by Merton. "Disinterestedness" is just a norm of bonding as such. A journal or prize that was known to be biased would lose some of its value for bonding. "Organized skepticism" is not so much a norm as a description of a situation in which participants recognize the inadequacy of the means they possess to judge the claims of science—the very situation that produces the demand for bonding. The term "organized" is an important qualification: there are actual means of bonding, such as degree granting and the like, between which the skeptic chooses. "Communism" or publicity is another matter entirely, and I think one on which, as I have suggested, Merton was simply in error. There are advantages to keeping trade secrets if they are secrets one can exploit. There is a patent mechanism for preserving the secrets' use and protecting it from copiers. Because science can be produced as a public performance or, sometimes, kept secret and used as a product, scientists have a choice—the choice is dictated by their interests and those of their funders, and does not always lead to making scientific results public. "Universalism" is a descriptive feature of the market and another way of expressing the political mythology of representation. If by some bizarre circumstance, scientists were confined to something like a sovereign buyer such as Stalin, it would be rational to be non-universalistic, as indeed Lysenko and his associates were, and of course Hitler's scientists were as well. Is this, or Islamic science, some sort of normative aberration? In the sense that granting epistemic sovereignty to any particular tradition or agent is a violation of the basic political mythology of science that is the foundation of its notion of representation, it certainly is. But universalism does not demand universal agreement, just the agreement of representatives speaking properly for science.

THE NEW SITUATION OF SCIENCE

The basic argument of this chapter has been simple. Bonding is an economically essential feature of science that is a result of the high cost of assessing alternatives personally. Bonding, certifying, accepting, using, and so forth are real acts, acts that are not at all cost free. In the end, however, the overall benefits are very close to those conferred by the rule of law and the reduction of transaction costs that the rule of law enables. The real scientific revolution is the revolution that substantially reduced those costs by the emergence of an effective bonding market, itself the product of incentives, notably incentives rooted in the imperative of making money out of the possession of knowledge.

Scientists and non-scientists alike rely on, or treat as information, things that scientists say without having any knowledge of the opinions of this handful of certifying figures, and the certifying figures are themselves certified and re-certified by the many and highly redundant indirect means discussed above. Instead, there are many certifying mechanisms of the sort I have described that the user does rely on, such as the fact of acceptance in a journal, the granting of research funding and support of the project, the high academic position of the person reporting the finding, and so forth. The striking development from the kind of *Gemeinschaft* of early science is that science is now able to proceed effectively by accepting the certifications and recognizing the certifying mechanisms of other groups in science. And, unlike face-to-face mechanisms, these mechanisms of certification can be extended in such a way as to permit an enormously complex division of labor in which no one's understanding extends very far. If we can trust the market for bonding to produce adequate bonders, we can trust the results of science where there are such markets. In short, it is the market for bonding in which we place our trust, and on which our trust in science properly rests.

From the point of view of this chapter, the basic question raised by the corporatization of science, and especially biotechnology, is whether the system described here is historically doomed—bound to an era of academic competition that perhaps has already passed its peak and is being transformed into something else entirely. The usual way of thinking about what it might turn into is a world that is indirectly dominated by the demands of investors, of the source of the funds necessary to produce science. Since these funds far outstrip the funds available through teaching, it stands to reason that they will become—as government funding became—the locus of competition. But government funding of science was in effect an extension of the academic system, in which academic prestige governed peer review and if anything simply made it more powerful. So the new question is this: is the autonomy of science in the sense of scientific control over the standards of science compromised by these new funding sources?

To begin to address this question it is perhaps useful to discuss some ways in which the academic-governmental system itself has sometimes gone wrong or been accused of going wrong. It is well known, for example, that there are critics of the HIV-AIDS connection who argue that the huge AIDS research establishment is committed to a hypothesis and refuses to fund other approaches. High-energy physics research facilities and telescopes, notoriously, are scarce resources: opportunities to do research are allocated by like-minded committees, with the effect that the possibilities of research are limited. When there are no alternative sources of funding, these committees are effectively monopoly buyers, and "market" competition disappears in favor of science by decision. Nuclear power researchers failed to preserve their independence from the industry (Morone and Woodhouse 1989). In many disciplines, notably economics and sociology, it has been argued that the power of certain top journals, together with the peculiarities of competition for space in those journals, has served to elevate particular styles of research and exclude others, thus distorting the standards of the disciplines and the disciplines themselves. In each of these cases there is a dominant player whose conduct dictates the conduct of others, including the standards of evaluation.

These problem cases raise some serious questions about whether the arrangement I have described in this chapter, in which a scientist's acting as an agent for science provides certification or what I have called "bonding" independently, competitively, and in different but overlapping ways, is vulnerable to a shift in the weights of forms of market power of the sort that corporate science represents. In its most advanced form, the form familiar to us, it created a powerful internal market and set of incentives that propelled the development of science, reduced the risk of bad science. But the "system" I have described is an oddity in the history of science. University science and the research university came to their position of dominance in science only during the twentieth century. The idea of scientific authorship and the system in which a scientist acting as an agent certified the science of others, which is so characteristic of twentieth-century science, was very weakly developed.[6]

It would be ironic, but hardly surprising, if the success of science governed by this evaluative market were to lead to the demise of the system itself. The system depends on mutual monitoring through implicit agency transactions. But corporations do not participate in this process. They don't benefit by editing journals, and the journals would probably not be trusted if they did. Yet the problems of monitoring and evaluation that this loose system solved do not vanish. The "information asymmetries" that always exist in science still exist. Investors may need, or come to need, more and different types of monitoring and information. Conflicts of interest would still arise over evaluations. And the fact that cash has already invaded the "old" system of bonding in the form of payments for evaluation, suggests that a surrogate for the old system of cashless "credit" is in the process of emerging. This will almost certainly be a system that is less "public" than academic evaluation was, and in which academic science and its scheme of competitive incentives is marginalized and made ineffectual, and its web of indirect devices replaced by more direct forms of monitoring and assessment. The real irony is that this replacement will almost certainly, and justly, command less respect by the consuming public. The strong resistance to genetically modified foodstuffs in much of the world testifies to the suspicion in which corporate science will likely be held. Replacing the old evaluative system may thus kill the goose that laid the golden eggs.

10 Expertise and the Process of Policy Making
The EU's New Model of Legitimacy

> With every advance in centralization the man who uses his hands is brought under subjection by the man who wields the sword or pen. The secretariat begins as the servant and ends as the master, as every executive officer in our dominions laments. It is inevitable. In a loose aggregate of small parts where every family must fend for itself, it is the man whose muscles are hard, whose hands are deft, and whose judgment sound that is valued most. . . . But when . . . social activities have to be coordinated from a center then it is necessary to pick out the pure brains, the men who specialize in thinking. For a thinker is really a man who spends his time making other people think as he does, and consequently act as he thinks. (Hocart [1936] 1970: 126)

This quotation comes from a book by the English anthropologist A. M. Hocart who wrote in the first half of the twentieth century and who ignored the trend in anthropology that placed exclusive emphasis on the study of whole primitive societies and rejected as unscientific the study of the process of civilization itself. The general principle Hocart enunciates here is unmistakably instantiated in the peculiar political phenomenon known as the European Community (EC).

Much of literature on the European Community, however, has emphasized the peculiarities of the community as a political form, and concerned itself with the question of how to make the European Community more like traditional models—more federal, or more "democratic." What I would like to argue instead is that the European Community is a political form that represents an extension of forms of rule that are found in embryonic form elsewhere in the western political tradition that are not "democratic," and that the emergence of these forms into a practical governing regime tells us more about what is wrong and also historically dead about liberal democracy than the ideal of liberal democracy, used as a standard of evaluation, tells us about the European Community. I will suggest that the vestments of parliamentary democracy are simply misleading about the nature of this regime, and perhaps irrelevant as a standard.

In a note to the passage quoted in the epigraph, Hocart commends Tocqueville's account, *in L'ancien Regime* Book II, of "the way in which the clerks have gradually bored their way from the center through the whole feudal structure leaving only the shell" (Hocart [1936] 1970: 126n46). In the text, he comments that, as regimes change, "those who cannot adapt themselves to change, fade into ceremonial attendants . . . [while] effective power passes into the hands of the clerks, in the old wide sense of the term" ([1936] 1970: 126). My concern here will be to distinguish the ceremonial from the effective, or as Bagehot put it the "dignified" from the "efficient," and the shell from the center.

The standard of liberal democracy is relevant with respect to the question of what sort of a political phenomenon the European Community is, though the relevance is negative. What I will argue is that the community is not, as it has sometimes appeared, merely a kind of peculiar executive department of a quasi-state with a quasi-parliament, but rather represents a distinct form of rule with the capacity to supplant liberal democracy. Indeed, I will argue, part of the point of the European Community, and perhaps its main point, is to provide an alternative political structure that is capable of dealing with issues that European national liberal democracies have been incapable of dealing with. Usually the way one understands a sentence like this would be in terms of "the national" part of the phrase "national liberal democracies." Obviously there are problems that national liberal democracies cannot solve precisely because they are merely national and this is what justifies the creation of supranational bodies through treaty. This feature of the European Community, however, masks a much more important phenomenon, namely the phenomenon pointed to by Hocart, in which intellectuals or more precisely specialists and experts, come to replace the political form that existed before centralization and to absorb to themselves functions and features of the national state, or of other less centralized political forms.

In what follows I will argue that the EC is intelligible as its own form of rule, unlike democracy but taking over the functions of democracy. It is a system with a non-democratic, or rather non-majoritarian, ideal of consensual agreement as the basis of action. It has a political class, which is integrated vertically from the European Union (EU) down to regional bureaucrats, and organized into categories corresponding to highly differentiated bodies of bureaucratic and technical expertise, which take over not only executive functions but also the functions of discussion. And it has its own distinctive approach to the problem of legitimacy, which is tied closely to the requirements of its distinctive ideal of agreement and to the work of its political class.

COMITOLOGY, AGENDA SETTING, AND UNANIMITY: EXPERTS AS THE POLITICAL CLASS OF THE EUROPEAN COMMUNITY

Commentators have often noted the peculiarity of many of the procedures that have evolved into standard practice in the course of the history of the European Community. One particular practice that has been central to

European Community politics at the treaty or constitutional level is the institutional tension between the federalist centralizing thrust of the community and the existence of checks on this thrust which constrain community activities and policies by demanding or strongly preferring unanimity in decision-making. This is sometimes traced to the contrast between the main precursors to the European Community—the European Coal and Steel Community, which had a "High Authority" and was supranational, and the Organization of European Economic Cooperation, set up to administer Marshall Plan money, which was purely intergovernmental and operated through negotiations between states (Tsebelis and Kreppel 1998: 56–57).

The significant "constitutional" events in the history of the European Community reflected the balance between the two principles, as well as their persistence. At the time of the French boycott from 1966 to 1970, requirements of unanimity still functioned in the traditional manner of treaties. The continued existence of the treaty itself required unanimity, and a state that wished to block the activities of the commission was in a position to do so. This particular feature of the constitutional structure of the European Community has continued to have very powerful effects, even as it was limited, reaffirmed for particular issues, and so on.

To simplify a long and familiar history, the present form of this compromise is the comitology procedure, by which conflicts between the Commission and the European Parliament, as well as issues of implementation of legislation, are referred to committees. To quote from the European Parliament itself,

> The committees which are forums for discussion consist of representatives from Member States and are chaired by the Commission. They enable the Commission to establish a dialogue with national administrations before adopting implementing measures. Committees base their opinions on the draft implementing measures prepared by the Commission. (European Commission 2004)

This is a product of the entrenched regulative ideal of unanimity. As one commentator put it, it is the "constitutional fudge which glues the Union together by filling in the fundamental gulf between federalism and intergovernmental cooperation" (Chambers 1999: 100). And in this and other forms it means instead that an enormous amount of activity must be dedicated to the achievement of unanimity.

One might naturally ask then who is doing the work of achieving unanimity and how is it achieved? The answer is precisely of the kind Hocart would have expected. The unanimity achieved is unanimity among experts or among policy makers who are experts but also function in some indirect or informal ways as national representatives. Much could be said about, so to speak, the sociology of negotiations under the expectation of unanimity between persons either formally representing different nations or informally doing so and formally and informally concerning themselves with the achievement of policies that would secure unanimity. In the first place this is work that, like diplomacy itself, creates its own culture and since the kind of unanimity that in fact is domain specific, which is to say is about certain topics such as telecommunications policy, the tendency is to turn such questions into matters of expertise; expertise being itself a form of unanimity seeking, because experts in effect have power if and only if there is unanimity with respect to what it is they are expert about.

The quest for unanimity is, in Kantian terms, a regulative ideal, that is to say something that one must always desire. It thus produces a specific political task: to produce these consensuses. The more effort required, the more central the activity in this class becomes. But in the European Community the business of reaching consensus—which is very different from the business of reaching consensus in a party system where there is majority voting in parliament, in which such phenomena as party discipline and personal advancement are central—rapidly takes on a life of its own. More importantly, however, is that the task is not, as in diplomacy, the general business of relations between nations involving the actual agendas of nations in relation to one another, but is rather broken into particular bureaucratic sub-groupings, such as telecommunications policy or drug regulation.

Here the relationships between this new class and the class of experts become much more transparent. It is an old saying that people in the same profession from different countries are more alike than people in these professions are like others in different professions from their own countries, and the same point holds in an even more extreme way in relation to expertise. In matters of business, for example, businesses operate across national boundaries, include multinational state workers and managers, are often also owned by groups with different national backgrounds, and so forth. Employment of individuals flows from company to company. So to be an expert in a particular domain, such as drug regulation or telecommunication policy, is typically to already share in a very rich body of non-national background knowledge and indeed to some extent to be operating in a setting in which nationality is irrelevant though national circumstances and situations are not. This is already the *de facto* situation of the expert. In addition to this, it may be the case that the decision-making activity itself requires disciplinary knowledge, for example, in pharmacology or chemistry, which is already largely internationalized. So we not only have a political class, but a class of specialists or experts who share a great deal of common knowledge and common experience, which is not shared at all with the public at large.

VERTICAL BUREAUCRATIC INTEGRATION: SUBSIDIARITY

The second distinctive feature of the European Community as a kind of political alternative to liberal democracy involves the relationships at the working level between European Community bureaucracies and national and regional bureaucracies. Federalism in its American form operated with clear distinctions between not only the powers of the constituent state and the powers of the federal government but also, in practice, in terms of distinctions between domains. The federal government basically was not in the business of doing the things that the state governments were in the business of doing. This changed after the US Civil War when the powers of the federal government expanded through changes in the Constitution and through the interpretation of the Constitution in ways that expanded the meaning of clauses in the Constitution. The structure of this kind of federalism depends on the fact that at each level—state, county, city—there are elected officials who control their own bureaucracies, which are organized in accordance with the specific functions of the type of government and differ from one another. In principle there are no direct links of authority from a federal agency to a corresponding state or local agency, and indeed the agencies have legally distinct functions.

Ultimately the revenue collecting powers of the federal government, particularly through taxation on income, greatly exceeded the capacity of states to generate revenue and this led to a relationship in which states could be governed by federal regulations if they accepted federal money for programs that benefitted the states, but which were designed in a way that reflected federal interests and federal views of particular problems. This undermined the principle of federalism by making it possible for the federal government to impose mandates as conditions for funds. Thus the primary link is fiscal and regulatory relations flowing from fiscal power rather than from the direct authority of the executive. Paralleling this relationship but similar to it in character are vertical regulatory relations between bodies whose primary power is regulatory and whose fiscal contribution is minimal. These are the agencies that can be claimed to be federal by virtue of expanded interpretations of federal powers.

It is this last form, which has been increasing in importance in the US for over a century, that is completely dominant in the European Community. In both settings it creates a situation in which a variety of bureaucracies are closely related with respect to the conferences they attend, the careers that are carried out through them, to the personnel, and the regulatory issues they address.

The structure of the European Commission is the place to start with this. The commission has a collegium of twenty commissioners, with twenty-three "Directorate General" offices. These are often run by experts. Appointments are by merit, but there are unofficial national quotas.

> Decision-making is open, access for interest groups is easy, and national bureaucrats are increasingly interrelated with commission officials in formal and informal working groups. This phenomenon, called *engranage*, includes about 25 percent of German officials in formal and informal working groups. (Matláry 1998: 67)

These are mainly interrelated at the regional level. In 1992 there were already about five hundred expert groups of a certain permanence, "where national and Commission civil servants work intensively together" (Wessels 1992: 46), and there are innumerable working groups (with national bureaucrats), advisory committees (with experts), and formal COREPER (Comité des Représentants Permanents) bodies with functional working groups.

The system is partly formal and partly informal, and reflects features of European bureaucracy. Bureaucratic expertise works in a way different from so-called independent expertise, precisely because of the feature of dependence. Experts in the European Community system are part of a career structure that often includes national bureaucracies which themselves are a career structure, and the career structure is strongly biased toward unanimity because those whose careers advance are those who are good at producing and securing unanimity. Commission experts deal with the same national experts time and again. The policy "language" is professional, is cast in expert terms, not in interest terms. The main business of achieving results in the face of different interests is concealed by this, but it is always present. Nevertheless the system "demands that participants in the process command the professional aspects of a quite often very technical problem" (Matláry 1998: 67).

Thus the principle of subsidiarity serves to involve national- and lower-level bureaucracies in the implementation of commission policies and initiatives through relationships that are cooperative rather than coercive, as in the American system, and which are in many contexts free from the pressure of public politics and public constituencies. The informed constituency on drug regulation is small; the public as a whole, insulated from the issues by complex national medical bureaucracies that make drug decisions, doesn't particularly understand its interests. The primary agencies whose decisions are affected are governmental agencies rather than individuals directly. So perhaps it is not surprising that business interests have considerably more influence on these activities and that the primary point of reference for bureaucrats in national states or health care administrations is the higher level technical environment shared with other countries and with European Community bodies themselves.

"COMMISSION" AS A FORM OF RULE

In what I have said here I have described some governmental mechanisms that ordinarily are found within liberal democracies, which I have suggested have acquired in the European Commission, and, I would argue, elsewhere, their own significance as alternative forms of rule. In this conclusion, I want to follow up this thought by making some more systematic points about liberal democracy and its limitations and discontent. The classical model of liberal democracy is government by discussion with political decisions being made on the basis of the results of discussion as measured through some sort of voting procedure. Representative democracy has representatives doing the discussing and engaging in discussions in their role as representatives with those that they represent. The executive, on this model, executes the laws that parliament or a representative body enacts. The extent to which this model was ever meaningfully descriptive of European parliamentary democracies is an open question. Many European countries simply inherited a bureaucratic structure instead of bureaucracies that were established in situations of strong monarchs and weak systems of representation in which the monarch and the bureaucracies had their own legitimacy and capacity to legitimate themselves apart from the representative bodies. Moreover, "discussion" was never a significant feature in European national politics because the parliamentary systems of each nation were organized around class parties, which had ideologies that were primarily designed, if that is the word, to enhance the solidarity of the class or religious groups whose interests they represented rather than to persuade unattached voters.

In short, the very existence of a predominantly class or religiously based party system that operated in parliament primarily in terms of coalition making effectively precluded government by discussion, and indeed discussion in the serious sense of discussion in which the parties to the discussion were open to being persuaded by the views of the other, at all. This meant that preexisting state bureaucracies, with their own, though limited, capacities for generating legitimacy and acceptance apart from the parliamentary system were significantly more powerful and autonomous than the category of executive in the traditional view of liberal democracy would permit. This bureaucratic power was also not limited by the judiciary as it was in the US. Consequently robust traditions of bureaucratic discretion and power persisted largely unaffected by "democracy."

Though European party style democracy in its stable post–World War II form was certainly a political triumph and a massive improvement on the weak parliamentary regimes prior to World War I, it was, nevertheless, a weak form of democracy. In particular, it was too weak and its legitimacy too fragile to successfully enforce difficult and unpopular state policies. States with a two-party system in which the parties can tacitly accept and impose, regardless of the hardships, a given policy despite a lack of popular support, are more powerful. In multi-party politics, in contrast, the content of political discussion expands. Someone is found to voice criticisms or raise issues. But at the same time there is typically no one in parliament to be persuaded, because the parties themselves are more likely to be well-disciplined and governed by rigid ideologies or interests.

In this setting one needs a powerful mechanism for removing difficult political decisions from electoral politics. The European Community, from its inception in the coal and steel negotiations, represented a means for doing precisely this, which is to say, displacing responsibility for unpleasant decisions onto an international body that could not be held as directly accountable and which was never elected in the first place. Such bodies could operate by a strategy of patience and through anticipating that the unpopular policies would eventually be accepted if they worked out. Time is an important political commodity that governments especially in unstable parliamentary regimes did not have, insuring that these regimes would have a strong interest in developing those mechanisms in order to avoid taking responsibility for these policies and measures.

There is of course nothing distinctly European about this pattern or even the mechanism of referring problems to treaties. The fact that international law treaties supersede state law is a convenient legal reason for this but the motivation is far more fundamental and the use of mechanisms of this sort occurs in many other contexts as well. Monetary policy, for example, was one of the great divisive public issues a century ago. In most countries this policy issue has been expertized, and given to a more or less independent body that is immune from immediate political pressure and given the capacity to wait and be patient. This kind of systematic surrender of political power by liberal democracies in order to move issues off the agenda is indeed so basic to twentieth century political practice that one might even regard it as a characteristic feature of present day liberal democratic regimes. Indeed, in this sense, they appear to be in a continual process of dissolution, or rather outsourcing and diminution of their political role.

PRECLUSIONARY LEGITIMACY

One kind of legitimacy comes from success in electoral contests in which participants present their ideas and plans and are voted in or out. The classic model of liberal democracy works just in this way: open public discussion, which proceeds in the expectation that the representatives of the voters will respond to public opinion, creates public opinion, which is then enacted into legislation by the representatives, who are motivated by the fact that elections are contested and adversarial to make promises in accordance with particular positions expressed in the course of public discussion, and implemented by an executive subject to the law. The system has numerous elements of discipline: representatives who ignore public opinion will risk non-election. The adversarial character of the struggle for power assures that discussion made in the expectation of judgment by voters will be serious and lively. Legitimacy is a result of the procedures of majoritarian voting, which are firmly entrenched as the standard for "democracy," as well as a by-product of the efforts of elected officials to secure personal followings.

Although this model is very far from the European Community model, one can ask similar questions about discipline, motivations for discussion, the nature of the policy end-game, and so forth for this system, and also where there are surrogates for the functions, especially the legitimation functions, of liberal democracy. The obvious differences are in the role of parliament. In both systems, there is "discussion" but the primary role of the European Parliament has to do with the end game—it is able to threaten a veto and negotiate changes in legislation. Its role is limited, however. The agenda is set by the commission, whose proposals in turn come from working groups within the commission that rely on experts. The end game requires, if not unanimity, something close to it, a fact repeatedly complained about in the EU's own documents (e.g., European Commission 2001b: 22, 29). Contention is thus avoided—contentious issues cannot be resolved by majorities, so there is no point in discussions that produce contention, except to sabotage proposals.

One effective strategy to adopt in this situation is to propose policies that have been pretested to assure that there are no national interests that will contest it and no experts or stakeholders who will be motivated to contest it by mobilizing support from a national representative or member of the European Parliament. We might call this preclusive legitimacy, since its aim is to preclude contention and allow proposals to be accepted unanimously or nearly so.[1]

One of the few constitutional documents from the time of classical liberalism to discuss the problem of expertise explicitly is John Stuart Mill's *Representative Government* ([1861] 1962), and the differences between Mill's notion of "council" and the guidelines for accessing expert advice of the EU are designed precisely for this purpose. Some dramatic differences are immediately obvious. For Mill as for the EU, council can be sought at any stage of the policy making process, and by any responsible decision-making body. But for Mill there is no suggestion that council need be anything more than private, that it need be public, that there should be a transparent procedure by which it is given, or that there is any "accountability" for council other than that which is demanded by the seeker of council, such as a legislator. Implicitly the relationship is personal and a matter of trust and honor.

For the EU, matters are entirely different. The language is public rather than private. Experts are increasingly understood as stakeholders, i.e., in terms of their conflicts of interest and rules for revealing conflicts of interest and their gender (Commission of the European Communities 2002: 12). *Departments*—remarkably—are given the following responsibility: to "consider how to promote an informed and structured debate between policy-makers, experts, and interested parties (e.g., workshops, consensus conferences), particularly on sensitive issues" (CEC 2002: 12). The process of advice giving should be transparent and divergent views and persisting uncertainties should be part of the report. Not only should responsible parties make decisions, they should justify the decisions and cite the evidence, and this responsibility extends not only to experts but to the commission itself, which is urged to not only take responsibility for the decisions, but to "be capable of justifying and explaining the way expertise has a been involved, and the choices it has made based on advice" (CEC 2002: 9–10) and not "hide behind experts" (2002: 9). But "accountability extends also to the experts themselves" (2002: 10).

It should be evident that the emphasis here on procedure, public access, and the creation of structured discussion indicates a fundamental change in function from "council" in the liberal sense. The acknowledgment that "the interplay between policy-makers, interested parties and the public at large is a crucial part of policy-making, and attention has to be focused not just on *policy outcome* but also on the *process* involved" (CEC 2002: 3) needs to be understood as an admission that this "interplay" is a full-fledged surrogate for the liberal model outlined above. The plea for greater openness and emphasis on process reflects considerations of legitimacy: these reforms amount to a shift to greater procedural or process legitimation as a solution to problems of legitimacy inherent in current European Community governance.

What are the concerns? They are well-expressed in the White Paper on European Governance (European Commission 2001b: 7): that despite the double democratic mandate through the EP and the council representing the individual member states, it is perceived to be unable to act effectively (for example, on food safety); that when it does act (for example, to improve quality of life) it does not get credit, which goes to national governments; that "'Brussels' is too easily blamed by Member States for difficult decisions that they themselves have agreed or even requested"; and that people do not understand the institutions or "feel the Institutions act as an effective channel for their concerns" (European Commission 2001b: 7).

These concerns lead to the constitutionally novel and odd result that the process of expert and stakeholder advice itself is given the burden of constructing procedures that respond to these problems—even to constructing a "discussing class," to use the term of Donoso Cortes, that is an alternative to the liberal "public." The problem of reaching out to local democracy is done through the principle of subsidiarity, which involves local and regional bureaucrats in the policy making process, is a similar kind of substitution. Local bureaucrats are "closer" to the people, to be sure, but only in an odd way, since the people typically have little effective control over these bureaucrats, who are heirs to the administrative structures of the absolutist state, insulated from politics, rather than accountable "representatives" in the sense of Mill.

The European party system has, as I have suggested earlier, served to interfere in the process of translating public discussion into law by making representation less direct. Here as well we find the system of expert advice coming into a new role as a surrogate for representation. The "Report of the working group 'Democratizing expertise and establishing scientific reference systems'" (European Commission 2001a) proposes the creation of new participatory mechanisms to allow for the scrutiny of expert opinions (2001a: 21) as well as suggesting ways of reforming the traditional model of expertise itself. "Procedures must be established to review expertise beyond the traditional peer community, including, for example, scrutiny by those possessing local or practical knowledge . . . sometimes referred to as 'extended peer review'" (2001a: ii). This is to redefine "peer" in a way that creates a new surrogate for the public and a new locus of discussion in place of the lost public discussion of classical liberalism—all in a quest for something that expertise, in classical liberalism, did not have and did not require, namely legitimacy.

This report notes that "'majoritarianism' is generally incompatible with the development and use of expertise" (2001a: 7), but at the same time claims to be engaged in a process of "democratizing expertise" that strengthens democratic institutions (2001a: 7). The argument for the creation of new participatory mechanisms should be understood in the light of this. These are alternatives to the democratic institutions of national and local democracy which are appropriate to the new political form of a vertically integrated expertized bureaucracy, which relates through a long series of "interfaces" between expert and manager groups (2001a: 24), whose "policy" activity is to provide proposals for European Commission regulation and legislation that can be accepted or avoid veto in a series of non-majoritarian steps to ratification at the commission and European Parliament. Neither the European parliament nor the commissions, the double legitimators of the EU, are sufficient to represent the public. Instead, it is recommended that procedures be created for "citizen's juries, consensus conferences, focus groups, and public hearings," modeled on such participatory forms as Danish technology panels, which legitimate in a novel way (European Commission 2001a: 21). So there is a transformed notion of the public and a transformed set of institutions through which the public is addressed.

One may well ask if this is a meaningful notion of the public, or if these are meaningful "public" institutions. One important finding of the best available study of these participatory bodies in national settings is that they have had no discernible impact on parliamentary debates or state actions (Hansen 2004). So these efforts are better understood as something other than a form of participation in the process of legislation.

Perhaps they should be understood as similar to the sorts of consumer testing efforts that focus groups are traditionally used for. To the extent they help legitimation, they are signs that "someone is listening," even if the listening has no effect. But there is a deeper problem here with the implicit notion of the public itself.

Can there be a meaningful notion of the public without a meaningful notion of accountability to this public, without reasonably direct mechanisms to enforce this accountability, and without the possibility of learning from the use of power? It is difficult to see how. But it is not so difficult to see how a consumer-testing model of public relations could be conceived as a useful adjunct to a process of rule organized around vertically integrated specialist bureaucratic expert cultures that are organized around technically specialized problems. The main problem faced by these bureaucracies is output legitimacy, that is to say results, as Fritz Scharpf argued in his classic work (1999). But as the governance paper acknowledged, the public cannot assess most of the intended results, or ascribe the results to the right agencies. Nor can they assess the technical claims made in the internal process of decision-making, and it is well known that public members of participatory panels have a strong tendency to defer to experts. The only results that the public can assess come in the form of scandals and other public relations failures. So an advance warning of public concerns is crucial; actual input, or participation, is not.

To be very blunt about it, the regime I have been describing here is a parallel to "democracy" in the traditional liberal sense. It can also serve, and does serve, as a surrogate for it. And it is being asked to become more of a surrogate, by providing substitutes for the absent public and absent discussion of EU policy making. The effect of this increasing surrogacy is to make the public activities of the EU even more ceremonial. We need only update Hocart slightly: those who cannot adapt themselves to change, fade into the ceremonial of the European Parliament and similar bodies, while effective power passes into the hands of the experts and expert stakeholders, who have the power to preclude alternatives.

11 Was Real Existing Socialism a Premature Form of Rule by Experts?

The history of Communism in the twentieth century, if the current orthodoxy is to be believed, was no more than a detour in a process in which history ends in a world of civil societies organized as liberal democracies that increasingly relate to each other following the model of liberal democracy itself, through the rule of law, collective discussion, the general recognition of human and civil rights, and so forth. In this image of world history, the worldwide dominance of liberal democracy is the culmination of a process that appears as a first draft in the Westphalian peace, which gradually spread through time, for example, through the internationalist ideology of Woodrow Wilson. In this teleological image of history, Communism appears as a developmental error, an error produced by an accidental combination of erroneous ideology and special circumstances of delayed development in certain countries that made them particularly susceptible to it.

In what follows, I propose to reconsider this version of the meaning of twentieth century Communism, especially, but I am afraid very abstractly, with reference to Eastern Europe and Russia. My concern will be with a three-part relationship, between the state, civil society, and expertise. I will argue that the system of real existing state socialism was a kind of experiment in the construction of a model of relating expertise, the bureaucratic state, and the political forces arising from "civil society." I will ignore, or rather bracket, the problem of the Soviet system itself and also the coercive character of Communist regimes, important as these issues are. My concern will be with civil society, or rather with an important but seldom discussed aspect of the problem of civil society, the place of non-governmental organizations in processes involving knowledge and expertise.

EXPERTISE AND THE STATE: FIVE MODELS

To clarify what I take to be the main issues here, let me simply identify five alternative structures of the relation between expertise and the state of the kind that actually existed in the late 1940s, at the moment that Eastern Europe became Communist. The descriptions are caricatures, but I trust that they will at least be recognizable. We may conveniently describe these alternatives as the Napoleonic, the German, the British, the Swedish, and the American. By the "Napoleonic" I mean to designate powerful centralized state bureaucracies with a formally separate system of specialized technical training; the Grande Écoles in the original model, in which the organizations of the state itself produced a need for expert, specialized civil servants, typically with high prestige and pay, and a specific ethic that is connected to their special education for service in a particular bureaucracy or group of bureaucracies.

This is a model of the appropriation of expertise in which political control is exerted from the top to the top, for example where political authority comes from a presidential political system and flows to a state bureaucracy in which careers are bound up with an internalized system of promotion and command, and are thus cushioned from politics, except in the sense of responding in a broad way to social and technical needs as defined, typically, from a national perspective. The characteristic "input" of locals to the process of decision-making is protest. The relevant bureaucracies respond to pressure, and seek to avoid protest, but they do not respond to local initiative. The end of the era in which the local notables exercised real or potential power in France came in 1848, and was decisive (Halévy 1974).

This model, minus the Grandes Écoles, is relevant to the Eastern European case, for it is a fair description of the system of rule of the Austro-Hungarian Empire. There were of course other differences, notably those that arose from the extent of decentralization of authority in response to the problem of nationalities. The Grandes Écoles developed an internal culture of national competitiveness that provided a progressive, expert element that the Austro-Hungarian Empire lacked. But both relied on central authority delegated to a class of bureaucrats without local allegiances whose careers were bound up entirely with the system itself. Expertise entered from the top or center, if it entered at all, into administration, and "politics" was something separate from expertise entirely.

The systemic problem of this scheme was protest: centralization, either in its broad French forms or its narrow, bureaucratically oriented Austro-Hungarian form, meant that policy was insensitive to local issues and problems, and the rigidities and distortions that resulted from the long lines of communication of public opinion meant that protest was the only means of getting a response. Implicitly, this meant that the bureaucracies were not merely administrative but political, engaged in the business of responding to and avoiding protest. Freed of practical political responsibility, local political movements, such as Serbian nationalism and Viennese anti-Semitism, devoted itself to "politics" in the sense of ideology, symbolism, or political theater.

The decentralization of the Austro-Hungarian Empire, however, meant that a remarkable variety of self-help associations could flourish: among these were the Moravian associations of sheep breeders and agriculturalists that were central to the creation of a connected set of research institutions in Brno (Brunn), eventually including university professorships and abbeys, that served as the research community in which Gregor Mendel made his genetic discoveries (Orel 1996). This Central European success story of the nineteenth century should dispel any thought that such institutions are limited to the "West." And this type of collective body has been revived in the more recent period. For example, groups of Polish agricultural producers have played a significant role in the reorganization of the Polish meat industry and the regulation of meat products. Part of the contribution of these groups to the processes of politics is knowledge; they possess specialized understandings of the activities that the state regulates and affects through its actions, and can serve as a counter or constraint on the claims of state bureaucratic experts by distributing specialized knowledge among institutions of different kinds, operating under different constraints than those of bureaucratic discipline and careerism.

In Britain, the system was one of parliamentary sovereignty, but at the same time, one in which a strong "professional" class of civil servants actually carried out the functions of the bureaucracy. Ministers came from Parliament, and they were in the classic sense amateur politicians; men, for the most part, who were men of the world, but who also had considerable experience in the raw politics of their own political party. The political parties generally were large and complicated organizational phenomena. The realities of bureaucratic life were familiar to any experienced party man.

Experts, however, posed difficult problems for the civil service. Although the civil service was professional with respect to career patterns, with respect to specialized knowledge it was an organization of amateurs: persons who were stringently selected, especially at the very top, on the grounds of their performance as students at Oxford and Cambridge in academic areas, such as the study of classics, that had no direct relation to the kind of task that they performed in the bureaucracy. What this meant was that bureaucratic decision-making had a high level of what might be thought of as cultural cohesion, which allowed for the extensive use of discretion.

The system had great strengths as an administrative tradition, but was nevertheless poorly adapted to the application of expert knowledge. In the 1930s, in particular, the technical problems of the siting of telephone and telegraph lines were critical. But it was necessary for the bureaucracy and civil service system to acknowledge and accommodate the existence of this kind of expertise, and in the system that existed this meant that someone who was part of the civil service cadre and had been promoted through the system needed to be put in charge of these technical decisions. It was not possible under the system simply to appoint an outsider with the relevant technical skills because this would have meant giving the outsider a high rank and a set of privileges within the civil service system for which their records did not qualify them. Thus, either some kind of special structure within the bureaucracy and outside the civil servant traditions had to be created—with all of the many problems attendant on this, including the fact that this new bureaucracy needed to operate in terms of rules and traditions of its own—or the problem needed to be granted to a separate body of some sort, such as a commission.

The problem was similar to the one faced by the military in wartime, and the solution there was to have experts "seconded" or temporarily assigned to generals and admirals and their staff to be used as seemed fit, in effect granting considerable personal discretion on a personal basis to particular experts who proved themselves to officers. This was obviously not a permanent solution; in fact, after the war the scientists who were crucial to British success for the most part went back to academic life. Like all solutions, it had weaknesses, in the sense that there were areas in which it was vulnerable to problems of particular kinds. In this case, it was prone to expert errors, errors made possible by the combination of expert status and administrative discretion and secrecy, and also to de facto dominance by professional associations, which used administrative discretion for their own ends to produce a system congenial to their interests, a situation well represented by the National Health Service.

Nevertheless, this was a system that was relatively responsive to local concerns and initiative. Parliamentary sovereignty, along with the fact that parliamentarians held cabinet positions, meant that the local concerns of members of Parliament could not be ignored. Ministers were directly accountable to Parliament; questions could be raised, votes could be refused and party positions could be contested, and, not surprisingly, ways to accommodate national policy and local concerns could be found. Members of Parliament functioned as local notables, and constituent service and local loyalty mattered in their election.

Another solution, which we might call the German solution, served, like the Napoleonic system, to integrate expertise into government bureaucracies and so turn experts into bureaucrats. But it differed both with respect to centralization and with respect to the existence of Grandes Écoles. The German solution was also different with respect to the relationship between the bureaucracy and politics. The bureaucracy was typically not neutral, but in fact embodied a well-developed political set of powers of its own and a considerable amount of bureaucratic secrecy and discretion, so much so that the bureaucracy amounted to the continuation of the empirical state as a kind of alternative to democratic politics rather than subordinate to democratic politics. But the German bureaucratic system had an additional flaw that was simultaneously its greatest virtue, the practice of promoting on merit within the bureaucracy people who were genuinely competent and expert with respect to the tasks of bureaucracy itself.

What this produced, certainly consistent with other German state traditions was what we might call expert bureaucracies, which typically held themselves to high standards, but standards of their own devising. The

German way was often systematically different from what was done in accordance with international standards, but, most importantly, there was nothing in the character of either independent expertise or independent amateurism that could effectively counter the expert claims and critically evaluate the experts' practices in the bureaucracy. The Grandes Écoles were in some sense outside the bureaucracy; in the German case, the bureaucracies themselves monopolized expertise and defined the categories of expert knowledge.

The very fact of the monopoly on expertise held by the bureaucracy created a systemic problem. Promotion and success in a bureaucratic career required conformity with the dominant climate of opinion within the bureaucracy. Mavericks who bucked the system could not rise in the bureaucracy, there were no alternative careers to which they could carry their expertise, and there was no hope of returning to a position with a change of political leadership. This meant that there simply were no external controls on bureaucratic power, except, rather oddly, in the powers of other bureaucracies with a political base in the cities or the Länder. So the German system avoided the problems of the centralization of political authority, and responded to local problems differently: the bureaucracies tended to legitimate themselves by respecting the expectations of local stakeholders directly, bypassing the formal democratic process, thus protecting itself from informed amateur criticism and informed criticism of associations. These stakeholders, of course, had expert knowledge as well: the monopoly of the state bureaucracies was never complete. But associations, such as trade groups, were accustomed to operating so closely with the ministries in this kind of stakeholder relationship that conflict was systematically avoided. This tended to confirm the power of the experts within the bureaucracies rather than to challenge them. Not surprisingly, the solutions that resulted from ministerial "leading" of stakeholders were not always consistent with what experts elsewhere believed, that is to say, with the best science or best policy.

The Swedish case, like the rest of Scandinavia, was a variant on this model, with a greater role for citizens. Problems tended to be defined by movements of citizens in the expectation of future state action or support. Experts played a characteristic role in this process. Once a problem had been politically defined, agricultural surpluses, for example, and a movement with some ideas of how to solve it had developed sufficient membership, experts played a role in identifying detailed policy solutions that the state could accept and implement. This model assumes a high level of grassroots initiative, a competent body of experts, and a responsive national state. It works as well as it does because of scale and because it is possible to borrow solutions tested elsewhere. The French problem of centralization and the German problem of choosing a unique and non-comparable alternative path thus do not arise. There is nevertheless a very striking feature of this system. The role of the expert is not to create a climate of opinion, nor to serve as technical advisor to a party (although this is certainly possible and consistent with the system, and was in fact a role played by the Myrdals, for example), but rather to solve a unique problem of policy, for which expertise is useful, but not in itself sufficient. This allows for a certain amount of creativity, in that it frees the expert from the limitations of the self-disciplining community of experts, and their self-limitations with respect to what is really known, without relying on a bureaucratic consensus enforced by the discipline inherent in bureaucratic careers.

The American case is too complex to deal with at length, but as with all such comparisons, the basic constitutional fact of federalism is central. In many respects, however, it is a mixture of forms, in which there is an element of overlap and competition. Expertise is not bound to particular bureaucracies, and few bureaucracies have the kind of autonomous power found in European bureaucracies. There is often an expert culture with a strong base in universities, which competes with bureaucracies, or works under competitive contract to them. Experts often speak directly to voluntary organizations and politicians to define policy, rather than to the state, which applies policy legalistically and contractually rather than through the exercise of discretion. A wide variety of centers of expertise and initiative compete to be heard in the policy process, and stakeholders typically exert influence through expert claims, that is by asserting their expertise to a public audience, rather than in negotiations, as in Germany. Market competition is the default mode of resolving conflicting claims, rather than regulatory power, and the characteristic problems of regulation involve the control of competition rather than the assertion of special state expertise. Nevertheless this market competition occurs in an environment in which there is a large array of intermediate associations, such as trade groups and local associations of citizens, in which knowledge is transmitted. This is not a process that produces uniformity directly, but it imposes consequences on those who do not adapt, and thus places significant pressures on local governments, local associations, and trade groups to respond by acquiring expertise.

THE PARTY OF EXPERTS

Leaving out the topic of ideology entirely, we can see the Soviet model and as I will show, this model pre-dates the Soviet era in Russia itself as a particular solution to the problem of expertise in relation to bureaucracy and politics. It is characteristic of bureaucracies that the mechanisms of promotion and careers back up the policies and rules by enforcing a kind of consistency in the use of discretionary power, consistency that is more or less cultural and more or less specific to the culture of the bureaucracy. Parties, whatever their aim, are themselves forms of discipline in which differences of opinion are subordinated to party goals, and party goals are themselves

Was Real Existing Socialism a Premature Form of Rule by Experts? 215

dependent on the achievement of a certain level of agreement on matters of opinion. Expertise amounts to a kind of mastery of a set of opinions with respect to some specified technical activity with a specialized content. There is an inherent problem of knowledge and power, the problem for those in power of securing trustworthy knowledge, and the problem for those with knowledge of securing the trust of those in power. The idea of a party of experts, a party whose features include expertise, is a solution to this problem. The potential conflicts between the three elements disappear: the three are united into one closely related unit.

Unity of this sort, however, comes at a price. Uniformity is characteristic of bureaucratic organizations; a kind of "groupthink" emerges.[1] Groupthink is both a virtue and a pathological feature of expertise—a pattern that depends on a number of forms of "soft discipline" operating together. In a system in which people exercise limited discretion under the gaze of others who judge the exercise of this discretion, it allows for consistency and avoids the reliance on punitive powers and overt authority, which would amount to simple authoritarianism; amateur decision-making, rather than decision-making backed by expertise. But if we combine the internal soft discipline of bureaucratic careerism with the discipline of subservience to party opinion and the additional discipline of that of the community of experts, we produce a peculiar combination that guarantees a very considerable degree of uniformity, in which a soft system of discipline with mutually supporting mechanisms of control effectively smothers alternative opinion and excludes outsiders. Ideology is relevant here. Communism was, in a peculiar sense, a form of the ideology of expert rule, which made as its centerpiece the full utilization of the powers of production, the conquest of nature, the claim to being scientific, the identification of party ideology with science and rationality, all of which were tremendously attractive to scientists in the West in the 1930s, so it should be no surprise that strong resistance was not the norm.

What does this have to do with civil society? A brief example from the area of agricultural history is relevant here. In pre–1914 Russia, a policy was promoted by the state to organize peasants into cooperative forms of production, credit, and consumption, following a pattern that was well established internationally. But this was, from the start, a policy in which the state sought to apply expert knowledge in order to reform peasants against the peasants' self- perceived interests—to tutor their preferences, in the phrase used by Phillip Kitcher—in order to bring about some higher result. The problem they faced was that the cooperatives, though they involved a quarter of the peasant households, did not work very well, and were "marked by high rates of default, assemblies that rarely met, boards that lacked links in their communities, and associations that lacked active involvement of their members" (Kotsonis 1999: 137).

A few quotations will suffice to show the authoritarian tendencies in this model of expertise. At a congress of *Zemstvos*, one expert speaker said:

"For the agronomist there can be no cooperatives as such. Cooperatives are for him only the means for achieving social and economic ends: the reorganization of the household" (quoted in Kotsonis 1999: 114). Another added that the goal was to "instill consciousness where it did not exist" (quoted in Kotsonis 1999: 114). The program required that the expert plays a political role. "Who, if not the agronomist, should correct the errors of the independent activity of incompetent cooperative leaders, and defend the cooperatives from village kulaks and enemies" (quoted in Kotsonis 1999: 118). The agronomist was thus in a kind of competition for authority with local notables, defined them as enemies, and spoke for the "true" interests of the peasant against the peasants' narrow individualism and profit seeking.

The model of expertise here is one in which civil society, represented by the leadership of the local community, is an irrational obstacle to progress, which the expert must overcome. It is only a short step from this image of the role of the expert to the idea of a disciplined expert party, using propaganda to bring about the needed tutoring of preferences to enlist support and eliminate opposition, in order to bring about the full application of the expert's knowledge. And it need hardly be added that by this logic the next need—coercion—is entirely justified. But it would be a mistake to overlook the significant role of education in this process. Success in this system for an individual came through becoming trained, and the Soviet regime put great emphasis on literacy and technical education. This was the soft side of rule by experts, and it had a profound effect. But in the context of a coercive apparatus, education was itself a form of rule. And it is not surprising that in much of Eastern Europe, a central aim of the Communist restructuring after the war was to train working class students in such areas as economics, and to place working class scholars and party loyalists in positions of power in the educational system to ensure that the apparatus of education did not turn into a locus of resistance to the state.

Yet there have been circumstances in which the kind of comprehensive application of expert power implied by this model seemed justified. An important element of the appeal of the socialist regimes in Eastern Europe in the post-war period reflected the trauma of unemployment in the 1930s. The Soviet Union was seen, during the post-war period, as the sole success story in the face of the world economic crisis of the 1930s, and it was generally believed that this was due to the effective implementation of planning as a means of rationally organizing the Soviet economy. Of course, the idea of planning was fashionable throughout Europe and even in the US. It was adhered to by Fascists and Nazis, but also by the Socialist parties in many of the smaller states. Hendrik DeMan, the socialist who turned Fascist in the course of the war, was an exponent of what he called *planisme*, and similar ideas gripped many scientists, especially in England, where a movement of scientists in support of socialist planning and the planning of science developed. This was a natural alliance, in a sense, because much of the admiration of the Soviet regime and of Communism had to do with the idea of technological conflicts with nature and the expansion of human powers. The war enhanced the reputation of planning, because under wartime circumstances all of the belligerents engaged in a massive amount of planning, economic controls, and extensive programs of technological development, based not on market competition or private initiative but on state direction. Planning in this sense implies comprehensiveness: there is no point to planning the economy without planning the inputs into the economy, and when these are inputs of human talent, this implies the planning of education and education for the purposes of the plan.

It is often said that the defining issue of the nineteenth century labor movement, and of the dominant socialist parties, was the shortening of workers' hours. After it was achieved, the movements fragmented, especially in the 1920s. From this perspective, the great depression of the 1930s was a political godsend, because it created a new issue of equal power, namely employment. This was precisely what Communism promised: to provide expert management of the economy in such a way that unemployment would cease to exist. Moreover, the promise had a grounding in Oscar Lange's famous economic theory of socialism (Lange and Taylor 1938). The theory was, on the surface at least, validation of the claims that expert planners could indeed abolish unemployment and at the same time produce all the benefits and efficiencies possible under capitalism.

Lange established that it was theoretically possible for socialist planners to set prices in a way that would mimic the effect of the market without introducing the lags and uncertainties characteristic of the adjustments made by the market to new information in the form of prices, and at the same time enable the redistribution of the "social dividend." If prices were defined by the experts, there would be no uncertainties, and prices could be adjusted without introducing uncertainties in ways that assured full employment.

The "planner" or expert in this model had a technical task which, in practice, would have been difficult to perform, but which in any case was never performed and was never intended to be performed. Planners focused instead on fixing prices and distributing income in a way that assured employment. This dispensed with the market, of course, but it also dispensed with the surrogate for the market that Lange had imagined as part of his model, and in practice unemployment was avoided by simply granting state-operated planned money from central funds to assure employment at levels necessary to avoid unemployment. What actually occurred, as Michael Polanyi shrewdly observed with respect to the Russian economy before the war, was a system in which planners listened to factory managers and took their estimates and integrated them into a "plan." The system was in practice polycentric, driven more or less by self-set goals, as well as the larger goal of providing employment. Yet it was an economy "run by experts" who were governed by various forms of soft discipline, and in which the relevant expert knowledge, the knowledge of managers, was fed into a planning bureaucracy governed by the same soft discipline. There is a sense in which it "managed" in name only; it had no independent expert grounds for making decisions, it could only collate them. But the system nevertheless did allow for the influence of expert opinion to be felt, and this had important consequences in such areas as health care. It was expert opinion on a leash, the leash of soft discipline of state bureaucracies together with the harsher discipline of the party, but it was expert opinion nevertheless.

IS THERE A LESSON?

In one sense, this system of rule by a party of experts with control of a real administrative structure was a fulfillment of the Saint-Simonian dream, in which the enlightened actually ruled. And it worked to bring about the main results it aspired to: unemployment was eliminated, and a certain level of technical sophistication and competence was reached and preserved. Why did it fail? It is easy enough to say that the experts were not really experts, that they were deluded by their ideology, that their ideology was false, that the principles, for example those espoused by Lange, were not actually applied, and so forth.

But this is too simple. Utilizing, assessing, and organizing expertise is always a problem for politics. There is always an agency or trust problem to solve. To judge the claims of an expert or a body of experts with respect to their absolute or scientific or metaphysical validity requires a God, or alternatively some sort of super expert, and not the ordinary citizens of real existing modern society. The Communist party assumed this role and failed, not surprisingly. Indeed, the Soviet model, understood purely as a scheme for organizing expertise, seems, if not doomed to fail, to be a high-risk system in which everything is bet on one order of things without mechanisms for either correction or for counterbalancing the system in case of error.

Nevertheless, the societies on which this model was tried were an attempt to reach out into a particular kind of future, a future with a significant role for expert knowledge. Perhaps the formula was, for the reasons I have indicated here, the wrong one. It is still quite unclear that anyone has discovered the right formula. Different administrative traditions and different institutional histories, some of them very particular, have enabled some countries and some political formations to handle expert knowledge successfully. But there may be some general lessons.

The Russian example mentioned above can serve as an ideal typification of a common situation in the present development of civil society in the least developed areas of post-Communist Europe, in which a passive and resistive group of subjects respond to an institution, such as an NGO, created or subsidized for their benefit for purposes largely defined by experts

Was Real Existing Socialism a Premature Form of Rule by Experts? 219

who represent central authority or Western development bodies. Much can be said about this commonplace situation, but I will restrict myself to a simple case, based on a comment made by one of the many critics of the present focus on civil society, who regards it as neo-liberal ideology, and who suggests that post-Communism has been a failure in which the benefits of worker solidarity in the former regime have been replaced by insecurity and insipid Western "civil society" institutions with no value. As one of these critics put it, "for many citizens it is far from clear that their rights have been enhanced in any substantive way: the reemergence of Rotary clubs is little consolation when you no longer have secure employment" (Hann 1996: 9). Aside from the problem of logic here—the fact that Rotary clubs are not labor unions and not in the business of enhancing employment rights—the comment indicates is a fundamental misunderstanding or bias with respect to what it is that civil society consists of; and as it happens one that obscures the problem of knowledge. Rotary clubs are paradigmatic bits of civil society—NGOs that fill the space between the family and the state. They serve the interests of businessmen, in that they enable them to meet socially and cooperate on service projects. But they serve a great many other familiar purposes: people who come together and are practiced in working together can transfer this skill and the relations of trust they embody to other domains. They have political potential that they would not otherwise have. They relate to one another as quasi-equals and democratically, in terms of formal procedures of decision-making, rather than in terms of competition or as members of families or parties. But they also serve as ready audiences for, and constraints on, experts, and thus are important instruments for the creation of relations between experts and the users of knowledge. A typical Rotary Club's activities include luncheons with speakers. The speakers are disproportionately drawn from the ranks of local bureaucratic experts, often in relation to policy concerns. So these meetings serve as a means of face-to-face transmission of knowledge, and allow for the expert and the members of the community to interact face to face as something like equals, under the rules of common membership and courtesy that the clubs embody.

Most of this is familiar from de Tocqueville. But de Tocqueville failed to grasp the knowledge aspect of these associations in the US, even at the time that he wrote. To an astonishing extent, the associations that he admired had, like the present–day Rotary clubs, significance as educational, or more precisely, knowledge transmission bodies. Masonic organizations such as the Eastern Star provided speakers who provided expert knowledge in a form that could be digested by the public. The famous American farmers' movement, The Grange, was structured on the model of the Masons, complete with quasi-medieval "ranks" for its members, like the Masonic degrees. But the ranks were based on the attainment of knowledge: to achieve a rank required one to have mastered a body of scientific agricultural knowledge. So these organizations were not only a machine for the production of civility, they were also part of a system of the personal transmission of expert knowledge. And citizens with knowledge could respond to the state not only as equals but also by dominating it: by holding its offices, by judging its office holders, and by initiating policy.

In this role, then, they were a means of the democratization of knowledge. Why democratic? In some settings, of course, alliances like the Masons and religious confraternities have been anti-democratic in effect, serving as a means of elite dominance. In the US, and more generally where there are a large number of such associations, the effect is otherwise. The number of organizations makes a difference when the groups overlap with respect to membership, so that people who found themselves excluded or out of sympathy with any one organization would belong to another organization with members from the first organization. Membership within the organizations was "democratic" in the sense that a certain degree of equality was assumed within the group (as these alliances were either fraternal organizations or modeled in some fashion on fraternal organizations). "Brotherhood" was the term that many of these associations used. A social world dense with such organizations was necessarily democratic in tone, since the overlap of fraternal memberships served to make almost everyone a member of a group that shared fraternal ties with a member of each of the other fraternal groups.

When they are sufficiently numerous and dense, they also serve as a means for producing a genuine public realm that respects the public/private distinction. A person who is a member of several organizations will be constrained by their ties to manage, outside of the political arena, conflicts of interest, or to promote means of performing basic political acts, such as distributing political positions, on grounds that avoid conflict, such as merit. Thus these organizations can serve as a countervailing force to the kind of local political clientelism that is characteristic of state-centered political orders. And much of what they can do is a matter of knowledge and information. By serving as a means of transmitting knowledge about the technical issues facing the state, they serve as a means of producing transparency, enabling the public to respond effectively, and to recruit other experts to countervail against the state's experts, if need be.

Thus, when we discuss the absence of civil society, it is not merely a matter of the number of NGOs, but of the capacities for political action that these organizations directly and indirectly serve to enhance: knowledge and access to knowledge, as well as the capacity to speak back to experts, are central to these capacities. It is very striking that development agencies in the Third World have been compelled to invent bodies that mimic these capacities in order to gain the cooperation of those whom they aim to help: to respect "local knowledge" claims and systems and democratize the development process by inclusion and respect for the knowledge of those affected by the development strategies, empowering them to talk back (cf. Frossard 2002: 140–41).

Was Real Existing Socialism a Premature Form of Rule by Experts? 221

So the Rotarians are a poor symbol of the triviality of the achievements of post-communist society. They are, instead, the paradigm of a kind of association that mediates between expertise and the people, and a creator of the kind of citizens who are capable of dealing with the state not as subjects but as competent and informed constrainers, as well as facilitators of the personal relations that allow for the flow of knowledge in both directions across networks of institutions. The state-directed organizations of the Communist period were designed to provide services, but to preclude the use of the organizations to talk back to the state. Whether they can be converted to these new purposes is an open question.

One must be wary of nostalgia here. Although it is difficult to see how to replace the kind of political education, the means of producing politically responsible citizens, which associations like the Rotarians provide, these may no longer play the central role they once did. There may be other means of personal transmission of knowledge that will come to take the place of these older forms. The kind of civil society that may be needed today is a kind that perhaps is best exemplified by a current example. In 2001, an Airbus crashed in New York City, and questions about the cause of the crash were not easily answered. The culprit seemed to be the rudder, but it was not clear whether this was a technical flaw or a human error, and it was also unclear which kind of technical flaw or human error could have produced the crash. A typical expert bureaucratic agency in the US, the National Transportation Safety Board, had the task of examining this question, and ordering remedies. But questions immediately arose about the validity of this agency's initial conclusion. In response, an activist created a website that allowed for a public discussion by experts of various kinds, including pilots and engineers, which permitted the questioning on a technologically equal level, that is to say on an expert level, of the conclusions of the expert bureaucracy. On the website, individuals expressed opinions different from the official ones. This is itself, of course, a form of civil association, and one that has many more elaborate analogues, such as the World Wildlife Federation and Greenpeace. There is a sense in which these organizations are the real analogues to nineteenth century civil society.

Where this leaves us with respect to the larger question of the development of civil society in Eastern Europe is not entirely clear, but it does pose a question about what sort of "civil society" is relevant. To the extent (and it is a large extent) to which these new forms of expert civil association are not national but are trans-national and heavily weighted toward the participation of the most technologically developed countries with the largest bodies of independent experts, it suggests that becoming part of this network may be the necessary response to the twenty-first century "expertised" state. The need for the personal transmission of knowledge at the local level is not likely to vanish, however, nor is the need for forms of expertise that counter the state's expertise. Traditional "civil society" institutions are not the only means of doing this, but to deal with the complexity of the knowledge demands of the modern state without them requires a substantial alternative administrative tradition and structure, such as the French or German systems. The *nomenklatura* represented a failed solution to a genuine problem, not merely an ideological aberration. The historical irony it suggests is this: a society that fully utilizes knowledge, something which the Communists aspired to, requires the independent institutions that it was so eager to destroy.

12 Blind Spot?
Weber's Concept of Expertise and the Perplexing Case of China

When Weber talked about the problem of the role of knowledge in society, he used a vocabulary in which the terms "experts" (*Experten*) and "specialists" (*Spezialisten*) are more or less interchangeable. His normative ideas on this subject were central to "Science as a Vocation," where he argues that:

> only by strict specialization can the scientific worker become fully conscious, for once and perhaps never again in his lifetime, that he has achieved something that will endure. A really definitive and good accomplishment is today always a specialized accomplishment. And whoever lacks the capacity to put on blinders, so to speak, and to come up to the idea that the fate of his soul depends upon whether or not he makes the correct conjecture at this passage of the manuscript may as well stay away from science. ([1919] 1946: 135)

This reflected his attitude toward literary intellectuals peddling *Weltanschauungen*, but it was continuous with his hostility during the value-freedom debate in the *Verein für Sozialpolitik* (cf. Simey 1966, cited in S. Turner and Factor 1984: 57–58) toward the claim of the economists of the historical school to provide "scientific" policy advice and his hostility to professorial prophets, both of whom, he claimed, mixed value choices, which were inherently non-rational, with the claims they could legitimately make as "scientists." When these texts were written the ideal of universal knowledge and of intellectual leaders such as Goethe, who could claim universal knowledge, was dying a painful death. It was still upheld in literary circles and in the thought of philosophers such as Heidegger. An underlying theme of these texts is scorn for literary intellectuals' ambitions to be political guides. These struggles of his last decade provided the highly fraught context for Weber's writing on China ([1920] 1951).[1]

In Weber's discussion of Confucianism in historical Chinese society, he was faced with a bureaucracy and a judiciary which was produced by a system of examinations on what he characterizes as literary subjects. His repeated use of the term "literary" is revealing. In a sense, the Confucian tradition represents the fulfillment of the fantasies of his literary critics: a stable functioning order ruled by the literati on the basis of literary expertise. For Weber this model was necessarily one which could not achieve or eventuate in rationality, and the non-rational character of this tradition and of Chinese civilization became his theme in the text. There are many peculiar issues around his conclusion which raise questions about the status and meaning of the notion of expertise itself. The issues are whether the category of expertise and the category of expert knowledge are categories with a kind of universal significance or rather merely socially variable categories for which there are fundamental possible alternatives, and whether "specialist" and "expert" are interchangeable concepts. The Chinese case represents a powerful example through which these questions can be considered.

"WESTERN RATIONALITY"

Weber, in the series of studies of which his book on China was a part, was concerned with the problem of the development of modem western capitalistic economic rationality that resulted in the rationalization of the world of work, which then carried over into the rest of life. There is, however, a strong element of circularity in Weber's general account of this problem, because of his growing insistence in his last writings, especially his lectures on world economic history ([1927] 1961), that the rational organization of works was a wholly distinctive historical phenomenon. Circularity arises because the various forms of rationalization that Weber argued are the conditions for modem capitalism are not quite what they might appear. In this text they are presented as "conditions" or causes:

> In the last resort the factor which produced capitalism is the rational permanent enterprise, rational accounting, rational technology and rational law, but again not these alone. Necessary complementary factors were the rational spirit, the rationalization of the conduct of life in general, and a rationalistic economic ethic. ([1927] 1961: 260)

But Weber speaks of them also as "the distinguishing characteristics of western capitalism," and even follows this with "and its causes" ([1927] 1961: 232), thus confirming the muddle.

The issue, however, runs even deeper than this particular confusion over causes and definitions: it reappears at the core of his project, in relation to rationalism itself. In his late introductory essay to the *Religionssoziologie*, which Gerth and Mills titled "The Social Psychology of World Religions" ([1915] 1946), Weber wrote that the sources of modern rationality in the West turn out to be distinctive elements of rationality that were always there in the West and were either absent or very incompletely present (and consequently never fully developed) elsewhere (1958: 13–15). There is a strong sense that Weber in this project never in fact found the differentiating causes that led to Western rationalism, but merely found fundamental differences reaching back to prior differences of more or less the same kind.

He could enumerate these differences, but not explain their appearance in history. It is striking that when he attempted to do so, he was caught up in problems over the rationality of the actions to be explained. His explanation of the relative unimportance of magic in the West, which is crucial to his comparison with China, was given in his discussion of ancient Judaism in the same series of studies. There he argued that more or less accidental peculiarities of the Jewish use of oracles resulted in the absence of magic and the development of "rational methods":

> The Levitical oracle required something quite different: the question had to be correctly put in order that the facts and God's substantive will be determined simply by lot. Everything depended on the way that the question was put, thus, the Levite bad to acquire a rational method to express problems to be placed before God in a form permitting answers of "yea" and "nay." Complicated preliminary questions had to be settled before they could be placed before God and, in many instances, this arrangement hardly left anything to be determined by oracle ... Particularly for private needs, the oracle inevitably became less and less important as against the rational case study of sins, until the theological rationalism of Deuteronomy (18:9–15) in substance discredited lot casting altogether, or at least ceased to mention it. . . . The oracle by lot is mentioned by Ezekiel (21:21) for Babylonia, but it bad, as far as is known, long since disappeared from priestly technique. It was not replaced by rational Torah teaching but by the collection and systematization of the *omina* and by *expert* priestly interpretation. (1952: 179, 180, emphasis added)

The idea that small events have large consequences is not unique to Weber. But in this case the explanation seems to presuppose the rationality it purports to explain: Without a "rational" or non-magical attitude to these rituals, in this case a kind of literal legalism, the Levites would not have "had to acquire a rational method to express problems." Nor would they have extended the rituals in a non-magical way, and would not have excluded alternative "magical" rituals from their religious practice, as they apparently did. So rationality comes first, before the thing that explains it, here and generally.

This becomes especially apparent in his discussion of China, in which one particular form of thought produces difficulties for Weber. The form is Confucianism, especially Confucianism in its role as the basis of the conduct of officials in the classical Chinese bureaucracy. In the face of this Weber was reduced to something that looked suspiciously like name calling with a series of references to nonrationality. Thus he says:

> There was no rational science, no rational practice of art, no rational theology, jurisprudence, medicine, natural science or technology; there was neither divine nor human authority which could contest the bureaucracy. Only an ethic congruent with bureaucracy could be created and this was limited solely by consideration of the forces of tradition in the sibs and by the belief in spirits. Unlike western civilization, there were no other specifically modern elements of rationalism standing either in competition or in support of bureaucracy. Western culture in China was grafted upon a base which, in the West, had been essentially overcome with the development of the ancient *polis*. Hence, the culture of this bureaucracy can be considered an experiment which approximately tests the rationalism of government by office prebendaries and its effects. Orthodox Confucianism resulted from this situation. ([1920] 1951: 151–52)

His explanation for this form of thought is that it is an ideology, an ideology of what he could only characterize in Western terms as a body of prebends, that is to say a body of appointed officials.

But what sort of ideology was it? It was difficult for Weber to locate this system within his standard scheme of forms of legitimacy. Weber's three types of legitimizing belief, each characterizing a form of rule, were traditional, charismatic, and rational legal. In spite of the fact that the Chinese bureaucracy assumed normal judicial functions, it was not rational-legal in the sense that it was based on law that was codified in the sense constitutive for the West through the Roman legal tradition. That is to say, a body of law which could then be reasoned about and reasoned from independently by trained lawyers to produce predictable legal outcomes. Nor was Confucianism "traditional" in its function as a guide to bureaucratic action for the simple reason that once a basis for authority is written it is, almost by definition, no longer "traditional" because it now constitutes an independent potential basis for action no longer connected to the authoritative interpretation by its elders for the community. And by definition, since written texts begin with historical authors, it is no longer believed in by virtue of having the prestige of having been adhered to since time immemorial. Nor is Confucianism charismatic in the normal sense. There is no guru with special supernatural powers demonstrated through the performance of miracles, which is the paradigm for nonmilitary charismatic leaders.

Weber was nevertheless compelled by his scheme of types of authority to identify the nonrationalism of Confucianism with something "legitimating" simply by virtue of the fact that it is a legitimating doctrine, a set of claims about the basis and propriety of authority that was in fact used to justify authority. His solution was to find charismatic elements in it, but this reasoning extended the notion of charisma in problematic ways, though at the same time revealing the kinship of Confucian education to other practices. He said, for example, that there is a charismatic moment in the form of education in which the teacher awakens the charisma within the student, a phenomenon he also suggested is characteristic of certain forms of noble education ([1920] 1951: 119).

> The charismatic procedure of ancient magical asceticism and the hero trials, which sorcerers and warrior heroes have applied to boys, tried to aid the novice to acquire a "new soul," in the animist sense, and, hence, to be reborn. Expressed in our language, this means that they merely wish to *awaken* and to test a capacity which was considered a purely personal gift of grace. For one can neither teach nor train for charisma. Either it exists *in nuce*, or it is infiltrated through a miracle of magical rebirth—otherwise it cannot be attained. ([1920] 1951: 119–20, emphasis in the original)

This solves the puzzle of how a form of knowledge ruled by a rigorous system of written exams could be "charismatic." But Weber's characterization of the Confucian bureaucratic ideology remains essentially a list of negatives and paradoxes.

EXPERTISE AND SPECIALISM

Although the China study appears in a series dedicated to the economic ethics of the world religions (and Weber does also discuss Buddhism and Taoism in this volume), we begin with classificatory problems. Confucianism is not in any usual sense a "religion." Nevertheless the role it plays in Chinese society as well as the practice of Chinese bureaucracy is in many critical respects the same as the role played by religion in Christian or Islamic societies, namely as both supplying an explication and justification of social practices and institutions as well as serving as the moral and political *lingua franca* or scheme of moral justification for members of that society.

In this respect, Confucianism is like a religion, and, moreover, its structure of interpretive authority is not so different from religions. This further muddles the issue about expertise. Interpretation of religious doctrine often involves religious specialists, persons whose interpretations are in some sense authoritative, whether it is through their possession of divine revelations or their scholarly mastery of the religious text, or through some special genealogical connection which granted special authority over these texts, as in the case of the Brahmins in the caste system or the Cohens and Levites of the Jewish tradition.

Weber's more fundamental problem, however, involves the association of bureaucracy and expert or specialist knowledge. It is a curious feature of Weber's writings that the terms "expert" and "specialist," which Weber used more or less interchangeably throughout his texts, nowhere appear in the concentration that they do in the text on ancient China. Weber was justifiably fascinated and disturbed by the anomaly of a "bureaucracy" which does not rely on specialists. Yet, as Weber made clear, the system depended on a rigorous system of examinations on a specific and coherent body of Confucian literature, subject to extensive scholastic interpretation. In superficial respects this knowledge is similar to other bodies of expertise. Yet the attitudes of the bureaucrats (whom he characterized as prebends!) are hostile to the kind of specialized knowledge that is the hallmark of bureaucratic organization in its Western form.

> The position of the office prebendary appears in ethically hallowed form. It is the one position becoming to a superior man because the office alone allows for the perfection of personality. Mencius reasons that without permanent income the educated man can be of constant mind only with difficulty, and the people not at all. Economic, medical, priestly income represent the "little path." This leads to professional specialization, a very important point and closely connected with what has been said above. The cultured man, however, strives for that universality which in the Confucian sense education alone provides and which the office precisely requires. This view characterizes the absence of rational specialization in the official functions of the patrimonial state. ([1920] 1951: 160)

And again,

> The Confucian aspirant to office, stemming from the old tradition, could hardly help viewing a specialized, professional training of European stamp as anything but a conditioning in the dirtiest Philistinism. This was undoubtedly the locus of much of the important resistance to "reform" in the occidental sense. The fundamental assertion, "a cultured man is not a tool" meant that he was an end in himself and not just a means for a specified useful purpose. ([1920] 1951: 160)

The contrast to his ideal-type definition of bureaucracy, in *Economy and Society*, is unmistakable:

> Office management, at least all specialized office management—and such management is distinctly modem—usually presupposes thorough training in a field of specialization. This, too, holds increasingly for the modern executive and employee of a private enterprise, just as it does for the state officials. ([1968] 1978: 958)

The anomaly is not really addressed by Weber, because in one sense there is nothing to address. The Chinese bureaucracy had many elements of bureaucracy as an administrative form and had them to such an extreme extent, for example, the centrality of written examinations for employment, that there was little question about the type of administrative form it was. The problem arose with respect to the question of knowledge, that is to say the type of knowledge that the examinations tested.

For Weber, the idea of testing bureaucratic applicants on the knowledge appropriate to a literary elite is on the face of it essentially arbitrary because the knowledge is not directly connected to the actual tasks of the bureaucrats. Nor is it connected to an ascending hierarchy of specialization in which the knowledge of beginners is built on by the knowledge of the specialist as it is in Western administrative law. So the problem of expertise, and particularly the problem of expertise as used in the bureaucrats' political and legal capacities, becomes Weber's focus. What he immediately discovered is that legal enactment and particularly law finding, that is to say, identifying the relevant applicable laws, is in the Chinese system, irrational. The laws are not organized nor was there an impulse to organize them, contrasting radically with the Roman legal tradition and the Justinian rationalization of law precisely through this process of codificational organization ([1920] 1951: 149). Nor was there a kind of specialist legal discourse, such as that of the European law professors who interpreted Roman law after its "reception" in the Renaissance, that would accompany a process of judicial appeal to higher and more legally authoritative courts. It was this feature of de facto finality of the bureaucratic judges' legal judgments that Weber argued could be understood in terms of the ideal type that he had constructed in connection with Islamic law, what he called Cadi justice.

Unfortunately, this characterization explains one mystery by substituting another, because Weber's characterization of Cadi justice, which he admits is an ideal type that is quite unlike the actual historical institution of the Cadi (who was constrained by divine sanction to rule on very narrow cases), but was rather a figment of the Western legal imagination that depicted the Cadi as a judge sitting under a palm tree bound by no law book or appeals court and thus free to rule as he pleased. The opposite was in fact closer to the truth, and the position of the Cadi was the undesirable one of enforcing divine law without discretion or human consideration. And this leads one to suspect that the ideal type of Cadi justice is not a possible, practical form of adjudication, but only a hypothetical limit case, and consequently was not the actual form of adjudication in Chinese law either ([1968] 1978: 1115).

Nevertheless Cadi justice, as Weber depicted it, is in some sense an element of all law, a point which Weber's sometime student Carl Schmitt elevated into a radical account of discretionary adjudication that is relevant here, at least in part because of Schmitt's interesting conclusion. Schmitt argued that there is always a gap between the generalities of the law and the peculiarities of cases, and that the role of adjudication or even of bureaucratic ruling was to use discretionary power to determine the application of principles ([1922] 1985: 31). Current philosophy of law has shed this view and its implications, claiming, in Ronald Dworkin's famous phrase, that there is always one right solution to legal questions. Schmitt argues what is in effect the exact opposite, namely that there is no rational-legal consideration that bears on the application of the law to particular cases. The gaps between the law and the particular are intrinsic to legality as such and ineliminable by any sort of legal enactment or principle of interpretation because any new law or principle faces the problem of application in new form without eliminating it. This led Schmitt to the view that the only source of consistency in the judicial process of applying the law was cultural rather than legal, that is to say that the shared prejudices of judges are made for legal consistency rather than anything "rational" or "legal." This appeal to culture is revealing because it suggests that culture might in some sense be, as it was necessarily for the discretionary situations that Schmitt described, a more or less sufficient basis of adjudication on its own.

This point bears in a peculiar way on Weber's problem of understanding the relevance of literary examinations on Confucius for bureaucrats and judges. It is at least an interesting hypothesis that the function of literary examination was precisely to produce something analogous to what Schmitt believed had been accidentally produced in Germany by the extra-legal selection of judges from a particular social class, namely a strong cultural similarity which made it possible for legal and bureaucratic decision-making to be coherent and to an extent sufficient to produce and sustain a form of bureaucratic and judicial rule despite the apparent lack of codification.[2]

With this the pieces begin to fall into place. If literary examinations perform the function of testing for the possession of the shared culture necessary for bureaucratic adjudication and for the predictable carrying out of bureaucratic directives, then the system of examining and training becomes the mechanism for reproducing the particular kind of knowledge necessary for and appropriate to the bureaucracy. The knowledge in question would then not be expert knowledge in the specialist sense, but expert knowledge in a "cultural" sense that also happens to be sufficient for and appropriate to the particular legal task of exercising judicial and bureaucratic discretion in a manner that is consistent with the decision of others and hence predictable.

What remains somewhat mysterious about this solution to the problem of the nature of Chinese bureaucratic knowledge is the question of the content of this knowledge. Schmitt says little about the content of the similarities between German judges that enabled them to make sense of the rules in the same way. But the impression one gets is that they are employing their discretion as conservative upholders of the existing social order and that their predictability takes the form of bias against particular groups and ideas, and toward resolutions to conflicts that favor particular kinds of people. In the Chinese case, however, the interests are created by the bureaucratic structure and the common ground is a result of the system of intense literary examinations itself. So the exams seem to function in the manner of bar exams for lawyers, but have non-legal, "cultural" content.

Schmitt's non-legal solution to the problem of legal indeterminacy depends on the idea that there is a radical disjunction in kind between a legal consideration and the discretionary considerations and prejudices that inform the application of the law or bureaucratic decision-making. And it is this disjunction that does not hold in the case of China, though Weber strives to make it appear that it does by insisting on the "literary" character of the exams. Confucianism, however, is neither simply a literary culture, nor a religion, nor a bureaucratic ideology, nor specialist expertise, but something that is all of these things and perhaps much more. So we are faced with a problem of elaborating an explanation of a systematically different non-western phenomenon through the multiplication of Western intellectual distinctions, a process that ends in defining problems rather than explaining them.

A better analogy might be made to some accounts of American constitutional law, which suggest that there is a background doctrine that is not legal in the narrow sense but rather a kind of political theory that evolves along with adjudication and is relied on by the courts (Barber 1993). Knowledge of this body of thought, which takes the form of interpretations of the deeper significance of precedents, is not legal knowledge in the technical sense, and not specialist knowledge either, but rather something shared by the most profound thinkers in the community of constitutional interpreters. It is at the same time, in a sense, also the philosophy of the community—but it is a deeper understanding of this philosophy than the man in the street possesses. It is not the same as a *Weltanschauung*, which is supposedly "shared," but rather it is something understood more deeply by some than by others who also live in accordance with it.

WHERE WEBER WENT WRONG

If we grant that Weber's interpretation went wrong, it is appropriate to ask why it did. There seem to be two reasons, one of which is conceptual, the other a failure of scholarship. I will consider these briefly. Weber, as we have seen, operated with a disjunction between rationality, embodied in expertise that is specialized, and the category of the nonrational. The way the distinction is applied has the effect of excluding the possibility of rational non-specialized knowledge. As I have noted, this was the point of contention in the dispute that became the "crisis of the sciences," which followed his speech "Science as a Vocation" ([1919] 1946), which dismissed various justifications and characterizations of the pursuit of knowledge and denied there was any sort of modern knowledge that was not the knowledge of specialists. In that text it is somewhat ambiguous as to whether he thinks that comprehensive cosmological rationality and knowledge is merely an absurd present aspiration or whether it was always a false aspiration, but the implication is that it was always an illusion. Thus the Platonic idea of knowledge of the forms as the highest and controlling form of knowledge is a model of possible expertise, which happens to have been based on epistemic error.

In the essay on China there is also a reference to Plato, which on the face of it is quite odd: "The Platonic ideal was established on the soil of the *polis* and proceeded from the conviction that man can attain fulfillment by being good at only one task" ([1920] 1951: 161). This would make it seem that philosophy, or that which corresponds to knowledge of the forms, is itself a form of specialized knowledge wrongly given political significance by Plato: an interpretation which would help Weber preserve his image of rationality as distinctly Western and his own picture of Western intellectual history as summarized in "Science as a Vocation" ([1919] 1946: 140–43). But of course Plato's image of the guardians was that they would be trained in an extended hierarchy of the non-manual forms of knowledge and that on reaching the top of the hierarchy they would have the highest and most comprehensive knowledge, knowledge of the forms, which included knowledge of the form of the good. Thus the guardians were not, for Plato, specialists in ethical theory, the "one task" at the top of the hierarchy of knowledge, but generalists, or at least masters of a hierarchy of types of knowledge.

In one sense, Weber's argument is persuasive: no one now thinks that there is general knowledge of the Platonic kind: today, even the philosophers concerned with the heirs to Plato's forms, perhaps logicians or metaphysicians, are specialists. The last flirtation in the West with the idea of philosophical leaders—Heidegger's idea that he could be "the leader of the leader," that is to say Hitler, ended in catastrophe. And the revival of the Platonic sense of philosophical rule by neo-Conservative followers of Leo Strauss, portrayed in Saul Bellow's roman à clef about Allan Bloom, *Ravelstein*, has led to its own difficulties. Knowledge here seems indistinguishable from ideology—a point to which I will return shortly.

As a sociological claim applied to the past, however, it is misleading. One can identify a large number of cases in which bodies of learning that were highly general served as the basis of community life. The rabbinical governance of Jews after the fall of Jerusalem under the Mishnah, for example, is a clear case in which a body of thought was developed to ethically regulate life and to serve juridical purposes that applied to many domains, from economics to purely religious questions, and we can retrospectively construct the "theory" behind these regulations (cf. Neusner 1990, 1991). Rabbinical learning was "specialist" and "expert" only in a sense that does not fit the Weberian model very well. The knowledge of Torah was specialized in the sense that it was knowledge of a text. But the realm of application was decidedly non-specialized. Moreover, it fits the model of the philosophy of the community. A similar claim could be made for Islamic jurisprudence.

Weber seems to be skeptical about the idea that these philosophies were an actually effective basis of rule. His model of philosophically grounded rule appears to be natural law. He listed natural law as a source of legitimacy rather than as a form of legitimacy, meaning that natural law or a coherent body of ethical belief could serve as a buttress for the claim of the state to authority, but that it was insufficient in itself to constitute a form of rule. In an important sense the skepticism is justified: rabbinical rule was a matter of communal self-governance under a secular, separate state, rather than an effective blueprint for an actual form of political and juridical authority. Islamic law, similarly, ordinarily did not suffice, but rather coexisted with the law of the state (cf. Coulson 1969: 58–76).

Justified or not, this proved to be something of a blind spot for Weber's followers in the period of Communism. Hans J. Morgenthau, one of Weber's most successful admirers, analyzed the dictatorship of Stalin in terms of the categories of charisma conjoined with bureaucracy. This characterization had the effect of omitting the role of ideology. Of course, there is a question, historically, about the significance of ideology in Communist regimes. But the problem here is different: it is rather that Weber's categories of legitimate authority, which are the basis for his classification of functioning political forms, do not include a form of authority that is ideological, and tend to treat ideological matters as though they had no political significance beyond the role of legitimating authority.

In short, neither Weber's sociology of authority nor his conception of genuine knowledge had a place for comprehensive philosophies of the community. China is a case in which Imperial authority was closely tied to the bureaucracy run by literati who gained office through the examination system. Weber struggled to describe this in terms of European categories. He did not see that the "literary" tradition as a community philosophy is binding on all the participants, including the emperor—as with the ideological state, and that the mechanism of examinations served the purpose of inculcating and giving prestige to this philosophy and its adepts. Instead, he saw it as an arbitrary method of securing offices for life, prebends, with no rationality of its own.

One reason for this perception was scholarly. The examination system was criticized by Chinese modernizers "who questioned whether memorizing the classics and writing poems and essays were really relevant to the tasks of government, charged that the system merely tested men's classical education, and asserted that the examination net failed to capture men who possessed genuine abilities and high moral character" (Miyazaki [1963] 1976: 124–25). Weber echoed these criticisms. But the system as it functioned, especially in the five centuries of the last imperial period when it stabilized (Elman 2000a: xvii), was not quite as Weber and the critics portrayed it.

The exams were not, however, limited to poetry, calligraphy, and the classics. Questions of policy and legal reasoning were an important part of the examination procedure (Elman 2000a: 42). The essays, in any case, were not mindless classicism. Elman discusses the rhetorical structure of one of the most famous of the essays (which were published and used as study guides and models) based on a passage from the *Analects* of Confucius that read "When the people have enough, how can the ruler have too little?," which deals with the "ruler's responsibilities to provide a livelihood for his people" (Elman 2000b: 381). To be sure, these essays were constructed according to complex formal rules. Nevertheless they contained chains of argument that are not unrecognizable in Western terms, and which were both sophisticated and relevant to governance. In this case, he notes, the argument was designed to show "how low taxes would increase the overall wealth of the realm, if it remained in the hands of the people" and also benefit the dynasty. The effect of the argument, as he puts it, was to lead to a conclusion that was counterintuitive, and "channeled into a literati discourse built around Confucius's vision of a polity pegged to the interests of the people" (Elman 2000b: 386).

The exams were not limited to a small group of office seekers, something that Weber's account does not make clear. Huge numbers of aspirants studied for these tests, and thus were educated in this vision of the polity, and in much more. Elman estimates that by the nineteenth century, when the population had grown over 300 million, there were 3 million candidates for every biennial exam (2000a: 237). Few succeeded. But the experience of studying for the exams was very widespread. And the intensity of study, along with the uniformity of the topics, must have had an unusually uniformity-producing effect.

When it is considered in detail, the examination system seems less irrational, less medieval, and less alien. Exams in the West have the same fetishistic quality, from the SAT, which is a major determinant of college admission in the US, to the Baccalaureate in France, and the same arbitrariness of content. Weber, himself educated in one of the most arbitrary and rigorous systems of literary education in history, should have recognized the similarities. The fact that he saw the exams primarily in terms of the power of the literati is perhaps a result of his commitment to conceptual categories for which Confucius was a poor fit.

As a western academic he did not see the absurdities of the Chinese system as a mirror for the absurdities of the academic rituals and distinctions of the West; if he had, he could have written a new *les Lettres persanes* to mock them. But although Weber was alleged to have had a sense of humor (Swedberg 2005: 119), this was not his style.

A deeper question of a more "philosophical" kind also emerges in connection with Weber's judgments of the irrationality of Chinese practice. Weber used the notion of rationality in multiple ways, which sometimes conflict: sometimes the notion is normative, as in "Science as a Vocation" and elsewhere, in contexts where he is making judgments about forms of knowledge or action, such as the return to religion in an age that has eaten from the tree of knowledge; sometimes it is used as an interpretive instrument, as when he describes the task of making sense of the military decisions of German Field Marshall Moltke, in which the problem is to explicate as rational decisions that might not on the surface appear to be rational and to show what remains to be accounted for in terms other than rationality; and descriptively as a classification device, used in causal contexts to identify causal conditions.

The classificatory use can be comfortably regarded, within Weber's own methodology, as necessarily ethnocentric—it is an audience of Westerners who are being helped toward understanding—and of no significance beyond its uses in making causal sense of the social world as described from an Occidental point of view. But in the China volume Weber repeatedly seems to go beyond this, a problem that becomes obvious when we come to the question of whether the body of Confucian thought represents genuine knowledge. If it does not, as Platonic knowledge of the forms does not, Weber can dismiss the idea that these bureaucrats are experts rather than literati whose selection for bureaucratic office through examinations is merely an arbitrary procedure. If it is real knowledge, it presents a problem. As an interpreter, Weber would have an obligation to make rational sense of it, rather than simply labeling it irrational. If he says that it cannot be made sense of, he raises the question of whether he has understood it. The judgment in this case has to be that Weber stopped short of fully understanding Chinese thought even within the limitations of the Occidental perspective he brought to it.

The solution to this conundrum is not to be found in Weber. Indeed, the question of whether his own methodology was founded on a choice that was irrational by his own lights has persisted as the major philosophical issue with his thought. Leo Strauss himself, of course, made this point with respect to "Classical Political Philosophy," by which he meant Plato and Aristotle, and argued that Weber had illegitimately ruled out the possibility of knowledge of the good ([1950] 1971: 36–78). The ruling out was illegitimate because to ground it would have required Weber to engage philosophically with the claims of classical philosophy, in other words make himself into a philosopher, rather than to presume that this kind of philosophy was now superseded.

There is another problem, however, that goes to the heart of Weber's notion of expertise. The doctrines Weber was keen to reject as failures to specialize and therefore develop were doctrines which aspired to comprehensiveness. But comprehensiveness is not merely a bad goal, an illusory end rooted in literati nostalgia for the universal intellectual, as Weber seems to suggest. It is a practical imperative. There is a need to aggregate the knowledge of the specialists in order to make rational decisions. Narrowing may lead to achievement, but achievements need to be made usable for the non-specialist, or for the ruler. One aspect of the kind of intellectual mastery that the Confucians sought, and which Plato sought in his account of the ideal city, was the capacity to stand at the top of the pyramid of knowledge and decide wisely. Whether one thinks of this as specialist knowledge—whether one can be an expert about expertise—is an interesting question, but here it is beside the point: someone must use the specialist knowledge of the expert and make it into a whole. And one suspects that one source of Weber's inability to see the point of Confucianism is connected to his failure to acknowledge the problem of aggregating knowledge.

Part IV
Collective Heuristics
Expertise as System

13 Double Heuristics and Collective Knowledge
The Case of Expertise

There is a burgeoning literature on social epistemology. Some of it purports to illuminate the problem of expert knowledge. Much of this literature applies epistemological theories, such as reliabilism, to expert claims, which are interpreted in terms of notions familiar to epistemology, such as testimony. Another body of literature is concerned with the contrast between individual and collective rationality or collective knowledge, and is concerned with issues of emergence, specifically with the claim that collective knowledge processes are different from and arrive at different and better results than individual knowledge acquisition. Many of these are discussions of collective rationality, and use formal methods. To do so, they typically simplify the issues by assuming independent individual judges. Independence implies epistemic independence, meaning that people act on their own knowledge. Discussions of the related problem of expertise typically follow the same pattern: expertise is compared to testimony, which the *individual* judges as reliable. The classic prisoner's dilemma is based explicitly on the mutual ignorance of the prisoners with respect to intentions. Both the social relations between the prisoners and the possibility of sharing knowledge are defined away. In this respect, these approaches follow standard economic theories, which assume information equality or otherwise assume the irrelevance of differences in quality of information between market participants in market transactions. Nor is there an easy alternative to these assumptions. Asymmetric information theorizing, for example, is technically difficult even in small scale transactions with limited dimensions of relevant information, such as theorizing the issues of agency in a used car purchase. Expanding these considerations and expanding considerations of variations between market participants makes calculating outcomes intractable.

My concern in what follows will be with cases of extreme "information asymmetry" in which members of the audience of the experts have knowledge that is different from the knowledge of experts. The knowledge is often relevant, and the decision by a member of the audience of the expert to accept or reject the expert's claims is not, as the models imply, based simply on beliefs about the reliability of the experts, but on the knowledge that the member of the audience already has, and has solid grounds for. In these cases, the better model for understanding how the member of the audience assesses the expert involves the content of the knowledge, not merely the evaluation of the expert. The member of the audience makes an epistemic judgment on the primary knowledge material, not merely on the credentials of the expert. My concern in this chapter will be to provide a way of thinking about these epistemic judgments. But this discussion will be mostly illustrative.

My primary aim will be to suggest a way of thinking about the aggregation of these judgments and how this aggregation can be understood. In the course of this I will treat the problem of expert knowledge as a special case of knowledge aggregation. My suggestion will be that the application of specific decision procedures, such as voting, produces, at the collective level, an emergent form of knowledge acquisition with its own features. Nothing about this account, however, requires an appeal to super-individual entities or processes, collective intentionality, and so forth. My point, rather, will be that to understand these processes it is necessary to eliminate some familiar prejudices about knowledge acquisition and our dependence on others. To put it in a slogan, my point is that "collective epistemology" or social epistemology has failed to be either sufficiently social or sufficiently epistemological. My approach will be to bring both back in, without resorting to appeals to collective facts.

THE BACKGROUND

Social epistemologists have long been concerned with cases in which collective decisions, through such means as judges voting on verdicts, differ from individual judgments. Philip Pettit formulates two of the standard assumptions of these cases as follows:

- you are amongst many people who face a certain question;
- you are all equally intelligent, equally informed, and equally impartial. (2006a: 179)

In normal social situations, neither of Pettit's assumptions hold, and in expert situations the exact opposite is assumed: that people who know something you don't are more intelligent, and may have fewer biases. Moreover, they claim to understand the question better than you do, a second-order claim with unusual epistemic properties: among other things, it undermines the usual ways of judging the claims of others as one understands them.

Pettit interprets the epistemic issues that arise when one's own opinion differs from the majority opinion as a normative problem: when should one defer to majority testimony and when should one not do so? To answer this, he adds to his standard assumptions about equal knowledge and the like:

- you, however, differ from most others in the answer you give;
- you are aware that these things [i.e. the full set of prior assumptions about equal intelligence, knowledge, and impartiality] are true. (2006a: 179)

If we begin with the question of how we would ever know that the people you are among "are all equally intelligent, equally informed, and equally impartial," we can see that these models are epistemically problematic. In this case, the problem of expert knowledge is excluded by definition: expert knowledge is precisely that case in which equality in intelligence, knowledge, and impartiality are denied by both the expert claiming expertise and the member of the expert's audience assessing it. So any direct application of these assumptions to the notion of expert knowledge will fail. They could apply only if the problem of expert knowledge is reduced to the problem of assessing expert "testimony," so that the question of when to defer to an expert becomes a problem of when to defer to majority opinion about the expert. As noted earlier, this way of understanding assent to expert claims strips the knowledge claims themselves of content, making the knowledge of the content possessed by the members of the audience irrelevant.

Another approach to the problem of aggregation involves the suspicion of systematic bias in the production of expert knowledge claims. Miriam Solomon has in mind the idea that gender biases and the like distort theory choice. Although this approach was originally motivated by feminist considerations, it applies more generally. Solomon constructs this as a problem of epistemic diversity, and, rather than dealing with expert authority, deals with the problem of theory choice in the scientific community as a model for epistemic decision-making generally. She suggests that what is needed is a means of eliminating the effects of biases by balancing biases against one another and demanding empirical support for all options (2006a: 37–38; cf. 2006b). This differs slightly from Pettit's approach, by assuming that despite being equally impartial, people have biases. But it also takes a valuable step in epistemologizing the problem of aggregation. "Theory choice by a community" is a collective procedure, although it is a theoretical construction of the observer rather than something that scientists collectively perform, as in voting. And the term "biases" does provide some, very minimal, epistemic content to the notion of epistemic diversity. But this is too small a step. The problem of bias is dwarfed by a much bigger problem of epistemic diversity: that we know different things and can understand different things.

DOUBLE HEURISTICS

The Pettit assumptions are simply false. The true, but difficult, situation is this. We know something already, about experts and what makes them acceptable, and also often about the content of their claims. Our knowledge is not "equal" to that of others, or the same as others. We have our own experiences, as well as practical and sometimes theoretical knowledge that either fits or fails to fit with the expert claims. The (descriptive rather than normative) epistemological problem is to understand this kind of knowledge and to understand how we rely on our knowledge of others—the social aspect—and how we use our own knowledge to assimilate it to what others know.

The literature in social epistemology has been dominated by technical solutions. But if one adds actual epistemology to the social, by considering how we use the content of the knowledge of others as distinct from simply accepting on trust, these solutions become unstable. A less technical, but more usable way of conceptualizing the problem would be this: to think of our use of the knowledge of others as governed by more or less standard heuristics, which may go wrong in abnormal situations, and thus have biases. To discuss this problem, however, one needs some sort of model. The image of the individual knower I propose to work with is itself a simplification, as it must be. But it is a simplification that allows for a discussion, however limited itself, of the general problem of knowledge aggregation. The model is this: the individual is limited, operates with complexity reducing epistemic strategies, arrives at knowledge, and makes knowledge judgments. The individual knower, in short, uses heuristics, which, like all heuristics, work in some situations and not others. They have biases and blind spots. This is hardly an innovative idea, of course. It is enshrined in the literature on empirical models of rational choice (Tversky and Kahneman 1974, 1981).

The value of this starting point is this: it provides us with a model for thinking of emergent and "collective" forms of the same thing. We can think of decision procedures, such as democracies, and aggregation mechanisms without collective decisions but with "collective" outcomes, such as markets, as themselves being heuristics. We can also think of procedures which function as if they were decision procedures, such as market decisions that put firms into bankruptcy, as heuristics. The market itself is not a heuristic, nor is a rule like majority voting. But it is a procedure which makes selections. If a procedure is understood as made up of people operating with particular heuristics that include heuristics about the knowledge of others and how to assimilate it, plus some sort of analogue to a decision, these emergent processes themselves can be understood to have normal situations in which they "work" and others in which their "biases"—biases being the source of the efficiency gained by heuristics—lead to bad results.

This notion of a "double heuristic" then allows us to conceptualize the issues that arise with, for example, the (now commonplace) claim that liberal democracy needs to be abolished to save the human race in the face of global warming. We can ask what sort of alternative collective heuristic there is, such as the heuristic of uncritical acceptance of the assertions of scientific experts, and what the biases of this heuristic might be; which is to say, to ask what the normal and abnormal situation is for this heuristic when it is understood as a heuristic made up of the aggregation of the heuristics of people judging experts with the biases of these heuristics, and of experts themselves making decisions with their biases.

Nevertheless, the contrast between individual and collective results is an important one, and can be generalized beyond voting examples. If we think of individual and collective procedures of dealing with questions, one thing is immediately obvious—a collective "decision," whether it is "the market decides," voting, or counting up the guesses about beans at the county fair, happens differently than individual decision. One makes up one's mind about a bean count, and decides to submit the estimate. The collective act of adding up the estimates and taking a mean takes place on a schedule. No "minds" are made up. The market makes pricing decisions continuously—buyers make them one at a time, sellers look at their stock and respond by changing prices. The collective result is a theoretical construction from the actual prices that are charged transaction by transaction. Juries deliberate and vote, in accordance with protocols and admonitions. Jurors decide they are persuaded when they reach an epistemic threshold of doubt that they individually determine by self-examination, but the collective threshold is unanimity or some other rule.

PUTTING EPISTEMOLOGY BACK IN

The problem of experts in politics has epistemic content, but the content is highly problematic. Both the literature in what Alvin Goldman calls "classical social epistemology" and the literature of the Mertonian sociology of science have focused on the authority of science. As I have noted, epistemologists, not fond of the term "authority," have construed the issue in terms of testimony. This allows authority to be interpreted in traditional philosophical terms, in this case in terms of reliability and therefore in terms of reliabilism, as an epistemology. Other social epistemologists have focused on cases in which collective knowledge is "better" than individual knowledge, or at least different. The model in these cases is guesses at the number of beans in a jar at a country fair: the mean is closer to the correct number than the individual guesses.

What is striking about these cases is their tractability to formal reasoning. One can put up a matrix of judges' votes, for example, and show that the collective result of the votes differs from individual votes (List and Pettit 2002). What is also striking is their inattention to content. Guesses about beans have little epistemic content. Moreover, one's knowledge of the guesses of others is irrelevant or assumed to be irrelevant.

But actual cases of judgments of expert opinions in political contexts are far richer, in a number of ways. The citizen has a variety of epistemic resources, including beliefs about the world, experiences, grounds for making judgments about the sources of claims, and personal knowledge to bring to the making of beliefs about the subject matter discussed by experts and of the experts themselves.

The classic discussion of this is Brian Wynne's paper "May the Sheep Safely Graze?" that considered the case of nuclear power experts making claims about the effect of radiation (1996). The sheep owners to whom the expert discussion was addressed were skeptical of the claims, based on their knowledge of the actual grazing habits of the sheep. This is a case of two kinds of knowledge fitting together. But the fitting together involved content, and the product of the fitting together would alter what each side believed, rather than merely combining independent estimates to create a third without altering at least the epistemic weight of the beliefs of one side or the other.

Assuming content away, using the model of bias and similar devices, does not help much with these cases. Empirically, content-free judgments about expertise based on the pure kinds of assessments involved in testimony—in the extremely abnormal and purified sense of testimony in which the reliability of the witness is the only consideration—are nowhere to be found. When people on a jury assess real testimony, they do so on the basis of their prior knowledge and actual experience of the world, as lawyers know very well, which is why they are careful to select juries that are as ignorant as possible about the topics they are going to hear testimony on.

A CLASSIC MODEL OF SCIENCE AS A COLLECTIVE HEURISTIC

Philosophy of science provides some models for thinking about "fitting together," such as Michael Polanyi's picture of science as a big jigsaw puzzle into which we each fit our little pieces of knowledge. Polanyi provided more than one, and the differences between his accounts are revealing with respect to the phenomenon of the relation between individual and collective heuristics. In the essays collected in *The Logic of Liberty*, he describes the collective process in terms of the

> adjustment of each scientist's activities to the results hitherto achieved by others. In adjusting himself to the others each scientist acts independently, yet by virtue of these several adjustments scientists keep extending together with maximum efficiency the achievements of science as a whole. At each step a scientist will select from the results obtained by others those elements which he can use best for his own task and will thus make the best contribution to science; opening thereby the field for other scientists to make their optimum contribution in their turn—and so on indefinitely. ([1951] 1980: 34–35)

This implies that what I am calling a heuristic—an efficient method for getting "collective" knowledge—results from individual contributions to a process of aggregating knowledge.

> The only way to get the job finished quickly would be to get as many helpers as could conveniently work at one and the same set and let them loose on it, each to follow his own initiative. Each helper would then watch the situation as it was affected by the progress made by all the others and would set himself new problems in accordance with the latest outline of the completed part of the puzzle. The tasks undertaken by each would closely dovetail into those performed by the others. And consequently the joint efforts of all would form a closely organized whole, even though each helper would follow entirely his own independent judgment. (Polanyi [1951] 1980: 35)

A collective process is defined by its decision procedure, which in these early writings Polanyi described as a "twofold condition," consisting of rapid publicity plus acclamation, in which

> each suggested new step can be readily judged as to its correctness or otherwise, and that each new step is rapidly brought to the notice of all participants and taken into account by them when they make their own next move. ([1951] 1980: 36)

Pure science, as distinct from applied science or technology, required this heuristic, rather than others.

Polanyi was arguing against planned science, which represented a distinct heuristic or set of possible heuristics. On the surface, planning seemed to be the perfect way to avoid waste in science and produce valuable results. A great deal of thinking, and a social movement of left-wing scientists in Britain, promoted planning generally, and the planning of science specifically, in the 1930s, as part of a general enthusiasm for the idea of planning. Polanyi's argument against planning had to do with the problem of knowledge.

> Put negatively, planning is simply impracticable, at least for the most important problems in science: No committee of scientists, however distinguished, could forecast the further progress of science except for the routine extension of the existing system . . . the points at which the existing system can be effectively amended reveal themselves only to the individual investigator. And even he can discover only through a lifelong concentration on one particular aspect of science a small number of practicable and worthwhile problems. ([1951] 1980: 89)

The argument against planned science then depends on an argument about the distribution of knowledge. Translated into our terms, the argument is this: knowledge in science is specialized, so a heuristic that depends on the knowledge of some small group or any collective decision-making process will lose the advantages that the specialist has in deciding how to pursue his or her own problems.

But science cannot avoid collective decision procedures. Money has to be doled out. In this respect it is necessary to construct another decision procedure. Here, notoriously, Polanyi and his sympathizers found the going more difficult. The process of doling out determines the content of the science that can be extended. So there is no escaping the consequences of the system of supporting science. The best that can be done is to have a system that retains the advantages of the heuristic described above.

> The pursuit of science can be organized . . . in no other manner than by granting complete independence to all mature scientists. They will then distribute themselves over the whole field of possible discoveries, each applying his own special ability to the task that appears most profitable to him. Thus as many trails as possible will be covered, and science will penetrate most rapidly in every direction towards that kind of hidden knowledge which is unsuspected by all but its discoverer; the kind of knowledge on which the progress of science truly depends. The function of public authorities is not to plan research, but only to provide opportunities for its pursuit. All that they have to do is provide facilities for every good scientist to follow his own interests in science. ([1951] 1980: 89–90)

With this general heuristic in mind, one can turn to problems of institutional design. This is the model that the Howard Hughes Medical Institute applies by giving six-year appointments on a principle of scientific promise with no restrictions on what the scientist will choose to do. The American National Science Foundation does this by evaluating proposals on merit by specialized panels. In each case, of course, many choices need to be made, each of which involves biases, biases which diminish the odds of science penetrating in some of the directions where hidden knowledge can be revealed.

The epistemology involved here is still individualistic: the discoverer seeks hidden knowledge individually. Verification is collective, by acclamation. Both of these are of course caricatures of the actual practice of science. But there is already a hint in these early writings of the problems of fitting knowledge together, which Polanyi later makes more central, in the idea of extension and the admission that specialization of a very extreme kind is characteristic of scientists. What disqualifies these scientists from making the kinds of general judgments about how science should be planned is this very specialization, and this also disqualifies them for the role of acclaiming scientific achievements. In some of his early writings, Polanyi spoke of the decision-makers in science as a group analogous to Plato's Guardians.

But the guardians were, so to speak, possessors of the most general knowledge; scientists, in contrast, are specialists. These were conflicts that he later resolved, in his classic essay "The Republic of Science" (1962).

The resolution is of interest not only because of its explicit appeal to the concept of spontaneous coordination, but because of the new kind of knowledge relation he identified as the connecting link between the specialized worlds of science. The new emphasis is especially relevant to "social epistemology," because Polanyi makes an explicit contrast between activities which are "coordinated" and those that are not. The examples favored by Pettit and Solomon are uncoordinated—the judges rendering verdicts and people guessing locations of submarines or numbers of beans in a jar are independent and take no account of the knowledge that others have. In science, Polanyi says, if people did this the scientists would deal with the problems set by the information available to all, but without knowledge of what the others were learning they would exhaust these problems and no progress would occur (1962: 54).

This is enough to show that science is a coordinated activity, "and it also reveals the principle of their coordination. This consists in the adjustment of the efforts of each to the hitherto achieved results of the others. We may call this a coordination by mutual adjustment of independent initiatives—of initiatives which are coordinated because each takes into account all the other initiatives operating within the same system" (Polanyi 1962: 54). The emphasis on coordination is new. And one soon sees why, when he considers the analogue to a decision procedure in science.

When Polanyi turns to the problem of explaining the way in which coordination works, he reasons in terms of what I have called here double heuristics. He introduces the image of the puzzle: "Imagine that we are given the pieces of a very large jig-saw puzzle, and suppose that for some reason it is important that our giant puzzle be put together in the shortest possible time" (1962: 55). Polanyi gives three examples of increasingly effective methods of doing this with a group of helpers. The first is independence, in which each person is given a few pieces to fit together: "Suppose we share out the pieces of the jig-saw puzzle equally among the helpers and let each of them work on his lot separately" (1962: 55). He remarks "it is easy to see that this method, which would be quite appropriate to a number of women shelling peas, would be totally ineffectual in this case, since few of the pieces allocated to one particular assistant would be found to fit together" (1962: 55). The second would be to supply each with copies of all the pieces, but still make them work independently: "We could do a little better by providing duplicates of all the pieces to each helper separately, and eventually somehow bring together their several results" (1962: 55). Polanyi's verdict is that "even by this method the team would not much surpass the performance of a single individual at his best" (1962: 55).

The best collective heuristic would be this, which Polanyi takes to be a model of the coordination heuristic for science itself. He goes on to note that self-coordination leads to unpremeditated results (1962: 55). Polanyi expands the thought with this image: "We may imagine this condition to be fulfilled for the fitting together of a jig-saw puzzle if each helper watches out for any new opportunities arising along a particular section of the hitherto completed patch of the puzzle, and also keeps an eye on a particular lot of pieces, so as to fit them in wherever a chance presents itself" (1962: 55). The "competence" in question is epistemic and localized. The person knows more about this little patch. But later in the text Polanyi admits that this has implications for the acceptance and evaluation of science.

From the point of view of discovery, the argument is the same. The result is a heuristic that is more effective than the others, at least with respect to speed. "The effectiveness of a group of helpers will then exceed that of any isolated member, to the extent to which some member of the group will always discover a new chance for adding a piece to the puzzle more quickly than any one isolated person could have done by himself" (1962: 55). The term "invisible hand" invites comparison to markets, and Polanyi suggests that the comparison is apt, but the conclusion should not be that science is a special case of markets, but that "the coordinating functions of the market are but a special case of coordination by mutual adjustment" (1962: 66). This notion of mutual adjustment, however, is a new emphasis. The contrast to the market is that in science the adjustment is to the publications of other scientists; in the market it is altered by competitors (1962: 56).

The motivations in science differ: "by contrast, the scientist responding directly to the intellectual situation created by the published results of other scientists is motivated by current professional standards" (Polanyi 1962: 56). Current professional standards, as we will see, play a special role. The choices about what lines of inquiry to follow that the scientist makes in the face of these standards, Polanyi admits, have an economic character. The scientist does not want to waste time on insoluble problems, or those that are too easy, or hypotheses that are implausible from the standpoint of present professional knowledge. But originality is prized by these professional standards.

The puzzle, from the point of view of the application of collective heuristics, is in the decision procedure, meaning in this case understanding how these standards are applied. As noted, Polanyi earlier seemed to rely on a kind of general acclamation. Now he recognizes the conflict between specialization and the idea that each scientist is omnicompetent to act as judge, and asks "how can an aggregate of such specialists possibly form a joint opinion? (1962: 59). The solution to this is of course to invoke a new collective heuristic, or what Polanyi calls an "organizational principle" (1962: 59). Crudely, there are scientists in adjacent areas of science who know enough to judge the work of the specialist, and this enforces consistency in the application of professional standards.

These relations of adjacency produce a network, which is the point at which we can interpret this as a collective heuristic. Polanyi puts this in his own terms:

> This network is the seat of scientific opinion. Scientific opinion is an opinion not held by any single human mind, but one which, split into thousands of fragments, is held by a multitude of individuals, each of whom endorses the other's opinion at second hand, by relying on the consensual chains which link him to all the others through a sequence of overlapping neighborhoods. (1962: 59–60)

But scientific opinion, even when it is distributed in this way (and Polanyi has more to say about whose opinions count most) is still opinion, as Polanyi always insisted. These procedures, and the collective heuristics system they create through their operation, are not epistemic guarantors of truth.

In his earlier writings Polanyi discussed the corruption of scientific opinion. In "The Republic of Science" he concedes that the system of control by the application of professional standards can lead to bad results. But on a collective level, it is, in our terms, the best heuristic. However, "Though it is easy to find flaws in [the] operation [of the organizational principles of this system], they yet remain the only principles by which this vast domain of collective creativity can be effectively promoted and coordinated" (1962: 61).

Evaluating these claims is not my concern here. This is an illustration of the basic concept of double heuristics. But a few points need to be made. Polanyi changes his ideas about the nature of the relations between areas of science in "The Republic of Science" by emphasizing the way in which specialists in adjacent areas evaluated new findings. He tells us little about their heuristics for doing so, though clearly his general ideas about professional standards are of the kind that has local variations and applications. The considerations Polanyi applies to science were also applied by him to the economics of planning, and this opens a related domain of inquiry.

Peter Boettke argued in *The Political Economy of Soviet Socialism* that the idea of central planning was applied in earnest only for the first decade after the Russian Revolution (1990). What emerged in its place was a collection of loosely related plans. The way the plans were collected and collated had little to do with the idea of central planning in the contemporary economics literature. The models of perfect knowledge that Oscar Lange (and even Frank Knight in response to Lange) had discussed when they examined the theoretical possibility of centralized socialist planning were completely unlike the actual process. Yet well into the 1940s, planning continued to be discussed in these theoretical terms, and the successes of the Soviet Union were taken to vindicate, in some sense, the theoretical possibility of a kind of virtual knowledge of demand. Polanyi himself pointed out that, although the planners got their knowledge in ways other than the open market, they were ways that were quite mundane. As David Prychitko notes,

> Polanyi argued that, as opposed to the theoretical model, the Soviet economy has been composed of numerous, conflicting planning centers—a "polycentric" as opposed to "monocentric" order. Coordination, to the extent that it occurred at all, took place not at the center of the planning hierarchy, but at the lower levels, among the individual enterprise managers who used their own discretionary authority and engaged in black market exchanges. Though the quantity and quality of outputs chosen and produced at the enterprise level became aggregated into a so-called central plan, and indeed were later published as a unified, centrally issued plan established by the directives of GOSPLAN (the Soviet central planning bureau), in fact the coordination of economic activities took place at the enterprise level, at the bottom of the hierarchy. (Prychitko 2002: 154n8)

Managers engaged in black market operations knew what the values of goods were, whether there was demand, and so forth (cf. Roberts 2005). These were imperfect means, but nevertheless means subject to real world discipline in the form of facts about prices. The managers used this information to plan their own production, and the planners aggregated these plans and tinkered with them. This was a system with its own epistemic biases, resulting in part from the limited knowledge of the contributing players. It was far from the ideal rationalized central planning. Nevertheless, it was a system that aggregated knowledge of diverse kinds into a collective result.

The most famous alternative to this form of centralized pseudo-planning in "Socialist" countries was the decentralized Yugoslavian system of worker self-managed productive units, which operated with limited market mechanisms for resources, and more or less open markets for the consumer goods. As Prychitko showed in *Marxism and Workers' Self-Management* (1991), these units, which purported to solve the problem of alienation by giving the workers control of what happened to the products they made, transferred the problems of planning and making market related decisions to the workers, or rather to workers' councils, which were supposed to be democratic, participatory, and to produce a decentralized bottom up control of the economy that eliminated the waste of financial speculation and advertising.

Democratic participation is a knowledge aggregation system. And comparing the scheme of aggregation of knowledge of an ordinary hierarchical firm to a democratically self-managed one, as Prychitko does, points out some interesting differences in how knowledge is shared. The workers had a greater propensity and incentive to share information about what was happening in their part of the production process, for example. But the workers were not especially willing to undertake the knowledge-related tasks of aggregating this knowledge, or taking responsibility for decisions—problems that would be solved in an actual case of democratic rule by rewarding winners in political competition. This points to a whole range of questions about how propensities and abilities to use and share knowledge differ among organizations, and thus to the epistemic problem of what sort of learners different organizations are, and what are the biases, efficiencies, and blind spots in the different "collective" information processing and aggregating heuristics that result from the way in which the organizations operate.

BILATERAL ASYMMETRIC CONSILIENCE

Fitting the pieces together is a metaphor, as is the term "network." Polanyi doesn't inquire into the epistemology of fitting together. What is the relevance of having the pieces fit, or having new knowledge in adjacent areas of science? Certainly it has some bearing on our sense that we are on the right track, that the previous steps leading up to the new knowledge were the correct ones, and so forth. This model suggests consilience of induction as both a ground for belief in "our piece" and the solution provided by the puzzle as a whole, but also suggests a model of collective outcomes of epistemic contributions that go beyond individual knowers. The "adjustments" which Polanyi stressed are also adjustments in what people believe and the weight they give to beliefs.

Other examples can be used to reveal the problematic results of interpretations of experiments which ignore the "social" cues on which we ordinarily and necessarily rely in coming to beliefs. It is nevertheless awkward to think epistemically about what fitting together might mean because the traditions of epistemology are individualist. To help this along, let me give an example of a non-individual epistemic notion. Here the (descriptive rather than normative) epistemological problem is to understand this kind of knowledge and to understand how we rely on our knowledge of others—the social aspect—and how we use our own knowledge to assimilate it to what others know.

Suppose that the doctor supplies a diagnosis that is based on your self-reported symptoms, but that also predicts symptoms that you did not report because you did not think they were relevant, but can now recognize as part of the syndrome. The situation is one of asymmetric knowledge, but also of distributed knowledge: the patient knows something the doctor doesn't as well as the reverse. They are different kinds of knowledge: the doctor supplies the means of fitting together without knowing in advance at least some fact that turns out to fit. This is consilience in the original Whewell sense of correctly predicting some novel fact that the theory was not constructed to account for (Whewell 1858: 88–90). In this case, the doctor was accounting for the symptoms that were presented.

This is different from reliabilism, also "social" and "epistemic" in a sense independent of judging testimony, yet which still reflects acceptance of the asymmetric knowledge of others. The basic thought is that the fact of consilience itself adds to the epistemic weight of the facts considered independently, in contrast to the aggregation and voting cases. The added weight is not something done by judging the expertise of the source, though this is part of the story. It is social because you don't get the epistemic payoff, namely consilience, without the social, in this case the acceptance as minimally weighty of the fact and content of the beliefs of others, which are then combined with one's own for the payoff.

In contrast, assessing testimony adds no epistemic weight, content, or predictive power to the original testimony—it is a subjective weighing of something else's epistemic weight (or "probative force," you can pick your favorite term). "Consilience" or what we might in this case call "Asymmetric Bilateral Consilience," is more than merely consistency with the diagnosis, which is another, weaker sense, (which might be the case where a jury rejects testimony based on their own knowledge of relevant facts that are not consistent with the testimony, which we could call "Asymmetric Bilateral Consistency"). But maybe we could do the world a favor and not call them anything fancy.

Like all heuristics, this one can go wrong, and typically "going wrong" means applying them under circumstances that don't work for reasons the user does not know. The place that this heuristic most obviously can go wrong is when the novel fact predicted by the expert is not as independent of the facts known to the non-expert as one or the other might believe. This would occur, for example, when both expert and non-expert are describing facts in accordance with a common but unacknowledged ideology, as when the non-expert reads an ideologically selective newspaper report and "discovers" that this fits an expert "truth" that is generated in a hidden way by the same ideology. The hypothesis of a hidden variable producing the facts, like the case of assumptions of independence in statistics, is normally one that is beyond the limits of the heuristic itself. And this raises questions about the way in which the heuristics we employ in assessing and giving weight to other people's opinions, for example, in the case of the problem described by Pettit of when to defer to majority opinion, are themselves potentially compromised. The heuristics are limited by our failure or inability to assess whether these opinions are indeed the result of more or less independent judgments of others, or are the product of a consensus produced artificially by some other means. This fits with the many social psychological experiments on conformity of the 1950s, to be discussed shortly, which showed how readily people would accept false beliefs if a group of which they were a part affirmed them. If the subjects of the experiments had known that there was a conspiracy by the members of the group to affirm these beliefs, or even, that they were not independently arrived at, they would have responded differently. In the case of the physician's diagnosis, the same point holds: if one's descriptions of one's own symptoms are influenced by the same therapeutic ideology as the physician, the independence of the two acts of description, one motivated from and derived from the physicians diagnosis, the other from the private experience of the patient, is an illusion.

Polanyi's puzzle model of science depends on giving epistemic weight to the beliefs of others, and "fitting" them in some way with their beliefs. What is fitting, in an epistemic sense? This strong kind of consilience is one example of fitting. Collective rationality, extended mind, etc. models locate the knowing in the collective knower. Polanyi's model doesn't do that: it relies on the notion of networks. But it also allows for, and indeed forces us to begin, thinking about the kinds of heuristics, both individual and (actually) collective rather than merely social, that are in fact employed, and how they produce the double heuristic pattern. Bilateral asymmetric consilience is a very strong source of epistemic weight. But it too makes some assumptions about independence: the scientific workers are supposed to be specialists working on their own little patch of science and thus uninfluenced by what is going on in the parts of the network, or the puzzle, that they are not working on. And this is not the only form of fitting: there can be heuristics that work using weaker heuristics, such as deference to scientific authority as such and consciously fitting our observations and beliefs to whatever appears as the consensus. But of course these heuristics have their own weaknesses and biases.

INFORMATION POVERTY AND CONSENSUS

As part of the training for American diplomats, they are shown a table of cutlery, with dozens of implements. Why? So they know how to use the right fork, and avoid a diplomatic gaffe. One could have expert knowledge of such things, but most of us, in the face of the problem of how to use a fork, use the simple heuristic "when in Rome, do as the Romans." This is suggestive. Isn't it normally right to accept what others believe, or to give it great weight? Isn't it a significant problem for a believer in "x" if others reject "x"? Doesn't this produce a potentially large explanatory burden?

Heuristics work in normal situations. This one would also work, unless one were copying the wrong person. Here we have heuristics as well: the Castilians who, according to the apparently false legend, started lisping because King Phillip lisped were following a heuristic, and successive generations followed them based on their own heuristic of talking like their betters. Does this make sense as a normative rule? Of course not, in the sense of an abstract approach to ethical truth. But this is misleading, as are a large number of psychology experiments which come to mind in these cases.

Here are a few more examples. Vance Packard, in the 1950s, gave the example of an umbrella for sale in a department store. At a low price, the umbrella failed to sell. The price was doubled, and it sold briskly. What is going on here epistemically? The question of whether an umbrella is any good is not one that we are ordinarily able to determine by looking at it. The heuristic that says "you get what you pay for" would lead you to think a cheaply priced umbrella was no good; a higher priced one would be good. Since this is the only information we have in this case, the rule misleads us.

The Asch conformity experiments involved subjects who were placed with a group of confederates who gave different measurements of a line. Asch wondered about the circumstances under which the subject would capitulate to the majority. He found that some people did, others were confused, and others were resistant. The findings were that if the confederates were unanimous, people conformed; if there were a few dissenters, or even an inconsistent dissenter, the rate of conformity dropped drastically. The Milgram experiments seemed to show a lot of conformity. But they can't even be run again because people would know what was going on. Subjects did question the experiment as it went on, but the experimenters were trained to fend the questions off.

The experiments are all about abnormal situations: settings are information poor, so that often the only added information is the beliefs of others; access to other opinions is manipulated; information costs are manipulated or high, so that only cheap information supports the outcome. So these are, from the point of view of normal heuristics, abnormal situations. They are useful only for revealing our normal heuristics. But they also show

that one can create abnormal situations that allow these normal social heuristics to be used against people. The problem, as indicated in connection with bilateral asymmetric consilience, is that the heuristics themselves, by definition, do not detect the abnormality of the situation. This is particularly important in relation to notions like consensus, which we know from these experiments to have powerful effects on people's belief: assumptions about the independence of the parties to the consensus are false, and the environment is information poor.

EXPERT KNOWLEDGE AND DEMOCRACY

We can think of the problems with which we began, the problem of expertise in liberal democracy, in terms relative to normal and abnormal heuristics rather than "truth." Simple models of democracy assume that people have interests, knowledge of the basic functions of government and information on how they are being carried out, and a capacity to assess the

Double Heuristics and Collective Knowledge 255

interests and motives of others. They operate to advance their own interests, and make common cause with those who can articulate interests that coincide with theirs, or are not in too great a conflict with theirs, or match their vision of a harmonious, decent society. But the heuristics they employ, according to various bodies of research, involve getting information from trusted sources, such as local influentials, rather than making these assessments on their own. This is a heuristic: trust those who you know to be well-informed, responsible, and with a stake in the same things you have a stake in.

"Influence," however, is a crude term, which implies some sort of occult psychological force. Perhaps, in these cases, it should be understood epistemically, in the manner of the physician. If the influential says things that imply things that the hearer knows, it should help strengthen both of their beliefs. Even the weak epistemic support provided by the fact that the influential, who is similarly situated, has these beliefs is still epistemic rather than a matter of occult psychology. Nevertheless the reliance on influentials is a heuristic with obvious biases. Some of these, under normal circumstances, are beneficial. They provide protection against such classic evils of democracy as demagoguery: if one is relying along with one's friends on one's local influentials, it is unlikely that waves of political enthusiasm for false prophets will overwhelm the system. At the same time, it is a heuristic that is relatively immune to totalitarian ideology: local influentials tend to think for themselves and not behave in a uniform manner. But it is also true that such a system is not especially receptive to assertions of expert authority that do not operate through trusted local influentials.

Of course, all of this is a greatly simplified model even of traditional democracies. Modern democracies are composed of people with memberships in a variety of groups, which operate in ways that differ, and have their own heuristics. Because of the sheer variety of heuristics found in different groups, the possible combinations of them in a collective procedure are also large. The problem of designing a decision procedure that produces good results given the individual heuristics of the participants is daunting. But posing the question in terms of double heuristics does allow us to give these questions some content. What if it is claimed that liberal democracy—because of its open discussion, which fails to adequately defer to scientific consensus—needs to be abolished or corrected by policing utterances about science in order to save the world by enacting proper policies on climate change? These are translatable into questions about the joint operation of individual and collective heuristics, and pose questions that might be solved by altering collective decision procedures to produce heuristics with different biases.

We can ask the same kinds of critical questions about the double heuristics involved in the production of collective expert opinion out of individual expert heuristics. Does scientific groupthink and grant-driven bandwagoning make science unreliable as a source of the kinds of facts that political bodies need to make? What if Ulrich Beck was right to complain that experts had a conservative epistemic bias, which led them to be skeptical about the evidence for risks, and to systematically under rate risks, and we have a system for collective decision-making that defers to experts? (Beck 1995). We magnify the error producing potential of the system in a specific direction. But if we have a system in which experts benefit by asserting risks, we have the opposite result.

In the end it will be clear that there is no such thing as a perfect heuristic, that each has blind spots or biases. We can also see what the "normal" situations are in which the heuristics can be said to be the best, and ask whether the situation we are in is abnormal, and perhaps requires a differently designed decision procedure which implies a different collective heuristic. There is no general solution to the problem of whether the situation in which the heuristic is applied is normal. But that is not the point. We will at least have a vocabulary in which to ask these questions, and ask them about historical cases which are similar, as well as to think about problems of institutional design. This is a failing of much present discussion of expertise and liberal democracy, which is concerned instead with the question of whether expertise is genuine.

It is also a failing of social epistemology to ignore the epistemic dimension of "the social," the fact that much of the content of our social relations with others involves epistemic weightings—indeed, it is hard to see anything in our social relations that does not involve changes in the weighting of our own beliefs on the basis of the actions and beliefs of others. Thinking in terms of double heuristics compels us to think about collective decision procedures in terms of the same problems of bias, selectivity, and so forth that characterize the individual knowledge related activities of which collective activity is composed.

14 Normal Accidents of Expertise

The organizational theorist Charles Perrow invented the term "normal accidents" ([1984] 1999) to apply to the kinds of failures that are inevitable in complex systems, such as chemical plants or nuclear plants, which are "coupled" in a tight way, meaning that when something went wrong in one part of the system it would have consequences for other parts of the system (Perrow [1984] 1999: 72, 89–100). Some of the consequences in such systems are predictable linear consequences of failures of components in the system. Others, which will be my main concern here, will involve multiple failures of components with unpredictable consequences.

These consequences can include catastrophic outcomes. Loosely coupled systems, such as an assembly process that is made up of several component assembly processes that operate independently but need to converge at the final assembly of a product, also fail, but they allow for more time to correct for failures and to invent responses. Tightly coupled systems are more sensitive: responses need to be immediate and routinized, which means that failures must be anticipated in advance. The failures that can be anticipated in advance are those for which redundant systems can be created or standard operating procedures for correction can be applied in the face of failure. Many failures in a coupled system, however, result from unanticipated interactions between elements of the system in the face of the failure of multiple elements of the system, which produces problems that cannot be solved by standard procedures. When tightly coupled systems fail in this way, the results can be catastrophic. Loosely coupled systems are more forgiving.

Producing expert knowledge is different from producing nuclear power or chemicals, but there are similarities. Error and error correction are a major element of what systems producing expert knowledge do, and they involve a complex division of labor which is also a division of knowledge: technical or expert knowledge of highly specialized kinds have to be brought together to make the system work. In some respects, however, producing expert knowledge and producing chemicals are especially similar. In big science there is always complex instrumentation that must be made to work and must be understood. Errors involving the functioning and design of instruments are endemic to big science. The technologies are often unique, cutting edge, and difficult to test in the conditions where they are designed to be used.

Unanticipated interaction effects have the potential to produce catastrophic results. There have been two major failures of expert communities in the last decade: the failure of the economics community to grasp the implications of the rise of various financial instruments in relation to mortgages and the alterations of mortgage policies, and the failure of the climate science community to anticipate the drop in the rate of temperature change over the last decade. These failures have been much commented on, and the discussion is still in the phase of lack of consensus—including a lack of consensus over whether there was a failure, or whether the failure was major or minor. Each involved complex interactions. It is appropriate to ask whether the model of normal accidents applies to these cases. In what follows, I will do no such thing, though I will return to the issues with climate science in the conclusion. It is clear, however, that much of the political discussion of experts and expert consensus is blind to the general problem of catastrophic expert failure, which will be my concern here. Of course, this issue relates to the problem of skepticism about experts, as it should. But the point of the chapter is to identify a specific problem that arises with systems producing expert knowledge.

THE QUESTION OF SYMMETRY: CAN SCIENCE STUDIES TALK ABOUT FAILURE?

Talk of "failure" and "error" in science studies invites quotation marks: according to the methodological principle of symmetry, failure and error are socially constructed in the same way as "true" scientific facts are. Is this consideration relevant here? The field has itself seen a sea change in the discussion of such topics, especially in relation to risk. Major figures such as Harry Collins and Bruno Latour have modified their views in order to avoid being seen as skeptics, particularly about global warming. Latour says that,

> I intended to emancipate the public from prematurely naturalized objectified facts. Was I foolishly mistaken? Have things changed so fast? In which case the danger would no longer be coming from an excessive confidence in ideological arguments posturing as matters of fact—as we have learned to combat so efficiently in the past—but from an excessive distrust of good matters of fact disguised as bad ideological biases! While we spent years trying to detect the real prejudices hidden behind the appearance of objective statements, do we now have to reveal the real objective and incontrovertible facts hidden behind the illusion of prejudices? (2004: 227)

Collins has claimed that we are in a third wave of science studies in which the reality of expertise is accepted. Michael Lynch suggests that the source of the problem, the symmetry thesis, itself be treated as problematic: He revises Bloor's famous formulation, to suggest a discovery program that "would be impartial with respect to truth or falsity, rationality or irrationality, success or failure [and symmetry or asymmetry]. Both sides of these dichotomies will require explanation" (Lynch 2010: 11–12). These are all efforts to problematize the problematizing device of symmetry itself. But is this necessary? And does it bear on the application of Perrow's argument to expertise?

Answering this requires a return to some fundamentals. The term symmetry derives from a distinction in explanatory form. Causal explanations are symmetric; teleological explanations are not. In a teleological explanation, there is a favored endpoint that does not require further explanation. The classic example is the Aristotelian theory of motion: an object seeks its appropriate final place (Taylor 1964: 21–25). Once it is there, there is no more motion, except for disturbances of the natural order. Objects "fall" in order to get to their place in the natural order. The order itself is explained by some higher principle. In the case of science, this kind of explanation involved truth or correctness and error. The history of science traditionally was written as a mixed history of truth and error. The truths, or at least the fact that scientists correctly believed in true facts, didn't require explanation—they had, so to speak, arrived at their natural end. Error, however, did require explanation.[1] In writings like Laudan's *Progress and its Problems* (1978), social explanations were given the task of explaining error, but not truth. Dispensing with symmetry meant dispensing with the favored status of correctness. But it also meant a change in the object of explanation. The teleological view ran together belief and truth: truth became a sufficient explanation for belief. The symmetric view was that truth was irrelevant to explanation of belief: beliefs were natural facts of their own, and in the real natural world of belief, explanations of true and false beliefs worked in the same way. Truth in a final sense was a separate matter.

One advantage gained by this convention of explaining belief rather than truth, and explaining symmetrically rather than using truth to explain belief, is to avoid retrospective bias—to recreate the situation in real time, as the scientists faced the issues in question. But this is symmetry about causes or explainers, not about the thing to be explained. The thing that was being explained was the naturalistic fact that people believed something to be true. Science studies scholars elaborated a complex vocabulary to describe taken-to-be-true facts without calling them true. In actor network theory, the way was to show that elements of the network had enrolled more additional elements in their network than other things. In Andrew Pickering's writings on practice, terms like "hypothesis" and "test," along with "failure," were replaced by the idea of the dialectic of resistance and accommodation (Pickering 1995: 22; S. Turner 1999b: 152–55). But the point of the explanations, terminological gimmicks aside, was precisely to account for the fact that some things were taken to be fact. So the objects of explanation of the asymmetric accounts and the symmetric accounts were the same: what science arrived at and took to be true. They were merely described differently. It is an additional, and problematic, thesis that descriptions using "true" and "fact" without quotations can never be justified, and even whether science studies itself can avoid appealing to these notions. This was the source of a large literature on reflexivity in the 1980s, and a response to the fascination in the same decade among philosophers of science with "scientific realism," which was the thesis that the beliefs of science were indeed true, and that this was the explanation of the success of science.

In the discussion of examples that follows, I will dispense with, or at least bracket, the convention of symmetry as well as abstract concerns about premature naturalization of facts. The cases I will discuss here are both cases in which what was taken to be true changed from a situation of confusion to one in which the relevant facts came to be taken for granted truths. The language of failure and error was employed, unproblematically, by the people involved in the state of confusion: the confusion was motivated by what they took to be failures, errors, contradictions, and the like. Trevor Pinch, in his study of one of these cases, uses the sanitizing term "perceived contradiction" (1986: 156). In this case the contradiction was perceived by everyone, and was there, so nothing is added by noting that it was "perceived." The dispute was about the meaning of the contradiction. There was no disagreement or confusion about the factual character of the events themselves or the fact that they were failures, in the banal sense of unexpected and unwelcome outcomes. The same, of course, cannot be said of discussions of climate science. In the case of climate science, there are people who deny that any failures of prediction have occurred. Yet in this case as well there is a more or less clear acceptance by virtually everyone that there has been an unexpected and unwelcome outcome, and active discussion of the meaning of this outcome. For this reason, I will suggest, the situation parallels the early moments of the cases I will describe in more detail.

Perrow's oxymoronic term "normal accidents" captures the core idea of explanatory symmetry without ever appealing to the term itself, or entangling him in the issues of reflexivity about facts. His point is to show that the same organized technical processes that produce success in a complex production technology also, as part of their "normal" operations, produce "accidents," namely, unintended outcomes that are unanticipated and also not corrected for by normal safety measures, such as redundant systems, pressure valves, shutoff mechanisms, circuit breakers, and so on. The effect of this is to redefine "normal" in relation to "accidents": to describe a class of accidents that arise from the "normal" organization of complex productive processes. The accidents he wants to "normalize" or treat symmetrically are accidents beyond those which the safety mechanisms for the discrete elements of the process ordinarily correct.

The point of this chapter is to extend this reasoning to expert systems: to show that it is "normal" for unintended and unanticipated outcomes to occur in expert systems that are not correctable by the usual safety mechanisms—meaning, in the case of science, such things as peer review, replication, and findings from related work in the network of science (cf. Polanyi [1946] 1964), and also to show that the problems are especially acute for tightly coupled expert systems. The cases I will discuss here—the failure of the Large Hadron Collider and the Homestake experiment—do not involve problematic asymmetries. The results of the Homestake experiment were unambiguously a "problem" for the science involved. No one seriously denied that something was wrong, somewhere: the predictions had failed. There was no favored solution: instead there was spirited and contentious disagreement. As Pinch showed, the disagreements about the meaning and importance of the failure were connected to the social locations of the participants and critics, especially their disciplinary background (1986: 172–75). But this point turned out to explain very little about the outcome of the controversy. The winners won for reasons familiar to STS (Science and Technology Studies) scholars: the main findings, which the experimenter obdurately held to, were eventually linked up to other experiments, and the claims of his critics, a few of which were plausible at the time that the main finding was a lonely anomaly, could not accommodate these experiments. One of the interpretations proposed showed how the results could be accommodated by changing the theory in a way that accorded with some earlier speculation in physics. It turned out to be correct.

In short, the critics of the experiment lost, whether one chooses to describe this loss "sociologically," philosophically, as was done at the time by Dudley Shapere in a prescient paper, "The Concept of Observation in Science and Philosophy" (1982), or in terms of the way the scientists themselves eventually came to understand the situation. In the cases of failure I will discuss here, the term serves equally for its STS sense and its sense in the language of the scientists themselves. Indeed, if these languages were not largely translatable, it would be impossible for STS to explain science. In using the terms in this way one need not violate explanatory symmetry. Truth is not used as an explanation, and using the terms does not amount to acting as an omniscient observer illegitimately taking sides or producing a Whig history in which the victory of the winners is construed as the inevitable outcome of the historical process. Symmetry is a convention that avoids these mistakes. But it is a convention that makes sense only in terms of the purposes it serves, and it serves these purposes in some contexts and not others. In the cases to be discussed here, artificially problematizing the language of error and failure, does nothing to change the explanation.[2] Symmetry about causes, in the form of Perrow's showing that accidents are the result of normal processes, does change the explanation, and it is this kind of symmetry that will be preserved in what follows.

CERN: NORMAL ACCIDENT?

The CERN Large Hadron Collider (LHC) is well known and no purpose would be served by describing it here. The system itself is a vast collection of electro-magnets—1,734 large magnets and 7,724 smaller corrector magnets. The magnets direct and accelerate proton beams placed in a tunnel cooled by superfluid helium, to produce collisions whose results are captured by detectors. The experiments require a massive amount of energy, and energy levels within the experiment itself are an order of magnitude higher than in previous accelerators. After its launch on September 10, 2008, it suffered a major failure on September 19, 2008, which has been extensively documented (Bajko et al. 2009; CERN 2008; Chalmers and Henderson 2008; Hill 2008; Rossi 2010). The LHC was shut down, a large effort was put into diagnosing the failure, and it was repaired, with the systems that failed replaced or cleaned and fixed, and redesigned. The failure occurred during powering tests of the main dipole circuit.

The symptom of the failure was a release of helium that heated the supercooled tunnel: a "quench." The initial response to the accident followed the pattern described by Perrow: confusion and a radical underestimation of the seriousness of the problem; the wrong outcomes are "not only unexpected, but are incomprehensible for some critical period of time" (Perrow [1984] 1999: 9). Although the leak of helium and the loss of helium were reported in the logbook, the fact that the fire brigade was called was entered but later deleted. "Sources" were initially upbeat:

> A CERN source who had initially feared that the incident could delay the LHC's operations by several weeks said hopes were rising during the afternoon that the damage was limited. "They just managed to bring back the compressors again, so who knows," the source said. "These guys make miracles and could bring back the system in a week." (Chalmers and Henderson 2008)

There were no miracles; further inspection found considerable and unexpected damage. Exactly the kind of confusion described by Perrow set in. An extensive investigation was launched, and preliminary report was made (CERN 2008), then a follow up report (Bajko et al. 2009).

The basic facts of the event as described in the reports and the subsequent explanations by the chief engineer for the project (Rossi 2010) were these. The cryostatic vacuum enclosure in which the experiments were conducted had a safety relief device that allowed for the release of helium into it in case of failure, but it was not designed for the pressures that developed, which were "considered 'beyond design'" (CERN 2008: 1), and it did not release helium at the rate needed to avoid damage to the system. In short, this was an anomalous event, not anticipated in the design. The mystery was the cause of the event. The proximate cause settled on by the investigators, with the caveat that, as the parts were destroyed in the accident, any conclusion must remain "speculative" was a defective bus connector between electromagnets. The components had been extensively tested, in accordance with normal procedures for preventing accidents, though it happens that the particular section that failed was the only one of eight that had not been tested. They had not, however, been tested with one another in the system itself. They were vulnerable to unanticipated interaction effects, and in this case one of the most mundane: an arc or short resulting from excessive resistance in one of the components.

The "normal" safety devices worked as designed. The power tripped off when resistance was detected and the relevant systems—the quench or helium detector and the energy discharge systems that rapidly powered down the system by inserting resistors—all worked as expected. In a second, however, an arc developed, blowing a hole in the helium enclosure and letting the helium into the beamline—several tonnes worth. This was an unanticipated interaction which involved two failures, which led to a third. The beam vacuum degraded and the insulation began to degrade in neighboring subsectors. When the pressure reached the level of atmospheric pressure the spring-loaded relief discs opened, and helium was released from the tunnel. But the release valves, not designed for this rate of escape, could not prevent the internal pressure from rising with such force that it pulled magnets from their supports and filled the tunnel with soot. This sequence was not evident at the time. As Lyn Evans, the project's leader, told *The Times*, "It was only by going back through the data that we see a signal that was considered insignificant at the time. A helium valve was opening and that's because the fault was drawing more and more helium to keep things cool, until it couldn't any more. The safety system was not good enough to cope" (Henderson 2009).

The electrical fault that led to the arc was presumably the result of improperly soldered connections, which in turn was the result of a decision to use a solder with silver and tin content, which had a higher melting point and didn't flow as easily as lead, resulting in bad connections. The decision to use this solder was based on a desire to protect the workers from lead. Given that the instrument required 1,200 tonnes of superconducting wire for the magnets alone, it is no surprise that there would be a short somewhere when the system was powered up. As the engineer in charge, Lucio Rossi, admitted, it occurred in a "relatively low-tech system," namely "an interconnection between magnets." But he argued that the nature of the problem reflected a complex set of "faults in design" that "even if comparatively trivial, are intimately connected with superconductivity and its subtleties" (Rossi 2010: 1). What interacted, in this case, was a set of faulty designs—the solder and the magnet connection, parts that worked as designed but failed in the unanticipated conditions, signals that were missed, valves that were not designed for the event as it occurred, and so forth. This was not a simple case of a part failing to work and its backup failing to work.

Other physicists familiar with such systems anticipated that failures of this general kind would occur. Their initial responses, unlike the CERN sources, were that the problems were no surprise. "It's what happens when you start up a big, superconducting machine," Judy Jackson, spokeswoman for the Fermi National Accelerator Laboratory outside Chicago, told the Associated Press. "Our impression is that what happened last Friday at CERN caught them more by surprise than it did us" (Hill 2008). The problem was not that there was a lack of normal measures, such as backup systems. "The thing about the LHC was it has not just caused a quench, but there are systems that are supposed to prevent it from melting and dumping helium," said Michael Harrison, who worked on Fermilab's Tevatron collider and designed and built the US's other superconducting collider at Brookhaven on Long Island. "So it was obviously something else that went on as well" (Hill 2008). The redesign and fix for the problem reflected the fact that multiple systems failed. New systems were designed to solve these problems (Henderson 2009).

WHAT IS KNOWLEDGE RISK?

We can identify three key places in this narrative of the accident where things went wrong or were at risk of going wrong because of errors or limitations of our own understanding. These are, to coin a phrase, knowledge risks: risks we incur in the course of acting on imperfect knowledge. The first involved the low-tech system, the bus, which failed because of the solder used in the connections. A decision to use a silver compound solder was made for safety reasons. The probability of an electric fault was increased by this decision. The increase was far greater than realized at the time of the decision. A second involved the failure to recognize the significance of the signal that the helium valve was opening. The third was the generic risk identified by Rossi: that strange things happen in relation to superconductivity. Knowledge risks are ubiquitous; there were hundreds, perhaps hundreds of thousands, of decisions made in the course of the construction of the collider that involved similar kinds of risks. Each of them might have gone wrong—failed to produce the expected results—for reasons that were not known to, or understood by, the decision-maker.

Science is a means of reducing knowledge risk, though only one means among many. Experience, tacit and explicit, also reduces knowledge risk: one prefers an experienced surgeon to the one with the most recent textbook and little experience. But science occupies a special role in relation to knowledge risks because it is a system for producing the knowledge that reduces these risks. Like any system, it has its own risks, and its own knowledge risks. It can be characterized in Perrow's terms, as loosely or tightly coupled. Classical science was a very loosely coupled system. There were many errors made by scientists, but there was plenty of time to correct errors, relatively few serious consequences of error (especially in pure science) and there were good mechanisms for correcting the errors. Much of the literature on science in the period after World War II, which looked backwards to science as it was before the war, was concerned with these corrective mechanisms. The fact that scientists had a career incentive to refute the conjectures of others (Popper [1963] 1965) and to replicate the work of others (Zuckerman and Merton 1971; Ziman 1978), plus the network-like, interdependent structure of science, which meant that errors would be detected as a result of the use of findings in adjacent areas (Polanyi [1946] 1964), were taken to be key to the error reduction process.

The science system and the institutions of science supported these processes. Science was a "liberal" institution, in which authority was always exercised indirectly. Scientific societies did not proclaim orthodoxies nor (except for a small number of incidents in which national societies intervened in controversies) attempt to settle questions of scientific truth directly. Consensus was allowed to develop on its own. And in some cases it took centuries to happen. Practices of peer review were developed, which facilitated the forming of consensus by excluding crazy and unscientific ideas from journals. But peer review had a light hand—it was understood to be a means of screening out obvious error rather than affirming one true answer.

The idea was that truth would emerge without coercion in a community of independent scientists forming their own ideas about what was true. The consensus that emerged was all the stronger for being uncoerced. It was also open to correction by the same means as it was formed—the unforced assent of competent practitioners. There were standards—standards of competence, for example. The club was exclusive, or at least excluded people. Academic positions were hard to come by. But accredited scientists were free to form their own opinions, pursue their own hunches, and report their results if they were not obviously erroneous, in the expectation that truth would emerge from the process of conjecture and refutation that was supported by the competition between scientists for reputation and recognition and from competition between research institutions to employ the most meritorious and visible scientists and associate themselves with their discoveries.

We can think of knowledge risk on the model of errors of hypothesis testing: the error of accepting false hypotheses on the basis of the data, and the error of failing to accept true ones. Both types of error were filtered out by this system, but slowly. The error of accepting false hypotheses was filtered in several ways, first by the system of publication, which relied on peer review of one kind or another to exclude obviously wrong assertions or obviously bogus findings; by the system of granting degrees and society memberships only to competent practitioners; and by the fact that there were career incentives, in the form of recognition and reputation, which rewarded scientists for disproving widely held scientific ideas. The error of failing to accept true hypotheses was corrected for by the need for scientists to produce novel findings: a true hypothesis was likely to be a fruitful one and scientists could not afford to ignore this fruit. Rivalry, indeed, meant that there were strong incentives to exploit new findings in one's own scientific work, and in exploiting the findings, one would either confirm them or find reasons to reject them.

What this loosely coupled science was good at was exploiting opportunities. The decisions on what research to do were made by scientists running labs, typically with a small group of students and technicians. Equipment was important, but relatively cheap and easy to obtain or make. It was possible for industries to sponsor labs—which were given relatively large amounts of freedom to work in an area of science, such as the textile chemistry supported lab run by Michael Polanyi in the 1930s—which allowed the lab's research to benefit the industry without being involved directly in the development of new products. What the German chemical industry paid for in this case was world-class expertise in physical chemistry as it related to a general area, and thiat is what they got.

There were other loosely coupled systems that had the same outputs: knowledge that enabled industrial production. Bell Labs was a model of a patient industrial organization. It required a strong sense of the goals of the organization and of the technology that could be improved by new and inventive science. Expectations were clear—scientists were paid to produce results that could be used. But the uses need not be immediate, and experience had shown that research in given areas of physics produced results that could be put to use along with many other results that either would never be used or that might remain curiosities for some time. These kinds of projects filtered out error in their own ways. In the case of Bell Labs, its scientists published and were an active part of the organized community of science itself. But the fact that they were expected to do research that eventually led to practical improvements in telecommunications meant that their results were often also tested in practice by other members of the Bell team.

This kind of loosely coupled structure contrasts with such tightly coupled projects as the Manhattan Project, where there was a high level of technical complexity, clear goals, many knowledge risks, and short time frames—in this case the pressure of war. This project succeeded. But the German and Japanese projects, which had the same goal, failed. In the German case, the failure was a result of mistaken ideas about the physics. It is worth recalling that Oppenheimer opposed the development of the H-bomb on mistaken grounds related to his own beliefs about the relevant physics (Thorpe 2006: 210), which were especially important because the knowledge in question was subject to secrecy restrictions that prevented it from being filtered for error in the classical way. This is suggestive: tightly coupled systems of knowledge production generate special kinds of knowledge risks, risks that arise when the filtering mechanisms change, which are analogous to the risks Perrow identifies for tightly coupled production systems.

VERY TIGHTLY COUPLED EXPERT SYSTEMS

In the 1960s a famous experiment, known as the Homestake experiment, was designed with the aim of empirically testing some basic physical ideas about solar neutrinos. The experiment began in 1970. The best physics of the time predicted that solar neutrinos would pass through the earth at a particular rate. But no one had ever tested this by seeing what happened inside the earth. The Homestake experiment was an attempt to do so. The experiment was conducted at the bottom of an abandoned gold mine in South Dakota. The design was itself complex because solar neutrinos are difficult to detect. The method was to build a huge vat and fill it with perchloroethylene, a chemical used in dry cleaning. The chlorine atoms were the means of detection: when a solar neutrino collided with a chlorine atom it produced a radioactive isotope of argon, which could be extracted by bubbling helium through the vat and used to estimate the number of neutrinos that had been captured.

It was widely believed at the time that this would be a crucial experiment—a test not only of ideas about solar neutrinos, but of the image of the world provided by particle physics. The results, however, were incomprehensible. The vat did detect the argon by-product, but it was detected at a rate far below what was predicted. Something was right, neutrinos were detected, but something had also gone seriously wrong. But what? The experiment depended on a reasonably well understood technology of collection, with an understood physical chemistry. The estimates were based on this stable knowledge—and the assumption that the knowledge risks were known and controlled. The model of the sun that was being tested was also well supported.

The Homestake experiment, like the CERN accident, involved a complex instrument and elements that depended on a variety of disciplines or sub-disciplines. The experiment thus involved both an epistemic problem and a social problem of organizing the decision-making involved in the construction of the experiment and its interpretation. The "social" problem is also epistemic: a problem of the aggregation of knowledge.[3] The knowledge relevant for the experiment was distributed among many people, with specialist knowledge and perhaps tacit knowledge that was not possessed by other members of the team working on the experiment. Moreover, and not surprisingly, critics of the experiment from different disciplines had different interpretations of what had gone wrong. Some even claimed, at first, that the discrepancy was not as significant as it appeared.

What brought these scientists together was the experiment, not common membership in a discipline. They needed to manage the fact that the experiment as a whole depended on a division of labor that was also a division of expertise. This was a relationship that differed radically from the relationship between competitors in a discipline. They were not, accordingly, motivated to refute one another's core scientific ideas, much less the work involved in the experiment—they were neither competent to do this, nor had any reason to, until the experiment failed. The enterprise they were engaged in was a cooperative one—it required some level of mutual understanding and trust. On the other hand, they were strongly motivated, both internally and externally, to defend the aspect of the experiment that was part of their expertise and for which they were responsible. The disciplinary knowledge that went into the experiment, from multiple disciplines, was entrenched. Raymond A. Davis, the experimenter, later recalled it this way: "My opinion in the early years was that something was wrong with the standard solar model; many physicists thought there was something wrong with my experiment" (2002). Indeed they did. They focused, as Perrow's model of normal accidents suggests they would, on the aspects of the experiment that routinely go wrong in experiments: possible errors in calculations and errors in the experiment itself. But, as Davis later said, they were unable to find the error. "Years of measurements produced consistent answers and many tests showed that there were no problems with experimental procedures" (2002). The experiment continued, with the same results—detecting only close to a third of the predicted results. Data collection ended almost a quarter century after it began, with no solution.

Trevor Pinch's history of this controversy recounts the stage of confusion, and it is characteristic of the kinds of accidents Perrow describes. Pinch quotes a summary of the 1972 Irvine Solar Nuetrino conference: "the critical problem is to determine whether the discrepancy is due to faulty astronomy, faulty physics, or faulty chemistry" (1986: 157). The four domains he outlines made a different proposal: that the argon was trapped in the tank by some unknown process, causing the detector to fail to collect all of the argon produced by the interactions with neutrinos (a problem of radiochemistry); that the nuclear cross-sections were based on extrapolations from high to low energy situations that may have been unwarranted (a problem of nuclear physics); the possibility that the neutrinos oscillate between three phases, so that only one phase is detected (a problem of neutrino physics); and the possibility that the flow of solar neutrinos is not steady because of mixing of outputs from the sun, which might produce long term anomalies (a problem of astrophysics) (Pinch 1986: 157–59).

Pinch's interpretation of the controversy revolved around such things as Davis's credibility and suggested that this was more important than the results themselves. His credibility was based largely on the fact that Davis took the criticisms seriously, and carefully tested and retested the processes himself in response to criticisms and suggestions (Pinch 1986: 175). But the crux of Pinch's interpretation involved the notion of interpretive flexibility, and the idea that there were resources in the theoretical background to the experiment that could be exploited to account for the results without getting rid of anything basic in the physics or the solar neutrino model itself. But his respondents put limits on this flexibility, by rejecting some interpretations as ad hoc because they were post facto interpretations designed to explain away the experiment rather than being well-grounded in actual physics. Interestingly, though Pinch dismissed the uses of ad hoc as inconsistent and just another sign of interpretive flexibility, one of the hypotheses that was not treated as ad hoc involved the issue of oscillations (Pinch 1986: 189), and indeed, as Pinch notes, "if we assume the evidential context of the experiment is neutrino physics then ideas such as neutrino oscillations seem to follow rather naturally" (1986: 194–95).

When Pinch wrote it made some sense to treat the "consensus" that there was a serious discrepancy as a "social accomplishment," to treat interpretive flexibility as an irreducible fact of science, and so forth. In retrospect, however, his account, and the disagreements and speculations he described, were part of the stage of confusion itself. The problem with the experiment was explained only later, in a (Schlattl) 2001 paper. The paper reported results with a new kind of detector, which was able to detect neutrino oscillation. The paper explained that only one of the three "flavors" that the neutrinos oscillated between could be detected by the methods in the experiment. This was the third that the results had consistently reported. The experiment itself had been sound. It lived up to the expectation that its results would be of fundamental significance, and Davis's hunch was correct. The significance turned out to be that the standard model of particle physics needed to change: neutrinos had been thought to be without mass and to be of the same type when they left the sun and when they arrived on earth. It was eventually solved by recognizing that neutrinos have mass and therefore can change type or oscillate, and did so in the course of traveling from the sun.

The stubbornness of this problem was a result of the interaction between two errors—the error of thinking that the detector would capture all of the neutrinos and the mistaken belief, deeply grounded in the standard model of massless neutrinos, that they did not oscillate. The two elements—the theory underlying the collection of data and the model that was being indirectly tested but was presupposed by the measurement procedures—combined to produce the incomprehensible results. Neither could be directly tested by the instrument Davis used. There was nothing "wrong" with the calculations, the chemistry, and the procedures themselves. It is normally preferable to have a theory of the experiment that is independent of the theory that is being tested, but this is not always possible. In this case, the solution required a technological deus ex machina.

270 *The Politics of Expertise*

The story of the Homestake experiment is comforting, if we look only at the beginning and the end. If we ignore the long period of confusion, the outcome conforms to the classical model. The problem was taken up by other labs. Finally a detector was invented that could detect the oscillating neutrino. There were career incentives for solving this problem, conjectures and refutations, and an ending which affirmed the significance of the original experiment—a Nobel Prize for Davis, the experimenter. The self-correcting machinery of science worked, though it took a long time to do so. If we look at the three decades of incomprehension, however, the picture is less comforting. The consensus of the scientific community was wrong in its initial reaction, and wrong for decades. As Davis later recalled, "Many distinguished physicists suggested explanations for the low solar neutrino flux that now seem fanciful" (2002). But these explanations were, for many years, treated as sufficient grounds to dismiss the experiment. The reaction of the "scientific community" is telling. The Homestake experiment was one of the highest profile and most anticipated experiments in the history of science. Davis was no Mendel toiling in obscurity. In the absence of a routine explanation for the results, the scientific community chose more or less to ignore them, and to accept as plausible explanations that were largely groundless, but conserved the standard model of the sun and the particle physics behind it. Rather than treating the results as a major anomaly that needed to be addressed and accounted for, the community lost interest in them.

The correction process prevailed. But the circumstances were unusual. Despite Davis's suspicions of the standard model, the hope of the funding agency was that the result would confirm the standard model. Yet when it did not, the experiment was not shut down. The anomalous results were important enough to continue to secure funding for the project for decades, perhaps in the hope that the experiment would correct itself. Davis, by his own account, was strongly motivated by his suspicion that the standard model was wrong. But if this had been the stated motive of the research, it would likely not have been funded. International competition was important as well. Scientists outside the US continued to work on the problem, and had different funding sources with less commitment to the consensus point of view and more willingness to take a chance on a topic that the experiment had opened up to new thinking. This was exceptional. It is difficult to get funding for a twenty-five-year-long experimental run with a complex and expensive design. Nor is funding readily available for refutations of the standard model. In this case, the funders probably were motivated by a desire to confirm the standard model, and to continue funding in order to account for the anomaly. In other cases where costs are high, such as time on expensive telescope systems, it has been claimed that only projects that fit with standard models get access. We may think of this loop—in which funding decisions restrict to the standard models the kinds of science that is done, which in turn justifies the funding decisions—as a way of tightening a loosely coupled system. But the effect of tighter coupling, as we have seen, is to produce a particular kind of knowledge risk—risk of failures that fall outside of those that can be corrected by standard operating procedures or technical solutions.

POLICY-ORIENTED SCIENCE AS A TIGHTLY COUPLED SYSTEM

One of the central elements of tightly coupled systems is time: there are short lags between events in the system. As a consequence, there is little time to make corrections other than those provided by routines, back-up systems, and standard operating procedures for error correction. The reason the classical model of science worked so well in correcting errors was that it had time—time for conjectures to be refuted, for alternative ideas to develop, and to get support from new findings. The classic model also supplied a motivation to do these things, and sufficient independence between sources of support to allow scientists the freedom to follow their hunches about what was wrong.

The anomalous finding was, from the point of view of the field, an accident. The accident was detected and recognized as significant in part because the experiment was conducted in a tightly coupled area of science, in which precise predictions were not only possible, but normal. Policy-oriented science, and one cannot help but think of climate science as an example of this, works very differently. It is a feature of this kind of science that it is time-limited, usually by the demands of the decisions that need to be made or by the desires of the participating scientists to have an impact on policy. It is also commonly the case that policy-oriented science is done by an artificially created community of scientists who share particular policy concerns, who make funding decisions about one another's work, and are bound up with one another in many other ways. Thus policy-oriented science truncates the processes of science in order to produce a needed consensus in a shortened time frame, in a situation where there are known to be gaps between the evidence and the decisions, policies, and practices they are supposed to guide.

The issues with these systems can best be understood by examining the institutions involved, which operate in ways that are different than "normal" science itself, or regulatory science. The institutions are familiar: in the United Kingdom, there are Royal Commissions. In the US, the National Academy of Sciences was created in 1863 to perform this service and produces a steady stream of reports in response to governmental requests as well as on its own initiative. The US National Institutes of Health (NIH) has a "Consensus Development Program" which holds major conferences with the key researchers in an area on nearly a monthly basis during the academic year on such topics as "Vaginal Birth after Caesarean" and "Enhancing the Quality of Colorectal Cancer Screening." The slogan of one of the programs for outreach sponsored NIH is "Mind the Gap: Bridging the Gap between Evidence and Practice." The website shows a white-coated medic stepping into a blank space—perhaps a street, perhaps the void (NIH 2009). The phrase and the image capture the issues nicely: the generic problem to which they are a response is the fact that the evidence is not enough to guide practice unequivocally, and that some sort of fraught step, even a leap, is needed to get from the evidence to practice. The reason for these institutions is this: the science alone—the "evidence" in this phrase—is insufficient, conflicting, or simply not in a form that can guide practice. But practice is necessary, ongoing, and consequential. So the process of bridging the gap needs to be helped along.

In one sense, these institutions can be treated as marginal to science itself. They are, in the famous phrase of Susan Star and James Griesemer (1989), boundary organizations, engaged in producing boundary objects, in the form of such things as commission reports that are usable for decision-makers or policy. But if we consider science as a knowledge production system that can be more or less tightly coupled, the role of these institutions becomes more relevant. Every major science funding system is concerned, increasingly, with the impact of research. Most of these systems now involve (a) large scale funding initiatives targeted at the production of knowledge relevant to politically important knowledge domains, and (b) specific requirements for describing and identifying impacts, including public impacts, in the text of proposals themselves. These are coupling devices: they assure that the research is coupled more closely to the rest of the science system, as well as to public goals. The public goals in question are the same kinds of goals, and usually the exact same goals, that these institutions—consensus conferences and commissions—are concerned with. Coupling research to impact is not voluntary, though the specific impacts are selected by the applicant. The effect of these practices, and many other related practices, is to create a more tightly coupled knowledge production system than the classic model. But to the extent that the system becomes more tightly coupled it becomes susceptible to risks, including knowledge risks, which are characteristic of tightly coupled systems.

NEW KINDS OF CONSENSUS

To be a policy research community is to promise some sort of expert knowledge about the policy problem, rather than mere advocacy of a policy supported by data. But to get to this goal in a timely manner, one that does not wait on the long process of consensus formation required by the classical, loosely coupled model, requires truncating the process of consensus formation. This is precisely the purpose of consensus seeking institutions, such as consensus conferences and commissions, and the goal of targeted funding systems. But there is a price to be paid in terms of knowledge risk.

Climate science is the field that today is the most visible example of a policy oriented science field that is tightly coupled. The history of the field provided by Spencer Weart (2003), which is a defense of the scientific credentials of the field and its legitimacy as science, bears this out. Weart describes the slow development of the subject under the conditions of loosely coupled science. In this phase, money to pursue key ideas, such as the study of the accumulation of CO_2 in the atmosphere, was scarce, and the interested scientists were able to do research on these topics only more or less by accident: the generous military funding of science in the 1950s, for example, provided some key elements (Weart 2003: 31). Geophysical research generally is "platform" science, because it requires big instruments, which in turn require extensive lobbying by researchers to acquire (2003: 40). Only when public fears were aroused (2003: 40–41) and the conservation movement picked up on the problem of global warming (2003: 44) did the money begin to flow freely.

Climate modeling is at the core of the study of global warming. And like CERN and the Homestake experiment, the materials that go into models come from a variety of scientific fields. The climate prediction outputs of these models were, not surprisingly, sensitive to assumptions, parameters, small variations inputs, and so forth. Weart recounts a long history of failure to make even plausible predictions, such as models that predicted that a doubling of CO_2 would produce a rise in global temperatures of 10°C or higher, as well as the fiasco of the predicted new ice age. Weart concedes that these "rudimentary" models were wildly wrong, though they were presented as quite serious policy relevant predictions at the time, by scientists such as Stephen Schneider, who are still active and still aggressively promoting the policy relevance of their current views (Weart 2003: 83). Weart's openly Whiggish perspective on these models was that "most research begins with flawed theories, which prompt people to make better ones" (2003: 84). He treats the fact that "a simple calculation (whatever problems it might have in detail) could produce a catastrophic outcome" (albeit on paper) as a "disturbing discovery" (2003: 84).

Weart makes the same points about the intertwined social and epistemic complexity of the science: communication between the relevant fields was a problem (2003: 125, 149). Thus aggregating climate-relevant knowledge was a problem, which was not matched by the controlling social structure of a discipline, as was the case with normal science, but done under a different structure. Climate itself, it was clear from the outset, "was a staggeringly intricate complex of interactions and feedbacks among many global forces" and that even relatively simple phenomena, such as the doldrums in the tropical seas, defied explanation (Weart 2003: 111). He concedes that this field does not operate as a normal scientific discipline does:

> The social structure is not cohesive. A community in one specialty cannot check the work of researchers in another branch of science, but

> must accept their word for what is valid. The study of climate change is an extreme example. Researchers cannot isolate meteorology from solar physics, pollution studies from computer science, oceanography from glacier-ice chemistry, and so forth. The range of journals they cite . . . is remarkably broad. This sprawl is inevitable. . . . But the complexity imposes difficulty on those who try to reach solid conclusions about climate change. (2003: 195).

Weart acknowledges that the models rely on ad hoc devices. They fit the actual climate, even roughly, "only because they had been laboriously 'tuned' to match it, by adjusting a variety of arbitrary parameters" (2003: 177). He also acknowledges that generating money for the field was intertwined with politics throughout: self-interest, emotional commitment, and the political cause of promoting action on the problem coincided (2003: 151).

> These abnormalities (compared to the classical model of disciplinary science) are, for Weart, justifiable on the grounds of time: "in the case of climate, waiting for a sure answer would mean waiting forever. When we are faced with a new disease or an armed invasion, we do not put off decisions until more research is done: we act using the best guidelines available" (2003: 198–99). This is the language of the NIH consensus conferences, and of commissions. In the absence of ordinary disciplinary controls, we must accept the claims of climate science on other grounds. Weart's own judgment of the correctness of the dominant views in climate science rests on his "feeling for where scientific claims are reliable and when they are shaky" (2003: 199), his belief that, "The few who contest [the] facts are either ignorant or so committed to their viewpoint that they will seize on any excuse to deny the danger" (2003: 199).

Accordingly, Weart closes the book with his own policy recommendations, and the following final sentence:

> The spirit of fact-gathering, rational discussion, tolerance of dissent, and negotiation of an evolving consensus, which has characterized the climate science community, can serve well as a model (Weart 2003: 201).

In short, it is these features of the climate science community that need to be replicated in the domain of policy, and at the same time provide an alternative ground for trust in the conclusions, distinct from the control of disciplinary "social structure."

This characterization of the climate science community has now been shown to be false in every respect as a result of the release of e-mails from the University of East Anglia's Climatic Research Unit (an institution Weart praises). It is now evident that facts were mishandled and suppressed, data withheld and lost, peer-review manipulated, a major effort made to discredit those who questioned the "consensus," and more—this group is now an example of what Polanyi called the corruption of science. The contrast between these e-mails and the period when this work was done by disciplinary science is striking. Thirty years ago I was given access to the editorial files of the Oceans and Atmospheres series of the *Journal for Geophysical Research*. The Atmosphere series, which is now separate, now advertises itself as one of the top ten most highly cited research publications on climate change over the past decade. Its sister journal *Geophysical Research Letters* is also among the top ten. At the time, the journal was a model of open discussion. Rejections were rare, although around 30 percent of the submissions were rejected, most of the rejections were because the papers were inappropriate (for example, engineering papers about platforms for science rather than science), or because the English was inadequate. The editor of the journal had a strong sense of serving a community, and because this was platform science, it was a well-defined community: the people who worked in or had access to the satellites and research vessels and sensors that were required to do the research. Novelty came largely from novel platforms, such as new satellites or technology. Tolerance was high and a paper could be accepted even if it was speculative, if the editor believed someone in the community might find it useful. Because this was platform dependent science there was a degree of prescreening: these projects had already gone through evaluations as grants or as applications to use the technology. But the field was well-funded, and there were multiple agencies in different countries supporting research, with no shared political agenda. The goal of the journal was to serve the community, and it erred on the side of inclusion. There were no instances of the kinds of peer-review manipulation discussed in the East Anglia e-mails, and virtually no negative reviews. "Consensus" under these conditions was not something that needed to be asserted or demonstrated. To the extent that consensus was an issue, it was the product of a loosely coupled system that minimized interventions designed to produce consensus.

TWO KINDS OF KNOWLEDGE RISK

Perrow argues that the people who operate complex systems think in the following way: they make initial choices about how to think about the accident situation in the face of ambiguous data. If the first steps they take are consistent with the choices they have made about how to think about the data, their mental model of the situation, they psychologically commit to the model and lose the skepticism they might originally have had. New data that are inconsistent with the model do not become reasons for reconsidering the model. Instead, they are seen as mysterious, unilluminating, or incomprehensible. The data are discounted. The similarity between this response and Kuhn's discussion of paradigms and the response of "normal science" to anomalies is striking. And it is a reminder that the problem of knowledge risk is not confined to tightly coupled systems of the kind discussed here. Disciplines, even the open structures defined by the classical model, produce intellectual conformity, which creates distinctive knowledge risks. The negative consequences of this conformity were more important to Kuhn's mentor James Bryant Conant, who noted the limitations of scientists: their tendency to groupthink, their proneness to hobbyhorses, and their tendency to over-rate the importance of their own disciplinary concerns (Conant 1952: 110–17, 176).

The traditional disciplinary model was fading even as Conant wrote in the late 1940s and early 1950s. The Homestake experiment itself was an example of what came to be called "Big Science." Science studies scholars have struggled to make sense of the new forms of science that have emerged since then, and especially in the last thirty years: terms like "technoscience," "Mode 2" (Gibbons et al. 1994), and "post-academic" science (Ziman 1996) have been invented to describe these new forms. Tight-coupling is a feature of this new mode of science. To some extent, the knowledge risks of disciplinary science and the knowledge risks of tightly coupled science overlap. But the differences do matter. Unlike disciplines, the new forms typically involve a complex division of intellectual labor involving multiple specialties and a "social structure," in Weart's sense, that serves to aggregate knowledge from these specialties to produce expert conclusions. The products of this kind of science embody this complexity. But complexity itself produces unexpected interaction effects that belong to no discipline. The expertise in question is about things that are not under any disciplinary domain. Consequently, the structures involve mechanisms of consensus production and control that differ from, and involve more overt use of authority, negotiation, and pidgin communication between specialties than in the model of disciplines with paradigms. The problem of aggregating multidisciplinary knowledge is not a problem that can be solved in any disciplinary way. The pressure to produce results leads to the de facto elimination or moderation of some of the means of correction provided by the traditional disciplinary model—what Robert Merton called organized skepticism is less effective when the objects of the skepticism are not disciplinarily defined. These new structures have many virtues. They produce results that can guide policy and innovation and produce objects that disciplinary science could not. But there is no epistemic free lunch. Each of these differences creates knowledge risk.

15 Expertise in Post-Normal Science

Evelyn Fox Keller, in a recent article, asked, "What Are Climate Scientists to Do?" (2011). Her concern is about the fact that people are skeptical about claims that climate scientists present as authoritative science. She makes the standard case: that the consensus is strong, that the opponents are paid off and acting on behalf of special interests, and that policy makers and politicians should accept the science and act accordingly. The problem is that they are not doing so. The question that needs an answer is, "What should the strategy of climate scientists be in the face of reluctance to accept the results of science?" This is a problem that goes to the heart of the question of the role of expertise in a democratic society, and more precisely a liberal democratic society, one in which public discussion matters. But it raises the question from a very specific perspective, namely the strategic perspective of the scientist committed to a particular set of policy relevant claims, or to a policy itself.

In recent years scientists and activists operating from this perspective have frequently expressed a normative claim: politicians should defer to the scientific consensus. The grounds for this have varied slightly, but the main idea is that the scientific consensus is either truth or the best approximation to truth that is available, and that politicians and the public are in no position to assess the validity of the claims made in the consensus and therefore should not do so. In its more extreme forms, this line of argument comes to the conclusion that if politicians do not accept the consensus, they are endangering the earth, and that the whole system of liberal democracy that allows them to do so needs to be abolished or radically reformed, for example by creating a new power of suppressing speech that is contrary to the scientific consensus.

The claim that the public should defer to a "consensus" as distinct from each person deciding, or assessing the credibility of the scientists and science, is a claim about science as a collectivity, or regime, which produces a "consensus." So this claim would need to rest on some justification for regarding this regime as a reliable or preferable source. What might this justification be? How can we assess scientific regimes epistemically? Does climate science deserve to be treated with this kind of deference? Or does climate science have features that make it less deserving of epistemic deference? These are live issues, and muddled ones, apart from the question of whether the claims themselves are true. But they are also issues that go beyond climate science to the general question of the reasons we have for accepting the products of different scientific regimes.

THREE CONCEPTS: POST-NORMALITY, COLLECTIVE HEURISTICS, COMPETENCE OF COMPETENCE

Much of what we know about how science works as an organized, collective enterprise comes from the history of science. But present science, and especially science related to climate change, differs in significant ways from science in the past. It has become common to call this new kind of scientific regime "Post-Normal Science." Normal science was the subject of the writings of Karl Popper, Thomas Kuhn and his mentor James Bryant Conant, Michael Polanyi, and Robert K. Merton. But by the time of the rise of big science, especially weapons physics, the conditions of science had changed. The great conundrum for the Congress for Cultural Freedom in 1953 was the question of how to organize, or even understand, a form of science that was driven by selective government subsidies and conducted in large national laboratories rather than in small academic ones. The problem of how to understand a form of science in which much of the information and decision-making was secret had already made the older account of normal science, with its emphasis on what Merton called "communism," the open sharing of scientific results, of dubious relevance. The new regime systematically replaced elements of the old regime, with potentially significant epistemic consequences.

The arms race supplied a great, and confusing, object lesson about the new form of science. The success of the Anglo-American effort to build the bomb, and the failure of the German one, was taken to vindicate a "democratic" approach to science, as distinct from the "authoritarian" German approach. The German effort foundered because the leading scientific figure made a basic miscalculation about the relevant physical possibilities and invested effort in the wrong approach. But the subsequent missile and space race seemed to give the clear advantage to the Soviets.

The distinction between normal and post-normal science is open to interpretation. Nevertheless, one can see, in broad outlines, some important differences between past science (and science that is still conducted in the old way) and the kinds of science that represent the new way. Terms like "technoscience," Mode 2 Science, academic and post-academic science, and the like have been proposed to mark the distinction between what science used to be, or was idealized to be, and whatever it is that science is today. The new forms of science are "context-driven, problem-focused and interdisciplinary" (*Wikipedia*, "Mode 2"). Traditional research, in contrast, is disciplinary, investigator initiated, and governed by established paradigms.

The relation between normal and post-normal science is not merely temporal: post-normal science is a reform, an attempt to solve problems with normal science. The main problems were these: specialization favored the pursuit of "academic" problems esteemed by specialists, without practical implications, and disinclined scientists to work on interdisciplinary problems that might have greater pay-offs, both practically and scientifically. From very early, the Rockefeller Foundation regarded disciplinary boundaries as an impediment to progress, especially to progress that would help solve practical problems, and funded accordingly. The new forms of science developed closely in relation to funding.

Normal science was a system with known properties, and in particular known epistemic properties. Post-normal science has different properties. Many of the special features of post-normal science reflect the removal of limitations and controls that were built into normal science. Specialization and peer review by specialists, for example, are maximized in normal science. In post-normal science, it is unclear who is a peer and the point is to produce or construct knowledge, or to answer questions, such as policy questions that specialists can't answer within the limits of their specialized methods, theories, and competences (Ziman 2000).

It is useful to think about these properties in these terms: just as individuals operate with heuristics that assure more rapid results, with some costs in the forms of biases and blind spots, institutional systems of knowledge production also can be understood as means of speeding up results. I call these collective heuristics. One can think of decision-making institutions in general in these terms: courts, legislators, bureaucracies, large technoscience projects, and corporations, even economic systems, each need to gather information, aggregate it, process it, and then apply it to decision-making situations. Each does so in distinctive ways, with different outcomes.

Much of the early "social" literature on science, by such writers as Michael Polanyi ([1946] 1964, 1951, 1958) and James Bryant Conant (1947, 1952), was concerned with the epistemic properties of science as a collective activity—with what I am calling its collective heuristics. Kuhn's *The Structure of Scientific Revolutions* ([1962] 1996) was the culmination of this literature: an account of how science as a community or set of communities revises its opinions. The picture they gave of what I am calling normal science—meaning normal science in the sense of science in the pre-atom bomb era rather than in the sense of the Kuhnian distinction with revolutionary science—was a system with certain features, and certain epistemic biases or failings.

Normal science was an ensemble of practices; arrangements; divisions of labor; disciplinary features, including what someone was trained in and what they were not; a journal system; a review system that varied by discipline and time; and various ways in which scientists made money and reputations. In what follows, it will be useful to start with the uncontroversial gross features of this system, compare them to the poorly understood present, and then focus on the distinctive institutional features of science, before turning to the problem of what sort of collective heuristics these systems produce. Some of the strains in the old system became evident with the case of J. Robert Oppenheimer and the H-bomb. The strains in the new system are evident in the controversy over anthropogenic climate change.

With this we can return to the puzzle raised by Evelyn Fox Keller, and ask whether there is a legitimate question about climate science as an institution, and by extension other forms of post-academic science. But this requires one more concept in addition to the normal post-normal distinction and the idea of collective heuristics. It is an issue of what in Continental legal systems is called competence-competence, in German "*kompetenz—kompetenz*," or in French "*competence sur la competence.*" In the case of courts, it is the competence to decide which questions one can decide. The US Supreme Court has this competence. Lower courts do as well, but only subject to the higher competence of the Supreme Court, which can curtail this competence both in individual cases and by rule. Constitutional courts in Europe normally do not have this competence: they get to rule on cases that are specifically given to them as part of their competence. But sometimes they can rule, as a recent German court did, that it had competence to over-rule European courts.

Science has an analogous problem, but with no formal solution. There is a system of vetting through journal publication and peer review plus replication and the testing of claims through their application in related settings in science. As we will see, these worked in a particular way in normal science—they were governed by what Merton called the ethos of science (1973a), as well as other considerations balancing the acceptance and rejection of ideas. But scientists are now called upon, and call on themselves, to make claims or answer questions that have a large technical component but are not "science" in this narrow sense. There is no system of controls of the same kind on these claims. In many areas of technoscience there are pragmatic standards of technical success: the drugs or machines need to work. But the same constraints do not apply to much of what scientists do in the name of science outside the traditional boundaries. Worse, there are communities of "science" oriented around practical and policy problems that are not generated by the normal growth of knowledge, and whole branches of science, under the heading regulatory science, that operate in this hybrid zone.

The problem of competence-competence is especially acute in these areas. The training of the scientists in question is normally technical and specialized. They are expected to use this narrow knowledge to make decisions, or give advice, about issues that are unquestionably related to this narrow base, but which go far beyond it. Normally the issues involve the kinds of interactions one would expect in an open environment, in contrast to the closed environment of the laboratory itself. But the processes in the open environment, their interactions, are not reducible to the knowledge of any specialty of science. By definition, the scientists who are called upon in these situations are asked to go beyond their competence. The issue of whether they are competent to decide what their competence applies to arises normally in this situation. And it is not an issue that can be solved within their competence, but a meta-issue that is beyond any technical specialism.

This meta-problem of competence, and the question of how to even discuss this problem, were brought to the consciousness of scientists in a particularly intense form after Hiroshima. Should scientists have done something different? Was it their business to control the products of their work? Were they responsible for what politicians did with it? Was this a collective problem, or a matter of individual conscience? Was it a matter of the ethos of science and what was good for science, or a matter of the scientist as citizen, governed by political obligation? But most important was the problem of whether scientists knew what to do, as scientists, as a consequence of their special knowledge.

One lesson of this episode, but a lesson obscured by politics and learned only partially and in long retrospect, was that nuclear physicists were not experts on international affairs, security, strategy, and the like, nor were they good judges of their Soviet counterparts. They were used by a highly sophisticated KGB and deluded themselves into thinking they were speaking freely as "scientist to scientist" in international exchanges. This was an episode of scientific hubris. But it was rooted in a real problem of competence: they did have technical competence about one aspect of the complex question of nuclear strategy and world peace. But this did not mean that they were competent to judge the limits or relevance of their competence.

This is a problem that is pervasive in scientific decision-making. One can give endless examples: I will return to an important one later in the chapter. But a few might be given here. Bernard Lovell, the father of radio astronomy and Nobel laureate, fought a battle against funding for DNA research in the 1950s, after the discovery of DNA, on the grounds that it was overrated in importance and without practical significance. Was this merely cynical and self-serving? Not at all. As we will see, Bernard Lovell's inability to grasp a different topic is a characteristic feature of specialized scientists of the normal science era. This pervasive inability—a lack of genuine competence-competence—has had problematic consequences for the whole era of "big science" that developed into post-normal science.

NORMAL AND POST-NORMAL

As the term "big science" suggests, there is no sharp line dividing normal from post-normal science: the two are idealizations or ideal-types with many intermediate or transitional forms. Some present science is still "normal" and there have been efforts to recreate normality for a few privileged researchers, for example, in the Hughes Medical Foundation. But the grant system and the exigencies of funding science inevitably push science in the direction of money, and political exigencies push the money in the direction of work with some anticipated practical payoff, or some policy significance.

The normal science ideal, seldom realized very lavishly, was that competent scientists should be given the funds to do what they decided was the best use of their time and effort. The constraints they were under were already given by the structure of competition in science itself—reputational rivalry, the need to make discoveries first, and the competition for positions, such as chairs or institute leadership positions that allowed scientists to pay for research, for junior positions, and thus to carry out their guesses as to what would produce discoveries. The result would be validated by the "scientific community," which was comprised of specialists (who were competent peers who would replicate and use the results) and scientists in related fields (who would apply or employ the results in their own work, and thus indirectly test them).

This was a system that worked largely through indirect means—another useful concept, derived from liberal political theory. Overt direction or decision-making by collective bodies representing science was minimized. Grants were introduced by such groups as the Rockefeller Foundation, in the 1920s and '30s, but at first these were "Block Grants" rather than project grants, which allowed decisions to be made about what lines of work to pursue at the level of the scientific institution rather than by the foundation. When they arrived, they supplemented facilities supplied by the university.

Scientists made money on the side, through industrial consulting, and often by using industrial money to support their own labs by doing work related to their primary research in the institute or university labs. This kind of work, even in surprisingly modern forms, had gone on in chemistry on a large scale since Justus von Leibig's fertilizer business. But this kind of work was not taken to be an end in itself. One could choose academic science as a vocation or leave it for industry. The structures were distinct, and reputation was the sole determinant of academic success. The university benefitted indirectly from ties to industry, but was not dependent on it and did not institutionalize these arrangements. Instead, the arrangements were left to the discretion of the scientist, whose interests were governed by the facts of reputational competition and their own financial interests; they were allowed to balance the two on their own.

Not surprisingly, some chose one over the other, for example by becoming full-time industrial chemists, or by working on areas without commercial application but with high reputational value, while others did both. The conflicts were real, but they did not affect the scientific validity of the results. The practical work was constrained by the fact that the discoveries needed to be made into something that actually worked. The chemists were not the judges of that; the market was. Similar issues arose in other fields, such as geology, with the same conflicts managed in the same ways. It was only the caesura of the Manhattan Project that changed all of this, in the direction of collective action and collective direction, or direct means.[1]

What is striking about American science policy of the early post-war period is the extent to which proposals for funding science attempted to articulate and preserve the conditions of normal science under the new circumstances that were being acknowledged. These were significant changes: big science was seen as necessary for national security, science in general was taken to have a crucial role in the national economy, and the state was seen as the necessary major source of funding for science. The initial proposal for a government "foundation" by Vannevar Bush reflected the desire to preserve the features of academic science but providing funds. As David Kellogg summarizes,

> Bush's proposed foundation rests on five principles: (1) long-range support for research; (2) an administrative agency composed solely of people selected for their "interest" and "capacity"; (3) a structure of grants provided directly to researchers outside the government; (4) "policy, personnel, and the method and scope of the research" left entirely to the grant recipients; and (5) foundation (not grantee) accountability to the President and Congress. (Bush 1945, quoted in Kellogg 2006: 8)

The conditions were preserved by providing barriers to political interference or control, to preserve what Michael Polanyi called the autonomy of science.

The autonomy of science, under various names, was a major concern of scientists in the 1930s, highlighted by the apparent politicization of science in Nazi Germany and by the Lysenko affair. These topics, and the larger question of what was called "the social relations of science," including the problem of the impact of science on society and the problem of the underutilization of science by industry, led to a flurry of organizing, counter-organizing, and manifesto writing, which was the source of many of the key ideas of science studies. One of these key ideas was that there was a specific "ethos" of science that distinguished it from other social forms and justified both its claim to autonomy, but also its claim to intellectual authority. Robert Merton summarized this ethos in terms of four norms or "institutional imperatives," which he calls *universalism, communism, disinterestedness*, and *organized skepticism* (1973b: 270).

"Universalism" means that there are no sectarian truths, such as Nazi or Socialist science, but also that science is open to talent. "Communism" means that scientific knowledge is shared. "Disinterestedness" means that scientists pursue scientific truth without regard for who benefits or what political stance or policy it favors. "Organized skepticism" means that scientists test the claims of other scientists and accept claims only after they have been through a process of critical examination.

The "ethos" is thus a guide to the norms of a kind of collective epistemic regime. If we ask the basic question of how epistemic regimes produce results we can see how this regime is supposed to work, and why this regime has its particular biases. How does academic science gather information, aggregate it, process it, and then apply it to decision-making situations? The gathering of information—the production of findings, experiments, observation, and so forth—is not directed by any central authority, but rather the indirect result of reputational competition between scientists. Scientists have their own pet ideas, hunches, and the like, which drive their personal research programs. These ideas conflict with those of other scientists who are their rivals, giving them incentives to test and correct the ideas of others. Getting one's ideas accepted is difficult, especially if they do not support or confirm established scientific beliefs.

Writers like Conant and Polanyi stressed the difficulty that new ideas and findings faced. They were concerned with ideas born out of time, or prematurely, meaning that the scientific community was not cognitively prepared to accept or understand them when they were introduced. This was a product of various features of science, but the result was that science was characterized by a kind of groupthink and was conservative—a set of basic ideas, once established, was difficult to change, and mere facts that did not fit, what Kuhn called anomalies, were not sufficient on their own to alter widely held beliefs, especially theoretical beliefs that were not directly tied to observation and experimental practice.

Nevertheless, reputational competition was based on discoveries, so originality was also prized in this system. Thus the information gathering part of the process was driven in a particular direction by reputational competition, namely in the direction of confirmation bias. This led to a distinctive collective heuristic dynamic, in which original work that could be strictly tested but which was largely in conformity with existing theory was highly valued and sought. Theoretical novelty was also prized, but it was more difficult to get novel theoretical ideas accepted.

How did knowledge get aggregated in this anarchic system? Polanyi contributed a nice image that fits with these distinctive biases toward both originality and confirmation. Science was like a large puzzle, which individuals could contribute a piece to, finding where it fits, and thus producing a larger and cohesive result. The knowledge required was specialized and no one needed to understand the puzzle as a whole. They just needed to know their own piece and find out where it fit. The fact of fitting was a kind of corroboration, because it showed that the piece was consistent with other pieces produced by specialists of other kinds.

The difficulty with this anarchic system, which the defenders of the autonomy of science never resolved, was that decisions had to be made concerning allocations of funds, choices of research directions to support, and so forth. Not every decision in a large and expensive system could be made on merit, thus leaving the investigator free to choose, as had been the case with pure academic science funded internally by universities or institutes.

In genuine academic science, unsullied by the grant system, there was no need for or possibility of "consensus" as the term later came to be used. Scientists accepted or did not accept findings or new theoretical ideas. There was a strain toward consistency, and debates and conferences to resolve conflicts between theories. Prizes were awarded when new ideas were accepted, though it is worth noting that even the Nobel Prizes normally were given for work done decades earlier and that acceptance was rarely instantaneous. In some cases academies of science stepped in to try to resolve outstanding disputes, but there were few mechanisms for gauging a consensus. Kuhn treats textbooks as representing the "paradigm," but even here there are disputes. Scientists routinely quibble with textbook formulations or reject them outright.

Even Kuhn acknowledged that revolutions won out over time, and that this was often generational time. In some cases, the winning out took several generations—the gene concept had a tortuous history with slow acceptance, skepticism, indecisive show-downs between rivals, and the possibility of careers in the area of plant-breeding and population genetics without reference to this central idea. Indeed, in a recent survey asking scientists for their views of definitions of the gene it was found that many disagree with textbook definitions, different fields define the term differently, and that there are residual disagreements within fields. This is what made the Lysenko affair itself possible: the "consensus" was weak and loose. Practical work in breeding could go on without it, and did.

Polanyi's picture of science as an enterprise of providing individual contributions to the solution of a big puzzle is interesting as a means of comparison. It is a picture of a collective heuristic, but it involves no general notion of consensus. Specialists, in the relevant field and adjacent fields for which a finding has implications, are the only audience that needs to accept or reject a finding. The only relevant consensus is about whether the piece fits the puzzle. And even this consensus is mere acceptance by enough scientists to treat the result as a solution. The important fact is that scientists go on as if the piece fits, and fit other pieces to it. The problem of competence-competence barely arises. Scientists are never called upon to make judgments outside of their specialized knowledge, or about issues that are very close to it.

POST-NORMAL SCIENCE AS THE SUBSTITUTION OF DIRECT MEANS

Polanyi's model is a way of picturing aggregation: the bringing together of scientific contributions into a larger cognitive unit. Kuhn's account of how paradigms are created is a model of processing information: turning this unit into a trainable core. In academic science, this was done without central direction, in a market-like atmosphere. Whether a textbook represented the field was a matter of whether it was used by many scientists in teaching. Application was a market matter as well. Scientists made money by consulting for or by working in industrial labs. The test was whether the product worked.

With big science, and the weapons projects that became central to physics in the post-war period, a new model emerged. Decisions allocating vast resources needed to be made. The merit of individual investigators was not sufficient, because the problems went beyond single specializations, involved workers and issues from multiple specialties, and required judgments beyond the competence of single scientists. Personal merit was not enough either, because judgments about the content of the science and its likelihood of working out and producing desired results became an increasingly large part of decision processes. This was a fundamental shift, which the advocates of autonomy found difficult to assimilate or assess.

Scientists, as the Bush proposal showed, attempted to preserve as much as possible of the ethos of academic science in this new situation. Decentralization, control by specialists, and an emphasis on the centrality of scientific merit were preserved in the proposal, and even, as we will see, in such areas of applied science as the decision processes on weapons systems. But pressures to produce results, and the increased importance of the grant system itself, eventually led to the use of more direct means. The reasons for these changes reflected the slowness and unsystematic applicability of "normal science."

The changes are not easily summarized, or even understood. But the basic pattern was that processes that were formerly governed by indirect means, such as the investigators making a free choice motivated through reputational competition, were now done by direct means, such as providing incentives for certain kinds of research. Each substitution of a direct for an indirect means was also the removal of a safeguard. The free choice of problems is a safeguard, though not a perfect one, against the confirmation bias of science noted by Kuhn, and the tendency to groupthink noted by Conant. Making grants contingent on the promise that they will add to knowledge, but in a way that confirms past science eliminates a range of possible research projects, including those that are most likely to produce alternative perspectives and anomalies.

The use of pure merit criteria by judging scientists, rather than scientific plans or ideas, is another safeguard against the cognitive prejudices of the granting agent or committee. This may seem like a small distinction, but the prevention of a direct link between the prejudices and preferences of a grant committee for particular ideas and outcomes and the decision to grant is a small but meaningful corrective to the bias to confirm. Removing these correctives "helps" overcome the "problems" of anarchy and free choice, but at a collective cognitive price. Removing it builds a new bias into the collective heuristic. Removing one after another, for example, by directing funds to particular topics that have been defined in terms of particular ideas, increases this price. And at each point of direct action there are cognitive issues of competence-competence, that is, questions about whether the decision-makers are competent to make the decisions they are making or to define the limits of their competence.

Bernard Lovell overreached his competence in attacking DNA research, but this is a kind of overreach that is endemic to scientific decision-making. His judgment was self-interested, but also ignorant—he was neither privy to the science as it was developing on the research front, as a specialist would be, nor did he, or perhaps anyone, have the capacity to predict future outcomes. Nevertheless, these decisions determine what kind of science will be done, and there are reasons for making direct decisions. Polanyi's critics made this point when they observed, with respect to his rejection of "planning" in science, that the system of decisions was itself a kind of planning (Bernal [1965] 1979; Max Born quoted in McGucken 1984: 290–91). To show the patrons of science that the money was being effectively spent it was useful to promise results, and therefore to assure that there would be results.

When we examine decision processes, however, the mirage of technical certainty vanishes. Even in the simple case of judging scientific projects rather than the scientific merit of individual scientists, there are issues of competence-competence. Judgments about whether an idea will work out are prospective judgments, or guesses about the future. We can have the most competent people make these guesses, but this does not mean that they are actually competent to make these guesses. The evidence on expert judgment generally suggests that predicting the future is a hazardous affair even for experts, and that experts overestimate their capacities to predict successfully (Tetlock 2006). A system of competing regimes rather than one single direct authority avoids the risk of making one bad choice, but at the cost of allowing many bad choices. And this was true of the Rockefeller Foundation's interdisciplinary projects: promising ideas went nowhere, despite the large sums invested.

OPPENHEIMER AND THE H-BOMB

Competence-competence becomes a larger issue when there is no competition: when a single choice is made, or needs to be made, through a direct process that involves no market, rivalry, or alternative. In this case, who is competent to make such decisions, and are they competent to judge their own competence? This kind of problem was central to the dismissal of Oppenheimer and the decision to build the H-bomb, an idea promoted by Edward Teller. The story is a complex one, in part because it involves all the phases mentioned above—gathering information, aggregating it, processing it, and applying it—along with significant issues with the use of direct means and their relation with indirect means, as well as issues of competence-competence.

Robert Oppenheimer was the father of the A-bomb, a revered physicist, a master scientific manager, and certainly the most authoritative voice on weapons questions anywhere. He was concerned, in the aftermath of the use of the bomb, with the political and administrative side of atomic research. Oppenheimer's writings are closely allied to the autonomy of science movement. He stressed the craft character of science, the distinction between science and technology, and the need for atomic science itself to proceed in an open academic setting. He also backed proposals for the internationalization of control over nuclear energy, and represented the scientific community to decision-makers.

Oppenheimer's fall was a central event in the developing relation of science to the state. In 1953, Oppenheimer was accused of being "in all probability an agent of the Soviet Union" by the recently resigned executive director of the Joint Congressional Committee on Atomic Energy, William Liscum Borden. His security clearance was stripped. In an attempt to clear his name, Oppenheimer appealed to the Atomic Energy Commission's Personnel Security Board. The board heard and examined allegations that Oppenheimer had obstructed the development of the H-bomb. But the evidence for obstruction was scant and confusing, and in the end Oppenheimer had been persuaded. In most respects, Oppenheimer seems merely to have done what scientists normally do: resist novel approaches and apply informed skepticism to Teller's ideas. What fatally undermined Oppenheimer, however, was the admission that he had lied in past security interviews. This raised questions about his integrity.

"Integrity" was not a particularly important concern for normal science. Fraud was rare, and, as Conant observed, even eccentric characters had to conform to social controls on experimenters: the fact that experiments were a public act, and open to scrutiny. In the new regime, however, integrity was an issue. Scientists were called upon not merely to accept or reject new ideas as individuals, but to exercise direct authority over the development of and investment in ideas. In this context skepticism and resistance, rather than being meritorious and part of the indirect testing mechanism for scientific ideas, could undermine the testing mechanism and the use of rivalry as a counter-balance to groupthink or set ideas.

Edward Teller, the father of the H-bomb, was a classic example of what Conant had in mind when he spoke of scientists being prone to having hobbyhorses. Teller had been obsessed with the idea of thermonuclear energy since 1940, and had honed his ideas throughout the Manhattan Project. The treatment of Teller's ideas, which eventually turned out to be correct, is the heart of the story.

Both Oppenheimer and Teller were acutely aware of the problems in continuing to get the epistemic benefits of the old regime under the bureaucratic conditions of the new regime. Oppenheimer was a master at the use of committees and in scientific discussions—persuasive, sharp, authoritative, and respected. Teller emphasized the need for rivalry, and promoted the idea of a second laboratory, preferably located at a university, but within the system of national laboratories, in order to enable them to compete and to overcome the risk of having research in an area governed by the set ideas of one lab and its bureaucracy. As he explained,

> Because secrecy imposed limits on how many scientists were permitted to offer advice or criticism, and because those overseeing the program at the political level were not always knowledgeable about the possibilities, it seemed vitally important to establish a separate, second weapons laboratory, a competitive younger sibling to Los Alamos. Being less well established, a second laboratory would be more likely to support innovation . . . and it would provide balance and the spur of competition to Los Alamos. (Teller 2001: 333)

Scientific discussion of the results and proposals of each lab was crucial. But if the discussion was of experimental results rather than the future prospects of ideas, the danger of shutting off promising avenues by committee decisions—decisions that were intrinsically beyond the actual scientific competence of their members—could be mitigated.

The issue with Oppenheimer that underlays the accusation against him was that it was clear that many scientists objected to the development of the H-bomb on moral or political grounds. The question was whether the scientists' moral scruples led them to make technical objections, thus obstructing the development of the bomb, which were politically motivated and technically faulty. As one might expect, the separation of technical and moral questions was an important firewall. Decision-makers and decision-making processes depended on the ability of decision-makers to rely on the technical advice—that it be unbiased, or in Merton's language "disinterested." But although the criticisms and advice were public, it was impossible to determine motivation. To be sure, people could spot self-interest. But political motivations were more difficult to separate.

Because the process of bomb-making substituted direct for indirect means at every stage, these issues arose in all the stages: gathering information was conditional on a decision to make and test bombs and invest the resources to run calculations—a year-long process—and run simulations on the primitive computers of the time. The processing of the knowledge was through discussion and the presentation of technical papers and proposals. The decisions to develop the weapon were cases of the aggregation of scientific and technical knowledge. The decision-makers had to assess technical advice given by many people. The decision to produce and deploy the bomb involved similar discussions that not only included, but were centered on, political and military considerations. In each case a direct means—committee decision, for the most part—was substituted for the

290 *The Politics of Expertise*

free acceptance and rejection of ideas over time characteristic of science. The urgency justified it, as did the goal. Building bombs is not a natural outgrowth of disciplinary science.

The case of the H-bomb decision illustrates something important about credibility. The very hint that a scientist was failing to observe the distinction between technical and moral opinions was enough to disqualify the advice. Oppenheimer accordingly, did whatever he could to defend himself against the charge of bias. In the end he endorsed the bomb as "technically sweet." The complaints, or suspicions, that brought Oppenheimer down, were suspicions about the process—suspicions that were difficult to dispel. Because he was an influential figure, he bore responsibility for the effects of his words.

In many respects this was a model open decision-making process, because two sides had their say. The process itself went far beyond Oppenheimer and involved promoters of the bomb agitating for its support. None of the participants in these debates were "competent" to make the relevant decisions, at least in the early stages. Oppenheimer, as Teller pointed out, was not an engineer, and the technical issues were in fact beyond his competence. It would have been better for him personally to have recognized this and not intervened in the process. But the general question of the technical feasibility of the project was one about which no one was an expert: like all complex projects, it involved knowledge from a variety of technical specialties.

CLIMATE SCIENCE

What generalizes from this case? In the H-bomb case we face a problem with the collective heuristics of a regime in which many safeguards have been removed, direct decisions replace the indirect means of individual decision-making by scientists, and competence-competence issues arise with each replacement. Yet this process preserved enough safeguards, including the manufacturing of competition between labs and open discussion among scientists, that the basic properties of the collective heuristic of physics—which resembled it in its papers, experiments, and discussions—were preserved, and controlled the committee decision-making process. The system was one which contained corrective mechanisms, in the form of weapons tests, but also public discussion of the physics and mathematics, as well as of other issues. The process allowed outsiders—in this case political appointees, to participate in decisions, choosing sides and making retrospective judgments based on experience. The system naturally involved self-interest, and the committee process was designed to counteract it. Openness of debate was the central means of filtering out bias resulting from self-interest—notably the hobbyhorses which scientists, focused on the use of their specialized knowledge, were prone to. These practices and institutional safeguards helped provide a balance between Type I and Type II error.

But the elimination of safeguards in the course of substituting direct means can easily produce more serious changes in the collective heuristics. A system of grants based on a false consensus on the prospects of future science that excludes alternatives, for example, has the effect of producing science that is intended to fit with this consensus. Without strong checks on this, an uncorrected bias toward confirmation is built in to the collective heuristic. The existence of this bias in "normal science" was extensively discussed by Kuhn. The grant system increases the bias, and thus the need to correct it.

How does climate science compare to H-bomb science with respect to the kinds of features that go into producing a collective heuristic? The differences are substantial. We can see them in two easy ways—first by comparison to the kinds of directly epistemic considerations that were part of Teller's view of how nuclear science should be organized. Teller was concerned with the balance between acceptance and resistance to new ideas: Oppenheimer, he thought, had been too resistant to his, and he was concerned with the problem of institutionalizing rivalry. Oppenheimer, for his part, promoted rigorous criticism and public discussion of the relevant ideas, and also promoted alternative paths. The thinking and practice of these bodies reflected this need for balance, and built surrogate institutions that would mimic normal science under the conditions of urgency of the war and then the arms race. Oppenheimer struggled both with non-scientific partisans of the H-bomb and the problem of clearly distinguishing moral and technical considerations. This depended on people accepting that as a matter of honor he would not have made technical objections that were motivated by moral biases. If in the end he failed, it was for reasons of personal integrity, his self-confessed idiocy of misleading security officers, which undermined the point of honor on which the acceptance of his advice as unbiased depended.

From the very early days of the history of climate science, there was an entirely different relationship between policy and science. In 1977 the World Climate Conference was organized in Geneva to review the state of knowledge of climate change and variability and the possibility of an anthropogenic role in it. The implied purpose of the conference was to provide policy relevant knowledge. In its statement, it went beyond this, to call not only for vast funding, but also for a policy of prevention. In 1985, a conference in Villah, Austria, claimed that there was now a scientific consensus, called for more research, including research on social and economic impacts, and for policy-makers to consider mitigation policies. In short, this was policy-oriented science from the first, which was directed at the goal of a consensus and a preferred set of policies.

One can see immediately the divergence between Oppenheimer's separation of the technical and moral and the climate scientists' willingness to advocate. But the divergence made sense in connection with the claims of such scientific activists as James Hansen, to the effect that climate change would doom mankind, and was the most important of all issues. If this were true, it followed that establishing and promoting a scientific consensus in support of the needed policies was not merely a matter of urgency, but a matter of such urgency that it overrode the kinds of considerations that formerly governed scientific practice.

The goal of successfully asserting consensus was a matter of urgency. There could be no waiting for the scientific community to come around. This meant that a tight definition of climate scientists, corresponding to the consensus, was needed, and that outsiders and critics could be dismissed. It also meant that "consensus" was to be produced by direct means: this was the purpose of the Intergovernmental Panel on Climate Change (IPCC). If we compare the IPCC to the atomic energy agencies, the differences are stark. The atomic agencies tolerated and encouraged both discussion and vigorous criticism, and even rivalry. They could afford to do so because the ideas were eventually tested. In climate science there are fewer internal rivals and less diversity of opinion: this would be inimical to the claim that the science is settled. Yet the field itself is muddy and there is no unambiguous testing.

Nevertheless, the results needed to be presented both as real science and as the product of a process that mimicked real science. At the heart of this needed to be the claim that there was some sort of effective corrective mechanism for error. The atomic scientists used criticism and discussion for this, but it may have slowed down the making of the right decisions. The IPCC provided a formal process, which included attempts at technical reviews of IPCC results by "independent" scholars and allowed for open criticism that required a response. But the reviews they actually conducted allowed the dominant voices in the research supporting the IPCC to control the review process. The need for consensus was allowed to override considerations of conflicts of interest and the lack of independence of the review process. Procedural anomalies, indeed, were characteristic of the IPCC and climate science in general.

The anomalies, and the issues about whether they are real anomalies, are partly revealed by comparing climate science to Merton's ethos. "Communism" involves the open sharing of scientific knowledge. The communistic norm refers to the sharing of scientific information among scientists and for the good of the scientific enterprise. In Merton's eloquent phrasing, "property rights in science are whittled down to a bare minimum by the rationale of the scientific ethic" (1973a: 272). The products of science are public property, and so the practice of scientists must affirm the public character of knowledge. "Secrecy," Merton wrote, "is the antithesis of this norm" (1973a: 273); scientists may not hoard the information they develop or the conclusions they draw, but they must freely share their results, methods, and materials (1973a: 273).

One of the ongoing issues in climate science, and one central to climategate, is the repeated refusal of climate scientists to provide the necessary information for critics, and the assertion of property rights to information. As Phil Jones put it,

> We have 25 years or so invested in this work. Why should I make the data available to you, when your aim is to find something wrong with it? (quoted in Montford 2011: 232)

Michael Mann invoked property rights:

> My computer program is a piece of private intellectual property, as the National Science Foundation and its lawyers recognize. It is a bedrock principle of American law that the government may not take private property "without [a] public use" and "without just compensation." (quoted in Montford 2011: 222–23)

Under pressure from an investigative committee, he then claimed that the program was on his FTP site. When the program was checked it was apparent that Mann had misrepresented the work he had done and cherry-picked the results (Montford 2011: 224–26).

The other side of this story is told by Oreskes and Conway in *Merchants of Doubt* (2010), who argue that the requests for data and information were merely forms of harassment. To make this charge is to impugn the motives of the critics, which is the central focus of the book by Oreskes and Conway. The claim is similar to the one made against Oppenheimer. Both allege an abuse of process. The Mertonian norm that is being invoked here is the norm of disinterestedness. Oreskes and Conway claim or imply that the scientists and critics—the doubt merchants of the title—are paid off or motivated by pro-market ideology. At no point do they consider that the grant system itself provides many incentives for conformity and silence, and few for dissent. Biasing interests are built into a system that rewards content rather than merit: this was the concern that motivated Polanyi.

Merton's most problematic norm, for climate science, is organized skepticism. As we have seen, the IPCC review process and the system of peer review are means by which climate science is subjected to skepticism. But skepticism about the larger project of confirming anthropogenic climate change is not admissible: skeptic is a term of derision. The "organized" part is the issue as well. Peer review has taken on a far more adversarial and problematic role in climate science. Problems about reviewing, the use of committees to advance agendas, and the like are chronic. The processes originated as indirect means of facilitating discussion: peer review was needed to say whether something was worth talking about, not that it was true, or, as a *Wall Street Journal* writer put it, "bullet proofed."

294   The Politics of Expertise

Substituting panels and committee decision-making for a situation in which belief and acceptance is not a matter of committee decision but the free adoption of ideas and results by persuaded scientists is a radical change. One of the members of the National Academy of Sciences expert panel assessing issues with the iconic hockey stick pattern describing hemispheric temperatures back to 1000 (cf. Mann 2012) described the process in these terms:

> We didn't do any research on this project, we just took a look at the papers that were existing and we tried to draw some kinds of conclusions from them. So here we had twelve people around the table, all with very different backgrounds from one another,

> and we just kind of winged it to see . . . that is what you do in that kind of expert panel. (quoted in Montford 2011: 262–23)

Calling both the results of this kind of expert process and the results of organized skepticism "science" is more than problematic, as it amounts to the acceptance of a radically different epistemic regime.

SHOULD WE BE PUZZLED BY THE FAILURE OF CLIMATE SCIENCE TO PERSUADE?

Imagine if the decision to pursue the H-bomb had been—as it very well could have been under only slightly different circumstances—a decision made in public with Oppenheimer and Teller representing different ideological viewpoints and associating themselves with different parties and social movements, speaking loudly, without dropping their mantle as scientists, for their cause. Perhaps they would have justified themselves by saying that the fate of humanity depended on the outcome, something that was not far from the truth. This would have "politicized" the decision.

It was very close to becoming this kind of conflict even within the secret world of academic science. But both Teller and Oppenheimer went out of their way to avoid this happening. Teller insisted to the end that he did not believe that Oppenheimer's obstructions, which Teller nevertheless deeply felt, were politically motivated. But Oppenheimer failed, in the eyes of his external enemies, because of his act of idiocy in lying to the security services, which called into question the honesty of his attempts to keep the scientific and the moral separate, and cast suspicion on his earlier "technical" opposition to the H-bomb.

If the atomic scientists would have behaved in this imaginary way, we would have been rightly skeptical about what we were being told in the name of science. Now transpose these same considerations to the conduct of James Hansen and other climate scientists. The alliances with political movements are open. Preferences for particular policy solutions—neither an area of expertise for these scientists nor necessarily linked to their claims about climate—are given freely and in extreme forms. Public figures endorse claims about science and the consensus with equal disregard for the separation of the scientific and the ideological. The ideological preferences are visible and extreme. The demands made are astonishing. And as climategate has shown, there are serious breaches of fair play with respect to such things as peer-review and an overwhelmingly partisan rather than disinterested attitude toward open discussion of the many anomalies in the standard account. Should we be skeptical?

Merton understood something crucial about the authority of science: that it derived in part from the constraints, the self-denying norms, which scientists imposed on themselves. Adherence to these norms is itself a solution to the competence-competence problem. The rules are ways of science defining its own limits, and thus its competence. Organized skepticism is one of the limiters: one cannot treat as established science that which has not passed through skeptical scrutiny within the institutional system of science. Disinterestedness means one cannot take political sides in the name of science; one must stick to what has been established scientifically.

Teller chafed at the surrogates for organized skepticism that he faced in the world of weapons research, but never at the need to face skeptics. He only asked for a fair hearing for his ideas. The record of climate science is quite different. Attacking critics, even editors who allow critical papers into print, stigmatizing scientists for raising questions, and refusals to supply relevant information have been characteristic of climate science. If we look at the adherence to self-denying norms in isolation from the question of whether the claims of climate science are true, this much seems clear: the fact that these issues have both been raised and the fact that climategate confirmed many of the suspicions of the critics is sufficient to raise questions about the authority of these scientists.

In an important sense, adherence to these norms is epistemically irrelevant: truth is truth, whether or not it is produced in accordance with the ethos of science, much less an ethos that is now firmly in the past. But in another sense it is not irrelevant. Climate science is a test of post-normal science. We know a great deal, however unsystematically, about normal science as a collective heuristic. We know little about post-normal science. The record is simply not there. Time will tell whether it is possible to get what Ziman called reliable knowledge if one bypasses the limits imposed by the ethos, and substitutes direct means and committee decisions for the slow process of scientific acceptance. And time will reveal the biases of this new collective heuristic.

Notes

NOTES TO THE INTRODUCTION

1. I have argued elsewhere, in relation to a similar kind of argument by Ian Hacking on child abuse, that the apparently startling "constructionist" elements of such problems as the medicalization of child abuse disappear when we take into account the actual problems faced by the participants, in this case the physicians who are called on to testify in abuse cases (S. Turner 1998). I suspect that a similar kind of argument could be made for the Foucaultian cases: the drama in these cases, as in detective stories, depends on omitting crucial facts about the participants' knowledge.
2. I discuss this case elsewhere (S. Turner 1997).

NOTES TO CHAPTER 1

* This chapter forms a part of a larger project, *Liberal Democracy 3.0* published by Sage in its *Theory, Culture & Society* series. Research for this project has been supported by the National Science Foundation Ethics and Value Studies and the Science and Technology Studies Programs.
1. There are exceptions to this, such as Steve Fuller's *The Governance of Science* (2000). In political science itself, the writings of Aaron Wildavsky (1995) and Charles Lindblom and Edward Woodhouse (1993) should also be mentioned. Each reflects the concerns of Robert Dahl (1993) with the competence of citizens.
2. The American system of "extension education" in agriculture is an example of this. It soon created a new kind of inequality between early adoptees and laggards.
3. The claims about the nature of intelligence to which the letter writer to Newsweek objected (Jaffe 1994), curiously, produced a similar kind of collective letter signed by a large number of prominent psychologists, designed to correct what they saw to be the alarming disparity between what was presented by journalists and commentators as the accepted findings of psychological research on intelligence and what psychologists in fact accepted. Here the issues were different: the accepted facts were simply not known to the journalists, who seemed to assume that the facts fit with their prejudices.
4. This is a large theme of the literature that inaugurated "professional" diplomacy and foreign policy analysis. Hans Morgenthau (1946), for example, stressed the idea that it was often a necessity for the leader to act against the democratic consensus with respect to foreign policy.

5. For a detailed theoretical account of the notion of discretionary power, see the discussion of the notion of decision in the work of Schmitt. Schmitt focuses on the puzzle of declarations of states of exception (or states of siege), which are not, by definition, governed by rules that fully define the conditions under which the decision-maker can act authoritatively. This is of course the same phenomenon as administrative discretion: the law is not, and perhaps cannot be, written to cover every contingency, so the bureaucrat, or judge, is given power to apply the law as he or she sees fit (Schmitt [1923] 1988: 31–34).
6. Elsewhere, I have discussed some other aspects of the problem of expert knowledge in relation to power. In "Forms of Patronage" (S. Turner 1990), I discussed the problem faced both by scientists and by governmental patrons in deciding whether to patronize scientists, and I suggested that there was a generic problem that arose from the fact that politicians and bureaucrats were not trained in a way that enabled them to judge the promises made to them by scientists. It is questionable whether scientists are able adequately to judge such promises, as they do, for example, in peer review decisions on grant applications. I pointed out in that paper that the knowledge possessed by scientific experts was so specialized and fragmented that there was no general threat of scientists or experts as a group supplanting democracy. In "Truth and Decision" (S. Turner 1989; Chapter 3 in this volume), I discussed the issue of the limitations of specialist knowledge in the face of ill-structured decisions of the sort that policy makers and politicians actually face. I noted that typically experts with different backgrounds framed issues in ways that conflicted, and that consequently there was no univocal expert opinion in such decisions. This speaks to the notion that "expert culture" is some sort of unified whole: clearly it is not.
7. Thinkers like Foucault and Habermas present a more serious challenge than Fish does when they attack the power of the public to judge, because this undermines the notion of democratic or liberal legitimacy itself. For Habermas, for example, the communication on which the legitimacy of uncontested as well as contested viewpoints is based may be "distorted," and its results therefore bogus. Foucault is even more direct. The beliefs that we share or accept widely as true as well as the (for him) small domain in which political contests occur are all essentially the product of non-consensual manipulation, or rather a kind of hegemonic intellectual influence which does not require conscious manipulators but which prevents the ordinary citizen from, to put it in somewhat different language, giving "informed consent" to the arrangements under which he or she is compelled to live.

For Foucault, the condition of religious believer, that is to say the voluntary acceptance of the authoritative character of that which cannot be understood, is realized in an involuntary way by the citizen: the religious believer voluntarily accepts mystical authority; the ordinary citizen is mystified into the acceptance of uncontested givens through which he or she is deprived of the volitional and cognitive powers necessary for citizenship. Foucault holds out no hope that there can be any escape from this kind of "control" and provides no exemptions from its effects, except perhaps to intellectuals who can recognize and protest against their fate, but who are politically irrelevant because they have no alternative to this fate. In Foucault, the experts and the public disappear simultaneously into the thrall of forms of discourse, which is constitutive of their mental world. In Habermas, in contrast, there is an exemption for experts, of a sort. The people who do the steering are not trapped within the limitations of the life-world that they steer. This is not to say that they are not limited, however, by the effects of distorted communication. But their limitations are different from the limitations of those they administer over. Their control cannot be truly legitimate because the consent that they depend upon is not genuinely "informed." Those who assent are governed by myths that preclude their being truly informed or informable.

As I suggest in the conclusion, both lines of argument depend on a kind of utopianism about the character of knowledge that social constructionism undermines.

NOTES TO CHAPTER 3

1. McCormmach (1982) provides an interesting novelistic presentation of this transformation from the point of view of an older physicist who could not accept the transformation going on around him.

NOTES TO CHAPTER 4

1. I omit any discussion here of the communications problems that resulted from those back channel dealings in which Ham's response may have been misunderstood by lower level engineers to mean that the issue had been taken care of. This is discussed in detail in Langewiesche (2003: 812).
2. A parallel case is presented by Charles Thorpe (2002: 539–46) in a discussion of the culpability of J. Robert Oppenheimer for defective advice with respect to the hydrogen bomb, which he was suspected of having opposed for political reasons. This long-discussed, never resolved case shows the difficulty of assigning responsibility for technical opinion.
3. Phil Engelauf, the formally responsible senior engineer, explained the response to the foam problem in this way: "We've had incidences of foam coming off the tank throughout the history of the program and the same management processes that I think got us comfortable that that was not really a safety of flight issue have been allowed to continue, rightly or wrongly." The problem had been analyzed by Boeing, but, as he put it, "we got the wrong answer on the analysis" (Harwood 2003a). The analysis, of course, came with many caveats and was not literally "wrong." The error was a meta-expert error, taking the available facts to be sufficient reason to ignore the foam problem.

NOTES TO CHAPTER 5

1. The question of Oppenheimer has been discussed at great length, even becoming the subject of a Broadway play. The decisive moment for Oppenheimer as a scientific advisor, however, was his opposition, on technical grounds, to the "Super," the hydrogen bomb, which he claimed would not work. At this point, the question of whether his political views influenced his technical advice became impossible to leave aside. When he was proved wrong, it became impossible to continue to trust him (Thorpe 2006).
2. Carl Schmitt articulated this viewpoint in *The Crisis of Parliamentary Democracy* ([1923] 1988), but the same attitudes are found far more widely.

NOTES TO CHAPTER 6

1. I will leave aside for this discussion an aspect of the political status of these figures that I have stressed elsewhere (e.g., S. Turner 1987, 2002, Chapter 9

in this volume)—the fact that they purported to act as representatives. Powell explicitly saw himself as representative of both the scientific community and of the democratic public; Althoff presumably saw himself as a civil servant, exercising the authority of the state.

2. All of the usual qualifications apply to this distinction. Results that appear to be part of the corpus may cease to be so on the basis of future scientific investigation. Moreover, the distinction is often hazy in practice. The difference between adding to the corpus of scientific knowledge and performing statistical analysis using scientific concepts, or coming up with findings that are potentially relevant to the corpus of scientific knowledge but not yet sufficiently understood to be part of that corpus, for example, is not always clear or acknowledged by scientists, who may loosely use the term "scientific." And investigations that employ the categories and concepts of the corpus of scientific knowledge without themselves being candidates for inclusion in this corpus, are not entirely and obviously distinct in practice from "basic" investigations. Nevertheless, there is a difference, however disputed in practice, that is acknowledged by scientists and forms part of their working self-concept and scheme of evaluation.

3. Elsewhere I have argued for an extended use of this term to include self-created bodies with claims to represent larger bodies of opinion, which can have a variety of roles in relation to state arrangements (cf. S. Turner 2002, Chapter 9 in this volume). This reflects the political reality that international NGOs, such as Greenpeace, play a role similar to official commissions in public discourse, and take on the same kinds of trappings of expertise.

4. The Tammany Hall bosses did not have the benefit of Robert Merton's later analysis of them as benign helpers to impoverished immigrants, and, as we shall see shortly, for the most part stood in the way of "reforms" that kept these same immigrants from dying of cholera. The distribution of contracts and jobs was their concern, and doubtless some of this benefitted the poor that the bosses protected. But the cost/benefit ratio of this arrangement was not very good, and in the case of cholera, its exploitative character was obvious. But so was its "Democratic" character, for most of the public health measures that were called for, such as the removal of pigs from the houses of citizens, were unpopular with the poor.

NOTES TO CHAPTER 7

1. The Kentucky survey may have fulfilled Kellogg's conception better than the Pittsburgh investigation. The fact that much of the funding for the Pittsburgh Survey came from the Russell Sage Foundation was something of an embarrassment to Kellogg, but he regarded it as a kind of demonstration project.

2. John McClymer argues that "social engineering" was a multiform intellectual and social movement of which the Pittsburgh Survey was an example (1980).

3. "Russell Sage Foundation Skeleton of Events in Chronological Order," Russell Sage Foundation (RSF) Papers, Box 3, Folder 20A, Rockefeller Archives Center, Pocantico Hills, North Tarrytown, NY (hereafter RAC).

4. However, the theme of workplace accidents and their importance as a cause of poverty had a long history in reform movements.

5. Robert W. DeForest to John Glenn, 23 April 1920, RSF Papers, Box 4, Folder 31, RAC; John Glenn to Robert W. DeForest, 27 April 1920, RSF Papers, Box 4, Folder 31, RAC. Kellogg complained that the research done with foundation support in the twenties was not publicized as the Pittsburgh Survey had

been. "One of the great foundations spent hundreds of thousands of dollars on an inquiry of vital public concern; the reports were run off by a commercial publisher in editions of 2,000—a tremendous reservoir of fact; a tiny spigot" (Kellogg and Deardorff 1928: 828).
6. Mary E. Richmond to Ada Sheffield, 24 August 1915, RSF Papers, Box 13, Folder 112, RAC.
7. Bruere's description of Pittsburgh's response to Prohibition includes a fascinating discussion of the use of gangs of young boys as bootleggers.
8. Part of the hostility of reform activists to statistics was a result of the fact that statistical studies routinely failed to justify their concerns.
9. M. E. Richmond to John Glenn, 16 March 1920, RSF Papers, Box 13, Folder 112, RAC.
10. Ayres, Address to Educational Society, Baltimore, 13 November 1914, RSF Papers, Box 13, Folder 118, RAC.
11. Kellogg never alludes to this problem of rejection of unsatisfactory survey results, though he once complained that the results of a study of race relations on the Pacific coast were not published because of a dispute between the ameliorist funders and the "scientific researcher" (Kellogg and Deardorff 1928: 829).

NOTES TO CHAPTER 8

1. L. L. Bernard and Jessie Bernard provide the classic discussion of the edifying model and its internal conflicts as embodied in the American Social Science Association ([1943] 1965: 545–607).
2. Parsons and some of the other sociologists of the era sought to integrate their conception of the social role of the man of knowledge (to take a phrase of the title of Florian Znaniecki's work on the subject [1940] 1965) into their general conception of modern society. The reflexive aspect of these conceptions is perhaps the best developed feature of the previous literature on the issue. Studies such as Alvin Gouldner's *The Coming Crisis of Western Sociology* (1970) have, however, concentrated on the supposed "legitimating" functions of sociological theorizing in relation to the public at large. There is a sense, as we shall see, that this was precisely the audience that they rejected. Our aim will be to examine the audiences they sought to put in the place of the public, and the tasks they sought to substitute for public "legitimation."
3. *The American Journal of Sociology* was conceived as a means to respond to this summons by contributing to the synthetic task implied by these conditions. It would also "attempt to translate sociology into the language of ordinary life..It is not supposed essential to the scientific or even the technical character of thought that it be made up of abstractly formulated principles. On the contrary the aim of science should be to show the meaning of familiar things, not to construct for itself a kingdom for itself in which, if familiar things are admitted, they are obscured under an impenetrable disguise of artificial expression. If sociology is to be of any influence among practical men, it must be able to put its wisdom about things that interest ordinary men in a form which men of affairs will see to be true to life. That form will frequently be the one in which not theorists but men of affairs themselves view the facts concerned. These men are then the most authoritative sociologists" (Small 1895: 13–14).
4. Mrs. Dummer, a Chicago philanthropist, also underwrote Thomas's research on the "unadjusted girl" during the 1920s and supported activities of the American Sociology Society.

5. Barnes left the academic world and became a newspaper columnist, until he was fired for his antiwar views at the beginning of World War II, and made a living from his books, which poured forth at a great rate on a variety of subjects. Ellwood wrote a series of articles denouncing the SSRC-funded versions of sociology as "Emasculated Sociologies" (1933) and a book attacking the philosophical premises of quantitative sociology designed to bring back the Wardian edifying sociology that SSRC sociology had supplanted. His *A History of Social Philosophy* (1938), a book-club selection, concluded with a discussion of the underlying contrast between the Wardian and Sumnerian views of the possibilities of social telesis. Sorokin, who was on good terms with Ellwood, also successfully published with conventional publishing houses for the larger public. His poor relations with his peers in the discipline are legendary.
6. The idea of sociological research as a mirror to hold to society for the purpose of edification did not disappear in the '20s. Ogburn's *Recent Social Trends in the United States* (1933) is an example of this genre on a national scale, as was *An American Dilemma* (Myrdal 1944). Yet from the work of the ISRR on, one can identify some shifts in the intended audience for sociological writing. Some of the shifts are consequences of incremental developments of methods. The dissertations by F. A. Ross on school attendance (1924) and T. J. Woofter on Negro migration (1920), which introduced multivariate correlations, partialling, and the familiar multivariate regression equation, were simply not readable, at least in their statistical portions, by the untrained. Partialling became the staple of the "sociological" side of the Institute for Social and Religious Research, though the publications of the ISRR were designed to minimize the technicalities in their presentation. This kind of work could not have been supported by a wide public audience.
7. George Lundberg's famous tract, *Can Science Save Us?*, was published in 1946. Even at this date, the argument for a "natural science of society" is utilitarian: "the best hope for man in his present social predicament lies in a type of social science strictly comparable to the natural sciences" (1946: 35). The problem, he believed, is in the persistence of "prescientific folkways" in our modes of public social discussion and the fact that as yet "we have about such questions very little positive knowledge—verifiable generalizations—of the type that we have in the other sciences and by virtue of which they perform their marvels" (1946: 7). This fact has decisive bearing on the ideal of edification: "whether education will help solve our social problems depends on the validity of what we teach. There is no doubt that much of what we teach on social subjects is worse that useless, because it consists merely of transmitting the errors, prejudices, and speculations of bygone generations. Unless knowledge is constantly tested and replenished through scientific research, education may be an enemy rather than an aid to social amelioration" (1946: 7).
8. The Bureau of Applied Scientific Research had itself shifted to government support by the '60s, but the model of the relation of the researcher to the sponsor was similar. The relation was contractual, the aims negotiated with the sponsor. In each case the sponsor ordinarily had an interest in the collection of the data or its analysis that was at variance with its use as "pure science." In some sense the proprietary research model survives in the work of Lazarsfeld students such as Rossi, especially in evaluation research.
9. The Lazarsfeld model was to use a survey project in two ways: to produce a proprietary document for the business or agency that paid for the research (and was typically overcharged), and to write an academic study using the same material (together with material added to the surveys for academic

purposes that the overcharging made possible). Some variation of this practice is characteristic of survey research even to the present day: when government agencies commission survey work, their aims and the reason the money is spent are systematically at variance with the aims of the sociologist who wishes to produce an academic study. The academic survey researcher resolves the conflict by producing both kinds of results. There are, of course, other models. A classic paper by Merton and Lerner discusses the issues of sociology as a policy science in a way that parallels Parsons' discussions but focuses more directly on the practical dilemmas of the empirical researcher, who, especially in government positions, is liable to become a "bureaucratic technician" (1951).

10. Rockefeller Foundation, Trustee Minute of 16 April 1930: 3. 200S, Harvard University, Industrial Hazards, 1929–30. RG 1.1, Series 200, Box 342, File 4069, Rockefeller Archive Center, Pocantico Hills, NY (hereafter RAC).
11. Having been an active member of the Rockefeller Foundation Board, Edsall had an intimate understanding of both the criteria and the tacit procedures used for assessing proposals.
12. The $875,000 allotted to Harvard represented about one-third of the entire amount given to the social sciences in 1930 ($2,617,000). Rockefeller Foundation, 1931: 1–4, Memorandum of 31 July entitled "Continuation of Limited Program in Support of Schools of Social Technology," in "Social Sciences' Program and Policy, August 10, 1931," RG 3, Series 910, Box 2, File 12, RAC.
13. Rockefeller Foundation, Trustee Minute of 16 April 1930: 3. 200S, Harvard University, Industrial Hazards, 1929–30, RG 1.1, Series 200, Box 342, File 4069, RAC.
14. This fund would eventually be used to support Douglass V. Brown's research in medical economics, Lloyd Warner's study of Newburyport, and a race relations study of Natchez, Mississippi. This somewhat broad interpretation of industrial hazards continually placed the committee at loggerheads with the officers of the Rockefeller Foundation, who felt that research of this kind had little bearing on industrial hazards.
15. The amount allocated to the Harvard Industrial Hazards Project was almost equal to the total amount ($888,000) given to five institutions for "general social science research" in 1930. (Rockefeller Foundation, "Continuation of Limited Program in Support of Schools of Social Technology.") Consistent with this distribution of support, E. E. Day, director of the Social Division, expressed to Mayo his conviction "that the program constitutes one of the best prospects we have in the general field of the social sciences in this country," and he looked for "large accomplishments during the ten-year period for which the new grant provides support. (E. E. Day letter to Elton Mayo, 14 May 1930, RG 1.1, Series 200, Box 34, File 4069, RAC).
16. These were the original words (likely penned by Frederick W. Gates) used to state the purpose of the foundation when it obtained a charter from the state of New York in 1913 (Collier and Horowitz 1976: 64–65). They have served as a continuous point of reference for policy matters throughout the life of the foundation.
17. Kohler describes how the scope for the social sciences had come to be defined by the end of the 1920s: "To increase the body of knowledge which, in the hands of competent technicians, may be expected in time to result in substantial control. To enlarge the general stock of ideas, which should be in possession of all intelligent members of civilized society. To spread appreciation of the appropriateness and value of scientific methods in the solution of

modern social problems" (1976: 511). Issues of control became paramount in the 1930s, in all likelihood because of the deepening depression.
18. Rockefeller Foundation, 1930, Trustee Minute of 16 April 1930: 3, 200S.
19. Rockefeller Foundation "Continuation of Limited Program in Support of Schools of Social Technology."
20. The grant to the Industrial Hazards Project amounted to almost 90 percent of the total funding ($980,000) in the field of industrial hazards and economic stabilization for 1930. Mayo's work in the Industrial Research Department of the University of Pennsylvania received support, beginning in 1923, from John D. Rockefeller Jr.'s personal fund "as a matter of special interest." It received yearly extensions until 1926, when support for Mayo's work was taken over by the LSRM (Bulmer and Bulmer 1981: 383).
21. Donham was able to convince President Lowell to approve the appointment of Elton Mayo as professor of industrial sociology in conjunction with a joint fundamental study of human relations in industry (Cruikshank 1987: 63).
22. This had been originally developed by Harvard law professor Christopher Columbus Langdell in 1870. Having been impressed by the method during his time as a law student at Harvard, Donham sought to adapt it to the Business School curriculum.
23. He had played a significant role in the formation of the Department of Industrial Hygiene in 1919 and in the founding of the School of Public Health in 1922, where he served as dean (in addition to his Medical School deanship).
24. David Edsall, 1929, "Statement" (for Mr. Lamb of the [Harvard] University publicity bureau), Deans' Subject File, Industrial Physiology, Francis A. Countway Library of Medicine, Boston, Massachusetts. (Harvard Medical School Deans's Subject File, 1899–1953, Rockefeller Gift for Industrial Physiology; hereafter FCL).
25. Mayo had observed that fatigue, as manifested in "morbid preoccupations," was attributable to imbalances between a worker's expenditure of energy and the demands of his work situation. Elton Mayo, 1929: 5, "The Human Factor in Industry," FCL.
26. Wallace Donham letter to David Edsall, 20 August 1929: 2, FCL.
27. Elton Mayo letter to E. E. Day, 5 May 1930, 200s, Harvard University, Industrial Hazards, 1929–30, RG 1.1, 200, Box 342, File 4069, RAC.
28. David Edsall letter to Elton Mayo, 22 April 1929, FCL.
29. David Edsall letter to Stanley Cobb, 26 August 1929, FCL.
30. Richard M. Pearce, Officer's Diary, 18–19 November 1929: 2, Visit to Harvard with Edward E. Day, 18–19 November, RG 12.1, Box 52, RAC.
31. Rockefeller Foundation, 1930, Trustee Minute of 16 April, 1930: 3. 200S.
32. Rockefeller Foundation 1931: l, Memorandum of 22 July entitled "The Social Sciences in 1930," RG 3, Series 910, Box 2, File 12, RAC.
33. Rockefeller Foundation 1930: 1. Trustee Minute of 16 April. 200S.
34. Mayo's teaching and research became the basis for a series of weekend workshops for business executives, organized and directed by Business School professor Philip Cabot, beginning in January 1935. Recruited "from the high but not the highest," the intent was to "influence those executives who would soon have greater responsibilities (Cruikshank 1987: 163).
35. Wallace Donham letter to David Edsall, 20 August 1929, FCL.
36. Lawrence J. Henderson, 1938: 4, "Draft-Committee on Industrial Physiology," Henderson Papers, Box 19, File 22, Faculty Papers of Lawrence J. Henderson, Manuscripts Department, Baker Library, Harvard Business School, Boston, Massachusetts. (hereafter BL).
37. Lawrence J. Henderson, 1938: 1, Statement to Rockefeller Foundation, Henderson Papers, Box 19, File 22, BL.

38. Although the Paretan language was distinctive, the underlying ideas themselves were not particularly original; nor was the idea that knowledge of equilibrating processes was the key to constructing an applied role for the social scientist. Giddings, for instance, had developed virtually the same line of argument in his discussion of "social telesis" (Giddings 1924: chap. viii).
39. As a recent article puts it: "Henderson's ideal of management, like Mayo's, consisted in discovering the informal organization of small work groups in the plants and redirecting their functional sentiments toward goals harmonious with the formal organization of the manager. The skilled administrator for Henderson was a kind of Hippocratic clinician who could patiently assist the natural tendencies of the social organism to restore its condition of spontaneous cooperation" (Cross and Albury 1987: 182).
40. Lawrence J. Henderson, 1938: 5.
41. The response by publishers to "Concrete Sociology" was lukewarm, and it never saw the light of day. While its rigor was respected, it was felt to be too austere to have any sort of general appeal.
42. The manuscript was referred to Henderson for critical comment, according to Parsons, "in connection with my appointment status" (Parsons 1970: 832).
43. Lawrence J. Henderson, 1938: 4.
44. His notion of the social system, as he later acknowledged, was influenced by Henderson's work on Pareto (Parsons [1951] 1964: vii).
45. Talcott Parsons, 1938: 8-9, "A Sociological Study of Medical Practice," Paper Presented at Sociology 23 Seminar, Sociology 23 Lectures, Box 23, Lawrence J. Henderson Papers, BL.
46. It is evident that the meaning of function for Parsons was purposeful activity. By virtue of consistent action along these lines, the equilibrium of the social system was to be maintained. This conception is seriously at odds with the commonplace view that Parsons viewed society as a self-equilibrating organism, whose functioning was automatic. His standpoint was not that of the passive biologist, but rather the activist medical practitioner, whose interventions would ensure the health of the social system.
47. For a more detailed account of the pattern variables and their significance for Parsons' theory of professionalization, see Buxton 1985.
48. These included the National Morale Committee of American Defense-Harvard Group, The Civil Affairs Training Program, and the Enemy Branch of the Foreign Economic Administration.
49. Talcott Parsons, 1941, Report of the Committee on National Morale, Parsons Papers, Correspondence and Related Papers ca. 1930-59, Box 3, Faculty Papers of Talcott Parsons, School of Overseas Administration Collection, Harvard University Archives, Cambridge, Massachusetts, (hereafter HUA).
50. Talcott Parsons, letter to Edward Hartshorne, 29 August 1941, Parsons Papers, Correspondence and Related Papers ca. 1930-59, Box 3, HUA.
51. Talcott Parsons, letter to James Conant, 8 February 1942, Parsons Papers, Correspondence and Related Papers, 1923-40, Box 15, HUA.
52. Talcott Parsons, letter to James Conant. 8 February 1942.
53. Talcott Parsons, Letter to James Conant, 8 February 1942.
54. Talcott Parsons, Letter to Kingsley Davis, 21 January 1943, Parsons Papers, Correspondence and Related Papers ca. 1930-59, Box 16, HUA.
55. Talcott Parsons, 1943, Memorandum on a Possible Sociological Contribution to the Proposed Training for Military Administration, School of Overseas Administration, Box 2, HUA.
56. Talcott Parsons, Letter to Marion Levy, 15 September 1943, Parsons Papers, Correspondence and Related Papers ca. 1930-59, Box 13, HUA.

57. The continuities with the older conception are still evident in this document, however. One of the other areas of interest was the study of the causes of "man's beliefs, needs, and emotional attitudes" so that "this knowledge may be used by the individual for insight and rational conduct," a characteristic "edifying" activity involving a wide public audience. The emphasis of the report, however, is on the difficulty of foundations in applying social science knowledge "in efforts to deal with social problems" that result from the lack of "well-recognized professions with established fields of expert jurisdiction to which laymen are accustomed to defer" (Gaither 1949: 114). The examples of past successful uses of "foundation aid" to deal with this lack included "the development of professional standards in such fields as medicine, education, public welfare and social service, library work, city management, psychiatry and clinical psychology, and personnel administration." Support served to "raise their standards of performance, improve their operating techniques, and increase their ability to use the resources of all types of research" (1949: 115).
58. Such as those of David Riesman, whose *The Lonely Crowd* was a major publishing success in the 1950s.
59. Donald Young was especially adamant that deans should not reward textbook authors, and he preferred a scientistic model of propaganda for the social sciences, in which popularizers would promote and explain the achievements of researchers, thus helping to make a case to the public for funding (1948). Such a work was in fact subsidized.
60. Ironically, the exception to this was Nixon, who, as vice president, supported expansion of the social sciences in the NSF.
61. The early generations of American sociologists, most visibly the generation of Odum and Ogburn, had a partial solution to this problem. They did not attempt to write "sociology" for a broader public, and divided their lives in ways that allowed them to be academic sociologists as well as reformers, public figures, and institution builders.

NOTES TO CHAPTER 9

* The writing of this chapter was supported by a grant from the National Science Foundation Ethics and Values Studies Program (SBR-6515279). Revisions were done at the Swedish Collegium for Advanced Studies in the Social Sciences and also with the support of a grant from the NSF Science and Technology Studies Program (SBR-9810900). I would like to acknowledge the suggestions of several commentators on earlier versions of this paper, especially including Phil Mirowski, George Alter, and Richard Swedberg.

1. An interesting internal study of this question was done in 1971 at the University of Chicago, when the university, responding to undergraduate student activism, considered converting to an entirely graduate institution, attempted to do this; the problematic character of the assumptions that the author, economist and dean David Gale Johnson, was forced to make may indicate something about the difficulties here, but also points the way to the possibilities of empirical analysis. Interestingly, at this time, which in retrospect is now considered a period of prosperity for the sciences (though shortly after the beginning of a sharp decrease in the rate of growth of funding), the sciences were not money makers for the university. This hints that as competition for funding became more intense and more universities competed, the sciences require even greater subsidies, and perhaps even that the increases in tuition in the following period, ultimately, through the complex cascade of cross-subsidization that is characteristic of universities, actually wound up supporting science.

2. Actually it is about the First Amendment, and the strange contrast between attitudes toward the regulation of newspapers and similar sources of opinion and the regulation of other products.
3. There is a good but small literature on peer review (cf. Chubin and Hackett 1990) and on ethical issues (La Follette 1992).
4. Elsewhere I have argued that it was fatally misleading for Polanyi to have used the word "knowledge" with respect to these competencies or skills (S. Turner 1994). As I have repeatedly pointed out since, "knowledge" used here is an analogical notion, but one in which the distinctive characteristics of knowledge are absent precisely because of the nature of the stuff that is being captured by the analogy (1999a, 1999b). Philosophers sometimes think of knowledge as justified true belief, for example, but the stuff that is being analogized is not, except analogically ("implicitly"), beliefs, and by definition neither warranted nor justified in the usual public sense of this term, and consequently not the sorts of things one can say are true. I have elsewhere suggested that the best one can do with these notions is to talk about the habits that one acquires by successfully going through certain kinds of public performances (1994). It is these habits that I have in mind with the problematic phrase "embodied knowledge." The issues here are primarily of importance to social theory and philosophy, but it is worth at least alluding to them to indicate that there is no easy way of eliminating them in favor of some simple substitute notion.
5. Latour's actor network theory (1987), from the point of view of this chapter, is in effect a description of the connections between parts of the process of the rise and fall of scientific ideas, but it is not an explanatory model. It works, to put it very simply, by a kind of inverted behaviorism. Rather than denying intentionality to human beings and explaining them and their interactions as though they were purely causal phenomena, as behaviorism attempted to do, actor network theory inverts this explanation and grants a kind of quasi-intentionality to all sorts of objects, including the subject matter of science, making networks into quasi-intentional conglomerations. Nevertheless, this actually explains nothing because the relevant intentions are not themselves explained by anything. What is right about the Latourian model is the denial of a point of epistemic sovereignty, such as "the scientific community." What is lost is any account of the intentions themselves, and how they relate to one another to produce the particular social forms that arise in science.
6. I am grateful to David Stodolsky for bringing the fascinating work of D. A. Kronick (1988) to my attention. Kronick discusses the evolution of authorship, and the previous use of anonymity and collective publication, and the demise of these alternatives to the present system. Kronick, however, uses the language of Merton, and thus runs together two things that from the point of view of the present chapter ought to be sharply distinguished: the collective nature of science and the act of publication of particular anonymous contributions by particular scientific collectivities. The latter I take to be a case of collective endorsement that effaces the contributor. Kronick seems to think of it as a microcosmic instantiation of the collective nature of science itself.

NOTES TO CHAPTER 10

1. The term is my own coinage, but the idea is well expressed in a passage from Armin Spoek's thesis, describing the way in which the German food ministry developed policy after the BSE scandal: the German response was to engage all relevant interests. According to one interviewee this was to provide an institutional setting in which both the consumer and the agricultural camps

would have to come to an agreement before presenting an institutionally harmonized position to the outside world (Spoek 2003: 35).

Such an agreement would preclude democratic contestation and the need for a majoritarian voting solution by maintaining the appearance necessary for legitimacy by precluding the alternatives that would have arisen in a parliamentary debate.

NOTES TO CHAPTER 11

1. The phrase is associated with Irving Janis, who applied it to faulty decision-making, such as Kennedy's decision to support the Bay of Pigs invasion and to the decision-making that went into the war in Vietnam (Janis 1982). It has been applied more recently to such fiascos as the *Challenger* disaster. These are American cases, but each represents a special kind of bureaucratic situation in which stakeholders function as a group and are in a position to ignore or exclude outside opinion, which is usually treated as incompetent or hostile. These decisions contrast with the more typical case in the US, in which federalism leads to conflicts of policy that bring to the surface issues on which outside experts as well as bureaucratic experts disagree in the public arena, often in the courts.

NOTES TO CHAPTER 12

1. The original publication was 1915. The Gerth translation is of a revised 1920 version.
2. This case has been made in extenso in a persuasive paper by Xiangyang (2006).

NOTES TO CHAPTER 14

1. Philosophers pointed out a large problem with this account: according to Taylor, intentional explanations were teleological and asymmetric. The intended end was the favored end of an intentional explanation. So there was a question of whether any account that relied, as the "Strong Programme" in the Sociology of Scientific Knowledge did, on ordinary intentional language, could ever be symmetric in the relevant sense (S. Turner 2010a). This discussion was framed in the now passé language of the problem of reasons and causes. But it has reemerged in the form of the concept of "normativity," where it has the same implications. The term "belief" itself, for example, has been claimed to be a "normative" concept that cannot be understood "causally" (Rouse 2002: 99).
2. The issues with this device are discussed in "Webs of Belief, Practices, and Concepts" (S. Turner 2010a).
3. I have discussed the problem of aggregation of knowledge and the issues with the social organization of aggregation elsewhere (S. Turner 2005, Chapter 4 in this volume). See especially "Political Epistemology, Expertise, and the Aggregation of Knowledge" (S. Turner 2007b, Chapter 2 in this volume).

NOTES TO CHAPTER 15

1. As with War Socialism, the use of direct means can be highly effective. The forcing of support for particular topics can also overcome biases in

the anarchic system. The main examples of this involve interdisciplinarity. Reputational competition is disciplinary. It motivates people to do "purely academic" research that impresses specialist peers but has no application or interest outside a narrow specialist community. The Rockefeller Foundation in the1920s and afterwards many other funding agencies fought against this tendency by preferentially funding interdisciplinary work, or by funding initiatives that drew scientists with particular skills into new areas. The great success was the phage group and the importation of physics into biological chemistry. There is a sense in which adding collective projects with different cognitive heuristics and therefore different cognitive biases is a corrective to the disciplinary system.

Bibliography

Abbott, Andrew. (1988). *The System of Professions: an Essay on the Division of Expert Labor.* Chicago: University of Chicago Press.
Allport, Gordon W. (1968). *The Person in Psychology: Selected Essays.* Boston: Beacon Press.
Allport, Gordon W., and, Helene R. Veltfort. (1943). "The Uses of Psychology in Wartime." *Journal of Social Psychology* (S.P.S.S.I. Bulletin) 18: 165–23.
Andersen, Svein S., and Kjell A. Eliassen. (1996). "EU-Lobbying: Between Representivity and Effectiveness." In S. Andersen and K. Eliassen (eds.), *The European Union: How Democratic is it?*, 15–69. London: Sage.
Aron, Raymond. (1985). *Clausewitz, Philosopher of War.* Translated by C. Booker and N. Stone. Englewood Cliffs, NJ: Prentice-Hall.
Bajko, M., F. Bertinelli, N. Catalan-Lasheras, S. Claudet, P. Cruikshank, K. Dahlerup-Petersen, R. Denz, P. Fessia, C. Garion, J. M. Jimenez, G. Kirby, M. Koratzinos, Ph. Lebrun (Chair), S. Le Naour, K. H. Mess, M. Modena, V. Montabonnet, R. Nunes, V. Parma, A. Perin, G. de Rijk, A. Rijllart, L. Rossi, R. Schmidt, A. Siemko, P. Strubin, L. Tavian, H. Thiesen, J. Ph. Tock, E. Todesco, R. Veness, A. Verweij, L. Walckiers, R. van Weelderen, and R. Wolf (CERN, Geneva, Switzerland) and Feher, S., R. Flora, P. Limon, and J. Strait (FNAL, Batavia, USA). (2009). "Report of the Task Force on the Incident of 19 September 2008 at the LHC," European Organization for Nuclear Research, 31 March. Accessed April 11, 2013, http://cds.cern.ch/record/1168025/files/LHC-PROJECT-REPORT-1168.pdf?version=1http://cdsweb.cern.ch/record/1168025/files/LHC-PROJECT-REPORT-1168.pdf.
Banfield, E. (1991). "Leo Strauss." In E. Shils (ed.) *Remembering the University of Chicago*, 490–501. Chicago: University of Chicago Press.
Barber, S. (1993). *The Constitution of Judicial Power.* Baltimore, MD: The Johns Hopkins Press.
Beck, Ulrich. (1992). *Risk Society: towards a new modernity.* Translated by Mark Ritter. London: Sage Publications.
———. (1994). "The Reinvention of Politics: Towards a Theory of Reflexive Modernization." In U. Beck, A. Giddens, and S. Lash (eds.), *Reflexive Modernization*, 1–55. Stanford, CA: Stanford University Press.
———. (1995). *Ecological Enlightenment: Essays on the Politics of the Risk Society.* Translated by Mark Ritter. Atlantic Highlands, NJ: Humanities Press.
———. (1997). *The Reinvention of Politics: Rethinking Modernity in the Global Social Order.* Translated by Mark Ritter. Cambridge: Polity Press.
Bellah, Robert, Richard Madsen, William Sullivan, Ann Swidler, and Steven Tipton. . (1985). *Habits of the Heart: Individualism and Commitment in American Life.* Berkeley: University of California Press.

Bibliography

Bellamy, Richard, and Alex Warleigh. (2001). *Citizenship and Governance in the European Union*. London: Continuum.

Berger, S. (1972). *Peasants against Politics: Rural Organization in Brittany 1911–1967*. Cambridge, MA: Harvard University Press.

Bernal, J. D. (1939). *The Social Function of Science*. Cambridge, MA: MIT Press.

———. ([1965] 1979). *The Social Sciences: conclusion*. Vol. 4 of *Science in History*. Cambridge, MA: The MIT Press.

Bernard, L. L., and Jesse Bernard. ([1943] 1965). *Origins of American Sociology: The Social Science Movement in the United States*. New York: Russell and Russell.

Biagioli, Mario. (1993). *Gelileo Courtier: The Practice of Science in the Culture of Absolutism*. Chicago: The University of Chicago Press.

Boettke, Peter. (1990). *The Political Economy of Soviet Socialism: The Formative Years, 1918–1928*. Norwell, MA: Kluwer.

Borradori, Giovanna. (2003). *Philosophy in a Time of Terror: Dialogues with Jürgen Habermas and Jacques Derrida*. Chicago: The University of Chicago Press.

Borrás, Susana. (2004). "Legitimate Governance of Risk at EU Level? The case of GMOs," paper presented at 4S & EASST Conference, Paris.

Brinton, Crane. (1939). "What's the Matter with Sociology?" *Saturday Review of Literature*, May 6.

Brody, Howard, Peter Vinten-Johansen, Nigel Paneth, and Michael R. Rip. (1999). "John Snow Revisited: Getting a Handle on the Broad Street Pump," *Pharos* (Winter): 2–8.

Brooks, Samuel P. ([1918] 1969). "The task of good citizenship." In James E. McCulloch (ed.) *Democracy in Earnest*, 15–23. New York: Negro Universities Press.

Brown, James Robert. (2001). *Who Rules in Science? An Opinionated Guide to the Wars*. Cambridge, MA: Harvard University Press.

Brown, Richard E. (1979). *Rockefeller Medicine Men: Medicine and Capitalism in America*. Berkeley: University of California Press.

Bruere, Martha Bensley. (1927). *Does Prohibition Work? A Study of the Operation of the Eighteenth Amendment Made by the National Federation of Settlements, Assisted by Social Workers in Different Parts of the United States*. New York: Harper and Brothers.

Bulmer, Martin. (1984). *The Chicago School of Sociology: Institutionalization, Diversity, and the Rise of Sociological Research*. Chicago: University of Chicago Press.

Bulmer, Martin, and Joan Bulmer. (1981). "Philanthropy and Social Science in the 1920's: Beardsley Ruml and the Laura Spelman Rockefeller Memorial, 1922–29." *Minerva* 19: 347–407.

Bulmer, Martin, Kevin Bales, and Kathryn Kish Sklar, (eds.). (1991). *The Social Survey in Historical Perspective. 1880–1940*. Cambridge: Cambridge University Press.

Buonanno, Laurie, Sharon Zablotney, and Richard Keefer. (2001). "Politics versus Science in the Making of the New Regulatory Regime for Food in Europe." *European Integration online Papers*, 5. Accessed March 18, 2013, http://eiop.or.at/eiop/texte/2001-012a.htm.

Burke, E. ([1790] 1955). *Reflections on the Revolution in France*. New York: Liberal Arts Press.

Bush, V. (1945). "Science, the Endless Frontier. A Report to the President on a Program for Postwar Scientific Research." Washington, DC: United States Government Printing Office. Accessed April 17, 2013, http://www.nsf.gov/od/lpa/nsf50/vbush1945.htm.

Buxton, William J. (1985). *Talcott Parsons and the Capitalist Nation-State.* Toronto: University of Toronto Press.
Buxton, W. J. and Stephen P. Turner. (1992). "From Education to Expertise: Sociology as a 'Profession.'" in T. C. Halliday and M. Janowitz (eds.), *Sociology and Its Publics: The Forms and Fates of Disciplinary Organization*, 373–407. Chicago: The University of Chicago Press. [Chapter 8 in this volume]
Cabbage, Michael. (2003). "NASA Managers Missed Chances to Take Closer Look for *Columbia* Damage," *Orlando Sentinel*, March 23. Accessed February 28, 2013, http://articles.orlandosentinel.com/2003-03-23/news/0303230050_1_shuttle-nasa-engineers-nasa-managers.
Cabbage, M., and G. Shaw. (2003). "*Columbia* investigation: Senators Take Turns Confronting NASA," *Orlando Sentinel*, September 4.
CAIB/NASA (2003) *Accident Investigation Team Working Scenario*, Sec. 12. p. I, August 7; see Sec. 5: 1–60. Accessed February 28, 2013, http://www.caib.us/news/working_scenario/default.html Cannon, Walter B. (1945). "Lawrence Joseph Henderson 1878–1942." *National Academy of Sciences Biographical Memoir* 23: 31–58.
CERN. (2008). "Follow up of the Incident of 19 September at the LHC," Press Release Geneva, December 5. Accessed April 1, 2013, http://press.web.cern.ch/press/PressReleases/Releases2008/PR17.08E.htm.
Chalmers, Matthew, and Mark Henderson. (2008). "CERN Delays Atom-Smashing over Magnet Fault." *The Times*, September 20. Accessed April 1, 2013, http://www.thetimes.co.uk/tto/news/world/article1967076.ece.
Chambers, Graham R. (1999). "The BSE Crisis and the European Parliament." In C. Joerges and E. Vos (eds.), *Politics*, 95–106. Oxford: Hart Publishing.
Chubin, Daryl E. and Edward J. Hackett. (1990). *Peerless Science: Peer Review and U.S. Science Policy*. Albany: State University of New York Press.
Clark, Andy. (1998). "The Extended Mind," *Analysis* 58(1): 7–19.
Coase, R. H. (1974). "The Economics of the First Amendment: The Market for Goods and the Market for Ideas," *American Economic Review* 64: 384–91.
Collier, Peter, and David Horowitz. (1976). *The Rockefellers: An American Dynasty*. New York: Holt, Rinehart, and Winston.
Collingridge, David. (1980). *The Social Control of Technology*. New York: St. Martin's Press.
Collingridge, David, and Colin Reeve. (1986) *Science Speaks to Power: The Role of Experts in Policy Making*. New York: St. Martin's Press.
Collins, Harry. (2010). *Tacit & Explicit Knowledge*. Chicago: The University of Chicago Press.
Collins, H. M., and Robert Evans. (2007). *Rethinking Expertise*. Chicago: The University of Chicago Press.
Collins, H. M., and Trevor Pinch. (1993). *The Golem: What Everyone Should Know About Science*. Cambridge & New York: Cambridge University Press.
Columbia Accident Investigation Board. (2003). *Columbia* Accident Investigation Board Report, , Vol. 1–6. Accessed February 28, 2013, http://www.caib.us .
Commission of the European Communities (CEC). (2002). "Communication from the Commission on the Collection and Use of Expertise by the Commission: Principles and Guidelines," COM (2002) 713 final. Accessed March 18, 2013, http://ec.europa.eu/governance/docs/comm_expertise_en.pdf.
Conant, James B. (1947). *On Understanding Science: An Historical Approach*. New Haven, CT: Yale University Press.
———. (1951). *Science and Common Sense*. New Haven, CT: Yale University Press.
———. (1952). *Modern Science and Modern Man*. Garden City, NY: Doubleday & Co.

Coulson, N. J. (1969). *Conflicts and Tensions in Islamic Jurisprudence.* Chicago: The University of Chicago Press.
Cross, Alan. (2003). "Drawing Up Guidelines for the Collection and Use of Expert Advice: The Experience of the European Commission." *Science and Public Policy* 30: 189–92.
Cross, Stephen J., and William Albury. (1987). "Walter B. Cannon, L. J. Henderson, and the Organic Analogy," *Osiris* 2nd ser. 3: 165–92.
Cruikshank, Jeffrey. (1987). *A Delicate Experiment: The Harvard Business School 1908–45.* Boston: Graduate School of Business Administration, Harvard University.
Dahl, Robert. (1993). "Finding Competent Citizens: Improving Democracy." *Current* 351: 23–30.
Dakss, Brian. (2009). "NASA Engineer Warned About Tires." CBS/ February 11, 2009, 8:49 PM Accessed July 16, 2013, http://www.cbsnews.com/2100-500258_162-540495.html
Darrah, W. C. (1951). *Powell of the Colorado.* Princeton, NJ: Princeton University Press.
Davis, Raymond A. (2002). "Autobiography," Nobelprize.org. Accessed April 1, 2013, http://nobelprize.org/nobel_prizes/physics/laureates/2002/davis-autobio.html.
Dicey, Albert Venn. ([1914] 1962). *Lectures on the Relations between Law & Public Opinion in England during the Nineteenth Century.* 2nd ed. London: Macmillan.
Donham, Wallace. (1931). *Business Adrift.* New York: Whittlesey House, McGraw-Hill.
Dreyfus, Hubert and Stuart Dreyfus. ([1985] 2004). "From Socrates to Expert Systems: The Limits and Dangers of Calculative Rationality." Berkeley: University of California. Accessed April 15, 2013, http://socrates.berkeley.edu/~hdreyfus/html/paper_socrates.html.
Eaton, Allen and Shelby Harrison. (1930). *A Bibliography of Social Surveys: Reports of Fact-Finding Studies as a Basis for Social Action; Arranged by Subjects and Locations.* New York: Russell Sage.
Ellwood, C. A. (1923a). *Christianity and Social Science: A Challenge to the Church.* New York: Macmillan.
———. (1923b). *The Reconstruction of Religion: A Sociological View.* New York: Macmillan.
———. (1929). *Man's Social Destiny in the Light of Science.* Nashville: Cokesbury.
———. (1933). "Emasculated Sociologies." *Social Science* 8: 109–14.
———. (1938). *A History of Social Philosophy.* New York: Prentice-Hall.
Elman, B. (2000a). "Classical Reasoning in Late Imperial Chinese Civil Examination Essays." *Journal of Humanities East/West* 20 & 21: 361–420.
———. (2000b). *A Cultural History of Civil Examinations in Late Imperial China.* Berkeley: University of California Press.
Elster, Jon. (2010). "Obscurantisme dur et obscurantisme mou dans les sciences humaines et sociales," *Diogène* 1: 231–47.
England, J. Merton. (1982). *A Patron for Pure Science: The National Science Foundation's Formative Years, 1945–57.* Washington, DC: National Science Foundation.
Etzioni, Amitai. (1967). "Mixed-Scanning: A 'Third' Approach to Decision-Making." *Public Administration Review* 22: 385–92.
European Commission (2001a) "European Governance, A White Paper," COM (2001) 428 final. Accessed March 18, 2013, http://eur-lex.europa.eu/LexUriServ/site/en/com/2001/com2001_0428en01.pdf.

———. (2001b). Report of the Working Group: "Democratizing Expertise and Establishing Scientific Reference Systems (Group I b)," R. Gerold, pilot; A Liberatore, rapporteur (White Paper on Governance, Work area: Broadening and Enriching the Public Debate on European matters). Accessed March 18, 2013, http://ec.europa.eu/governance/areas/group2/report_en.pdf.

———. (2004). "Glossary Inforegio English" (comitology). Accessed March 18, 2013, http://ec.europa.eu/regional_policy/archive/glossary/glos2_en.htm.

Evans, Richard J. (1987). *Death in Hamburg: Society and Politics in the Cholera years 1830–1910.* Oxford: Clarendon Press.

Feyerabend, Paul. (1978). *Science in a Free Society.* London: New Left Books.

Fish, Stanley. (1994). *There's No Such Thing as Free Speech and It's a Good Thing, Too.* New York: Oxford University Press.

Flyvbjerg, Bent. (1998). *Rationality and Power: Democracy in Practice.* Chicago: The University of Chicago Press.

Fosdick, Raymond Blaine. (1952). *The Story of the Rockefeller Foundation.* New York: Harper.

Foskett, John M. (1949). "The Frame of Reference of Ward's Dynamic Sociology." *Washington State University Research Studies* 17: 35–40.

Frossard, D. (2002). "How Farmer-Scientist Cooperation is Devalued and Revalued: A Philippine Example." In D. A. Cleveland and D. Soleri (eds.), *Farmers, Scientists and Plant Breeding: integrating knowledge and practice,* 137–59. New York: CABI Publishing.

Fuller, Steve. (2000). *The Governance of Science.* Buckingham, UK & Philadelphia, PA: Open University Press.

Gaither, H. Rowan. (1949). *Report of the Study for the Ford Foundation on Policy and Program.* Detroit: Ford Foundation.

Galpin, C. J. (1920). *Rural Life.* New York: Century.

——— (1938). *My Drift into Rural Sociology: Memoirs of Charles Josiah Galpin.* University: Louisiana State University Press.

Gaston, H. E. (1920). *The Nonpartisan League.* New York: Harcourt, Brace and Howe.

Geiger, Roger L. (1986). *To Advance Knowledge: The Growth of American Research Universities, 1900–1940.* New York: Oxford University Press.

Gerth, H., and C. W. Mills (eds.). (1946). *From Max Weber: Essays in Sociology.* New York: Oxford University Press.

Gibbons, Michael, Camille Limoges, Helga Nowotny, Simon Schwartzman, Peter Scott, and Martin Trow. (1994). *The New Production of Knowledge: The Dynamics of Science and Research in Contemporary Societies.* London: Sage.

Giddings, Franklin H. (1922). *Studies in the Theory of Human Society.* New York: Macmillan.

———. (1924). *The Scientific Study of Human Society.* Chapel Hill: University of North Carolina Press.

Giere, Ronald N., and Barton Moffatt. (2003). "Distributed Cognition: Where the Cognitive and the Social Merge." *Social Studies of Science* 33(2): 301–10.

Gieryn, Thomas. (1994). "Boundaries of Science." In Sheila Jasanoff, Gerald E. Markle, James C. Petersen, and Trevor Pinch (eds.), *Handbook of Science and Technology Studies,* 393–443. Newbury Park, CA: Sage/4S..

Gieryn, Thomas F., and Anne Figert. (1986). "Scientists Protect their Cognitive Authority: The Status Degradation Ceremony of Sir Cyril Burt." In Gernot Buhme and Nico Stehr (eds.), *The Knowledge Society,* 67–86. Dordrecht, Holland: Reidel.

Goetzmann, William H. (1966). *Exploration and Empire: The Explorer and the Scientist in the Winning of the American West.* New York: Norton.

Gouldner, Alvin. (1970). *The Coming Crisis of Western Sociology.* New York: Basic Books.
Gullander, A. (1948). *Farmers Co-operation in Sweden.* London: Crosby, Lockwood & Son.
Habermas, Jürgen. (1973). *Theory and Practice.* Translated by John Viertel. Boston, MA: Beacon Press.
———. ([1985] 1987). *The Theory of Communicative Action.* Vol. 2. Translated by Thomas McCarthy. Boston, MA: Beacon.
Hacking, Ian. (1991). "The Making and Molding of Child Abuse." *Critical Inquiry* 17: 253–88.
Halévy, D. (1974). *The End of the Notables.* Middletown, CT: Wesleyan University Press.
Halvorsen, T. (2003). "Better Analysis Needed for Critical Flaws," *Florida Today*, August 26.
Hann, C. (1996). "Political Society and Civil Anthropology." In C. Hann and E. Dunn (eds.), *Civil Society: Challenging Western Models*, 1–26. London: Routledge.
Hansen, Janus. (2004). "Framing the Public: Participation in GM Controversies." Paper presented at the 22nd Nordic Sociology Conference, Malmö, Sweden, August 20–22.
Haraway, Donna. (1984–85). "Teddy Bear Patriarchy: Taxidermy in the Garden of Eden, New York City, 1908–1936." *Social Text* 11: 20–64. Reprinted in Haraway, *Primate Visions: Gender, Race, and Nature in the World of Modern Science*, 26–59. New York: Routledge, 1989.
Harrison, Shelby. ([1912] 1985). "A Social Survey of a Typical American City." In *The Social Survey: papers by Paul Kellogg, Shelby M. Harrison and George T. Palmer*, 2nd ed. New York: Russell Sage Foundation, 18–32. New York: Russell Sage.
Harrison, Shelby. (1930). "Introduction: Development and Spread of Social Surveys." In Allen Eaton and Shelby Harrison, *A Bibliography of Social Surveys. Reports of Fact-Finding Studies as a Basis for Social Action; Arranged by Subjects and Locations*, pp. xi-xlviii. New York: Russell Sage.
Hartshorne, Edward Y. (1941). "German Youth and the Nazi Dream of Victory." New York: America in a World of War, Pamphlet No. 12.
Harwood, W. (2003a). "Ham Overcome by Emotion when Describing Anguish." *Space Flight Now*, July 22. Accessed February 28, 2013, http://spaceflightnow.com/shuttle/sts107/030722ham/.
———. (2003b). *CBS News Satus Report* STS-107, 9:00 PM, July 22. Accessed February 28, 2013, http://cbsnews.cbs.com/network/news/space/STS-107_Archive.html.
Henderson, Mark. (2009). "Large Hadron Collider to Run through the Year in Higgs Boson Race," *The Times*, June 5. Accessed April 1, 2013, http://www.timesonline.co.uk/tol/news/science/article6431714.ece.
Hershberg, James G. (1993). *James B. Conant: Harvard to Hiroshima and the Making of the Nuclear Age.* New York: Alfred A. Knopf.
Hill, Josh. (2008). "CERN Shutdown: Predictable?" *The Daily Galaxy*, September 29. Accessed April 1, 2013, http://www.dailygalaxy.com/my_weblog/2008/09/cern-shutdown-l.html.
Hine, Robert V. (1984). *The American West: An Interpretive History*, 2nd ed. Boston: Little, Brown.
Ho, Mae Wan. (2000). "The Precautionary Principle is Coherent." *Institute of Science in Society*, October. Accessed Mar 21, 2013, http://www.i-sis.org.uk/precautionary-pr.php Hobsbawm, Eric. (2006). "'Red science': A Review of J. D. Bernal, *The Sage of Science*," *London Review of Books*, March 9.
Hocart, A. M. ([1936] 1970). *Kings and Councillors: An Essay on the Comparative Anatomy of Human Society.* Chicago: The University of Chicago Press.

Hyneman, Charles. (1944). "The Army's Civil Affairs Training Program." *American Political Science Review* 38: 342–53.
Jachtenfuchs, Markus. (2001). "The Governance Approach to European Integration." *Journal of Common Market Studies* 39: 245–64.
Jacobs, Struan. (1997–98). "Michael Polanyi and Spontaneous Order 1941–1951." *Tradition and Discovery* 24(2): 14–27.
Jacoby, Russell. (1987). *The Last Intellectuals: American Culture in the Age of Academe*. New York: Basic Books.
Jaffe, Naomi. (1994). "Letters." *Newsweek*, November 21: 26.
James, D., P. O. Walker,, and D. J. Grosch. (2004). "SwRI Ballistics Tests Help Investigators Determine the Cause of *Columbia* Loss." Accessed April 11, 2013, http://www.swri.org/3pubs/ttoday/fall03/LeadingEdge.htm.
Janis, I. (1982). *Groupthink: Psychological Studies of Policy Decisions and Fiascos*. 2nd ed. Boston: Houghton Mifflin.
Jasanoff, Sheila. (1995). *Science at the Bar: Law, Science, and Technology in America*. Cambridge, MA: Harvard University Press.
Jensen, Michael C., and William H. Meckling. (1976). "Theory of the Firm: Managerial Behavior, Agency Costs, and Ownership Structure." *Journal of Financial Economics* 3: 305–60.
Johnson, Guy, and Guion Johnson. (1980). *Research in Service to Society: The First Fifty Years of the Institute for Research in Social Science at the University of North Carolina*. Chapel Hill: University of North Carolina Press.
Keller, Evelyn Fox. (2011). "What Are Climate Scientists to do?." *Spontaneous Generations: A Journal for the History and Philosophy of Science* 5(1):19–26.
Kellogg, David. (2006). "Toward a Post-Academic Science Policy: Scientific Communication and the Collapse of the Mertonian Norms." *International Journal of Communications Law & Policy* 11. Accessed April 10, 2013, http://ijclp.net/old_website/11_2006/pdf/ijclp_01_11_2006.pdf.
Kellogg, Paul. ([1912] 1985). "The Spread of the Survey Idea." In *The Social Survey: papers by Paul Kellogg, Shelby M. Harrison and George T. Palmer*, 2nd ed. New York: Russell Sage Foundation. Reprinted from *The Proceedings of the Academy of Political Science* 2, no.4 (July 1912): 1–17.
Kellogg, Paul, and Neva R. Deardorff. (1928). "Social Research as Applied to Community Progress." *Proceedings of the First International Conference on Social Work*. Paris: lmprimé Union (July 9–13): 784–831.
Kelly, John. (2003). "Foam Hitting Orbiter Nothing New: Concern Over 'In-Flight Anomaly' Gradually Diminished Over 20 Years." *Florida Today*, August 26, 2003. Accessed July 17, 2013. http://www.columbiassacrifice.com/pages_support/$news.htm
Kitcher, Philip. (2001). *Science, Truth, and Democracy*. New York; Oxford: Oxford University Press.
Kohler, Robert E. (1976). "A Policy for the Advancement of Science: The Rockefeller Foundation, 1924–29." *Minerva* 16(4): 480–515.
Komesar, Neil K. (1994). *Imperfect Alternatives: Choosing Institutions in Law, Economics, and Public Policy*. Chicago: The University of Chicago Press.
Kotsonis, Y. (1999). *Making Peasants Backward: Agricultural Cooperatives and the Agrarian Question in Russia, 1861–1914*. New York: St. Martins Press.
Kronick, D. A. (1988). Anonymity and Identity: Editorial Policy in the Early Science Journal. *Library Quarterly* 58: 221–23.
Kuhn, T. S. ([1962] 1996). *The Structure of Scientific Revolutions*. 3rd ed. Chicago: University of Chicago Press.
La Follette, Marcel C. (1992). *Stealing into Print: Fraud, Plagiarism, and Misconduct in Scientific Publishing*. Berkeley and Los Angeles: University of California Press.

Lange, O., and Taylor, F. M. ([1938] 1964). *On the Economic Theory of Socialism.* Minneapolis: University of Minnesota Press.

Langewiesche, W. (2003). "*Columbia*'s Last Flight: The Inside Story of the Investigation, and the Catastrophe it Laid Bare." *The Atlantic Monthly,* November 2003: 58–88. Accessed April 15, 2013, http://www.theatlantic.com/past/docs/issues/2003/11/langewiesche.htm.

Lansing, Al. (1956). "He Built a Bridge from Science to Everyday Life." *Saturday Review* 39: 42–43.

Latour, Bruno. (1987). *Science in Action: How to Follow Scientists and Engineers through Society.* Cambridge: Harvard University Press.

———. (2004). "Why Has Critique Run Out of Steam? From Matters of Fact to Matters of Concern." *Critical Inquiry* 30(2): 225–48.

Laudan, Larry. (1978). *Progress and its Problems: Towards a Theory of Scientific Growth.* Berkeley: University of California Press.

———. (1984). *Science and Values: The Aims of Science and their Role in Scientific Debate.* Berkeley: University of California Press.

Leusner, J. (2003). "*Columbia*: The Final Report." *Orlando Sentinel,* Wednesday, August 22. Accessed April 15, 2013, http://www.billnelson.senate.gov/news/details.cfm?id=244565&.

Leusner, J., K. Spear, and G. Shaw. (2004). "NASA Avoids Pinning Blame for *Columbia*." *Orlando Sentinel,* February 15. Accessed April 15, 2013, http://articles.orlandosentinel.com/2003-09-14/news/0309140446_1_okeefe-culture-columbia-disaster.

Lindblom, Charles E. (1979). "Still Muddling, Not Yet Through." *Public Administration Review* 39: 517–26.

Lindblom, Charles E., and Edward J. Woodhouse. (1993). *The Policy-Making Process.* 3rd ed. Upper Saddle River, NJ: Prentice Hall.

Lippman, Walter. (1920). *Liberty and the News.* New York: Harcourt, Brace and Hone.

———. (1922). *Public Opinion.* New York: Macmillan.

List, Christian, and Philip Pettit. (2002). "Aggregating Sets of Judgments: An Impossibility Result." *Economics and Philosophy* 18: 89–110.

Lubove, Roy. (1965). *The Professional Altruist: The Emergence of Social Work as a Career.* Cambridge: Harvard University Press.

Lugg, Andrew. (1978). "Disagreement in Science." *Zeitschrift für allgemeine Wissenschaftstheorie* 9: 276–92.

Lundberg, George. (1946). *Can Science Save Us?* New York: Longmans, Green.

Lynch, Michael. (2010). "The Checkered Career of Symmetry in Recent Social Studies of Science." Paper presented April 15 at the Fiftieth Anniversary Celebration, Boston Colloquium for Philosophy of Science, Center for Philosophy & History of Science, Boston University.

Lynd, Robert S., and Helen Merrell Lynd. (1929). *Middletown: A Study in American Culture.* New York: Harcourt, Brace.

Lytle, Tamara. (2003). "O'Keefe Makes Probe more Independent." *Orlando Sentinel,* February 13. Accessed February 28, 2013, http://articles.orlandosentinel.com/2003-02-13/news/0302130124_1_okeefe-ties-to-nasa-columbia-disaster.

Maddox, Robert James. (1995). *Weapons for Victory: The Hiroshima Decision Fifty Years Later.* Columbia: University of Missouri Press.

Malin, James C. (1956). *The Grassland of North America: Prolegomena to its History with Sddenda.* Lawrence, KS: James C. Malin.

Mann, Michael. (2012). *The Hockey Stick and the Climate Wars: Dispatches from the Front Lines.* New York: Columbia University Press.

Manning, Thomas G. (1967). *Government in Science: The U.S. Geological Survey, 1867–1894,* Lexington: University of Kentucky Press.

Matláry, Janne Haaland. (1998). "Democratic Legitimacy and the Role of the Commission." In A. Føllesdal and P. Koslowski (eds.), *Democracy and the European Union*, 65–80. Berlin: Springer-Verlag.
McClymer, John. (1980). *War and Welfare: Social Engineering in America, 1890–1925*. Westport, CT: Greenwood Press.
McCormmach, Russell. (1982). *Night Thoughts of a Classical Physicist*. Cambridge, MA: Harvard University Press.
McGucken, William. (1984). *Scientists, Society, and State. The Social Relations of Science Movement in Great Britain 1931–1947*. Columbus: Ohio State University Press.
Merton, Robert. (1942). "A Note on Science and Democracy." *Journal of Legal and Political Sociology* 1: 15–26.
———. (1973a). "The Normative Structure of Science." in *The Sociology of Science: Theoretical and Empirical Investigations*, 254–66. Chicago: University of Chicago Press.
———. (1973b). *The Sociology of Science*. Chicago: The University of Chicago Press.
———. (1976). *Sociological Ambivalence and Other Essays*. New York: Free Press.
Merton, Robert K. and Daniel Lerner. (1951). "Social Scientists and Research Policy." In Daniel Lerner and Harold D. Lasswell (eds.), *The Policy Sciences*, 282–307. Stanford: Stanford University Press.
Mäki, Uskali. (1997). "Free Market Economics of Economics: Problems of Consistency and Reflexivity." Paper presented to the New Economics of Science Conference, Notre Dame, Indiana, March 13–16.
Mill, John Stuart. ([1859] 1975). *On Liberty*. New York: Norton.
———. (1861). *Representative Government*. London: Parker, Son, and Bourn. West Strand. Accessed February 26, 2013, http://www.constitution.org/jsm/rep_gov.htm.
Miller, David (ed). (1985). *Popper Selections*. Princeton, NJ: Princeton University Press.
Mills, C. Wright. (1959). *The Sociological Imagination*. New York: Oxford University Press.
Mirowski, Philip. (2009). "Why There is (as yet) No Such Thing as an Economics of Knowledge." In Harold Kincaid and Don Ross (eds.), *Oxford Handbook of Philosophy of Economics*, 99–156. Oxford: Oxford University Press.
———. (2012). "The Unreasonable Efficacy of Mathematics in Economics." In Uskali Mäki (ed.), *Philosophy of Economics, Handbook of the Philosophy of Science*, vol. 13, 159–197. Amsterdam: North-Holland.
Mitroff, Ian. (1974). *The Subjective Side of Science: A Philosophical Inquiry into the Psychology of Apollo Moon Scientists*. Amsterdam: Elsevier.
Miyazaki, I. ([1963] 1976). *China's Examination Hell: The Civil Service Examinations of Imperial China*. Translated by Conrad Shirokauer. New York: Weatherhill.
Montford, Andrew W. (2011). *The Hockey Stick Illusion: Climategate and the Corruption of Science*. London: Stacey International.
———. (1976). *Sociological Ambivalence and Other Essays*. New York: Free Press.
Moore, Barrington. ([1954] 1966). *Terror and Progress-USSR*. New York: Harper and Row.
Morgenthau, Hans J. (1946). *Morgenthau, Scientific Man vs. Power Politics*. Chicago, IL: The University of Chicago Press.
Morone, Joseph G. and Edward Woodhouse. (1989). *The Demise of Nuclear Energy? Lessons for Democratic Control*. New Haven: Yale University Press.
Mulkay, M. J. (1976). "Norms and Ideology in Science." *Social Science Information* 15: 637–56.

Myrdal, Gunnar (with the assistance of Richard Sterner and Arnold Rose). (1944). *An American Dilemma: the Negro Problem and Modern Democracy.* New York: Harper.
National Institutes of Health (NIH). (2009). Medicine: Mind the Gap; an NIH Seminar Series. Accessed April 17, 2013, http://prevention.nih.gov/mindthegap/.
Nelson, Lowry. (1969). *Rural Sociology: Its Origin and Growth in the United States.* Minneapolis: University of Minnesota Press.
Neusner, J. (1990). *The Economics of the Mishnah.* Chicago: The University of Chicago Press.
———. (1991). *Rabbinic Political Theory.* Chicago: The University of Chicago Press.
Oakeshott, Michael. ([1947–48] 1962). "Rationalism in Politics." In *Rationalism in Politics and Other Essays,* 1–36. London: Methuen.
———. (1962). *Rationalism in Politics and Other Essays.* London: Methuen.
———. (1975). *On Human Conduct.* Oxford: Clarendon Press.
Ogburn, William (ed.). (1933). *Recent Social Trends in the United States: Report of the President's Committee on Social Trends.* New York: McGraw-Hill.
Orel, V. (1996). "Heredity before Mendel." In *Gregor Mendel: The First Geneticist,* trans. S. Finn, 7–35. New York: Oxford University Press.
Oreskes, Naomi and Erik M. Conway. (2010). *Merchants of Doubt: How a Handful of Scientists Obscured the Truth on Issues from Tobacco Smoke to Global Warming.* New York: Bloomsbury Press.
Ouchi, William G. (1981). *Theory Z: How American Business Can Meet the Japanese Challenge.* Reading, MA: Addison-Wesley.
Parsons, Talcott. ([1937] 1968). *The Structure of Social Action.* New York: Free Press.
———. ([1942] 1964). "Propaganda and Social Control." In *Essays in Sociological Theory,* rev. ed., 142–76. New York: Free Press.
———. ([1945] 1964). "The Problem of Controlled Institutional Change." in *Essays in Sociological Theory,* rev. ed., 238–74. New York: Free Press.
———. ([1951] 1964). *The Social System.* New York: Free Press.
———. (1959). "The Profession: Reports and Opinion." *American Sociological Review* 24: 547–59.
———. (1969). *Politics and Social Structure.* New York: Free Press.
———. (1970). "On Building Social Systems Theory: A Personal History." *Daedalus* 99(4): 826–81.
Pearce, Richard M. (1929). "Officer's Diary. 18–19 November. Visit to Harvard with Edward E. Day. 18–19 November." RG 12.1, Box 52, Rockefeller Archives Center, Pocantico Hills, North Tarrytown, NY.
Penick, James L., Jr. (1965). *The Politics of American Science: 1939 to the Present.* Chicago: Rand McNally.
Pennington, H. (2003). "We Don't Lack Skill, Just Political Will." *The Times Higher Education Supplement,* October 3. Accessed April 15, 2013, http://www.timeshighereducation.co.uk/features/we-dont-lack-skill-just-political-will/180194.article.
Perrow, C. ([1984] 1999). *Normal Accidents: Living with High Risk Technologies.* New York: Basic Books.
Peters, Richard. (1956). *Hobbes.* Harmonsworth, UK: Penguin Books.
Pettit, Philip. (2006a). "When to Defer to Majority Testimony—and When Not." *Analysis* 66(3): 179–87.
———. (2006b). "No Testimonial Route to Consensus." *Episteme: A Journal of Social Epistemology* 3(3): 156–65.
Pianin, E. (2003). "Congress Scrutinizing Manned Spaceflight." *Washington Post,* September 4. Accessed February 28, 2013, http://www.highbeam.com/doc/1P2-287903.html.
Pickering, Andrew. (1995). *The Mangle of Practice.* Chicago: The University of Chicago Press.

Pinch, Trevor. (1986). *Confronting Nature: The Sociology of Solar-Neutrino Detection*. Dordrecht: D. Reidel Publishing Company.

Pitkin, Hannah. (1989). "Representation." In Terence Ball, James Farr, and Russell Hanson (eds.), *Political Innovation and Conceptual Change*, 132–54. Cambridge: Cambridge University Press.

Polanyi, Michael (1941–43). "The Autonomy of Science." *Manchester Memoirs* 85(2): 19–38.

———. ([1946] 1964). *Science, Faith and Society*. Chicago: The University of Chicago Press.

———. ([1951] 1980). *The Logic of Liberty: Reflections and Rejoinders*. Chicago: University of Chicago Press.

———. (1958). *The Study of Man*. Chicago: The University of Chicago Press.

———. (1962). "The Republic of Science," *Minerva* 1: 54–73.

Popper, Karl. ([1963] 1965). *Conjectures and Refutations: The Growth of Scientific Knowledge*. New York: Harper & Row.

Powell, John Wesley. (1962). *Report on the Lands of the Arid Region of the United States: With a More Detailed Account of the Lands of Utah*. Cambridge, MA: Harvard University Press.

Price, Don K. (1965). *The Scientific Estate*. London & New York: Oxford University Press.

Prychitko, David. (1991). *Marxism and Workers' Self-Management: The Essential Tension*. New York: Greenwood Press.

———. (2002). *Markets, Planning, and Democracy: Essays after the Collapse of Communism*. Northampton, MA: Edward Elgar.

Reisner, Marc. (1986). *Cadillac Desert*. New York: Viking.

Riesman, David, Nathan Glazer, and Reuel Denney. (1950). *The Lonely Crowd*. New Haven: Yale University Press.

Roberts, Paul Craig. (2005). "Polanyi the Economist." In Struan Jacobs and Richard Allen (eds.), *Emotion, Tradition, Reason: Essays on the Social, Economic and Political Thought of Michael Polanyi*, 127–32. Aldershot, UK: Ashgate.

Robertson, David. (1994). *Sly and Able: A Political Biography of James F. Byrnes*. New York: Norton.

Rosenberg, Charles E. (1962). *The Cholera Years: The United States in 1832, 1849, and 1866*. Chicago: University of Chicago Press.

Ross, Frank A. (1924). *School Attendance in 1920*. Washington, DC: Government Printing Office.

Rossi, Lucio. (2010). "Superconductivity: Its Role, its Success and its Setbacks in the Large Hadron Collider of CERN." *Superconductor Science and Technology* 23(3): 1–17.

Rouse, Joseph. (2002). *How Scientific Practices Matter: Reclaiming Philosophical Naturalism*. Chicago: The University of Chicago Press.

Russell, Bertrand. ([1950] 2009). "Philosophy for Laymen." In *Unpopular Essays*, 21–32. New York: Routledge.

St. Petersburg Times. (2003). "Senators seek blame for NASA staffers." September 4. Accessed February 28, 2013, http://www.sptimes.com/2003/09/04/news_pf/Worldandnation/Senators_seek_blame_f.shtml.

Saunders, David. (2006). "The Judicial Persona in Historical Context: The Case of Matthew Hale." In Conal Condren, Stephen Gaukroger, and Ian Hunter (eds.), *Early Modern Europe: The nature of a contested identity*, 140–59. Cambridge: Cambridge University Press.

Sawyer, K. (2003). "*Columbia*'s 'smoking gun' was obscured." *Washington Post*, August 24; CAIB Report, August 26, 2003, 1: 125. Accessed February 28, 2013, http://www.caib.us/news/report/volume1/default.html.

Schiesl, Martin. (1977). *The Politics of Efficiency: Municipal Administration and Reform in America: 1880–1920*. Berkeley: University of California Press.

Schlattl, H. (2001). "Three-Flavor Oscillation Solutions for the Solar Neutrino Problem." *Physical Review* D, 64. 013009 (June). Accessed April 3, 2013, http://prola.aps.org/abstract/PRD/v64/i1/e013009.

Scharpf, Fritz. (1999). *Governing in Europe: Effective and Democratic?* Oxford: Oxford University Press.

Schmitt, Carl. ([1922] 1985). *Political Theology: Four Chapters on the Concept of Sovereignty*. Translated by George Schwab. Cambridge, MA: The MIT Press.

———. ([1923] 1988). *The Crisis of Parliamentary Democracy*. Translated by Ellen Kennedy. Cambridge, MA: The MIT Press.

———. ([1932] 1996). *The Concept of the Political*. Translated by George Schwab. New Brunswick, NJ: Rutgers University Press.

Schmitter, Philippe C. (2000). *How to Democratize the European Union . . . And Why Bother*, Lanham, MD: Rowman & Littlefield.

Schudson, Michael. (1997). "Cultural Studies and the Social Construction of 'Social Construction': Notes on 'Teddy Bear Patriarchy.'" In Elizabeth Long (ed.), *From Sociology to Cultural Studies: new perspectives*, 379–99. Oxford: Blackwell.

———. (2006). "The Trouble with Experts—and Why Democracies Need Them." *Theory and Society* 35: 491–506.

Schumpeter, Joseph. ([1942] 1950). *Capitalism, Socialism and Democracy*. New York: Harper & Row.

Scott, Roy V. (1970). *The Reluctant Farmer: The Rise of Agricultural Extension to 1914*, Urbana, IL: University of Illinois Press.

Scully, Roger. (1997). "The European Parliament and the Co-Decision Procedure: A Reassessment." *The Journal of Legislative Studies*, 3: 58–73.

Shapere, Dudley. (1982). "The Concept of Observation in Science and Philosophy." *Philosophy of Science* 49(4): 485–525.

Simon, Herbert A. (1977). *Models of Discovery and Other Topics in the Method of Science*. Dordrecht, Netherlands: D. Reidel.

Simey, T. S. (1966). "Max Weber: Man of Affairs or Theoretical Sociologist?." *Sociological Review* 14: 303–27.

Small, Albion. (1895). "The Era of Sociology." *American Journal of Sociology* 1: 1–15.

Small, Albion, and George Vincent. (1894). *An Introduction to the Study of Society*. New York: American Book Company.

Smithe, S. (1873). *Grains for the Grangers: Discussing all Points Bearing on the Farmers' Movement for the Emancipation of White Slaves from the Slave-power of Monopoly*. Chicago: Union Publishing Company.

Snow, C. P. (1961). *Science and Government*. Cambridge, MA: Harvard University Press.

Social Science Research Council (SSRC). (1933). *Decennial Report: 1923–1933*. New York: Social Science Research Council.

Solomon, Miriam. (2006a). "Groupthink Versus the Wisdom of Crowds: The Social Epistemology of Deliberation and Dissent." *The Southern Journal of Philosophy* 44: 28–43.

———. (2006b). "Norms of Epistemic Diversity." *Episteme: A Journal of Social Epistemology* 3(1–2): 23–36.

Spoek, Armin. (2003). "'Uneasy Divorce' or 'Joint Custody'? The Separation of Risk Assessment and Risk Management in Food Policy." Unpublished thesis, University of Sussex.

Star, Susan L. and James R. Griesemer. (1989). "Institutional Ecology, 'Translations,' and Boundary Objects: Amateurs and Professionals in Berkeley's Museum of Vertebrate Zoology, 1907–39." *Social Studies of Science* 19(4): 387–420.

Stegner, Wallace. (1962). *Beyond the Hundredth Meridian: John Wesley Powell and the Second Opening of the West*. Boston: Houghton Mifflin.

Stigler, Stephen M. (1986). *The History of Statistics: The Measurement of Uncertainty before 1900*. Cambridge, MA: The Belknap Press of Harvard University Press.

Strauss, L. ([1950] 1971). *Natural Right and History*. Chicago: The University of Chicago Press.

Sunstein, Cass. (2005). *Laws of Fear: Beyond the Precautionary Principle*. Cambridge, MA: Cambridge University Press.

Swedberg, R. (2005). *The Max Weber Dictionary: Key Words and Central Concepts*. Stanford, CA: Stanford University Press.

Taylor, Charles. (1964). *The Explanation of Behavior*. New York: Humanities.

Teller, Edward. (2001). *Memoirs: A Twentieth Century Journey in Science and Politics*. Cambridge, MA: Perseus Publishing.

Tetlock, Philip. (2006). *Expert Political Judgment: How Good is it? How Can We Know?* Princeton, NJ: Princeton University Press.

Thorpe, C. R. (2002). "Disciplining Experts: Scientific Authority and Liberal Democracy in the Oppenheimer case." *Social Studies of Science* 32: 525–62.

———. (2006). *Oppenheimer: The Tragic Intellect*. Chicago: The University of Chicago Press.

Timmermans, Stefan. (1999). *Sudden Death and the Myth of CPR*. Philadelphia, PA: Temple University Press.

Tocqueville, Alexis de. ([1835] 1969). *Democracy in America*. Edited by J. P. Mayer, Translated by George Lawrence. Garden City, NY: Doubleday & Company, Inc.

Tsebelis, George, and Amie Kreppel. (1998). "The History of Conditional Agenda-Setting in European Institutions." *European Journal of Political Research* 33: 41–71.

Turner, Fredrick Jackson. (1962). *The Frontier in American History*. New York: Holt, Rinehart & Winston.

Turner, Stephen. (1986). "The Sociology of Science in its Place." *Science and Technology Studies* 4: 15–18.

———. (1987). "The Survey in Nineteenth-Century American Geology: The Evolution of a Form of Patronage." *Minerva* 25(3): 282–330.

———. (1989). "Truth and Decision." In Daryl Chubm and Ellen W. Chu (eds.), *Science off the Pedestal: Social Perspectives on Science and Technology*, 175–88. Belmont, CA: Wadsworth. [Chapter 3 in this volume]

———. (1990). "Forms of patronage." In S. Cozzens and T. F. Gieryn (eds.), *Theories of Science in Society*, 85–211. Bloomington: Indiana University Press.

———. (1994). *The Social Theory of Practices: Tradition, Tacit Knowledge, and Presuppositions*. Chicago: University of Chicago Press.

———. (1996) "The Pittsburgh Survey and the Survey Movement: An Episode in the History of Expertise." In Maurine W. Greenwald and Margo Anderson (eds.) *Pittsburgh Surveyed: Social Science and Social Reform in the Early Twentieth Century*, 35–49. Pittsburgh, PA: University of Pittsburgh Press.

———. (1997). "'Net effects': A Short History." In V. McKim and S. Turner (eds.), *Causality in Crisis*, 23–45. Notre Dame, IN: University of Notre Dame Press.

———. (1998). "The Limits of Social Constructionism." In I. Velody and R. Williams (eds.), *The Politics of Constructionism*, 109–20. London: Sage.

———. (1999a). "Searle's Social Reality." *History and Theory* 38: 211–31.

———. (1999b). "Practice in Real Time." *Studies in the History and Philosophy of Science* 30: 149–56.

———. (1999c). "Universities and the Regulation of Scientific Morals." In John M. Braxton (ed.), *Perspectives on Scholarly Misconduct in the Sciences*, Columbus: Ohio State University Press.

———. (1999d). "Does Funding Produce its Effects? The Rockefeller Case." In Theresa Richardson and Donald Fisher (eds.), *The Development of the Social*

Sciences in the United States and Canada: The Role of Philanthropy, 213–27. Stamford: Ablex Publishing.

———. (2001). "What is the Problem with Experts?." *Social Studies of Science* 31(1): 123–49. [Chapter 1 in this volume]

———. (2002). "Scientists as Agents." In Philip Mirowski and Esther-Mirjam Sent (eds.), *Science Bought and Sold*, 362–84. Chicago: University of Chicago Press. [Chapter 9 in this volume]

———. (2003a). "The Third Science War. James R. Brown, *Who Rules in Science: An Opinionated Guide to the Wars* and Philip Kitcher, *Science, Truth, and Democracy*." *Social Studies of Science* 33(4): 581–611.

———. (2003b). *Liberal Democracy 3.0: Civil Society in an Age of Experts*. London: Sage Publications.

———. (2004a). "Quasi-science and the State." In N. Stehr (ed.) *The Governance of Knowledge*, 241–68. Piscataway, NJ: Transaction Books. [Chapter 6 in this volume]

———. (2004b). "Speaking Truth to Bureaucratic Power: Three National Responses to Cholera." *Technikolgenabschätzung*: Theorie und Praxis 3(13): 57–62. http://www.itas.fzk.de/deu/tatup/inhalt.htm.

———. (2005). "Expertise and Political Responsibility: The *Columbia* Shuttle Catastrophe." In Sabine Maasen, and Peter Weingart (eds.), *Democratization of Expertise? Exploring Novel Forms of Scientific Advice in Political Decision-Making*, 101–21. Kluwer: Dordrecht. [Chapter 4 in this volume]

———. (2006) "Was Real Existing Socialism a Premature Form of the Rule of Experts?." In Sven Eliaeson (ed.), *Democracy and Civil Society East of the Elbe*, 248–61. London: Routledge. [Chapter 11 in this volume]

———. (2007a). "The Social Study of Science before Kuhn." In Edward J. Hackett, Olga Amsterdamska, Michael Lynch, and Judy Wajcman (eds.), *The Handbook of Science and Technology Studies*, 3rd ed., 33–62. Cambridge, MA: MIT Press.

———. (2007b). "Political Epistemology, Expertise, and the Aggregation of Knowledge." *Spontaneous Generations: A Journal for the History and Philosophy of Science* 1(1): 36–47. [Chapter 2 in this volume]

———. (2008a). "Balancing Expert Power: Two Models for the Future of Politics." In Nico Stehr (ed.), *Knowledge and Democracy: Is Liberty a Daughter of Knowledge*, 119–41. New Brunswick, NJ: Transaction. [Chapter 5 in this volume]

———. (2008b). "Expertise and the Process of Policy Making: the EU's New Model of Legitimacy." In Sven Eliason (ed.) *Building Civil Society and Democracy in New Europe*, 160–75. Cambridge: Cambridge Scholars Publishing. [Chapter 10 in this volume]

———. (2010a). "Webs of Belief, Practices, and Concepts." *Archives européennes de sociologie* 51: 397–421.

———. (2010b). "Normal Accidents of Expertise. *Minerva* 48: 239–58.

———. (2012). "Whatever happened to knowledge?" *Social Studies of Science* 42: 474–80.

———. (forthcoming 2014). "Functionalism, Field Theories, and Unintended Consequences." In G. Manzo (ed), *Paradoxes, Mechanisms, Consequences: Essays in Honor of Mohamed Cherkaoui*. Oxford: Bardwell Press.

Turner, Stephen, and Regis Factor. (1984). *Max Weber and the Dispute over Reason and Value: A study in Philosophy, Ethics, and Politics*. London: Routledge & Kegan Paul, Ltd.

Tversky, Amos, and Daniel Kahneman. (1974). "Judgment under Uncertainty: Heuristics and Biases." *Science* 185 (27 September): 1124–31.

———. (1981). "The Framing of Decisions and the Psychology of Choice." *Science* 211 (30 January): 453–58.

Vaughan, D. (1996). *The Challenger Launch Decision: Risky Technology. Culture and Deviance at NASA*. Chicago: University of Chicago Press.
Wald, Lillian. (1927). "Introduction." In *Does Prohibition Work? A Study of the Operation of the Eighteenth Amendment Made by the National Federation of Settlements, Assisted by Social Workers in Different Parts of the United States*, ix-x. New York: Harper and Brothers.
Weart, Spencer. (2003). *The Discovery of Global Warming*. Cambridge, MA: Harvard University Press.
Weber, Marianne. ([1926] 1975), *Max Weber: A Biography*. Translated and edited by Harry Zolm. New York: Jon Wiley and Sons.
Weber, Max. ([1915] 1946). "The Introduction to the Sociology of Religions." In H. Gerth and C. W. Mills (eds.), *From Max Weber: Essays in Sociology*, 267–301. New York: Oxford University Press.
———. ([1919] 1946). "Science as a Vocation." In H. Gerth and C. W. Mills (eds.), *From Max Weber: Essays in Sociology*, 129–56. New York: Oxford University Press.
———. ([1920] 1951). *The Religion of China*. Translated by Hans Gerth. New York: The Free Press.
———. ([1927] 1961). *General Economic History*. Translated by Frank H. Knight. New York: Collier Books.
———. (1952). *Ancient Judaism*. New York: The Free Press.
———. (1958). *The Protestant Ethic and the Spirit of Capitalism*. Translated by Talcott Parsons. New York: Charles Scribner's Sons.
———. ([1968] 1978). *Economy and Society: An Outline of Interpretive Sociology*. Edited by Guenther Roth and Claus Wittich. Berkeley: University of California Press.
Wessels, W. (1992). "Staat und (westeuropaische) integration: die fushionsthese." In M. Kriele (ed.), *Politische Vierteljahrschrift* 23 (special issue).
Whewell, William. (1858). *Novum Organon Renovatum: Being the Second Part of the Philosophy of the Inductive Sciences*. 3rd ed. London: John W. Parker and Son.
Wikipedia. "Mode 2." Accessed April 10, 2013, http://en.wikipedia.org/wiki/Mode_2.
Wildavsky, Aaron. (1995). *But Is It True?: A Citizens Guide to Environmental Health and Safety Issues*. Cambridge, MA & London: Harvard University Press.
Wing, Frank E. ([1914] 1974). "Thirty-Five Years of Typhoid Fever: The Economic Cost to Pittsburgh and the Long Fight for Pure Water." In Paul U. Kellogg (ed.), *Wage-Earning Pittsburgh*, reprint ed., 163–86. New York: Arno Press.
Woods, T. A. (1991). *Knights of the Plow: Oliver H. Kelley and the Origins of the Grange in Republican Ideology*. Ames, IA: Iowa State University Press.
Woofter, Thomas Jackson, Jr. (1920). *Negro Migration: Changes in Rural Organization and Population of the Cotton Belt*. New York: W. D. Gray.
Wootton, Barbara. (1945). *Freedom under Planning*. Chapel Hill: University of North Carolina Press.
Worster, Donald. (1979). *Dust Bowl: The Southern Plains in the 1930s*. New York: Oxford University Press.
———. (1985). *Rivers of Empire: Water, Aridity, and the Growth of the American West*. New York: Pantheon.
Wouk, Herman. ([1951] 1979). *The Caine Mutiny*. Boston: Little Brown.
Wynne, Brian. (1996). "May the Sheep Safely Graze? A Reflexive View of the Expert-Lay Knowledge Divide." In S. Lash, B. Szersynski, and B. Wynne (eds.), *Risk, Environment, and Modernity: Towards a New Ecology*, 44–83. London: Sage Publications.

Xiangyang, Q. (2006). "Comparative Lawmaking, Legal Rationality and Weber." Unpublished paper, The Law School of Sichuan University, China.
Young, Donald. (1948). "Limiting Factors in the Development of the Social Sciences." *Proceedings of the American Philosophical Society* 92: 325–35.
Ziman, John. (1968). *Public Knowledge.* New York: Cambridge University Press.
———. (1978). *Reliable Knowledge: An Exploration of the Grounds for Belief in Science.* Cambridge; New York: Cambridge University Press.
———. (1996). "Is Science Losing its Objectivity." *Nature* 382(6594): 751–54.
———. (2000). "Are Debatable Scientific Questions Debatable?" *Social Epistemology* 14(2–3): 187–99.
Znaniecki, Florian. (1965). *The Social Role of the Man of Knowledge.* New York: Octagon Books.
Zuckerman, H., and R. K. Merton. (1971). "Patterns of Evaluation in Science: Institutionalization, Structure and Function of the Referee System." *Minerva* 9 (January): 66–100.

Index

A
Aalborg, 12, 102–4, 107, 111
accidents. *See* normal accidents
Addams, Jane, 148
A-bomb, 5, 12, 47–48, 98–100, 278, 288; interim committee, 96–100. *See also* atomic scientists; Ban the Bomb movement
accountability, 67, 75, 91–92, 118, 125, 205–7; and democracy, 82, 100, 115–16; and expertise, 17, 73–74, 112; political, 71, 94, 110–11
agency theory, 9, 15, 188, 195, 218, 239. *See also* principal agent theory
agricultural expertise, 1, 68, 111, 213, 215, 219; science, 66, 121–22, 211
Allport, Gordon, 168–70
Althoff, Friedrich, 125
amateur, 31, 33, 112, 211, 213, 215
ambiguity, 66, 75, 82–93, 92
American Journal of Sociology (AJS), 157
American Political Science Association, 159
American Social Science Association, 155
American Sociological Society, 157
anomalies, 292, 295; Kuhn, 276, 284, 286; and science, 262–3, 268, 270–71
area studies, 32–33, 173
arid lands (US), 11, 62–63
Aristotle, 70, 235
Army Corps of Engineers, 67
asymmetric bilateral consilience, 252–54
asymmetry. *See* information; knowledge
Atomic Energy Commission, 288
atomic scientists, 46, 87–88, 96–97, 110, 193; nuclear experts, 244, 292
audience, 11, 26–27, 31, 33, 119, 235; and legitimacy, 9, 24–25; and political discussion, 108; for science, 191, 285; for social surveys, 142, 150; for sociology, 156–60, 166–67, 170, 173–77. *See also* expert/audience relations
Austin, John, 114
Austro-Hungarian Empire, 210
authority, 21–22, 63–65, 158, 186, 215, 243; cognitive, 22–27, 30, 39, 186; political, 26, 32, 213, 233. *See also* science
Ayres, Leonard, 140, 149–50

B
Baltimore (David) Affair, 43
Ban the Bomb movement, 101
Barnes, Harry Elmer, 159
Beck, Ulrich, 13, 114–18, 123–24, 126, 129–31, 135–37, 256
belief, 18, 38, 44, 166, 185, 259, 298n7, 306n57, 308n1; and bureaucracies, 34–35; and conformity, 252–56; and decision-making, 56–61, 239, 244; justified true, 7–8, 22, 252, 307n4; legitimating, 50, 226, 233; and politics, 9, 47–48, 107–11; and science, 53–55, 84, 184, 251, 260, 266, 284, 294
Bell Labs, 266

Index

Bellah, Robert, 177
Bentham, Jeremy, 112
Berlin, Isaiah, 48
Bernal, J. D., 47
biases, 10, 12, 49, 80, 175, 258–59, 308–9n1; and certification, 192–93; collective, 108, 126; and decision-making, 98, 241, 289; epistemic, 240, 250–51, 255–56; expert, 4, 72, 74, 97, 99, 125, 241; and heuristics, 242–44, 246, 253, 279, 295; and science, 284, 286, 289–91, 293; racial, 35, 230. *See also* interests
A Bibliography of Social Surveys (Eaton), 142–43
big science. *See* science
Bismarck, Otto von, 120
Bloor, David, 259
Boards of Health, 134
Boettke, Peter, 249
bonding, 9, 186, 188; economics of, 194–96; and science, 10, 14, 189–93. *See also* certification; legitimacy
boundary organizations, 130–31, 272, 274
Britain, 93, 118, 212; civil service, 12–13, 32–33, 48, 102, 117, 119, 132, 210. *See also* cholera
Broad Street pump. *See* cholera
Bruere, Martha Bensley, 148, 301n7
Bureaus of Labor Statistics, 159. *See also* Massachusetts Bureau of Labor Statistics
bureaucracies, 22, 32, 34, 48, 80, 117, 129, 228; culture of, 122; expert, 73, 93, 104; independence, 94; and politics, 212; state, 120, 203. *See also* Britain; Chinese; consensus; Denmark; France; Germany; United States
bureaucratic politics, 94, 102, 108, 110, 129; and asymmetric power, 103–4; and planning, 105–7; and power, 130–37
bureaucratic state, 112, 209
bureaucratic tradition, 4, 12, 32, 112, 129, 134
Bush, George W., 45, 97
Bush, Vannevar, 283, 286
Byrnes, James S., 96, 98–100

C

The Caine Mutiny (Wouk), 6
Canute (King), 26
Carnegie, Andrew, 27, 139
Carnegie Corporation, 174, 178
Carnegie Institute, 142
case study method, 71, 145, 166–67, 225
Catholic Church, 10, 42–43
centralization (state), 125, 197, 198, 210, 212, 213
CERN (Large Hadron Collider), 261–64, 267, 273
certification, 5, 14, 31–32, 118; cost of, 187–88; and experts, 36, 73; and science, 8, 23–24, 188–95. *See also* bonding; licensure
The Challenger Launch Decision (Vaughan), 90
Challenger shuttle, 83, 87, 90, 92
Chamber of Commerce, 104, 106–7, 113
Chapin, F. Stuart, 161
charisma, 50, 226–27, 233
Charity Organization Societies (COS), 27, 147, 149
Cherwell, Lord. *See* Lord Cherwell
the Chicago School, 160
China, 30, 100, 172, 223–35; bureaucracy, 5, 9, 223, 226–36
Cholera Commission for the German Empire, 132
cholera epidemic, 13, 48, 125, 128–37, 300n4; Broad Street Pump, 129; Evans, Richard, 130, 132; General Health Board (UK), 130, 132; New York Sanitary Commission, 129, 134–35; Saint James Parish Committee, 133–134, 137. *See also* Hamburg cholera epidemic; London; New York Sanitary Commission; Snow, John
Churchill, Winston, 96
city planning. *See* urban planning
civil service, 33, 102, 117, 119, 211–12
civil society, 209, 215–16, 218–21
Clausewitz, Carl von, 54
climate change, 41–42, 44, 49, 242, 255, 277–80; climate science, 45, 258, 260, 271, 273–75, 290–95
Coase, Ronald, 182
Cobb, Stanley, 164–65

cognitive authority. *See* authority
Collins, Harry M., 37–38, 258–59
Columbia Accident Investigation Board (CAIB), 74–76, 79, 88–92
Columbia shuttle, the, 11, 72–73, 75, 82–84, 87. *See also* NASA
Columbia University, 29–30, 112
commissions, 27, 45, 47, 71, 300n3; and decision-making power, 129–37; and experts, 48, 73–75, 102, 212; and knowledge society, 126. *See also* boundary organizations; cholera; European Commission
committees, 22, 74, 92, 95, 195, 199, 293; regulatory, 128; technical, 48, 288–9, 290; as tribunals, 108. *See also* A-bomb (interim committee); cholera; science
Committee on National Morale, 168–71
Communism, 5, 9–10, 49, 193, 209, 215–19, 222, 233, 283
communism, 184, 191, 193, 278, 292
community survey. *See* social survey
competence, 26, 69–70, 74, 218, 265–66; and bonding, 188; and bureaucracy, 102, 104, 106, 117, 121; and experts, 17, 73, 80, 84, 86–87
competence-competence (*kompetenz-kompetenz, competence sur le competence*), 280–81, 285, 287–88, 290, 295
competition, 61, 67, 124, 248; and experts, 13, 48, 214; and politics, 98, 109, 112, 226, 251; and science, 131, 180, 191–92, 265, 270, 282–90; and science funding, 124, 194–95, 306n1
Comte, Auguste, 50
Conant, James Bryant, 13, 96, 136, 168, 170–71, 288. *See also* Kuhn, Thomas
"The concept of observation in science and philosophy" (Shapere), 261
Concept of the Political (Schmitt), 41
Condorcet, Nicolas de, 50
conformity, 84, 131–33, 175, 252, 254, 293; bureaucratic, 122, 213. *See also* groupthink; hobbyhorse
Confucianism, 9, 223–36
Congress for Cultural Freedom, 278
consensus, 3–4, 114, 125, 142, 150, 198–99, 252–4; bureaucratic, 9, 35, 48, 135–36, 214; and climate science, 277, 291–2; expert, 45, 49, 80, 258; and democracy, 47, 116, 255; managerial, 79–90; production, 97, 114–15, 135, 200, 271–6; scientific, 36, 40, 42, 82, 126–28, 137, 265, 269–71, 270, 285, 295; of stakeholders, 47, 111. *See also* decision-making
Consensus Development Program (NIH), 271–72
consilience, 251–4
controversy studies (science), 37
cooperation, 114, 131, 167, 173, 199, 220; civic, 106–7, 124, 129–30; political, 94, 103, 137
Cooperative Extension Service (US), 121
Cooperative Movement, 156
Cortes, Donoso, 206
council, 19, 82, 89, 250; and experts, 71–72; Mill's notion of, 71, 205–6
creation science, 18–19, 53
C-SPAN, 45
culture as explanation, 90–91
cultural studies, 19, 35

D

Danish bureaucracies. *See* Denmark (Planning)
DARPA (Defense Advanced Research Projects Agency), 129
Darwinism, 36, 41
Daugherty, Bob, 81
Davis, Raymond A., 268–70
Day, Edmund E., 163–64
Deardorff, Neva, 138, 141, 147
Death in Hamburg (Evans), 130
decision-making, 1, 8–9, 11, 13, 60, 199, 211, 272, 289–90; bureaucracy and, 4, 34, 231; collective, 77, 240, 246, 248, 255–56, 267; and democracy, 50, 71; expert, 2, 9, 45–47, 69–70, 73, 76, 131, 136, 208, 215; and policy, 56; political, 38, 64, 94, 101, 104, 123, 294; public, 71–72, 135; science and, 53–54, 56–59, 61, 67, 125, 186–88, 282–82, 287. *See also* A-bomb (interim committee); delegation; expertise

DeForest, Robert W., 147
delegation, 117–18, 120, 137, 187; to bureaucracies, 128–129, 210; to experts, 38–39, 45, 72, 86, 88, 118; of powers, 116–17, 119–21, 123–24, 131; and science, 125–126. *See also* authority; decision-making
DeMan, Hendrik, 216
democratic politics, 1–2, 12, 22, 46, 71, 111, 212
democratic rule, 17, 21, 50
democracy, 34, 40, 47, 49, 68, 109; and expert knowledge, 24, 32, 42–43. *See also* liberal democracy; parliamentary democracy; science
Denmark (Planning), 5, 12, 19, 102–3
discussion, 29, 39, 123, 128–29, 199, 202, 209, 221; and liberal government, 117; political, 108–110; public, 49, 114, 130–31, 135, 204, 255. *See also* experts
disinterestedness, 29, 113, 168; norm of science, 184, 193, 283, 293, 295
DNA research, 281, 287
Dr. Ruth (Westheimer), 25, 29
Does Prohibition Work? (Bruere), 148
Donham, Wallace, 162–66
Douglas, Mary, 175
Drinker, Philip and Cecil, 162, 165
Dummer, Ethel, 158
Durkheim, Émile, 4–5
Dworkin, Ronald, 230

E

Eastern Europe, 209–10, 221
Eaton, Allen, 138, 142–43
Economy and Society (Weber), 228
Edsall, David, 162, 164–65
Ehrlich, Paul, 43–45
Ellwood, Charles, 14, 157, 159, 178
embodied knowledge, 1, 7–8, 190–91, 231
epistemology. *See* social epistemology
equality, 18–19, 22, 32, 220; epistemic, 17, 50, 239, 241. *See also* expertise
error, 9, 24, 54–55, 80, 82, 271; expert, 44–45, 73–75, 257; hedgehog, 48; and science, 257–60, 271. *See also* knowledge risk

European Commission, 202, 205–7
European Community (EC), 197–205
European Parliament, 199, 205, 208
European Union (EU), 5, 198, 208
EU White Paper on European Governance, 206
evaluation of expertise, 240–41; economics of, 180, 186–87, 189, 195–96. *See also* certification; licensure
Evans, Lyn, 263
Evans, Richard. *See* cholera
examination systems, 48, 223, 228–31, 233–35
expert/audience relations, 9, 11, 24–25, 27–31, 214, 219, 239–41; with professionals, 33, 160, 174, 176
expert claims, 5, 21, 32, 34, 37, 84, 100, 119, 138; assessing, 8, 88; and disinterestedness, 113; and policy, 29, 41, 46; and responsibility, 73; trust and, 9, 86; validity of, 22, 36. *See also* bias; error; legitimacy
expert error. *See* error
expert knowledge, 6, 144–45, 211, 218, 224, 272; and bureaucracies, 104, 213, 230; and ideology, 20, 21; and non-experts, 115; *peuple eclaire*, 114; politics and 1, 35, 93; production of, 150, 257–58; and representative government, 101, 205, 207; soviet system and, 215; and stakeholders, 116, 213. *See also* cholera; experts (rule); legitimacy; liberal democracy; peer review; social epistemology
expert opinion, 9, 18, 71, 73, 78, 80–81, 84, 87, 129; aggregating, 79, 88, 255; and bureaucracies, 122; and decision-making, 69, 71, 96, 136; and policy, 45, 110; vs. public, 121
expert systems, 1, 257, 261, 265–66, 271–73
Experten (experts), 3, 223
experts, 18–19, 26, 141, 206, 239, 243, 252, 258; authority of, 22–25, 34, 77, 40, 137, 241 bureaucracies and, 1, 13, 30–31, 76–78, 93–94, 131, 210–22; class of, 44–45, 48, 200, 258; and commissions, 201–2, 205;

community and, 145–46, 198;
cultures, 20–22, 24, 207, 214;
democracy and, 34–35, 42–43,
46–47, 49; and policy, 29,
32–33, 45, 102; and politics,
95–96; power of, 3, 12, 17, 73,
112, 134–35; rule by, 17, 43, 47,
50, 215–16; subsidized, 27, 29,
35, 150, 167, 173–74, 178; types
of, 25–26. *See also* cognitive
authority; scientific expertise
expertise, 33, 35, 86, 129, 138, 200,
213, 224, 259, 276; authoritarian, 215–16; bureaucratic, 104,
112, 198, 202; and civil society,
205, 207, 209; delegation to,
116–18; forms of, 11 inequality of, 3; limits of, 1, 84; and
politics, 93, 95, 108; and policy,
69; and professionalization,
122; production of, 5, 30; and
responsibility, 76, 79, 81; internationalization of, 135–36. *See
also* decision-making; democracy; error; evaluation; experts;
legitimacy; medical expertise;
meta-expertise; scientific
expertise; social work; technical
expertise
"Expertise and political responsibility," (S. Turner), 11
explicit knowledge, 7, 9, 19, 34, 264

F
Fabian socialism, 93
facts, 23, 30, 38, 56, 59, 130; experts
and, 33, 46, 95, 113, 117, 240;
fact-surrogate, 85; ideology and,
21, 35, 37; neutral, 20, 39, 41,
54; and power, 96–98; science
and, 18, 69, 127–28, 183; and
values, 53, 56–57
Farr, William, 132–33
Fermi National Accelerator Laboratory, 264
Feyerabend, Paul, 17–18, 38
First Amendment (US), 25–26
Fish, Stanley, 20, 35–38
Flexner, Abraham, 30
Flexner report (medicine), 14
Flyvbjerg, Bent, 12, 102–13
"Forms of patronage" (S. Turner),
298n6
Ford Foundation, 32, 174

Fosdick, Raymond, 167–68
Foucault, Michel, 6, 19, 20, 35, 39,
112
France (bureaucratic traditions),
32–33, 113, 213, 222
French *Economistes*, 114
Fry, Luther, 160
funding, 29, 160–63, 279; bureaucratic, 102–3; of expertise, 27,
29; government, 1, 63, 65, 115,
174, 195, 201; of social sciences, 147, 158, 173–74, 176.
See also Rockefeller Foundation;
science funding; social survey;
subsidization

G
gatekeeping, 185, 192
Gehman, Harold (Admiral), 91–92
Gemeinschaft (community), 194
General Health Board (UK). *See*
cholera
geological surveys. *See* US
Geophysical Research Letters, 275
Germany, 112, 131, 136–37, 172–73;
bureaucracies, 9, 12–13, 32,
103, 107, 119–20, 129–33,
209–14, 222; military and
science, 116, 283; *Sonderweg*
(exceptionalism), 129. *See also*
Hamburg cholera epidemic;
Weimar politics
Giddings, Franklin H., 29, 156–57,
159
Gilbert, G. K., 63
Glenn, John (Russell Sage Foundation),
147
global warming. *See* climate change
Goldman, Alvin, 243
governance, 10, 114–115, 206, 208,
232–34; and expertise, 93;
professional, 34, 112, 124. *See
also* science
Grande Ecoles, 32, 210, 212–13
Griesmer, James, 272
groupthink, 82, 215, 255, 276, 284,
286, 288
Guston, David, 130

H
H-Bomb, 41, 266, 280, 287–91, 294
Habermas, Jürgen, 39, 85, 114; expert
cultures, 20, 21–22, 24, 25, 32,
35; ideal speech, 40, 86

Habits of the Heart (Bellah), 177
Hacking, Ian, 35
Ham, Linda, 76–78, 80–81, 87–89. See also *Columbia* shuttle; NASA
Hamburg cholera epidemic, 13, 129, 130–32, 136
Hansen, James, 292, 295
Haraway, Donna, 19
Harrison, Shelby, 138, 142–43, 145, 147
Hartshorne, Edward, 168–71
Harvard University, 156, 168, 172; sociology, 14, 161–62, 164–66. See also Industrial Hazards Project; Rockefeller Foundation; Rockefeller philanthropies
hedgehog error. See error
Heidegger, Martin, 223, 232
Heisenberg, Werner, 136
Henderson, Lawrence J., 162, 164, 166–69, 173. See also Mayo/Henderson model of social-scientific research
Henry Street Settlement, 148
heuristics, 242–3, 247–9, 255, 279; collective, 280, 284, 295. See also competence-competence
hidden knowledge, 6, 25, 179, 246, 252, 258
high politics, 12, 94–99, 112
Hiroshima, 281
Hitler, Adolf, 100, 193–94, 232
HIV-AIDS, 195
Hobbes, Thomas, 23, 120, 123
hobbyhorse, 84, 95, 136, 276, 288, 290
Hocart, A. M., 197–199
Hollings, Ernest (Senator), 74, 78, 92
Homestake Mine experiment, 261, 267, 270, 273, 276
homesteading, 11, 62–68
horse-trading (political), 47, 108–9, 111, 113
Hotz, Robert, 92
Howard Hughes Medical Institute, 246, 282
Hull House Maps and Papers, 139

I
The Iconoclast (Ward), 156
ideal-speech situation, 40, 85
identity politics, 50
ideology, 19, 36–37, 175, 209–10, 253, 255; bureaucratic, 226–27, 231–33, 252; expert knowledge as, 20–21, 215, 218–19; of planning, 12, 93, 102, 107–8; and science, 38, 100, 184, 186, 293
ill-structured problems, 57, 59–61, 66, 68–70
"immaculate conception" (of science), 37–40
Industrial Hazards Project, 161–67. See also Harvard University; Mayo/Henderson model of social-scientific research
information, 3, 80, 84, 292, 293; aggregation, 9, 11, 251, 279, 284–85, 287, 289; asymmetry, 59, 182–84, 188, 194, 196, 239, 247, 250–54, 259–60; hidden, 33, 95, 278; and markets, 9, 46, 217; and politics, 94, 97–98, 120. See also knowledge aggregation; ill-structured problems
Institute of Social and Religious Research, 160
institutions of delegation. See delegation (of powers)
interest group, 19, 36, 128–129, 136, 137, 201
interests, 102–10, 113, 185–86, 193; and bias, 48, 97, 293; collective, 126; conflicts of, 9, 56–57, 118–19, 137, 184, 205; and decision-making, 60, 64; and democracy, 254–55; experts and, 4, 29, 35, 42, 97, 202; vs. knowledge, 50; and stakeholders, 47
Intergovernmental Panel on Climate Change (IPCC), 292–93
interim committee. See A-bomb
Intergovernmental Panel on Climate Change, 49
Islamic law, 229, 233
Islamic science, 36, 194

J
Japan, 48, 97–100, 129
Jasanoff, Sheila, 37–38, 119
jigsaw puzzle model of science. See science
Johnson, Lyndon, 100
Jones, Phil, 293
Journal for Geophysical Research, 275
Judaism, 225, 227, 232
junk science, 118–119

Index 333

justified true belief. *See* belief

K

Keller, Evelyn Fox, 277, 280
Kellogg, David, 283
Kellogg, Paul "The spread of the survey idea," 139
Kellogg, Paul, 28–29, 138–51, 300–301n5, 10
Kentucky survey, 139, 300n1
Kitcher, Philip, 4, 41, 47, 215
Knight, Frank, 249
knowledge, 48, 209, 219–21, 223, 242, 267–68, 280asymmetry, 85–86, 182–83, 188, 196, 251–52; collective, 8, 239, 253; equality/inequality of, 3, 17, 19, 50, 239, 241; individual, 246, 256; organization of, 4–5, 7, 9, 13; specialized, 257; transmission of, 218. *See also* belief (justified true); knowledge distribution; embodied knowledge; expert knowledge; information; risk; scientific knowledge; tacit knowledge
knowledge aggregation, 8, 13, 50, 235–36, 240, 252; forms of, 10–11; problems of, 5, 13, 45–46, 241, 267; and representative democracy, 47, 250; and science, 48, 284–85, 289. *See also* heuristics; information
knowledge distribution of, 2–3, 5–6, 8, 11, 45–47, 69–70, 79, 245, 251
knowledge society, 126, 184. *See also* commissions
Koch, Robert, 132, 136
Kuhn, Thomas, 55, 84, 276, 278–79, 284–86, 291

L

Lange, Oscar, 218, 249
Lambright, Harry, 90
L'Ancien Regime Book II, (Hocart), 197–98
Large Hadron Collider. *See* CERN (Large Hadron Collider)
Latour, Bruno, 258
Laudan, Larry, 259
Laura Spellman Rockefeller Memorial (LSRM), 146–48, 150, 162
law, 225–6, 229–31, 233
Lazersfeld, Paul, 161–62

Left, the, 102, 111–112, 124
legal traditions, 229–30. *See also* Dworkin, Ronald; Schmitt, Carl
legitimacy, 1, 2, 15, 30, 198, 206–8, 233; and climate science, 273; and cognitive authority, 23, 30, 39; and the EU, 197, 203, 205–7; and experts, 24–26, 36, 121; and liberal democracy, 24, 49, 204–5, 208, 298n7; of science, 9, 12, 14, 35–36; Weber and, 226, 233. *See also* certification; licensure; trust
Lenin Peace Prize, 101
liberal democracy, 10, 16, 39–40, 110, 118, 197–198, 200, 202–4, 208–9, 242, 277;and expertise, 19, 25, 47, 113, 129, 137, 254–55; Germany and, 172–173. *See also* liberalism
liberal political theory, 19, 39, 282
liberalism, 20, 29, 32, 71, 108, 111, 207. *See* also democracy; experts (authority); Schmitt, Carl
licensure, 118, 123–124. *See also* certification; bonding
life-world, 21–22
literati, 223, 229, 231, 233–5
Lippman, Walter, 42–44
The Logic of Liberty (Polanyi), 244–46
London. *See* cholera
The Lonely Crowd (Riesman), 178
Lord Cherwell (Frederick Lindemann), 96
Lord Russell-Johnston, 110
Lovell, Bernard, 281, 287
Ludendorff, Erich, 72
Luhmann, Niklas, 3
Lynch, Michael, 259
Lynd, Robert, 160, 177
Lysenko, 193, 283–84

M

Mach, Ernst, 55
magic, 225, 227
Maki, Uskali, 182
managerial responsibility, 74, 76–77, 80–81, 84, 87–92
Manhattan Project, 99, 266, 283, 288
Mann, Michael, 293
the market, 214, 217, 287, 293; and aggregation of knowledge, 10,

46; and bonding of science, 190–94; and experts, 48, 137, 119, 137, 214, 239; and information, 2, 9, 217; mechanisms, 124, 250; and politics, 47, 108–9, 111, 113; and science, 125, 179, 180, 182, 187–91, 195, 283, 286; and sociology, 157, 159. *See also* heuristics; licensure
Marshall Plan, 199
Marxism and Workers' Self-Management (Prychitko), 250
Masonic organizations, 219–20
Massachusetts Bureau of Labor Statistics, 156
the Matthew effect. *See* Merton, Robert
"May the sheep safely graze?" (Wynne), 244
Mayo, Elton, 162–65, 168
Mayo/Henderson model of social-scientific research, 162–66, 168, 169
McCormack, Dan, 78
medical expertise, 82–83, 122, 168–70, 176; and social science, 166; and state powers, 118. *See also* licensure; professionalization
medicine, reform of, 14, 30–31
Merchants of Doubt (Oreskes and Conway), 293
Merriam, Robert, 31
Merton, Robert, 22–24, 183, 276, 278, 295, 300n4; and the Matthew effect, 189; and norms of science, 184, 187, 191, 193, 280, 283, 289, 292–93
meta-expertise, 80, 82, 86–87, 89, 91
Middletown (Lynds), 178
Mill, James, 114
Mill, John Stuart, 71, 85–86, 114, 205–6
Mills, C. Wright, 159, 175
Mishra, Aneil, 91
Mitroff, Ian, 184
Mode-2 Science, 276, 278
Moltke, Field Marshal Count, 120, 235
Morgenthau, Hans, 233, 297n4
Murray, Henry, 162, 168–70
Myrdal, Gunnar, 214

N
NASA, 11, 47, 73–74, 78–79, 81, 84, 86–92. *See also* Vaughan, Dianne

National Academy of Sciences (US), 271, 294
National Institutes of Health (US), 127, 271
national morale, 168–170, 172
National Science Foundation, 115, 126, 177, 246
neutrality, 17, 19, 21–22, 25, 32, 35, 39, 168
New York Academy of Medicine, 135
New York Bureau of Municipal Research, 138
New York Citizens' Association, 134–35, 137
New York City Charity Organization Society (COS), 138
New York Council of Hygiene and Public Health, 134–35
New York Geological Survey, 2
New York Sanitary Commission. *See* cholera
New York Tenement Commission, 27
Nobel Prize, 2, 120, 136, 181, 186, 270, 281, 285
nomenklatura, 222
non-experts, 3, 23, 39, 115
the non-rational, 223–26, 231, 134–35
normal accidents, 74, 90, 257, 260–62, 268
notables, 30, 131, 136, 141–42, 210, 212, 214, 216, 255
"A Note on Science and Democracy" (Merton), 183–84
nuclear weapons. *See* A-bomb; atomic scientists

O
Oakeshott, Michael, 93, 102, 108, 111–12
Odum, Howard, 159, 177
Ogburn, William, 160
O'Keefe, Sean, 75, 78, 90–92. *See also* NASA
On Liberty (Mill), 85
On War (Clausewitz), 54
Oppenheimer, Robert, 41, 100, 266, 280, 287–91, 293, 294, 299n1, 2
oracles, 49, 225
organizational behavior theory, 90–92, 176
Organization of European Economic Cooperation, 199
organized skepticism, 184, 193, 283, 193–95

P

Packard, Vance, 254
Palmer, George, 138
paradigm, 55, 84, 276, 285. *See also* Kuhn, Thomas
Pareto Seminar (Harvard), 166–67
Park, Robert, 160
parliamentary democracy, 71, 110, 112–113, 120, 197, 203–4, 212; and consensus, 200; and discussion, 20–21, 117, 207; Scandinavian, 109. *See also* European Parliament
Parsons, Talcott, 3, 156, 161–67
parties, 113, 206; of experts, 35, 49, 205, 214–15; political, 20, 47, 72, 104, 107–10, 203, 211, 216
patronage, 1–2, 27, 30, 177–78
Pauling, Linus, 83
Pearce, Raymond, 165
Pearson, Karl, 42, 47
peer review, 58, 192, 261, 266, 298n6; and consensus, 125–26, 265, 275; and expert knowledge, 73, 207; and post-normal science, 279–80, 282, 295; and science, 127–28, 179–80, 183, 186, 191, 195, 261. *See also* climate change
Pennington, Hugh, 87
Perrow, Charles, 257, 259–62, 265, 268, 275
Perry, Clarence, 140
Pettenkofer, Max von, 131–32, 135
Pettit, Philip, 240–42, 247, 252
peuple eclaire, 114
philanthropy, 27, 31. *See also* Rockefeller philanthropies
Pickering, Andrew, 259–60
Pinch, Trevor, 37–38, 260, 268–69
Pittsburgh Survey, 13, 28, 138–51, 158, 300–301n2, 5, 6
planning, 93–94, 103–8, 124, 174, 287; economics, 245, 249; soviet, 217–18, 250. *See also* bureaucratic politics; urban planning
Plato, 4, 232, 235–36, 246
Polanyi, Michael, 8, 131, 217, 266; and post-normal science, 283–87, 293; and science, 131, 244–51, 253, 275
The Polish Peasant, 158
Political conflict, 95, 108, 110–11
political responsibility, 45, 73, 76, 82, 96, 98–99, 210; personal, 72, 74–75, 77–80, 89–92
political science, 112, 159
politics. *See* bureaucratic politics; high politics; protest politics; representative government
policy related sciences 8, 56–57, 60–62, 66–70, 112, 155, 302–3n9
The Political Economy of Soviet Socialism (Boettke), 249
Popper, Karl, 55, 57, 278
post-normal science, 15, 277–95
power, 12, 22; bureaucratic, 130–37; and planning, 106–7; royal, 113, 117, 120. *See also* delegation; power/knowledge
power/knowledge, 3–7, 112
Powell, John Wesley, 62–70, 125, 156
prebends, 226, 228, 233
President's Commission on Efficiency and Economy, 145
principal agent theory, 182–86, 188–89
prisoner's dilemma, 239
professionalization, 14, 27, 30–34, 157, 165, 167, 177; and planning bureaucracies, 106, 112; of sociology, 160–61, 174–75. *See also* public administration; Rockefeller Foundation; social work
Progress and Its Problems (Laudan), 259
Prohibition, 147–149
propaganda, 169–171
protest politics, 100–102, 110
Prychitko, David, 250
public administration, 15, 30–31, 33, 139, 150, 161, 174; and expertise, 210–12
public discourse/dicussion, 30, 36, 45, 49, 59, 88, 97, 131; and legitimacy, 204; and politics, 20–21, 39, 59, 206–7, 221, 277; and science, 116, 130, 290–91. *See also* discussion
public health, 124, 132, 134–135, 150, 176, 300n4
public intellectual, 13–14, 160
Public Lands Commission, 64
public participation, 102, 105–6, 108, 121, 250; and knowledge

Index

transmission, 219–20; and science, 116, 118
public sphere, 43, 50, 167

Q
quasi-science, 123, 125–28

R
racism, 18–21
rationalism, 49, 108, 111; and politics, 93, 102–103, 112
"Rationalism in politics" (Oakeshott), 93, 111
rationality, 20, 56, 60, 109, 215; and Chinese bureaucracy, 224–26, 229, 231, 234–35; collective, 239, 253; and planning, 93, 103, 106–7; and power, 12, 101, 105
Ravelstein (Bloom), 232
reform organization, 139, 142, 145–51
reliabilism, 239, 243, 252
religion, 18, 20
The Reluctant Farmer (Scott), 121
Render, Barry, 91–92
Religionssoziologie ["The social psychology of world religions"] (Weber), 224
representation, 76, 94, 104, 106, 128, 186; and agency, 187–188; and expertise, 73–74
Representative Government (Mill), 71, 205–6
representative government, 9, 203–4
"The republic of science" (Polanyi), 247–49
responsibility. *See* managerial responsibility; political responsibility
Richmond, Mary, 27, 140, 147, 149
Riesman, David, 177
risk, 22, 58–59, 61, 120–21, 256; knowledge, 4, 10, 264–67, 271–72, 275–76; and science, 131, 188–90, 258
Risk Society (Beck), 114
Rocha, Alan, 79
Rockefeller Foundation, 31, 35, 139, 279, 282, 287; Columbia University and, 29–30; Harvard University and, 162–63, 165, 167, 171–72; professionalization of the social sciences, 148, 150, 161, 163
Rockefeller, John D., 139

Rockefeller philanthropies, 5, 14, 31–32, 112, 139, 177. *See also* Laura Spellman Rockefeller Memorial (LSRM)
Rohrabacher, Dana (Representative), 92
Rosenberg, Charles, 134–35
Ross, E. A., 156–57
Rossi, Lucio, 263–64
Rotary Club, 219, 221
Rowntree, Seebohm, 139
Royal, Ségolène, 49–50, 112–13
rule, forms of, 197, 202, 216. *See also* experts
Ruml, Beardsley, 147
rural sociology, 139, 150, 158
Russell, Bertrand, 57–58
Russell Sage Foundation (RSF), 27–29, 138, 140, 142, 149, 174, 300–301n1, 3; Charity Organizations Department, 147
Russia, 209, 214, 215, 217–18
Russian Research Center, 32, 173

S
Sage, Olivia, 147
Saint James Parish Committee (London), 129, 133–34, 137
Saint-Simon, Henri de, 50
Scandinavian bureaucracies, 103, 107, 112, 213
Schmitt, Carl, 20, 23, 37–38, 40, 46, 73, 229, 298n5; and German law, 230–31
Schneider, Stephen, 273
Schudson, Michael, 42–44
Schumpeter, Joseph, 26
science, 18, 101, 121, 180–182, 215, 217, 279; authority of, 4, 110, 122, 125, 277 (*see also* authority (cognitive); big science, 257–58, 276, 278, 281–83, 286; public character of, 53–56; democracy and, 5, 118, 120; failure and, 258, 260, 262–64; governance of, 114–16, 118, 123, 126, 129–31, 136, 187; jigsaw puzzle model of, 244–45, 247–48, 251, 253, 284–85; normal, 275–78, 295. *See also* anomalies; atomic scientists; audience; belief; bonding; climate change; consensus; error; science funding; market; peer

review; quasi-science; skepticism (organized); specialists; trust
science funding, 2, 19, 124–29, 179–82, 195, 270–73, 275, 282–85, 287, 291; state, 18, 115
science studies, 4, 37, 39, 103, 181–82, 258–60, 276
"Science as a vocation" (Weber), 223, 231–32, 234–35
science, technology, and society tradition. *See* STS
scientific community, 61, 270, 277, 279–80, 282, 284, 292
scientific expertise, 1, 6, 37, 101, 249
scientific knowledge, 4, 8, 53, 55–56, 120, 125, 159; and politics, 93; as public good, 179, 182–183, 190
Scientists' Movement, 100
settlement houses, 148, 156
sexism, 18–20
Shapere, Dudley, 261
Sierra Club, 29
Simon, Herbert, 57
Simon, Julian, 44
skepticism, 109, 233, 275, 285, 288; about experts, 44, 46, 119, 258; organized, 184, 193, 276, 283, 293–95
Small, Albion, 157–59, 170, 177
Snow, C. P., 67, 96
Snow, John, 48, 129, 133–35, 137
social action, 147, 158, 167, 168
social constructionism, 39–40
social control, 163, 167–170
social epistemology, 7, 239–43, 246, 251, 267
Social Forces, 177
social psychology, 170–173
The Social Psychology of World Religions (Weber), 224
social reform, 27–31, 112, 141, 145, 151, 177; research, 138–140, 143–144, 146–150, 158
Social Science Abstracts (Chapin), 161
Social Science Research Council (SSRC), 31, 147–48, 155, 159–63, 165, 167, 173–75
social sciences, 2, 29, 55, 89–90, 144–48, 166, 177; and propaganda, 170–71. *See also* medical expertise; Rockefeller Foundation
social survey, 28, 138–41, 146, 149–50; survey movement, 5, 13, 142–43, 158–59. *See also* US; Pittsburgh Survey; Russell Sage Foundation; Springfield Survey; Syracuse Survey
Social Survey movement. *See* social survey
social work, 28; as engineering, 29, 140–44; expertise, 145–47; professionalization of, 139–40, 149–51
The Sociological Imagination (Mills), 175
sociology, 155–178; academic, 163, 175, 177, 178; subsidized, 160–61. *See also* professionalization
Sociology 23 (Harvard), 166–68
sociology of science, 43–44, 243, 283
Solomon, Miriam, 241, 247
Sorokin, Pitrim, 159
Soviet Union, 214–18, 249, 288. *See also* Russia
specialists, 11, 56, 69, 114, 117, 198, 267; class of, 200; and community, 198; and science, 8, 246–49, 253, 279, 284–87; technical, 81; Weber and, 223–32, 236, 246
Spezialisten (specialists), 3, 223
"The spread of the survey idea" (Kellogg), 139, 144
Springfield Survey, 142–43, 147
Staatswissenschaft, 112
stakeholders, 13, 47, 102–6, 111, 115–16, 134, 213; experts as, 205–6, 208
Stalin, Joseph, 41, 93, 120, 193, 233
Star, Susan, 272
Stewart, William, 63–64
Strauss, Leo, 232, 235
STS (Science and Technology Studies), 90, 261
Structure of Social Action (Parsons, Talcott), 167
The Structure of Scientific Revolutions (Kuhn, Thomas), 55, 84, 279
survey. *See* social survey
the survey idea. *See* Kellogg, Paul
Sweden: bureaucracy, 210, 213. *See also* Scandinavian
Syracuse Survey, 143

T
tacit knowledge, 1, 3, 7–8, 267

Taft, William Howard, 64
Taliban, 42–43
technical expertise, 69, 72–75, 78–82, 87–90, 117, 198, 208, 211; and politics, 93, 102
technoscience, 276, 278–80
Teller, Edward, 287–91, 294
Thomas, W. I., 158
Three Mile Island, 120
Tizard, Henry, 96
Tocqueville, Alexis de, 2, 134, 197–98, 219
Truman, Harry, 115, 126
trust, 2, 14, 47, 184–85, 255; distrust, 119–120, 258; and expert claims, 9, 43, 72, 86, 215; and legitimacy, 5; and politics, 97–98, 117–18, 205, 218–19; and science, 122, 125, 194, 268
truth to power, 4, 97
Turner, Frederick Jackson, 62

U
unanimity, 198–200, 202
Understanding the Tacit (S. Turner), 1
Union of Concerned Scientists, 101
United Kingdom, 116, 271
United States, 119, 134, 201, 203; bureaucracy, 12, 67, 210, 214, 221; Congress, 45, 48; National Transportation Board, 221; science policy, 62, 112, 116. *See also* democracy, liberal democracy, National Institutes of Health, National Science Foundation
US Geological Survey, 63, 125, 158
universalism, 168, 184, 187, 193–194, 283
University of Chicago, 31, 160. *See also* Chicago School
University of North Carolina, 31
urban planning, 5, 102, 104–108

utopianism, 84

V
Van Kleek, Mary, 140
Van Rensselaer, Stephen, 2
Vaughan, Dianne, 11, 90
Veblen, Thorstein, 159
Verein für Sozialpolitik, 223
Vietnam War, 100
von Leibig, Justus, 121, 282

W
Wald, Lillian, 148
Ward, Lester F., 155–56, 159
Weart, Spencer, 273–76
Weber, Max, 3, 49, 72, 107, 125; and expertise, 223–236. *See also* specialists
Weick, Karl, 90
Weimar politics, 20
well-structured problems. *See* ill-structured problems
Weltanschauungen (worldviews), 223, 231
Western Insurgent Movement, 145
Westheimer. *See* Dr. Ruth (Westheimer)
"What Are climate scientists to do?" (Keller, Evelyn Fox), 277
Whitehead, Henry, 133
Wing, Frank, 142
Wilson, Woodrow, 209
Wootton, Barbara, 108
World Climate Conference, 291
World War I, 96, 156, 203
World War II, 32, 84, 96, 136; post-, 155, 160, 171, 216, 283, 203, 265, 286
Wouk, Herman, 6
Wynne, Brian, 116, 244

Z
Ziman, John, 295